REPRODUCTIVE RIGHTS AND JUSTICE STORIES

Edited by

MELISSA MURRAY
Professor of Law
New York University School of Law

KATHERINE SHAW
Professor of Law
Benjamin N. Cardozo School of Law

REVA B. SIEGEL
Nicholas deB. Katzenbach Professor of Law
Yale Law School

LAW STORIES SERIES®

FOUNDATION
PRESS

Law Stories Series is a trademark registered in the U.S. Patent and Trademark Office.

© 2019 LEG, Inc. d/b/a West Academic
    444 Cedar Street, Suite 700
    St. Paul, MN 55101
    1-877-888-1330

West, West Academic Publishing, and West Academic are trademarks of West Publishing Corporation, used under license.

Printed in the United States of America

ISBN: 978-1-68328-992-0

Table of Contents

REPRODUCTIVE RIGHTS AND JUSTICE STORIES

Introduction

This volume brings together important cases involving the state regulation of sex, childbearing, and parenting. These twelve cases, some canonical and some far less known, span topics involving contraception, abortion, pregnancy, and parenthood. The chapters tell their stories using a wide-lens perspective that illuminates the complex ways law is forged and debated in social movements, in representative government, and in courts.

As a field, "reproductive rights and justice" is relatively new, and its contours are quite broad, encompassing the various ways law shapes the decision "whether to bear or beget a child"[1] and the conditions under which families are created and sustained. Some of the cases included in this volume are very much part of the constitutional law canon; more are not. Until recently, these cases have not often been conceived of as part of a unified *field* of law.[2]

This volume remedies that oversight. Reading this group of cases together makes visible forms and effects of reproductive regulation that are less evident when the cases are read in isolation or in their more familiar doctrinal contexts. The framework of "reproductive justice" highlights the intersecting relations of race, class, sexuality, and sex that shape the regulation of reproduction. It examines the many ways law shapes the choice to have, as well as to avoid having, children. The volume addresses decisionmaking about contraception and abortion—the traditional subject matter of "reproductive rights"—in this larger reproductive justice framework, and locates this body of law alongside cases that consider a wider range of issues, including sterilization, assisted reproductive technology, pregnancy discrimination, the criminalization of pregnancy, and access to reproductive health care.

This "Law Stories" book is nontraditional in a second sense. Many of its chapters narrate the cases in ways that de-center courts. To be sure, the chapters tell stories about the individual litigants and lawyers behind important cases. But the stories recognize courts as but one of many institutions in our constitutional democracy, and they show how conflicts over law unfold in the institutions of civil society (medicine, religion, media), in democratic politics (social movements, political parties, and representative government), as well as in the courts. The stories feature ordinary women and men struggling with laws that govern the ways they

---

[1]   Eisenstadt v. Baird, 405 U.S. 438, 453 (1972).

[2]   The publication of the first casebook on the topic, MELISSA MURRAY & KRISTIN LUKER, CASES ON REPRODUCTIVE RIGHTS AND JUSTICE (2015), was an important development for the field; this volume complements and furthers that project.

make families, and show how members of the community, government officials, lawyers, and judges respond. In the process, these stories situate litigation histories in a larger social field, revealing the interplay of bottom-up and top-down forces that provoke, shape, and legitimate judicial decisions, and the role that struggle over courts and rights plays in forging new norms.[3]

This book is being published at a pivotal moment for this area of law. In 2018, Justice Anthony Kennedy, a long-standing voice in the U.S. Supreme Court's disposition of reproductive rights and justice cases, retired, and was replaced by Brett Kavanaugh. Past changes in the Court's membership have deeply shaped this body of law, as stories in this volume show. The retirement of Justice Kennedy and his replacement by Justice Kavanaugh will surely shape the dynamics of the Supreme Court in ways that will have important repercussions for this field. But the account of law and social change contained within these pages suggests that while the Supreme Court is an important player in these debates, it cannot settle the future of this body of law today any more than it could a generation ago. As importantly, many of the law stories in this volume involve questions of reproductive rights and justice in areas of constitutional law, employment discrimination law, and family law that will be less dramatically affected by the change in the composition of both the Supreme Court and the lower federal courts.

We have decided to organize the chapters in this volume in chronological order, rather than by subject matter. This format highlights the lived horizon in which women and men encounter—and struggle with—questions of reproductive rights and justice, and the ways American law has responded at different eras in the nation's history. But chronological order is just one way to make sense of the stories about rights, justice, and various forms of law-making inside and outside of the courts collected in these pages.

* * *

The first chapter, Melissa Murray's exploration of *Griswold v. Connecticut* (1965), tells the story of a case that has long been viewed as a stalwart of the constitutional law and reproductive rights canon. *Griswold* held that a Connecticut law criminalizing the use of contraception violated the right to privacy protected by the due process clause of the Fourteenth Amendment. The contraceptive ban challenged in *Griswold* carried a criminal penalty; and, critically, Estelle Griswold and Lee Buxton were arraigned, charged, and tried before a court for violating it. The chapter argues that in overlooking *Griswold*'s criminal law antecedents, we have overlooked many things. We have missed an opportunity to locate this decision within the broader context of the

---

[3]   *See generally* Reva B. Siegel, *Community in Conflict: Same-Sex Marriage and Backlash*, 64 UCLA L. REV. 1728 (2017); Robert Post & Reva Siegel, Roe *Rage: Democratic Constitutionalism and Backlash*, 42 HARV. C.R.-C.L. L. REV. 373 (2007).

criminal law reform debate that was taking place in the 1950s and 1960s—one that sought to limit the state's use of criminal law as a means of policing and enforcing compliance with majoritarian sexual mores. In doing so, we have failed to appreciate that the case was not simply about birth control, but also about designing limits on the state. Recuperating *Griswold*'s place in the criminal law reform debate brings these interests into focus—and makes it easier to discern the notion of privacy as a bulwark against the state's efforts to compel moral conformity. But perhaps most importantly, focusing on the criminal law aspects of *Griswold*'s history allows us to glimpse the similarities between the present day and the period that preceded *Griswold*. Then, as now, access to contraception remains uneven, especially for those who lack the personal resources to fund their contraceptive use. As importantly, the stigma and disapproval that once attended contraceptive use can still be expressed—albeit in more muted ways—in the new forms of state regulation that have emerged to replace the criminal ban struck down in *Griswold*. These insights make clear the limitations of decriminalization as a means of law reform, and underscore the many vehicles, beyond the criminal law, that the state may deploy in its efforts to enforce a particular vision of sex and sexuality.

In the second chapter, Neil Siegel tells the story of *Struck v. Secretary of Defense* (1971), a little-known case that was litigated by Ruth Bader Ginsburg, but never decided by the Supreme Court because it was declared moot. Susan Struck was an Air Force Captain whose pregnancy and religious refusal to have an abortion subjected her to automatic discharge from the Air Force. As Siegel shows, Ginsburg's brief in Struck's case highlights a path not taken in the development of the Supreme Court's equal protection doctrine on sex discrimination. In *Struck*, Ginsburg underscored the vital links between pregnancy discrimination and sex discrimination, and between sex discrimination and restrictions on access to contraception and abortion, at a time when the Justices did not understand the relationships among these practices. The brief came at a very early point in the development of equal protection law on sex discrimination—in 1972, just after the Court had held for the first time in American history that a sex classification violated the Equal Protection Clause, and before the Court's decision in *Roe v. Wade*. Only by registering where constitutional law was and where it would imminently head when Ginsburg litigated *Struck* can one entirely grasp the significance of Ginsburg's brief—and the implications of its subsequent neglect. In more recent decades, the Court has—to a significant, albeit incomplete, extent—gained an appreciation of the relationships among the practices that Ginsburg identified.

In the next chapter, Linda Greenhouse and Reva Siegel offer a fresh account of *Roe v. Wade* (1973). Greenhouse and Siegel do not begin with a litigation history or even a drama featuring familiar characters (Sarah Weddington, Linda Coffee, and Norma McCorvey). Instead they start their story in the 1960s, showing how debate over abortion changed shape in politics in the years before courts played a prominent role. This early history provides resources for thinking about polarization of abortion and the logic of abortion's constitutionalization. The authors show how concerns about race and class helped drive the early efforts toward abortion reform; examine the late appearance of feminist claims for abortion's decriminalization and the fierce resistance they provoked; and explore opposition to abortion's decriminalization in the years before *Roe* when the movement was predominantly centered amongst Catholics in the Democratic party and large numbers of evangelical protestants and Republicans had yet to join the cause. Born in politics, with courts barely in view, the debate over abortion ultimately reached judicial dockets in the form of new claims on the Constitution's longstanding guarantees of liberty, equality, and life. Greenhouse and Siegel examine the claims on the Constitution that *Roe* acknowledged, as well as competing arguments that the Justices were, initially at least, unable to hear. Ultimately, the Court was moved by these arguments for and against the abortion right, and reasoned from them two decades later when the Court reaffirmed a significantly revised version of the *Roe* framework in *Planned Parenthood v. Casey*. As the first case in a long line to reach the Supreme Court, *Roe* did not initiate the abortion conflict, and just as clearly did not end it. One of the few Supreme Court decisions that ordinary Americans can name, for some it is a symbol of judicial overreach; for others, it represents the courts' ability to protect individual rights in the face of mobilized political opposition. And, as Greenhouse and Siegel show, the story of *Roe* continues, a conflict that the Court can structure, but not settle.

Deborah Dinner next offers a reading of the equal protection case *Geduldig v. Aiello* (1974), which held, the year after *Roe*, that laws regulating pregnancy do not classify on the basis of sex sufficiently to trigger heightened judicial scrutiny under the Equal Protection Clause. Dinner's chapter situates the case within the context—and conflicts—of the American welfare state. The chapter explains that this constitutional case concerned a question that continues to vex legal and political culture. Does sex equality require the public to assume responsibility for sharing the costs of reproduction, much as we pool other risks that threaten family support (e.g. unemployment or accidents)? In the late 1960s, working women and activists confronted the limits of the U.S. welfare regime that had developed over the course of the twentieth century. Both public social insurance schemes and private employer-sponsored benefits were designed to support male breadwinners. Childbearing workers were an anathema within these schemes' gendered logic, and they excluded maternity from coverage. After labor feminists failed in the 1940s and 1950s to secure new forms of social security, including paid maternity leave, feminist legal reformers in the late civil rights era turned to a new legal tool: sex discrimination law. They analogized between pregnancy and temporary disability to force the inclusion of pregnancy within the public and private dimensions of the welfare regime. Prior to the realization of heightened scrutiny for sex-based classifications, feminist attorneys brought lawsuits challenging the gender stereotypes that underpinned both public and private employers' exclusion of pregnancy from temporary disability insurance. Yet the Supreme Court's 1974 decision in *Geduldig* held that pregnancy-based classifications did not necessarily constitute a violation of constitutional sex equality. Although the Pregnancy Discrimination Act of 1978 now makes clear that pregnancy discrimination constitutes sex discrimination in violation of Title VII, Dinner argues that this significant body of law is insufficient. The nation's failure to recognize that gender equality demands an expansion of the welfare state, in ways that would socialize responsibility for the costs of pregnancy and childbirth, continues to harm low-income families today.

The next chapter introduces a case that will be new to most readers—*Madrigal v. Quilligan* (1978), an unpublished decision from a California federal district court refusing to fully remedy sterilization abuse in the early 1970s. As Maya Manian describes in harrowing detail, *Madrigal* involved ten women (the Madrigal Ten) who filed a lawsuit alleging that medical personnel at the Los Angeles County USC Medical Center systematically coerced Mexican-American women into submitting to sterilization. Although the district court refused to award damages to the Madrigal Ten, the case dramatically altered public consciousness and public policy on coerced sterilization. Despite their loss in the damages phase of the litigation, the Madrigal Ten catalyzed efforts to strengthen California's regulations for ensuring voluntary consent to sterilization. In addition, the *Madrigal* litigation inspired the anti-sterilization abuse movement in California and helped to shape Chicana feminism in the 1970s. The case galvanized Chicana feminist activism in ways that highlighted tensions between mainstream white feminists focusing on reproductive rights and women of color focusing on reproductive justice. The Chicana activists brought the still nascent framework of reproductive justice to the forefront, incorporating concerns about discrimination along intersectional lines of gender, race, poverty, and immigration status—all issues at play in the *Madrigal* case, and all of which still resonate today.

Debates over sterilization also play an unexpectedly central role in Khiara M. Bridges' detailed story of *Harris v. McRae* (1980), in which the Supreme Court upheld the constitutionality of the Hyde Amendment, which prohibits the use of federal funds for abortions desired by Medicaid recipients. Although this funding restriction disproportionately burdens women of color, who are overrepresented among those living in poverty, the lawyers who challenged the Hyde Amendment failed to invoke race, class, or gender in their arguments against the law. The chapter explains the reasons for this erasure, identifying the precedent laid down by the Burger Court as responsible for rendering illegible claims that sound in race, class, or gender. As importantly, Bridges draws connections between advocacy against the Hyde Amendment and the growing opposition to sterilization abuse, highlighting the ways in which activists argued that by refusing to fund indigent women's abortions but covering the cost of their sterilizations, the federal government made it more likely that low-income women of color would choose sterilization in order to avoid unwanted pregnancies. Both *McRae* and *Madrigal* thus highlight the ways in which state power has been wielded, not just in the familiar direction of preventing abortion and encouraging pregnancy, but by using coercion to limit or punish family formation by marginalized groups.

Serena Mayeri's treatment of *Planned Parenthood v. Casey* (1992) showcases the interplay of social movement activism, legal and political advocacy, and the evolution of constitutional doctrine. In the 1980s, abortion opponents chipped away at *Roe v. Wade* by passing carefully-crafted state-level restrictions, advocating for a more lenient constitutional standard of judicial review, and supporting presidential candidates who would appoint more conservative judges. By the time Pennsylvania's Abortion Control Act reached the Supreme Court in 1992, *Roe* seemed doomed. But in a surprise decision authored by three Republican appointees, the Court reaffirmed *Roe*'s core holding while upholding all but one of the Pennsylvania restrictions. Abortion rights advocates succeeded in vanquishing spousal notification requirements, arguing successfully that they reflected an archaic vision of marriage inconsistent with modern equal protection law and posed dangers to survivors of intimate partner violence. Feminist advocates and scholars persuaded the Court to see abortion rights as a matter of women's autonomy, dignity, and equal citizenship as well as privacy, and so helped place abortion rights on firmer constitutional footing. But opponents of abortion persuaded the Court to dilute the standard of review applicable to abortion restrictions from strict scrutiny to the "undue burden" standard, and to elevate the state interest in protecting potential life, allowing for many more restrictions that limit access to reproductive health care for poor women, rural women, and women of color. The lessons activists on both sides of the abortion debate learned from *Casey* continue to reverberate today, as an increasingly conservative Court appears poised to further erode abortion rights and access.

In *Pregnant While Black: The Story of* Ferguson v. City of Charleston, Priscilla Ocen tracks one of the most notorious efforts to criminalize the reproductive choices of poor black women and the ways in which law failed to adequately address the various reproductive harms these women experienced as a result. Beginning in 1989, at the height of the moral panic surrounding crack cocaine, staff at the Medical University of South Carolina drug tested poor black pregnant women without their consent. The drug testing was part of a program developed in coordination with local law enforcement, ostensibly in an effort to promote fetal rights. Feminist lawyers, horrified by stories of black women being dragged from their hospital beds, sought to challenge the hospital's policy as a violation of the right to procreation, equal protection, and privacy, and in so doing, underscored the policy as part of a larger state effort to regulate the reproductive choices of black women. In 2001, the Supreme Court struck down the policy as a violation of the Fourth Amendment's right to be free of unreasonable searches. The Court's narrow framing of the legal question, however, left open the question of whether states may punish women for their behavior while pregnant. As a result, in the years since *Ferguson*, pregnant women, disproportionately those who are poor and black, continue to be prosecuted for crimes ranging from child neglect to murder.

In the next chapter, Samuel Bagenstos examines Chief Justice Rehnquist's surprising opinion for the Court in *Nevada Department of Human Resources v. Hibbs* (2003). In upholding the family-care provisions of the Family and Medical Leave Act (FMLA) as a proper exercise of Congress's authority to enforce the Fourteenth Amendment, the *Hibbs* Court endorsed key tenets of what the chapter calls feminist universalism—the notion that sex equality is best served by rules and policies that reject differentiation between women and men. The chapter traces the way that many American feminist legal advocates moved toward universalism in the 1970s and 1980s—a process that culminated in the enactment of the FMLA in 1993. The chapter then shows how Rehnquist—hardly known for his embrace of legal feminism up to that point—relied heavily on feminist universalist arguments in *Hibbs*. Rehnquist's embrace of universalism is perhaps ironic. Even at the time *Hibbs* was litigated, evidence was accumulating that the FMLA's universalist approach was insufficient to achieve the underlying goals of disestablishing gender-role stereotypes and promoting equal opportunities for women and men throughout society. In this regard, *Hibbs* at once reflects the triumph of the feminist universalist project and its limitations.

Pregnancy at work is front and center in Katherine Shaw's chapter on *Young v. UPS* (2015), the Supreme Court's most recent case on the meaning of the Pregnancy Discrimination Act of 1978. When UPS driver Peggy Young became pregnant, her doctor recommended that she not lift more than 20 pounds for the duration of her pregnancy. UPS refused to accommodate her limitation—although it accommodated many other employees with non-pregnancy-related limitations—forcing her to take unpaid leave and eventually to lose her health insurance. The lower courts in Young's case, like most lower courts across the country, analyzed her PDA claims in a comparative framework, concluding that the failure to accommodate *some* nonpregnant employees insulated UPS from liability for its refusal to accommodate pregnancy. In Young's case, the Court corrected that distortion of the PDA, holding that a pregnant worker like Young *could* make out a claim of pregnancy discrimination where an employer provided accommodations to a sizable number of other employees. Peggy Young's win was an important victory for pregnant workers—a victory that suggests the appeal of pregnancy across political lines. As Shaw explains, the legal fight to protect women who become pregnant and wish to remain pregnant, while also continuing to work, has produced unlikely coalitions of individuals and organizations that take starkly different views on many other issues involving reproductive rights and justice. Young's litigation team and amicus supporters reflected both liberal and conservative voices; so did the 6–3 majority her case produced, recalling the PDA's enacting coalition nearly forty years earlier. In this regard, *Young* may point the way to the prospect of unexpected—yet durable—legal and political coalitions around issues like paid leave, subsidized childcare, and additional protection against pregnancy discrimination at the state and local level.

Cary Franklin tells the story of *Whole Woman's Health v. Hellerstedt*, the 2016 case in which the Court invalidated a Texas law (H.B. 2) that imposed onerous regulations on abortion providers—and not on providers of other medical procedures of equal risk—in the name of protecting women's health. The chapter focuses not only on the Court's decision, but on actors such as Americans United for Life (AUL), an influential advocacy group partly responsible both for H.B. 2 and for the broader constitutional strategy that produced it. As Franklin explains, AUL has been tremendously successful in restricting women's access to abortion in recent years by pursuing an incremental strategy that aims to "hollow[ ] out *Roe*," not by challenging it directly but by promoting ever-stiffer abortion regulations and persuading courts to weaken constitutional protections for the abortion right. One of the chief ways AUL has pursued these goals is by casting abortion regulation as woman-protective, asserting that such regulation shields women and fetuses alike from a greedy and unscrupulous abortion industry. During the legislative debates over H.B. 2, legislators opposed to the law disputed its claims to protect women's health. They argued that there were no legitimate health justifications for the law, that it would actually hurt women by driving reproductive healthcare clinics out of business, and that the state's poor track record when it came to protecting women's health undermined its claim to be acting for that reason here. The central question in *Whole Woman's Health* was whether the Court would defer to the legislature's assertion that it was acting to protect women's health or whether it would probe whether the regulation actually yielded health benefits. The Court did the latter: It examined whether Texas's law actually served the state's interest in protecting women's health, and how the law affected women's ability to exercise the abortion right. By scrutinizing the law and finding that the balance of interests weighed heavily in favor of invalidation, the Court handed AUL and other anti-abortion forces a defeat. But it did not take long for those forces to regroup, in preparation for the next round of battles over abortion rights.

In our final chapter, Douglas NeJaime maps the legal question of parental recognition onto evolving principles of sexual orientation equality. He does so through the lens of *Brooke S.B. v. Elizabeth A.C.C.*, a groundbreaking 2016 New York Court of Appeals decision. While LGBT advocates have long argued for more expansive approaches to parenthood that would protect parents and children in a range of families, in recent years they also have urged courts to protect the children of same-sex parents specifically and thereby vindicate principles of sexual orientation equality. This chapter shows how an emphasis on sexual orientation equality can shape approaches to parental recognition in ways that yield recognition for some families—namely, same-sex couples and others using assisted reproductive technologies (ART)—while leaving other families in an uncertain state—namely, families in which the nonbiological parent did not participate in the decision to have the child but nonetheless raised the child. This distinction illustrates differences in standards that distinguish between *intent* and *function*. Intentional parenthood focuses on the decision to have a child, while functional parenthood focuses on the act of raising the child. The *Brooke S.B.* court adopted an intentional standard, and connected its approach to respect for same-sex couples' families and to emergent constitutional and family-law principles of sexual orientation equality. Nonetheless, the court explicitly left open the possibility of a functional test that would reach beyond the same-sex parents before it. Accordingly, both *Brooke S.B.* and subsequent developments—including decisions relying on and extending *Brooke S.B.*—have made New York a state in which same-sex and other nonbiological parents have multiple routes to parental recognition. New York is not alone in this regard: about half of states now recognize an unmarried nonbiological parent as a legal parent through an intentional or functional standard. Other states have resisted these reforms and have continued to limit parentage, presenting a new frontier for reproductive rights and justice.

1

Melissa Murray*

Sexual Liberty and Criminal Law Reform: The Story of *Griswold v. Connecticut*

Estelle Griswold, the Executive Director of the Planned Parenthood League of Connecticut (PPLC), could not have been more delighted. Just two days after she opened a Planned Parenthood birth control clinic at 79 Trumbull Street in New Haven, Connecticut, two police detectives were knocking on the door, seeking permission to search the premises.[1] For most, the prospect of welcoming police scrutiny would be unfathomable. But police scrutiny is exactly what Griswold and Lee Buxton, a Yale Medical School obstetrician and the clinic's medical director, hoped for when the clinic opened its doors on November 1, 1961.[2]

Just a few months earlier, the United States Supreme Court had dismissed a constitutional challenge to Connecticut's birth control ban on the ground that, although the law was on the books, it was rarely enforced—a crucial fact that "deprive[d] these controversies of the immediacy which is an indispensable condition of constitutional adjudication."[3] Despite the Court's pronouncement, Griswold and Buxton knew that the 1879 Connecticut law, which proscribed both using contraception and counseling others about contraception,[4] was a real imposition in the lives of Connecticut citizens, and not simply a case of

---

* Professor of Law, New York University School of Law. Many thanks to Douglas NeJaime, Kate Shaw, and Reva Siegel for their helpful comments and suggestions, and to the participants in our Fall 2017 convening, where I received tremendously insightful feedback. Caitlin Millat and Dylan Cowitt provided outstanding research and editorial assistance. All errors are my own.

[1] *See* DAVID J. GARROW, LIBERTY AND SEXUALITY: THE RIGHT TO PRIVACY AND THE MAKING OF *ROE V. WADE* 202–03 (1998).

[2] *Id.* at 201.

[3] Poe v. Ullman, 367 U.S. 497, 508 (1961).

[4] The Connecticut ban consisted of two statutory provisions. Under the first provision, "any person who uses any drug, medicinal article or instrument for the purpose of preventing conception shall be fined not less than fifty dollars or imprisoned not less than sixty days nor more than one year or be both fined and imprisoned." Conn. Gen. Stat. § 53–32 (1958 rev.). Under the second provision: "Any person who assists, abets, counsels, causes, hires or commands another to commit any offense may be prosecuted and punished as if he were the principal offender." Conn. Gen. Stat. § 54–196 (1958 rev.).

"harmless, empty shadows."[5] Although the law was rarely enforced against private physicians, who often prescribed contraception to their patients,[6] it *was* used to prevent the operation of publicly-available birth control clinics that would make contraception accessible to those without the means to secure private medical care.[7] And because the state allowed a health exception to the law, which permitted condoms, but not oral contraceptives or diaphragms, to be sold throughout the state, the ban also imposed particular burdens on Connecticut women.[8] With these harms in mind, Griswold and Buxton opened their clinic in the hope that "someone will complain and that the State Attorney in New Haven will act to close the center."[9]

Now, as she ushered Detectives Blazi and Berg into her office, Griswold could not contain her excitement. In the ninety-minute police interview, she did most of the talking. As Blazi took notes, Griswold eagerly proffered multiple copies of the clinic's literature and pamphlets, all of which scrupulously detailed the clinic's services and operations (including the procedure for fitting and instructing women in the use of a diaphragm and contraceptive jelly).[10] Throughout the interview, she made clear her strong hope that she would be charged and prosecuted for violating the law, thereby creating the ideal conditions for a constitutional challenge.[11]

On November 10, she got her wish. Circuit prosecutor Julius Maretz issued arrest warrants for Griswold and Buxton. Accompanied by one of their lawyers, Catherine Roraback, the pair appeared at police headquarters that afternoon to surrender. Their crime? Aiding and abetting the violation of the Connecticut statute by providing women with instruction on and materials for contraception.[12]

Although it would require her arrest and a criminal prosecution, in the end, Estelle Griswold achieved her desired outcome. In 1965, the

---

[5]   *Poe*, 367 U.S. at 508.

[6]   Lori Ann Brass, *An Arrest in New Haven, Contraception and the Right to Privacy*, YALE MED., Spring 2007, at 16, 16; Jonathan T. Weisberg, *In Control of Her Own Destiny: Catherine G. Roraback and the Privacy Principle*, YALE L. REP., Winter 2004, at 39, 40.

[7]   *See* Cary Franklin, *The New Class-Blindness*, 128 YALE L.J. 2, 22–24 (2018) (discussing the law's impact on public birth control clinics). In this regard, *Griswold* was part of a long effort to secure access to birth control for all citizens, not simply those with access to private physicians. As Jill Lepore notes, "[f]rom the start, the birth control movement has been as much about fighting legal and political battles as it has been about staffing clinics, because, in a country without national healthcare, making contraception available to poor women has required legal reform." Jill Lepore, *Birthright*, NEW YORKER, Nov. 14, 2011, at 49.

[8]   *See* Neil S. Siegel & Reva B. Siegel, *Contraception as a Sex Equality Right*, 124 YALE L.J. F. 349, 353–54 (2015) (discussing the way in which the law traded on well-worn gendered stereotypes about sex and parenting).

[9]   *See* GARROW, *supra* note 1, at 201.

[10]   *Id.* at 203.

[11]   *Id.* at 203–04 (noting that Griswold told detectives "she welcomed arrest and a chance to settle the question of the Connecticut State Statute's legality").

[12]   *Id.* at 206–07.

Supreme Court's decision in *Griswold v. Connecticut* struck down the Connecticut birth control ban and famously announced a right to privacy emanating from the "penumbras" of various constitutional guarantees.[13] Since then, *Griswold*'s logic has underwritten a broader commitment to reproductive rights—one that has expanded the right to contraception,[14] secured a woman's right to choose an abortion,[15] and paved the way for legal recognition of same-sex marriages.[16]

For a case that stands at the core of the constitutional law canon, *Griswold* is surprisingly spare—the majority opinion occupies a mere seven pages in the U.S. Reports. Critically, its spareness is not limited to its length. *Griswold*'s logic, some have argued, is conceptually underdeveloped, inviting a multitude of interpretations. For some, *Griswold* is a meditation on the relationship between enumerated and unenumerated rights.[17] For others, it is a reproductive rights case, laying a foundation for greater recognition of bodily autonomy.[18] It has also been cast as a sex equality case, underscoring the gendered nature of the Connecticut contraceptive ban and gesturing toward the relationship between privacy and equality.[19] For still others, it stands as a warning about the perils of judicial overreaching and creating rights out of whole cloth.[20]

This Essay offers an alternative interpretation of *Griswold*—one that has been woefully overlooked. Although we have come to regard it as a constitutional law case, or as a reproductive rights case, at bottom, *Griswold* was a criminal law case. Put differently, despite the majority's

---

[13]   381 U.S. 479, 484 (1965).

[14]   Eisenstadt v. Baird, 405 U.S. 438 (1972).

[15]   Roe v. Wade, 410 U.S. 113 (1973).

[16]   Obergefell v. Hodges, 576 U.S. ___, 135 S. Ct. 2584 (2015).

[17]   *See* David Helscher, Griswold v. Connecticut *and the Unenumerated Right of Privacy*, 15 N. ILL. U. L. REV. 33, 58 (1994) (arguing that *Griswold* is "significant for giving breadth and life to the idea that individuals have rights inherent in their existence, in being human and in being persons"); *see also* Robert G. Dixon, Jr., *The* Griswold *Penumbra: Constitutional Charter for an Expanded Law of Privacy?*, 64 MICH. L. REV. 197, 198 (1965) (noting that the *Griswold* opinion "ranged broadly through the Bill of Rights" to identify where the right to privacy was "directly or peripherally protected").

[18]   *See* Lackland H. Bloom, Jr., *The Legacy of* Griswold, 16 OHIO N.U. L. REV. 511, 534 (1989) (maintaining that *Griswold* "came to stand—in doctrine as well as in fact—for a relatively broad principle of constitutionally protected autonomy with respect to contraceptive and procreative matters").

[19]   *See* Siegel & Siegel, *supra* note 8, at 350 ("Because *Griswold* was decided before the sex equality claims and cases of the 1970s, the *Griswold* Court did not expressly appeal to equality values in explaining the importance of constitutionally protected liberty . . . . Yet as some contemporaries appreciated, in protecting decisions concerning the timing of childbearing, the *Griswold* Court was protecting the foundations of equal opportunity for women, given the organization of work and family roles in American society.").

[20]   *See* Robert H. Bork, *Neutral Principles and Some First Amendment Problems*, 47 IND. L.J. 1, 9 (1971) ("*Griswold*, then, is an unprincipled decision, both in the way in which it derives a new constitutional right and the way it defines that right, or rather fails to define it."); *see also* Michael J. McConnell, *Ways to Think About Unenumerated Rights*, 2013 U. ILL. L. REV. 1985, 1989 (2013) (characterizing *Griswold*'s reasoning as "turning somersaults in an unpersuasive attempt to ground the right of married couples to use contraceptives in the First, Third, Fourth or another part of the Fifth, Amendments").

discussion of penumbras and privacy, *Griswold* was, first and foremost, a case about prosecutions and policing. The challenged Connecticut statute carried a criminal penalty; and, critically, Griswold and Buxton were arraigned, charged, and tried before a court for violating it.

More importantly, *Griswold* was not simply a decision conjured out of whole cloth, as critics have suggested. Rather, it was a case born of and rooted in a criminal law reform movement that sought to design limits on the state's authority to police and enforce sexual mores. In this regard, Griswold and Buxton's constitutional challenge was not merely about expanding access to birth control, but also part of a broader effort to reimagine the state's use of criminal law as a means of enforcing moral conformity. Although criminal law has routinely been used to mark the boundary between licit and illicit sex, not all uses of the criminal law for regulating sex and sexuality have been viewed as desirable. Generally, the use of criminal law for marking and punishing coercive and nonconsensual sex has been deemed acceptable and appropriate, while criminal law's use in marking and punishing consensual sex—particularly between two adults—has encountered more skepticism. The facts of *Griswold* bear this out.

In overlooking *Griswold*'s criminal law antecedents, we have neglected this important aspect of the case and its legacy. This Essay recovers this history and situates *Griswold* in this historical debate about the scope and limits of the state's authority to use the criminal law to enforce moral and sexual conformity. Expanding *Griswold*'s narrative to include its ties to the criminal law reform movement brings into focus the concerns about contraceptive access that predated *Griswold*—and continue to shape the contemporary debate over public funding for contraception. As importantly, the contrast between the 1960s, when the state used the criminal law to curtail contraceptive access and use, and the present, when contraceptive use is lawful but access to contraception remains uneven, calls into question decriminalization's efficacy as a means of law reform.

PRIVACY AND CRIMINAL LAW REFORM

Since the founding, American jurisdictions have relied on the criminal law to regulate sex and sexuality.[21] Crucially, however, the state's efforts to regulate sex and sexuality focused primarily on criminalizing sex outside of marriage. On this account, the criminalization of contraceptive use did not occur until the period following the ratification of the Fourteenth Amendment, amidst fears about the decline in the birth rate among native-born white women. In 1873, as part of a broader "Purity" campaign, Congress passed the Comstock Act, which criminalized the use of the federal postal service for

---

[21] *See, e.g.*, State v. Green, 1 Kirby 87 (Conn. Super. Ct. 1786) (upholding conviction for violation of adultery statute, which provided that "if any man be found in bed with another man's wife, the man and woman so offending, being thereof convicted, shall be severely whipt [sic], not exceeding thirty stripes.").

distribution of contraception and other "obscene" materials.[22] In the aftermath of the Comstock Act, roughly half of the states promulgated their own "mini-Comstock laws," criminalizing contraceptive use and codifying the view that sex and procreation were inextricably linked.[23] Enacted in 1879, under the sponsorship of P.T. Barnum, the circus promoter who was then serving in the Connecticut legislature,[24] the contraceptive ban was part of this wave of "Comstockery." But even as it was part of the postbellum effort to combat declining birthrates, the ban, which codified the view that sex *should* be procreative, was part of a broader state effort to define the boundaries of normative sex and sexuality under laws prohibiting fornication, adultery, sodomy, and abortion. Critically, few questioned the state's power to legislate sexual mores, as the regulation of sexual morality was widely acknowledged to be within the scope of the state's police power to promote the health, safety, and general welfare of citizens.

include Griswold case — Blackmun specifies that state still has pwr to regulate sexuality in ways beyond birth control

But by the 1940s and 1950s, scholars were beginning to question this traditional authority. In two groundbreaking sex studies, *Sexual Behavior in the Human Male* and *Sexual Behavior in the Human Female*, Indiana University's Alfred Kinsey drew back the curtain on the intimate lives of everyday Americans. As Kinsey explained, Americans routinely engaged in sexual acts and practices that violated the criminal laws of most jurisdictions.[25] The problem was not the acts themselves, which, in Kinsey's view, were commonplace and therefore "normal," but rather a religiously-inflected legal regime that criminalized these acts in the name of morality. *is issue w/ separation of church + state?*

Kinsey's research revealed not only the gulf between the law's expectations and the people's actual practices, but also the fact that most of these morality-tinged prohibitions went unenforced. If they were enforced, it was done selectively, targeting vulnerable populations. As such, these statutes "instilled cynicism toward the law," diminishing respect for the legal system.[26] Not content simply to note the disjunction between law's expectations and the reality of quotidian life, Kinsey began

---

[22]   Comstock Act, ch. 258, 17 Stat. 598 (1873) (repealed 1909); *see also* Reva B. Siegel, *Reasoning From the Body: A Historical Perspective on Abortion Regulation and Questions on Equal Protection*, 44 STAN. L. REV. 261, 314–15 (1992). For a discussion of the "purity campaign" waged by Anthony Comstock and the Committee for the Suppression of Vice, see Margaret Blanchard, *The American Urge to Censor: Freedom of Expression Versus the Desire to Sanitize Society—From Anthony Comstock to 2 Live Crew*, 33 WM. & MARY L. REV. 741, 745–49 (1992).

[23]   Siegel & Siegel, *supra* note 8, at 350–51.

[24]   GARROW, *supra* note 1, at 16.

[25]   WILLIAM N. ESKRIDGE, JR., DISHONORABLE PASSIONS: SODOMY LAWS IN AMERICA 1861–2003 109 (2008) (discussing Kinsey's presentation of a discussion paper entitled "Biological Aspects of Some Social Problems," which argued that the law was divorced from the reality of intimate life and calling for law reform).

[26]   LEIGH ANN WHEELER, HOW SEX BECAME A CIVIL LIBERTY 106 (2013).

advocating for legal reform. Private, consensual sexual acts, he argued, should be beyond the purview of the criminal law.[27]

Kinsey's was not the only voice challenging the state's authority to use criminal law to enforce traditional sexual mores. In 1954, in response to a series of controversial prosecutions of prominent Londoners on charges of homosexual sodomy, the British Parliament convened the Wolfenden Committee. Tasked with considering the ongoing efficacy of laws criminalizing homosexual sodomy and prostitution, the Committee issued a report to the British Parliament recommending the decriminalization of consensual same-sex sodomy.[28] In doing so, the Report emphasized limits on the state's authority to criminalize private, consensual conduct, noting that "there must remain a realm of private morality and immorality which is, in brief and crude terms, not the law's business."[29]

The Wolfenden Report prompted a series of debates between the legal philosopher H.L.A. Hart and Lord Patrick Devlin, a prominent conservative on Britain's High Court, on the role that majoritarian social mores should play in the criminal law.[30] Devlin argued that, irrespective of harm or injury to persons or property, the criminal law legitimately could be used to discourage deviations from commonly held notions of morality.[31] In response, Hart argued that although the criminal law could be used to address immoral acts that posed harm to third parties or property (like murder or theft), it should not be used to criminalize all departures from majoritarian mores, including departures from conventional mores regarding out-of-wedlock sex.[32]

Meanwhile, on the other side of the Atlantic, the American Law Institute (ALI), a group of prominent lawyers, judges, and legal scholars charged with clarifying and simplifying the American common law, was also launching its own effort to reform and modernize American criminal law. Led by Columbia Law School professor Herbert Wechsler, the ALI's Model Penal Code (MPC) project sought to draft a modern criminal code that could be adopted in whole or in part by individual states. Although the MPC's drafters would consider a wide range of reforms, they took particular interest in laws governing sexual offenses. In doing so, the drafters were influenced by Kinsey's research and the Wolfenden Report.

---

[27]   *Id.* at 105.

[28]   THE WOLFENDEN REPORT: REPORT OF THE COMMITTEE ON HOMOSEXUAL OFFENSES AND PROSTITUTION ¶ 62, at 48 (Stein & Day 1963). Notably, the Committee recommended the continued criminalization of prostitution.

[29]   *Id.* ¶ 61, at 48.

[30]   *See* Mary Anne Case, *Of "This" and "That" in* Lawrence v. Texas, 2003 SUP. CT. REV. 75, 123–24 (noting that the Hart-Devlin debates were a response to the Wolfenden Report).

[31]   *See* PATRICK DEVLIN, THE ENFORCEMENT OF MORALS 2–3 (1965).

[32]   *See* H.L.A. HART, LAW, LIBERTY AND MORALITY 57 (1963). Understood as a major exposition of themes at the heart of criminal law, the Hart-Devlin Debates were excerpted in leading criminal law casebooks of the day. *See* BREST, ET. AL., PROCESSES OF CONSTITUTIONAL DECISIONMAKING 1382 n.12 (7th ed. 2018).

Specifically, the MPC drafters worried that laws criminalizing private sexual conduct between consenting adults intruded too far into private life. As importantly, they were sensitive to concerns that enforcing victimless sex offenses diverted scarce public resources from more pressing criminal justice issues, like rising rates of violent crime.

At the ALI's annual meeting in 1962, a draft of the MPC was presented to the membership for approval. The draft urged substantial changes in the laws governing adultery, fornication, prostitution, abortion, contraception, and private acts of sodomy between consenting adults. Under the proposal, fornication and adultery would no longer be criminalized, nor would the use and distribution of contraception. State regulation of abortion would be liberalized to permit "therapeutic" abortions in cases of rape, incest, and harm—broadly conceived—to the mother. Criminalization of sodomy would be reserved for circumstances involving force and/or public conduct. Eventually approved by a vote of the ALI's membership, the ALI's effort to reform sexual offenses also spawned similar legislative reform efforts in other jurisdictions, including Illinois and New York.[33]

CREATING CONSTITUTIONAL PRIVACY

Critically, these calls for criminal law reform—from Alfred Kinsey's work to the Wolfenden Report and the MPC draft—all emphasized a sphere of private, intimate life secluded from state oversight and insulated from criminal regulation. By the 1950s and 1960s, the concept of a zone of privacy beyond the state's regulatory ambit began to coalesce in ways that were meaningful for both criminal law reform and the effort to liberalize access to birth control.

In two cases concerning the scope of constitutional protections for criminal defendants, the United States Supreme Court began exploring the idea of a zone of privacy into which the government could not intrude. *Rochin v. California* involved a criminal conviction based upon evidence obtained when police officers entered the bedroom of a suspect and his wife, forcibly opened the suspect's mouth to remove recently swallowed materials, and ordered the "forcible extraction of his stomach's contents."[34] Concluding that the officers' actions "shock[ed] the conscience," the Court reversed the conviction, holding that evidence obtained through such "brutal conduct" violated the Fourteenth Amendment's Due Process Clause.[35]

Nearly a decade later, *Mapp v. Ohio*[36] offered the Court an opportunity to elaborate the contours of the constitutional protections established in *Rochin*. Like *Rochin*, *Mapp* involved an intrusive search of

---

[33]   ESKRIDGE, JR., *supra* note 25, at 123–24 (2008); *see also* Melissa Murray, Griswold's *Criminal Law*, 47 CONN. L. REV. 1045, 1051–52 (2015).

[34]   342 U.S. 165, 172 (1952).

[35]   *Id.* at 173.

[36]   367 U.S. 643 (1961).

an individual's home. Brandishing a fabricated warrant, Cleveland police officers initiated a thorough search of Dollree Mapp's home, including her bedroom, her "child's bedroom, the living room, the kitchen and a dinette," ultimately discovering a cache of pornographic material in a trunk. Although Mapp disclaimed ownership of the trunk and its contents, she was arrested, prosecuted, and found guilty of "knowingly having had in her possession and under her control certain lewd and lascivious books, pictures, and photographs" in violation of state law. Despite the fact that it was nominally an obscenity case, Mapp's ACLU lawyers argued that the state's intrusion into the private sphere—Mapp's home—was, by itself, a constitutional violation. In overturning Mapp's conviction, the Court seemed receptive to this line of argument. Referencing *Rochin*, the *Mapp* Court articulated a "freedom from unconscionable invasions of privacy" rooted in the Fourth and Fifth Amendments.[37]

Although *Rochin* and *Mapp* were principally concerned with procedural protections for criminal defendants, criminal law reformers interested in substantive limits on the state's use of the criminal law saw great promise in the Court's assertion that "the security of one's privacy against arbitrary intrusion by the police is implicit in the concept of ordered liberty."[38] In 1964, at the ACLU's Biennial Conference in Boulder, Colorado, Harriet Pilpel, who would later serve as general counsel for both the ACLU and Planned Parenthood, sought to bring together the logic of privacy, criminal law reform, and the ACLU's efforts to secure civil liberties in the face of the government's nascent "war on crime."[39] The ACLU's neglect of sex laws in its conception of civil liberties was, in Pilpel's view, regrettable and shortsighted. "An intelligent appraisal of the sex laws," she implored the ACLU, "could aid in the war on crime by carving out a definition of crime behavior which there is no rational or social, i.e. *secular*, reason for making criminal—behavior in private between consenting adults."[40] On this account, unless and until the ACLU was willing to take on sex laws as part of its broader agenda to secure civil liberties, these laws would "continue to be, as they are now, a dagger aimed at the heart of some of our most fundamental freedoms."

For Pilpel, the concept of privacy could be used to bridge the ACLU's efforts to secure civil liberties in cases like *Rochin* and *Mapp* and the effort to reform criminal sex laws, including birth control bans. On this account, privacy was not simply a means of securing procedural rights in criminal cases, but rather was a substantive limit on the state's authority to use the criminal law to regulate private conduct and enforce morality. Now, as the federal government launched a national war on crime, the

---

[37] *Id.* at 657.

[38] *Id.* at 650 (quoting Wolf v. Colorado, 338 U.S. 25, 27–28 (1949)).

[39] Harriet Pilpel, Civil Liberties and the War on Crime, Biennial Conference of the American Civil Liberties Union, 71 ACLUP, 1964.

[40] *Id.*

interest in a right to privacy as a bulwark against an encroaching state had become even more urgent. In light of the government's keen interest in cracking down on crime, outmoded sex laws posed an enormous threat. As Kinsey had earlier noted, morals-driven sex laws were easy to violate and, more troublingly, were prone to selective enforcement against vulnerable and marginalized communities. In this regard, a constitutional right to privacy could provide both procedural protections for criminal defendants *and* substantive limits on the state's authority to criminalize certain conduct.

CHALLENGING THE CONNECTICUT STATUTE IN THE STATE HOUSE AND THE COURTHOUSE

The language of the criminal law reform movement—and privacy in particular—came to frame efforts to reform and repeal the Connecticut contraceptive ban. By the late 1950s, birth control activists were eager to harness the logic of the criminal reform effort—and the underlying interest in privacy as a bulwark against the state—to challenge prohibitions on contraception. In a provocative 1955 advertisement, the PPLC underscored that the Connecticut contraceptive ban was about more than access to birth control. The ad, which depicted police officers hiding under beds, warned that "[a] policeman in every home is the only way to enforce this law." In doing so, the ad suggested that the law's enforcement *demanded* the state's presence in the most intimate recesses of the home. In this regard, the ad emphasized that, in allowing the state into the home to police sexual mores, the law imposed upon the rights and privacy of *all* citizens, not just women in need of birth control.

PPLC attacked the law through legislative advocacy *and* litigation. The earliest effort at judicial reform came in the 1940 case *State v. Nelson*, which sought to read into the statutes an exemption that would allow physicians to prescribe contraceptives to married women. On appeal, the Connecticut Court of Errors declined to follow this interpretation of the law, upholding the convictions of two doctors and a nurse under the 1879 law.[41] Still reeling from the loss in *Nelson*, a few years later, PPLC launched a new challenge, seeking an exemption for physicians in circumstances where pregnancy would pose a danger to the patient's life.[42] As before, the Connecticut high court held that the statute contained no implied exceptions for prescribing contraceptives in situations where pregnancy would endanger a patient's life. The case was appealed to the United States Supreme Court, which dismissed the matter on standing grounds.[43]

On the advocacy front, over the course of fifteen years, PPLC, in tandem with Planned Parenthood Foundation of America (PPFA), would make sixteen attempts to revise or repeal the contraception ban in the

---

[41]   126 Conn. 412, 11 A.2d 856 (1940).

[42]   *See* Tileston v. Ullman, 26 A.2d 582 (Conn. 1942), *appeal dismissed*, 318 U.S. 44 (1943).

[43]   Tileston v. Ullman, 318 U.S. 44 (1943).

legislature. Initially, these legislative efforts focused on complete repeal. When this strategy failed spectacularly, the birth control movement refocused its efforts on a more modest reform—legislating an exception to the law that would allow physicians to prescribe contraception to married women—the kind of exemption it unsuccessfully sought to read into the law in *Nelson*. Although this alternative would have the practical effect of freeing physicians from the threat of criminal prosecution, it would only make contraceptives available to those with access to private physicians.[44] Despite this limitation, the modest reform was seen as deeply threatening, and conservative forces, in tandem with the Catholic Church, stubbornly thwarted this effort at legislative reform.[45]

After years of pressing the legislature, PPLC eventually conceded defeat. Recognizing that the Catholic Church and conservative groups would continue to resist legislative reform, PPLC, now under the leadership of its energetic new executive director Estelle Griswold, launched new plans for yet another court challenge—one that would reach the U.S. Supreme Court, where it would be successfully resolved on the merits. PPLC envisioned a new legal challenge that would focus both on doctors who wished to advise patients about birth control, *and* on married couples for whom pregnancy would entail serious health risks and complications.

To achieve its goals, PPLC partnered with Yale Law School professor Fowler Harper and recent Yale Law School graduate Catherine Roraback[46] to bring a lawsuit. Harper and Roraback worked with Lee Buxton, PPLC's medical director, to recruit as plaintiffs married couples for whom a pregnancy posed a severe risk to the wife's health and life.[47] The case—*Poe v. Ullman*[48]—argued that the Connecticut contraceptive ban violated the patients' and physicians' due process rights under the Fourteenth Amendment. In making this claim, Harper and Roraback, with input from national ACLU lawyers Harriet Pilpel and Morris Ernst, elaborated the privacy arguments glimpsed in *Rochin* and *Mapp*, contending that the Connecticut law was a significant intrusion into intimate life.

---

[44] For a discussion of the socioeconomic consequences of the contraception ban, see Cary Franklin, Griswold *and the Public Dimension of the Right to Privacy*, 124 YALE L.J. F. 332 (2015).

[45] *See* GARROW, *supra* note 1, at 137–43.

[46] After her work challenging the contraceptive ban, Roraback would continue litigating on behalf of reproductive rights in Connecticut. She litigated a string of cases challenging Connecticut's criminal ban on abortion, leading to the law's invalidation by a three-judge panel in 1972, just a few months before *Roe v. Wade. See* Abele v. Markle, 351 F. Supp. 224 (D. Conn. 1972). In challenging the Connecticut abortion statute, Roraback "started developing some of these ideas that a woman has a right to control her own destiny." Weisberg, *supra* note 6, at 42. Meaningfully, these strains of women's liberation had been largely absent in the *Griswold* litigation.

[47] Weisberg, *supra* note 6, at 40.

[48] 367 U.S. 497, 508 (1961).

In addition to the pseudonymous *Poe* plaintiffs, Harper and Roraback also recruited two married Yale Law students, David and Louise Trubek, to front an ancillary legal challenge to the ban.[49] If the *Poe* plaintiffs presented a more traditional view of marriage, with breadwinner husbands and homemaker wives, then David and Louise Trubek were a point of departure—as were their legal arguments. Like the *Poe* plaintiffs, the Trubeks appealed to privacy in challenging the ban, but their privacy arguments also struck notes of sex equality.[50] For the Trubeks, access to contraception was not a matter of (the wife's) life or death—pregnancy posed no known health challenges to the couple. Instead, their interest in contraception was rooted in their desire to plan their family in a manner that made sense for their marriage, and, just as importantly, allowed both of them to establish and build careers as practicing lawyers. As they explained in their briefs, access to contraception would allow them the space and autonomy to make crucial decisions about how their marriage would be organized, including how to plan a family in a way that made sense for both of their legal careers.[51] On this account, marital privacy was not simply about excluding the state from the most intimate aspects of daily life; it was a precondition for structuring marriage along more egalitarian lines. In this regard, in both *Poe* and *Trubek v. Ullman*, the privacy argument sparked by the criminal law reform movement and tested in the context of procedural protections for criminal defendants was now deployed to challenge a substantive criminal law in registers that sounded in both liberty and equality.

In the end, the Supreme Court dismissed both cases. Treating the papers filed in *Trubek* as a petition for certiorari, the Court declined to review the case.[52] *Poe v. Ullman* was dismissed on jurisdictional grounds, with the Court concluding that because there was no threat of enforcement, the case was not yet ripe for review.[53] Still, the *Poe* plaintiffs' privacy argument resonated with Associate Justices William O. Douglas and John Marshall Harlan—although not necessarily as a limit on *all* state uses of the criminal law. In considering the Connecticut ban, Douglas imagined a world where "full enforcement of the law . . . would reach the point where search warrants issued and officers appeared in bedrooms to find out what went on."[54] Such an invasion of "the innermost sanctum of the home," in Douglas' view, constituted "an invasion of the privacy that is implicit in a free society."[55]

---

[49]   Trubek v. Ullman, 165 A.2d 158 (Conn. 1960).

[50]   *See* Melissa Murray, *Overlooking Equality on the Road to* Griswold, 124 YALE L.J. F. 324, 326 (2015).

[51]   *See* Complaint at 2, Trubek v. Ullman, 367 U.S. 907 (1961) (No. 847).

[52]   *Trubek*, 367 U.S. 907.

[53]   367 U.S. at 508–09.

[54]   *Id.* at 519–20 (Douglas, J., dissenting).

[55]   *Id.* at 520–21.

Although Harlan agreed that the Connecticut ban presented an imposition on privacy rights,[56] his dissent also forthrightly engaged the question of the state's authority to legislate morality.[57] Critically, Harlan did not dispute the state's authority to legislate in order to promote its "people's moral welfare," including laws that prohibited "adultery, homosexuality, fornication and incest."[58] But the Connecticut ban, which "determined that the use of contraceptives is as iniquitous as any act of extra-marital sexual immorality" was "surely a very different thing indeed from punishing those who establish intimacies which the law has always forbidden and which can have no claim to social protection."[59]

Both Douglas and Harlan echoed aspects of the broader criminal law reform debate that had raged over the last fifteen years. Should the state use the criminal law to police morality? And, if the state could use the criminal law to police morals, how far could it go to do so? Did the Constitution impose any restraints on the exercise of state police power in intimate life? For Harlan, state regulation of sexual morality was permissible, but the state's authority was not unfettered. The state could not go so far as to intrude upon marriage, an institution that the state valued, protected, and promoted as the licensed site of sex and sexuality. Douglas, although he did not endorse state criminal regulation of adultery and fornication, also appeared convinced that state intervention into the home to police contraceptive use violated the Constitution.

Because it dismissed *Poe v. Ullman* on jurisdictional grounds, the Court did not have the opportunity to consider these questions against the backdrop of the federal Constitution. However, soon after the Court's decision in *Poe*, the PPLC opened a birth control clinic in New Haven.[60] As expected, the birth control clinic drew law enforcement attention. In just a few days, Griswold and Buxton were arrested and charged under Sections 53–32 and 54–196, setting the stage for *Griswold v. Connecticut*.

As *Griswold* made its way through the Connecticut legal system, it became clear that this litigation was unlike the prior legal challenges. As an initial matter, Griswold and Buxton had different legal representation. Of the lawyers who had represented the plaintiffs in *Poe v. Ullman*, only Catherine Roraback remained on the *Griswold* legal team. Fowler Harper, who had spearheaded the *Poe* and *Trubek*

---

[56]   *See id.* at 553 (Harlan, J., dissenting) (rejecting "the intrusion of the whole machinery of the criminal law into the very heart of marital privacy, requiring husband and wife to render account before a criminal tribunal of their uses of that intimacy").

[57]   *See id.* at 539 ("In reviewing state legislation, whether considered to be in the exercise of the State's police powers, or in provision for the health, safety, morals or welfare of its people, it is clear that what is concerned are the powers of government inherent in every sovereignty. Only to the extent that the Constitution so requires may this Court interfere with the exercise of this plenary power of government.") (internal quotations and citation omitted).

[58]   *Id.* at 552–53.

[59]   *Id.* at 553.

[60]   *See* Mary L. Dudziak, *Just Say No: Birth Control in the Connecticut Supreme Court Before* Griswold v. Connecticut, 75 IOWA L. REV. 915, 936 (1990).

challenges and argued *Poe* before the Supreme Court, succumbed to cancer in 1965. Thomas Emerson, Harper's Yale Law School colleague, took up the cause, joining Roraback to defend Griswold and Buxton.[61]

The change in representation was not the only difference. As they pushed toward the Supreme Court, Emerson and Roraback refined their legal strategy. Again, privacy figured prominently as a limit on the state's authority. Critically, however, Griswold, Buxton, and their amici bolstered the privacy claim with other arguments that were rooted in the larger debate about criminal law reform and state enforcement of morals. In their briefs, the appellants went beyond privacy to explain that morals legislation, like the Connecticut laws at issue, was prone to arbitrary and discriminatory enforcement.[62] The concern with selective and discriminatory enforcement had also loomed large in the ALI's efforts to reform sexual offenses in the MPC. Indeed, Emerson and Roraback seemed to be parroting the concerns that the ALI drafters, Pilpel, and others had long articulated about the abuse of sexual offense laws when they noted that the challenged Connecticut statutes could be used "for blackmail, or for paying off a grudge, or for harassment of an unpopular citizen. It is not capable of rational administration."[63]

In addition to these concerns about selective enforcement, Emerson and Roraback argued that the challenged Connecticut statutes had the perverse effect of encouraging other criminal behavior. As they explained in their brief on behalf of Griswold and Buxton, "[t]he statutes tend to produce an increase in the number of illegal abortions." This point was likely due to the input of PPFA, the parent organization to the PPLC, which also assisted Emerson and Roraback and wished to link concerns about the birth control ban with broader concerns about family planning and population control. Indeed, PPFA filed its own amicus brief[64] in which it elaborated this concern. As it explained, as an alternative to contraception for married couples, abstinence was unrealistic and undesirable—and was likely to lead to more objectionable criminal conduct, like adultery, prostitution, and abortion.

Importantly, all of these arguments had been raised throughout the criminal law reform debate. Although it focused on the constitutionality of the contraceptive ban, as it headed to the Supreme Court, *Griswold* also bore the imprint of the criminal law reform movement and its interest in designing limits on state authority.

---

[61] *See* GARROW, *supra* note 1, at 230–32 (describing Fowler's transition of the case to his "longtime friend and colleague Tom Emerson" as he succumbed to his illness).

[62] Brief for Appellants at 70–71, Griswold v. Connecticut, 381 U.S. 479 (1965) (No. 496).

[63] *Id.* at 71–72.

[64] Brief and Appendices for Planned Parenthood Fed'n of Am. as Amicus Curiae, Griswold, 381 U.S. 479 (No. 496), 1965 WL 115612.

PRIVACY AND MORAL CONFORMITY

On June 7, 1965, the Court announced its 7–2 decision invalidating the Connecticut ban and announcing a right to privacy that, in the majority's view, emanated from the penumbras of the "specific guarantees in the Bill of Rights" and inhered in the marital relationship.[65] It was perhaps unsurprising that privacy figured so prominently in the decision. After all, the *Poe* dissenters, who now formed the core of the Griswold majority—with Douglas writing for the Court—had emphasized the idea of a space insulated from state encroachment. Further, Emerson and Roraback raised the privacy principle in their briefs—and did so in a manner that sounded in the register of criminal law reform. Specifically, they emphasized the idea of privacy as an essential feature of limited government. As they explained in their brief before the Court:

> The concept of limited government has always included the idea that governmental powers stopped short of certain intrusions into the personal and intimate life of the citizen. This is indeed one of the basic distinctions between absolute and limited government. Ultimate and pervasive control of the individual, in all aspects of his life, is the hallmark of the absolute state. A system of limited government safeguards a private sector, which belongs to the individual, and firmly distinguishes it from the public sector, which the state can control.[66]

Although the majority opinion embraced the notion of privacy as a bulwark against an encroaching state, it tethered the right to the institution of marriage and the marital couple—an abrupt departure from the individual-focused conception of privacy cultivated in the criminal reform debate. While Emerson and Rorabeck discussed marriage in their briefs, they did so to augment a broader argument about the right of all citizens to be secluded—in most places, but especially in the home—from the all-encompassing authority of the state. To this end, the appellants' brief, like the briefs filed in *Mapp* and *Rochin*, highlighted marriage and privacy, but harnessed these concepts to a more robust notion of individual rights. On this account, privacy's protections were not reserved exclusively for married couples, but were "a vital element" of the Constitution's efforts to "safeguard[ ] the private sector of the citizen's life,"[67] whether in marriage or outside of it.

For the *Griswold* majority, however, marriage provided a limiting principle for the newly announced right to privacy. The court recognized that an implicit right to privacy could logically license a wider range of sexual conduct, including more controversial crimes like sodomy, adultery, and fornication. In a likely effort to cabin its reach, Douglas'

---

[65]   381 U.S. at 484.
[66]   Brief for Appellants, *supra* note 62, at 79.
[67]   *Id.*

majority opinion rhetorically linked the privacy right with marriage and underscored that the challenged Connecticut laws were problematic not because they invited the state to demand moral conformity by intruding too far into the lives of citizens, but because they "operate[d] directly on an intimate relation of husband and wife and their physician's role in one aspect of that relation."[68]

But even as marital privacy undergirded *Griswold*, there were telling nods throughout the opinion to the criminal reform debate's interest in designing limits on the state's use of the criminal law. As an initial matter, the opinion's conclusion spoke directly to the question of restraining an intrusive state. Musing "[w]ould we allow the police to search the sacred precincts of marital bedrooms for telltale signs of the use of contraceptives?," the response was emphatic: "The very idea is repulsive."[69] The idea of jackbooted police officers marching through the bedroom was likely no coincidence. The provocative image recalled the facts of *Mapp v. Ohio*—a decision that Douglas had favorably cited only a few pages earlier. In referencing *Mapp*, and sketching the sinister image of the police in the bedroom, Douglas doubled down on an idea that the criminal law reform movement had championed: a right to privacy in the most intimate aspects of life.

But a space of seclusion from state intrusion was not the only link between the *Griswold* opinion and the criminal law reform movement. In defending the newly articulated right to privacy, Justice Douglas dispelled claims that there were no precedents for unenumerated rights by meticulously cataloging earlier cases, like *Meyer v. Nebraska*, *Pierce v. Society of Sisters*, *NAACP v. Alabama*, and *West Virginia State Board of Education v. Barnette*. In pairing *Griswold* with these earlier cases, which concerned parental rights and associational rights, Douglas was not simply aligning the right to privacy with other recognized constitutional guarantees. All of these earlier decisions concerned challenges to the state's attempt to enforce—often by resort to criminal law—conformity among its citizens. For example, *Meyer* struck down a Nebraska law that, in an effort to ensure that English, rather than the native languages of newly arrived immigrants, "should . . . become the mother tongue of all children reared in [the] state,"[70] criminalized German instruction in public schools. In *Pierce*, the Court invalidated a ballot initiative that, in seeking to cultivate a common American culture and ethos,[71] made it a crime for parents to send their children to private and parochial schools.

---

[68]   *Griswold*, 381 U.S. at 481.

[69]   *Id.* at 485–86.

[70]   Meyer v. Nebraska, 262 U.S. 390, 398 (1923).

[71]   In both *Meyer* and *Pierce*, the challenged laws were animated by anti-immigrant, nativist impulses. *See* Paula Abrams, *The Little Red Schoolhouse:* Pierce, *State Monopoly of Education and the Politics of Intolerance*, 20 CONST. COMMENT. 61 (2004).

In both cases, the Court took a dim view of the state's attempts to "foster a homogenous people"[72] and "standardize . . . children."[73]

The laws struck down in *West Virginia State Board of Education v. Barnette* and *NAACP v. Alabama* also spoke to government efforts to compel conformity among its citizens. In *Barnette*, the Court struck down on First Amendment grounds a state resolution requiring public school students to salute the American flag.[74] In *NAACP v. Alabama*, the Court held that the state could not require the NAACP to disclose the names of its members.[75] In both cases, the Court emphasized First Amendment protections for those dissenting from majoritarian viewpoints, whether the dissenters were Jehovah's Witnesses expressing their antipathy for the Pledge of Allegiance, or members of the NAACP, an unpopular political group in 1950s Alabama.

With this in mind, Douglas' invocation of these cases was not simply about implied fundamental rights, but rather intimated an affinity for the underlying logic of the criminal law reform movement. In all of these cases, the Court recognized the individual's right to be nonconforming, whether in terms of the state's educational program or the individual's political life. Put differently, all four cases framed the logic of privacy in terms of limiting the state's authority to enforce moral, educational, and political conformity among citizens.

In 1972's *Eisenstadt v. Baird*, the Court would elaborate *Griswold*'s subtle nod to individual freedom and constitutional protection from state efforts to compel moral conformity. There, the Court invalidated a Massachusetts law prohibiting contraceptive use by unmarried persons, and expanded *Griswold*'s privacy logic beyond the marital couple to focus instead on "the right of the individual, whether married or single, to be free from unwarranted governmental intrusion into matters so fundamentally affecting a person as the decision whether to bear or beget a child."[76] In so doing, the Court recuperated the understanding of privacy as an individual right against state encroachment that undergirded the criminal law reform debate and the appellants' briefs in *Griswold*. A year later, in *Roe v. Wade*, the Court would further underscore the individual nature of the privacy right, concluding that the right to privacy "is broad enough to encompass a woman's decision whether or not to terminate her pregnancy."[77]

---

[72]   *Meyer*, 262 U.S. at 402.

[73]   Pierce v. Soc'y of Sisters, 268 U.S. 510, 535 (1925).

[74]   W. Va. State Bd. of Educ. v. Barnette, 319 U.S. 624 (1943). As the Court noted, "[f]ailure to conform [with the resolution] is 'insubordination' dealt with by expulsion. Readmission is denied by statute until compliance. Meanwhile the expelled child is 'unlawfully absent' and may be proceeded against as a delinquent. His parents or guardians are liable to prosecution, and if convicted are subject to fine not exceeding $50 and jail term not exceeding thirty days." *Id.* at 629 (footnotes omitted).

[75]   357 U.S. 449 (1958).

[76]   Eisenstadt v. Baird, 405 U.S. 438, 453 (1972).

[77]   410 U.S. 113, 153 (1973).

But while *Eisenstadt* and *Roe* extended the privacy right to the individual, they did so by focusing on procreation—an act that, for many, was consonant with *Griswold's* focus on marriage. As *Griswold* and the right to privacy came to be understood as inextricably bound to marriage and procreation, they became unmoored from the broader conversation about the criminal regulation of morals and the state's authority to compel conformity. Indeed, this more limited understanding of privacy as "a fundamental individual right to decide whether or not to beget or bear a child," rather than a broader notion of sexual liberty and restraint on state authority, was evident in the Court's decision in *Bowers v. Hardwick*,[78] a 1986 challenge to a Georgia sodomy prohibition. In rejecting the claim that *Griswold* and its progeny conferred a right to engage in private consensual same-sex sodomy, the *Bowers* majority insisted that there was "[n]o connection between family, marriage, or procreation . . . and homosexual activity."[79] In this way, *Griswold's* invocation of the "sacred precincts of [the] marital bedroom[ ]" transformed it from a case about limits on state intervention in intimate life into a case that was almost exclusively about preventing state interference with marriage and procreation. Indeed, it was this more limited framing that allowed *Griswold*, and its articulation of a protected zone of privacy, to coexist alongside *Bowers*' repudiation of that zone for those deemed ineligible for marriage and incompatible with procreation.

But *Griswold's* effort to design limits on the state did not go unnoticed by all members of the *Bowers* Court. In a stirring dissent, Justice William Brennan focused on the right to privacy as a protection for those who did not conform to majoritarian norms. As he explained:

> The fact that individuals define themselves in a significant way through their intimate sexual relationships with others suggests, in a Nation as diverse as ours, that there may be many 'right' ways of conducting those relationships, and that much of the richness of a relationship will come from the freedom an individual has to choose the form and nature of these intensely personal bonds.[80]

On this account, the right to privacy was about providing space for non-conformity and limiting the state's effort to demand compliance with social and sexual mores.[81]

---

[78]   478 U.S. 186 (1986).

[79]   *Id.* at 191.

[80]   *Id.* at 205.

[81]   Brennan would echo these themes more forthrightly in his dissent from the plurality opinion in *Michael H. v. Gerald D.*, 491 U.S. 110, 141 (1989) (Brennan, J., dissenting) ("We are not an assimilative, homogeneous society, but a facilitative, pluralistic one, in which we must be willing to abide someone else's unfamiliar or even repellent practice because the same tolerant impulse protects our own idiosyncrasies. Even if we can agree, therefore, that 'family' and 'parenthood' are part of the good life, it is absurd to assume that we can agree on the content of those terms and destructive to pretend that we do. In a community such as ours, 'liberty' must include the freedom not to conform."). Similarly, Justice John Paul Stevens' dissent in *Bowers* also emphasized "the origins of the

It would take almost twenty years for these concerns to come to the fore in the Court's jurisprudence and its conception of the right to privacy. In 2003's *Lawrence v. Texas*, the Court confronted another challenge to a state statute criminalizing same-sex sodomy.[82] The case, like *Griswold* before it, prompted arguments about the state's use of the criminal law to police and enforce traditional sexual mores. In overruling *Bowers* and invalidating the challenged statute, the *Lawrence* majority appeared to expand *Griswold*'s notion of privacy beyond marriage to include adult relationships, whether married or not. But critically, *Lawrence* went even further to explicitly delineate limits on the state's use of criminal law as a means of policing sex and enforcing morals and moral conformity. As the *Lawrence* majority framed the issue, the question was "whether the majority may use the power of the State to enforce [majoritarian sexual mores] on the whole society through operation of the criminal law."[83] That issue seemed well settled. Writing for the majority, Justice Kennedy explained that socio-legal developments over "the past half century" reflected "an emerging awareness that liberty gives substantial protection to adult persons in deciding how to conduct their private lives in matters pertaining to sex."[84] As evidence of this "emerging awareness," the majority cited, among other developments, the MPC, which "made clear that it did not recommend or provide for 'criminal penalties for consensual sexual relations conducted in private.' "[85]

Five years after *Lawrence*, a federal appellate court would harness this logic to invalidate a criminal law prohibiting the sale of sex toys. In striking down the law, the appellate court aligned its decision with *Lawrence*, and, perhaps less obviously, *Griswold*. As it explained, "the State here wants to use its laws to enforce a public moral code by restricting private intimate conduct . . . . because the State is morally opposed to a certain type of private consensual intimate conduct."[86] Although the court did not reference it explicitly, one could not help but imagine *Griswold*'s visceral image of the police officer in the bedroom. Married or not, *Griswold* and its progeny were rightly understood as going beyond procreation and abortion to design sharp limits on the state's authority to impose conformity in intimate life.

CONCLUSION

Today, *Griswold v. Connecticut* is regarded as a stalwart of the constitutional law canon. This is fitting, as the decision's articulation of a right to privacy set in motion a "privacy revolution" that ultimately

---

American heritage of freedom—the abiding interest in individual liberty that makes certain state intrusions on the citizen's right to decide how he will live his own life intolerable." *Bowers*, 478 U.S. at 217 (internal citations and quotations omitted) (Stevens, J., dissenting).

[82]   539 U.S. 558 (2003).

[83]   *Id.* at 571.

[84]   *Id.* at 559.

[85]   *Id.* at 572.

[86]   Reliable Consultants, Inc. v. Earle, 517 F.3d 738, 746 (5th Cir. 2008).

reshaped constitutional law and its understanding of individual rights. But *Griswold* was not simply a constitutional law case; it was also a criminal law case, and its place in the criminal law canon should be recognized. Indeed, the privacy revolution that *Griswold* birthed was one that was rooted in the criminal law reform movement and its efforts to limit the state's ability to use the criminal law to enforce moral and social conformity. On this account, *Griswold*'s privacy revolution was one that relied on decriminalization as a means of limiting state authority in intimate life. In *Griswold*'s wake came *Eisenstadt v. Baird, Roe v. Wade,* and *Lawrence v. Texas*—all cases in which the right to privacy was marshaled to invalidate state criminal prohibitions designed to compel conformity with majoritarian sexual mores.

The question of course is whether limiting the state's use of criminal law in intimate life is sufficient to limit the state's authority to compel moral and sexual conformity. Today, more than fifty years after *Griswold* began the process of decriminalizing contraception, access to contraception remains a subject of intense debate and contestation in the United States. Most recently, much of this debate has focused on the contraceptive mandate of the Patient Protection and Affordable Care Act of 2010 (ACA). The law, enacted as part of President Barack Obama's sweeping health care reforms, requires health insurance plans to cover a wide variety of preventative health services. Recognizing that, historically, women's out-of-pocket costs for preventative services have been higher than men's, the ACA explicitly required that women's preventative health services—including contraceptive coverage—be included among those services that health insurance plans must provide without cost. Critically, this "contraceptive mandate" also included accommodations for religious houses,[87] and eventually, non-profits and closely-held corporations that objected to contraceptive coverage on religious grounds.[88] In October 2017, the Trump Administration, after failing to legislatively repeal the ACA, issued administrative rules that offer an exemption to the contraceptive mandate to any employer that objects to covering contraceptive services on the basis of sincerely-held religious beliefs or moral convictions.[89]

The effect of these developments on access to contraception is undeniable. By allowing objecting employers to shift the cost of contraception to consumers, the exemptions make contraception—especially certain forms, like the intrauterine device (IUD)—cost-prohibitive. Accordingly, some fear that the exemptions will impede access to contraception by making certain forms of contraception too

---

[87]   45 C.F.R. § 147.132(a)(1)(i)(A).

[88]   *See* Zubik v. Burwell, 136 S. Ct. 1557 (2016) (non-profits); Burwell v. Hobby Lobby Stores, Inc., 134 S. Ct. 2751 (2014) (closely held corporations).

[89]   Moral Exemptions and Accommodations for Coverage of Certain Preventive Services Under the Affordable Care Act, 82 Fed. Reg. 47838 (Oct. 13, 2017).

costly for women to obtain privately.[90] These material concerns about financial accessibility, interestingly, mirror many of the concerns that shaped the debate over contraception in the years preceding *Griswold*.[91]

Beyond recalling the accessibility concerns that preceded *Griswold*, the challenges to the contraceptive mandate suggest that the state has many options, beyond the criminal law, for compelling compliance with majoritarian sexual mores. By withholding public support for contraceptive access, whether through direct legislation or by allowing objectors to shift the cost of coverage, the state can continue to demand compliance with sexual mores that discredit contraception and non-procreative sex. Obviously, these civil and administrative restrictions are different in principle from the criminal ban struck down in *Griswold*. But in practice, these rules may accomplish the same goal as the criminal ban: precluding widespread access to contraception. And, as importantly, these forms of civil regulation communicate, albeit less robustly, the stigma and disapproval that undergirded criminal prohibitions.[92]

This is all to say that in overlooking *Griswold*'s criminal law antecedents, we have overlooked many things. We have missed an opportunity to locate this decision within the broader context of the criminal law reform debate that was taking place in the 1950s and 1960s—one that sought to limit the state's use of criminal law as a means of policing and enforcing compliance with majoritarian sexual mores. In doing so, we have failed to appreciate that the case was not simply about birth control, but rather, about designing limits on the state.

Recuperating *Griswold*'s place in the criminal law reform debate brings these interests into focus. It makes clear that *Griswold* and the right to privacy it announced was not conjured out of whole cloth, as critics suggest, but rather emerged out of a concerted effort to theorize and enforce limits on the state's use of criminal law. With this context in mind, the theme of privacy as a protection for nonconformity is easier to discern, even amidst the opinion's lofty paean to marriage and the marital couple.

---

90   GUTTMACHER INSTITUTE, DESPITE LEAVING KEY QUESTIONS UNANSWERED, NEW CONTRACEPTIVE COVERAGE EXEMPTIONS WILL DO CLEAR HARM (Oct. 17, 2017), *available at* https://www.guttmacher.org/article/2017/10/despite-leaving-key-questions-unanswered-new-contraceptive-coverage-exemptions-will; *see also* Robert Pear et al., *Trump Administration Rolls Back Birth Control Mandate*, N.Y. TIMES (Oct. 6, 2017), https://www.nytimes.com/2017/10/06/us/politics/trump-contraception-birth-control.html; Complaint for Declaratory and Injunctive Relief at 14–15, Massachusetts v. U.S. Dep't of Health & Human Servs., No. CV 17-11930-NMG, 2018 WL 1257762 (D. Mass. Mar. 12, 2018) (citing estimations that tens of thousands of women could lose access to contraception as a result of the exemptions, resulting in over $18 million in out-of-pocket costs for care).

91   *See, e.g.*, Brief and Appendices for Planned Parenthood Fed'n of Am., supra note 64, at *21, Griswold v. Connecticut, 381 U.S. 479 (1965) (No. 496) (discussing the impact of the Connecticut ban on low-income women).

92   *See* Melissa Murray, *Rights and Regulation: The Evolution of Sexual Regulation*, 116 COLUM. L. REV. 573 (2016).

But perhaps most importantly, when we focus on the criminal law aspects of *Griswold's* history, we are able to glimpse the similarities between the present day and the period that preceded *Griswold*. Then, as now, access to contraception remains uneven, especially for those who lack the resources to privately fund their contraceptive use. As importantly, the stigma and disapproval that once attended contraceptive use can still be felt—albeit in more muted forms—in the new forms of state regulation that have emerged to replace the criminal ban struck down in *Griswold*. These insights make clear the limitations of decriminalization as a means of law reform, and underscore the many vehicles, beyond the criminal law, that the state may deploy in its efforts to enforce a particular vision of sex and sexuality.

2

Neil S. Siegel*

The Pregnant Captain, the Notorious REG, and the Vision of RBG: The Story of *Struck v. Secretary of Defense*

This chapter tells the story of an unfamiliar case that ought to be widely known. It is about a woman, Captain Susan Struck, whose pregnancy and religious refusal to have an abortion subjected her to automatic discharge from the Air Force. The story is worth telling for at least three reasons.

First, the plight of the pregnant captain at its center deserves to be honored by collective memory.

Second, the story reveals a great deal about the vision of gender equality possessed by her advocate before the Supreme Court: Ruth Bader Ginsburg. Ginsburg briefed that 1972 case, *Struck v. Secretary of Defense*, in anticipation of a Supreme Court argument that she was to have given. Before oral argument could occur, however, the federal government waived Captain Struck's discharge and abandoned its policy of automatically discharging women for pregnancy, thereby mooting the case and avoiding a Supreme Court opinion.

Third, and most importantly, the story illuminates how the Constitution speaks to gender equality today. In *Struck*, Ginsburg underscored the vital links between pregnancy discrimination and sex discrimination, and between sex discrimination and restrictions on access to contraception and abortion, at a time when the Justices did not understand the relationships among those practices. The brief came at a very early point in the rise of the constitutional sex discrimination tradition—just after the Court had held for the first time in American history that a sex classification violated the Equal Protection Clause.

---

* David W. Ichel Professor, Duke Law School. I am grateful to Ruth Bader Ginsburg for an illuminating interview—and much more. I am also indebted to Reva Siegel, who has written about the themes in this chapter for many years and who has taught me more about gender equality than anyone besides my daughters. I thank Deborah Dinner, Cary Franklin, Serena Mayeri, Melissa Murray, Douglas NeJaime, and Kate Shaw for instructive comments, and Bo Stewart for outstanding research assistance. Portions of this chapter draw from Neil S. Siegel & Reva B. Siegel, *Struck by Stereotype: Ruth Bader Ginsburg on Pregnancy Discrimination as Sex Discrimination*, 59 DUKE L.J. 771 (2010).

Only by registering where constitutional law was and where it would imminently head when Ginsburg litigated *Struck* can one entirely grasp the profound importance, boldness, and insightfulness of Ginsburg's brief—and the implications of the Court's subsequently proceeding to neglect its message. In more recent decades, the Court has—to a significant, albeit incomplete, extent—gained an appreciation of the relationships among the practices that Ginsburg identified. And Ginsburg the Justice, in speaking for the Court, has brought a *Struck*ian perspective to bear in her interpretation of the intermediate scrutiny standard for sex classifications. Given recent changes in the composition of the Court, however, the future remains deeply uncertain.

STRUCK'S STRUGGLE WITH THE AIR FORCE AND LOWER COURTS

Captain Susan R. Struck was an unmarried career officer in the United States Air Force who became pregnant in 1970 while serving as a nurse in the Vietnam War.[1] Upon learning of her pregnancy, the Service ordered her to McChord Air Force Base in Washington State, where a disposition board hearing was held pursuant to federal statute and Air Force regulations.[2] At the hearing, and in an application for a waiver of her discharge, she declared her intention to give the child up for adoption when she gave birth, and she explained that her accrued leave time of sixty days more than sufficed to cover the temporary period of disability she anticipated after she gave birth.[3]

The Air Force, however, pursuant to a regulation then in effect, required her to choose between having an abortion and leaving the military.[4] The regulation stated that "[a] woman will be discharged from the service with the least practical delay when a determination is made by a medical officer that she is pregnant," and that "[t]he commission of any woman officer will be terminated with the least practical delay when it is established that she . . . [h]as given birth to a living child while in a commissioned officer status."[5] A 1971 amendment provided that "Discharge Action will be cancelled if Pregnancy is Terminated."[6] "I would love to have it known," Ginsburg recently shared, "that during the Nixon administration, Armed Forces bases were offering abortions to women in service and to dependents of men in service."[7] Notably, military policy

---

[1]   Brief for the Petitioner at 3, Struck v. Sec'y of Def., 409 U.S. 1071 (1972) (No. 72–178), 1972 WL 135840.

[2]   *Id.* at 3–4.

[3]   *Id.* at 4.

[4]   *See id.*

[5]   Air Force Reg. 36–12(40) (1970).

[6]   Struck v. Sec'y of Def., 460 F.2d 1372, 1376 (9th Cir. 1971) (quoting Part I.C of 1971 Amendments to Regulations).

[7]   Interview with Ruth Bader Ginsburg, Assoc. Justice, Supreme Court of the United States, in Washington, D.C. (July 21, 2017) [hereinafter Ginsburg Interview].

toward abortion at the time was both more permissive and more coercive than civilian policy.

The choice offered by the Air Force was no choice for Captain Struck, a practicing Roman Catholic for whom abortion was not an option.[8] Rather than accept the end of her career, she sued to prevent the discharge with the help of lawyers for the American Civil Liberties Union in Washington.[9] By contrast, the male service member who participated in conceiving the child with Struck did not require legal counsel. "I think the father of the child was known," Ginsburg recently recalled, "but nobody took any adverse action against him."[10]

Captain Struck was able to secure from the courts a stay of her discharge each month, including with the help of Justice William O. Douglas.[11] But she lost on the merits before Judge William Goodwin of the Western District of Washington, who granted the government's motion to dismiss her complaint.[12] As Judge Goodwin remarked from the bench, "Somebody said that [women are a little more difficult when they are pregnant than when they are not], that there is some change in their personality, and their capabilities. It could well be that the Air Force felt that when they formulated their policy and rules . . . ."[13] (That statement may strike readers today as eye-popping, but Ginsburg was not surprised at the time.[14]) Captain Struck, who had remained on active duty while stationed at McChord Air Force Base, appealed to the United States Court of Appeals for the Ninth Circuit. While her appeal was pending, Captain Struck was transferred to Minot Air Force Base in North Dakota.[15]

During her entire period of service in the Air Force, Captain Struck "maintained an excellent work record."[16] Colonel Max B. Bralliar, the Commanding Officer of Minot Air Force Base who supported her efforts to obtain a waiver of her discharge, reported that Captain Struck " 'demonstrated excellent ability in the performance of the managerial aspects of the work units and an excellent knowledge and application of nursing care principles.' "[17] He also underscored her " 'highly dedicated, professionally correct and mature attitude.' "[18] The government nonetheless denied her request for a waiver, explaining that the provision

---

[8] Brief for the Petitioner, *supra* note 1, at 56.

[9] *Id.* at 4.

[10] Ginsburg Interview, *supra* note 7.

[11] Brief for the Petitioner, *supra* note 1, at 5–7.

[12] *See id.* at 5.

[13] *Id.* at 35 n.29 (quoting Judge William N. Goodwin, Transcript, Struck v. Secretary of Defense, Jan. 29, 1971, at p. 23).

[14] Ginsburg Interview, *supra* note 7.

[15] Brief for the Petitioner, *supra* note 1, at 5.

[16] *Id.*

[17] *Id.* at 6 (quoting Colonel Bralliar).

[18] *Id.* (again quoting Colonel Bralliar).

amending the challenged regulation to provide for waiver requests took effect after she was ordered discharged.[19]

A three-judge panel of the Ninth Circuit unanimously affirmed Judge Goodwin's order dismissing Struck's complaint.[20] In the panel's view, "the necessity for, or at least the high degree of rationality of [the regulation] shows plainly through the fabric of this case."[21] Although Struck had not argued that she was entitled to remain in an active theater of military operations, the appellate court reasoned that if the hospital where Struck worked in Vietnam had been attacked, "a not improbable consequence might have been that the Captain, as a result of injury or shock might have suffered a miscarriage, and become a patient instead of a nurse" and so "a liability and a burden to the Air Force" rather than "a useful soldier."[22] She was thus "removed from the fighting zone, for the good of the service and of herself and her unborn child."[23] The panel also dismissed Struck's equal protection claim, stating that "a relevant physical difference between males and females justifies their separate classification for some purposes."[24] The panel deemed it irrelevant that no other physical condition requiring a period of disability—such as a broken leg, or drug or alcohol abuse (which might not be temporary)—resulted in mandatory discharge. Nor did it matter that a male officer who participated in conceiving a child was free—indeed, encouraged with extra benefits—to continue his Air Force career as a parent.[25]

The panel denied Struck's petition for rehearing and the full court denied rehearing en banc by a vote of eight to five.[26] The panel was, however, no longer unanimous. Dissenting from the denial of the rehearing petition, Judge Benjamin C. Duniway relied upon the Supreme Court's intervening decision in *Reed v. Reed*, which had invalidated a sex classification for the first time by declaring unconstitutional an Idaho statute that preferred men over women as administrators of estates.[27] In Duniway's view, "[i]t is not enough to say that there are physical differences between men and women, or that men and women are not fungible."[28] That was because "centuries of human experience attest to the reality that pregnant women work throughout their pregnancies," and "neither the fact of work nor the fact that one is paid for work has

---

[19]   *Id.*

[20]   Struck v. Sec'y of Def., 460 F.2d 1372, 1377 (9th Cir. 1971).

[21]   *Id.* at 1376.

[22]   *Id.* at 1375.

[23]   *Id.*

[24]   *Id.*

[25]   *See* Brief for the Petitioner, *supra* note 1, at 55 ("Parenthood among servicemen is not deterred, indeed additional benefits are provided to encourage men who become fathers to remain in service.").

[26]   460 F.2d at 1377–78.

[27]   404 U.S. 71 (1971).

[28]   460 F.2d at 1378 (Duniway, J., dissenting).

any necessary relationship to maternal and infant health."[29] He emphasized that no other physical condition occasioning a temporary period of disability resulted in mandatory discharge, and he saw no reason to believe that pregnancy disables women more than other temporary conditions such as a fractured leg, for which the Air Force mandates medical leave, not discharge.[30] "If this be rational," he wrote, "nothing is rational!"[31] He likewise declared irrational the distinction the regulation drew between male and female biological parents of children: only the mother was declared unfit to serve.[32] Although she "was never able to corroborate this," Ginsburg "was given to understand that [Ninth Circuit Judge] Shirley Hufstedler had a lot to do with—she wasn't on the panel—persuading Judge Duniway to write the dissent and then helping him."[33]

GINSBURG'S ARGUMENTS BEFORE THE SUPREME COURT

Struck headed next to the Supreme Court, where she was represented by Ruth Bader Ginsburg in her capacity as general counsel for the ACLU's Women's Rights Project.[34] Ginsburg recently described several litigation efforts on behalf of women's rights at the time:[35] "[O]ne major effort was to get rid of barriers based on pregnancy," both for military service members[36] and for "pregnant schoolteachers [who] were forced out on maternity leave."[37] Another major effort was "reproductive choice."[38] A third was a "whole range of discrimination against women in the Armed Services."[39] Captain Struck's case implicated all of those efforts.

During the summer of 1972, Ginsburg and ACLU Legal Office staff counsel Joel M. Gora "spent many hours" (as she later recounted) drafting Struck's petition for certiorari, one they "hoped would engage the Court's attention."[40] In the previous year, "the ACLU had taken on, along with *Struck*, several other cases challenging the rule, then maintained by all the Armed Forces, requiring pregnant service members to choose between

---

[29]   *Id.* at 1379.

[30]   *Id.*

[31]   *Id.*

[32]   *See id.* at 1380.

[33]   Ginsburg Interview, *supra* note 7.

[34]   *See generally* Amy Leigh Campbell, Raising the Bar: Ruth Bader Ginsburg and the ACLU Women's Rights Project (2003).

[35]   The quotations in this paragraph come from Ginsburg Interview, *supra* note 7.

[36]   *See, e.g.,* Gutierrez v. Laird, 346 F. Supp. 289 (D.D.C. 1972).

[37]   *See, e.g.,* Cleveland Bd. of Educ. v. LaFleur, 414 U.S. 632 (1974). For a history of the activism that produced this decision, see generally Deborah Dinner, *Recovering the LaFleur Doctrine*, 22 Yale J.L. & Fem. 343 (2010).

[38]   *See, e.g.,* Roe v. Wade, 410 U.S. 113 (1973).

[39]   *See, e.g.,* Frontiero v. Richardson, 411 U.S. 677 (1973).

[40]   Ruth Bader Ginsburg, *A Postscript to* Struck *by Stereotype*, 59 Duke L.J. 799, 799 (2010).

abortion and ouster from the military."[41] Struck's case, however, was
their "frontrunner."[42] A shrewd litigator who brought cases she could win,
Ginsburg wanted *Struck* to be the first constitutional pregnancy
discrimination decision by the Supreme Court. Captain Struck's
challenge to the terms of her military service raised questions about
pregnancy in the workplace. Could a woman carry her pregnancy to term
and keep her job at a time when it was commonplace for employers to fire
pregnant employees or force them to take mandatory leave?[43]

Ginsburg also wanted *Struck* to be "the first reproductive choice
case."[44] That was because Captain Struck "chose birth," so "there would
be sympathy for her position."[45] Ginsburg recently explained why she
regarded *Struck* as an ideal vehicle for raising both sides of the issue of
reproductive choice:

> Susan's case was so tremendously sympathetic on every level.
> It was . . . her government saying you can have your work or you
> can give birth. You can't do both . . . . Her case was part of the
> effort to remove barriers to pregnant women but also her case
> just teed up the choice question.[46]

Ginsburg thus viewed *Struck* as about both the right to terminate a
pregnancy and the right to continue one.[47] The latter right was important
in part because coerced sterilization was then of particular concern to
poor women of color, who were pressured or surgically compelled to stop
having children by doctors and social welfare agencies in different parts
of the country.[48]

Ginsburg and Gora "aimed to present the issue of reproductive choice
through [Captain Struck's] eyes and experience. Captain Struck chose

---

[41] *Id.*

[42] *Id.*

[43] *See supra* note 37; *see also* Comment, *Mandatory Maternity Leave: Title VII and
Equal Protection*, 14 WM. & MARY L. REV. 1026 (1973).

[44] Ginsburg Interview, *supra* note 7.

[45] *Id.*

[46] *Id.* Atmospherically, it likely helped Ginsburg's chances before the Court that
Struck was a middle-class white woman who intended to give the baby up for adoption, not
a poor woman of color who sought to raise the child on her own.

[47] *See* Dinner, *supra* note 37, at 385–86 (discussing the emphasis of Ginsburg and
other legal feminists in the early 1970s, including in *Struck*, on the right to bear children,
and not just the right to abortion).

[48] *See* REBECCA M. KLUCHIN, FIT TO BE TIED: STERILIZATION AND REPRODUCTIVE
RIGHTS IN AMERICA 1950–1980, at 7, 94–113 (2011) (documenting the changes in, and the
spread of, forced sterilization practices in the late 1960s and early 1970s through newly
created federal family planning programs); *see also* LINDA GREENHOUSE & REVA B. SIEGEL,
BEFORE ROE V. WADE: VOICES THAT SHAPED THE ABORTION DEBATE BEFORE THE SUPREME
COURT'S RULING 45–46, 49–54 (2012), https://documents.law.yale.edu/sites/default/files/
beforeroe2nded_1.pdf (documenting concerns about forced sterilization among poor women
and women (and men) of color during the late 1960s and early 1970s). For an examination
in this volume of forced sterilization of Mexican-American women during the 1970s, see
generally Maya Manian, *Coerced Sterilization of Mexican-American Women: The Story of
Madrigal v. Quilligan, in* REPRODUCTIVE RIGHTS AND JUSTICE STORIES 97 (Melissa Murray,
Katherine Shaw & Reva B. Siegel eds., 2019).

birth, but her Government made that choice a mandatory ground for discharge."[49] They filed the petition on July 31, 1972, and they "were elated that fall, when the Court, on October 24," agreed to hear the case.[50]

From then until December 4, when Ginsburg filed her merits brief, "the full presentation of Captain Struck's case was [her] principal project."[51] Also signing the brief were Melvin L. Wulf, Gora, and Brenda Feigen Fasteau of the ACLU in New York, and Robert T. Czeisler of the ACLU in Washington State.[52] The brief challenged the Air Force regulation on three grounds.

First, Ginsburg argued that governmental regulation of pregnant women presumptively violated equal protection when such regulation enforced the sex roles and stereotypes of the separate-spheres tradition— the longstanding system of sex roles that defined men as independent breadwinners and women as dependent caregivers in ways that subordinated women. Ginsburg challenged Struck's discharge for pregnancy as perpetuating that tradition:

> The central question . . . is whether the Air Force . . . may call for immediate discharge of pregnant women officers (whether detection of pregnancy occurs at 8 days or 8 months), unless pregnancy terminates soon after detection, while granting sick leave for all other physical conditions occasioning a period of temporary disability.[53]

Ginsburg was subtly implying that Struck had "picked the wrong form of recreation" in Vietnam—that is, sex instead of drugs or alcohol—an idea that "came from Susan."[54] From where Struck stood, there was no defending that difference in treatment:

> It is petitioner's position that *this distinction reflects arbitrary notions of woman's place wholly at odds with contemporary legislative and judicial recognition that individual potential must not be restrained, nor equal opportunity limited, by law-sanctioned stereotypical prejudgments.* Captain Struck seeks no favors or special protection. She simply asks to be judged on the basis of her individual capacities and qualifications, and not on the basis of characteristics assumed to typify pregnant women.[55]

As Ginsburg presented it, the government's discrimination against pregnant officers was a paradigmatic case of the sex-role restrictions that

---

[49]   Ginsburg, *supra* note 40, at 799.

[50]   *Id.*

[51]   *Id.*

[52]   *See* Brief for the Petitioner, *supra* note 1. Ginsburg wrote the brief herself. Ginsburg Interview, *supra* note 7.

[53]   Brief for the Petitioner, *supra* note 1, at 14.

[54]   Ginsburg Interview, *supra* note 7.

[55]   Brief for the Petitioner, *supra* note 1, at 14 (emphasis added).

subordinated women. Because the Air Force viewed pregnant officers through traditional sex-role stereotypes, Ginsburg insisted, it excluded all pregnant women from employment, rather than conditioning eligibility on ability to work.[56] Struck's own case illustrated that "many women are capable of working effectively during pregnancy and require only a brief period of absence immediately before and after childbirth."[57] The government, however, did not make individualized determinations. Instead, it barred all pregnant women from serving, putatively to protect them.[58] Regulations that purport to protect pregnant women by forcing them to stop working, Ginsburg sharply observed, "have in practice deprived working women of the protection they most need: protection of their right to work to support themselves and, in many cases, their families as well."[59] Thus, "mandatory pregnancy discharge reinforces societal pressure to relinquish career aspirations for a hearth-centered existence."[60]

The sex-role stereotypes shaping the Air Force regulation were perhaps most visible in its sex-differentiated approach to parenting. The regulation defined the terms of service so as to require a choice between employment and parenthood—for women only.[61] Although "men in the Air Force are not constrained to avoid the pleasures and responsibilities of procreation and parenthood,"[62] Ginsburg observed, Struck "was presumed unfit for service under a regulation that declares, without regard to fact, that she fits into the stereotyped vision . . . of the 'correct' female response to pregnancy."[63] "The discriminatory treatment required by the challenged regulation," Ginsburg elaborated, "reflects the discredited notion that a woman who becomes pregnant is not fit for duty, but should be confined at home to await childbirth and thereafter devote herself to child care."[64]

The regulation evaluated pregnant women as a group rather than as individuals, and it prohibited the employment of officers who became mothers, while allowing the employment of officers who became fathers. The regulation's prescriptive assumptions about pregnant women defined women's family role so as to make women dependents and second-class participants in core activities associated with citizenship. "[P]resumably well-meaning exaltation of woman's unique role in bearing children," Ginsburg urged, "has, in effect, denied women equal opportunity to develop their individual talents and capacities and has impelled them to

---

[56]   *Id.* at 16–21.

[57]   *Id.* at 35.

[58]   *Id.* at 16–21, 34–37.

[59]   *Id.* at 36.

[60]   *Id.* at 37.

[61]   *Id.* at 55.

[62]   *Id.* at 48.

[63]   *Id.* at 50–51 (internal quotation marks omitted).

[64]   *Id.* at 52.

accept a dependent, subordinate status in society."[65] Increasingly, Americans were recognizing that laws imposing that traditional role on women violate women's right to equal protection.[66] "In very recent years," Ginsburg explained, "a new appreciation of women's place has been generated in the United States. Activated by feminists of both sexes, legislatures and courts have begun to recognize and respond to the subordinate position of women in our society and the second-class status our institutions historically have imposed upon them."[67]

Although focusing on equal protection, Ginsburg advanced two additional challenges to the Air Force regulation. First, she argued that the regulation violated Struck's right to privacy as protected by the Due Process Clause. "Imposition of this outmoded standard upon petitioner," she urged, "unconstitutionally encroaches upon her right to privacy in the conduct of her personal life."[68] Relying on the Court's recent decisions protecting the right to use contraception, *Griswold v. Connecticut*[69] and *Eisenstadt v. Baird*,[70] Ginsburg argued that the regulation "substantially infringes upon her right to sexual privacy, and her autonomy in deciding 'whether to bear . . . a child.'"[71] In response to the Air Force's suggestion that it was aiming to discourage reproduction by service members, Ginsburg noted that the Service provided additional benefits to new fathers to encourage them to continue serving.[72] "The woman," by contrast, "serves subject to 'regulation'; her pursuit of an Air Force career requires that she decide not to bear a child."[73]

Ginsburg also invoked the Free Exercise Clause of the First Amendment, which bars government from "prohibiting the free exercise [of religion]."[74] She emphasized that "the challenged regulation operates with particularly brutal force against women of [Struck's Catholic] faith."[75] That was because "[t]ermination of pregnancy prior to the birth of a living child was not an option [she] could choose." In sum, "the

---

[65]   *Id.* at 38; *see id.* at 38–45 (discussing Hoyt v. Florida, 368 U.S. 57 (1961); Goesaert v. Cleary, 335 U.S. 464 (1948); Muller v. Oregon, 208 U.S. 412 (1908); and Bradwell v. State of Illinois, 83 U.S. (16 Wall.) 130 (1873)). A similar sentence appears in Ginsburg's brief in *Frontiero. See* Brief of ACLU as Amicus Curiae at 34–35, Frontiero v. Richardson, 411 U.S. 677 (1973) (No. 71–1694). She "worked on *Frontiero* and *Struck* simultaneously." Letter from Ruth Bader Ginsburg, Assoc. Justice, Supreme Court of the U.S., to Neil S. Siegel (Mar. 31, 2009) (on file with author).

[66]   *See* Brief for the Petitioner, *supra* note 1, at 16–32.

[67]   *Id.* at 26–27.

[68]   *Id.* at 52.

[69]   381 U.S. 479 (1965).

[70]   405 U.S. 438 (1972).

[71]   Brief for the Petitioner, *supra* note 1, at 54 (quoting *Baird*, 405 U.S. at 453).

[72]   *See id.* at 55 (quoted *supra* note 25).

[73]   *Id.*

[74]   U.S. CONST. amend. I.

[75]   Brief for the Petitioner, *supra* note 1, at 56.

regulation pitted her Air Force career against ... her religious conscience."[76]

GRISWOLD'S SUCCESSFUL EFFORTS
TO MOOT THE CASE

Solicitor General Erwin Griswold, representing the Air Force, was concerned about his client's prospects before the Court. Griswold "recommended that the Air Force waive Captain Struck's discharge and abandon its policy of automatically discharging women for pregnancy."[77] The Air Force took his advice. "[A]s if synchronized," Ginsburg explained, "the Air Force waived Captain Struck's discharge on the eve of our submission."[78] Griswold then moved to dismiss the case as moot.[79]

Research has not revealed why Griswold thought the government's position was untenable. In his remarks at the 1973 Judge Advocate General's Conference, he intriguingly stated that "in this day and age, our position was hopeless," and that "[a]s things have developed in our society, the case was a poor one to litigate."[80] He did not elaborate. Perhaps he regarded coercion of abortion as an inadvisable context in which to vindicate the government's asserted interests in the area of pregnancy discrimination.[81] Although Ginsburg never spoke with him about *Struck*, she recently opined that "he thought there was real loss potential. Plus, he thought it was wrong because they changed the regulation prospectively at the same time that he persuaded them to waive her [discharge.]"[82]

Fatefully, the Supreme Court never heard oral argument. It vacated the judgment of the Ninth Circuit and remanded the case to that court "to consider the issue of mootness in light of the position presently asserted by the Government."[83] "It was the right decision for the Air Force, and good news for Captain Struck and other service members caught in the same bind," Ginsburg observed in retrospect.[84] "But," she

---

[76]   *Id.*

[77]   Ruth Bader Ginsburg, Assoc. Justice, Supreme Court of the U.S., Advocating the Elimination of Gender-Based Discrimination: The 1970s New Look at the Equality Principle, Address at the University of Cape Town, South Africa (Feb. 10, 2006), https://www.supremecourt.gov/publicinfo/speeches/sp_02-10-06.html.

[78]   Ginsburg, *supra* note 40, at 799.

[79]   Memorandum for the Respondents Suggesting Mootness, Struck v. Sec'y of Def., 409 U.S. 1071 (1972) (No. 72–178). For Ginsburg's response to the motion, see Opposition to Memorandum for the Respondents Suggesting Mootness, *Struck*, 409 U.S. 1071 (1972) (No. 72–178).

[80]   Erwin N. Griswold, *Appellate Advocacy*, 1973 ARMY LAW. 11, 15, 16 (1973).

[81]   *Cf.* Janice Goodman, Rhonda Copelon Schoenbrod & Nancy Stearns, Doe *and* Roe, *Where Do We Go from Here?*, 1 WOMEN'S RTS. L. REP. 20, 35 (1973) (describing *Struck* as arising "in the area of coercion"). Notably, however, Griswold did not mention coerced abortion in his 1973 remarks.

[82]   Ginsburg Interview, *supra* note 7.

[83]   Struck v. Sec'y of Def., 409 U.S. 1071 (1972) (vacating and remanding for consideration of mootness given the government's change in position).

[84]   Ginsburg, *supra* note 40, at 799.

added poignantly, "an ideal case to argue the sex equality dimension of laws and regulations governing pregnancy and childbirth had slipped from our grasp."[85] Although conceding she might be "indulg[ing] in wishful thinking," she remained persuaded that, "[h]ad the Court considered Captain Struck's case, with the benefit of full briefing and oral argument, a dreadful mistake might have been avoided."[86] "After homing in on Captain Struck's plight," she reflected with enduring exasperation, "what rational jurist could have declared adverse discrimination based on pregnancy not sex-based discrimination at all!"[87] In that instance as in so many others, the path of constitutional doctrine was contingent, not inevitable. Individual actors made critical moves that influenced the subsequent course of the law.

THE LIGHT *STRUCK* SHEDS ON GINSBURG'S VISION OF GENDER EQUALITY

Ginsburg's *Struck* brief has been neglected[88] not only because the Court did not decide the merits, but also because, shortly thereafter, the Justices in *Geduldig v. Aiello* rejected an equal protection challenge to a policy of pregnancy discrimination.[89] The brief's neglect is unfortunate; it richly illustrates Ginsburg's approach to sex discrimination—an approach she would bring with her when she joined the Court, including when speaking for the Court. During her Supreme Court confirmation hearing in 1993, Ginsburg sought "to explain how [her] own thinking developed on [the] issue" of sex discrimination. She recalled Captain Struck's story, "a case involving a woman's choice for birth rather than the termination of her pregnancy." "The *Struck* brief," she recalled, "marks the time when I first thought long and hard about [sex discrimination]."[90]

Ginsburg's advocacy in *Struck* demonstrates that, along with several other feminist lawyers of the era, including Wendy Williams (whose brief in *Geduldig v. Aiello* also argued that pregnancy regulation is sex-based state action triggering equal protection scrutiny)[91] and Susan Deller Ross (who provided the Equal Employment Opportunity Commission (EEOC)

---

[85] *Id.*

[86] *Id.* The "dreadful mistake" to which Ginsburg was referring was the Court's decision in *Geduldig v. Aiello*, 417 U.S. 484 (1974), which is discussed below.

[87] Ginsburg, *supra* note 40, at 799.

[88] *See* Reva B. Siegel, *Comments, in* WHAT ROE V. WADE SHOULD HAVE SAID: THE NATION'S TOP LEGAL EXPERTS REWRITE AMERICA'S MOST CONTROVERSIAL OPINION 244, 245 (Jack M. Balkin ed. 2005).

[89] 417 U.S. 484, 496–97 (1974) (holding that the Equal Protection Clause permitted California to exclude from its disability insurance program the risk of disability resulting from normal pregnancy).

[90] *Nomination of Ruth Bader Ginsburg to Be Associate Justice of the Supreme Court of the United States: Hearing before the S. Comm. on the Judiciary*, 103d Cong. 205–06 (1993) [hereinafter *Ginsburg Hearing*] (statement of Judge Ginsburg).

[91] *See* Brief for Appellees at 24, Geduldig v. Aiello, 417 U.S. 484 (1974) ("As with other types of sex discrimination, discrimination on the basis of pregnancy often results from gross stereotypes and generalizations which prove irrational under scrutiny.").

with arguments that pregnancy discrimination implicated equal protection),[92] Ginsburg viewed pregnancy discrimination as a core case of sex discrimination. She did so, moreover, at a time when the question was open and plaintiffs were bringing pregnancy discrimination claims under the Equal Protection Clause or Title VII of the Civil Rights Act of 1964, both inside and outside the military. Before *Geduldig*, the EEOC accepted that claim.[93] In *Struck*, Ginsburg understood pregnancy discrimination as sex discrimination because she saw that laws enforcing sex roles of the separate-spheres tradition were compromising the "equal citizenship stature" of women. As a Justice, Ginsburg often uses that phrase,[94] and her commitment to equal citizenship stature has been described as the defining characteristic of her inclusive constitutional vision.[95] The *Struck* brief illuminates the origins and contents of that vision.

Ginsburg's *Struck* brief makes clear that she views some, but not all, regulation of pregnancy as discriminatory, just as she opposes some, but not all, forms of gender differentiation by the government as an equal protection violation. Ginsburg neither mechanically rejects the potential relevance of differences between the sexes nor invariably embraces them. At bottom, the *Struck* brief suggests, Ginsburg contests legally enforced sex-role differentiation because she views the prevailing system of differentiation as perpetuating the subordinate status of women.[96] "Heading the list of arbitrary barriers that have plagued women seeking equal opportunity," she thus insisted, "is disadvantaged treatment based on their unique childbearing function."[97] The harm Ginsburg perceived was not simply the restriction imposed on one woman's opportunities, but the "disadvantaged treatment" regularly inflicted on women because of

---

[92] *See* Reva B. Siegel, *Constitutional Culture, Social Movement Conflict and Constitutional Change: The Case of the De Facto ERA*, 94 CALIF. L. REV. 1323, 1385, n.169 (2006); *see also* Ruth Bader Ginsburg & Susan Deller Ross, *Pregnancy and Discrimination*, N.Y. TIMES, Jan. 25, 1977, at A33 ("Employers will continue to regard women as people who neither need nor want to remain in the labor market for more than a temporary sojourn. Traditional states of mind about women's proper work once the baby comes are difficult to abandon, even for gray-haired jurists.").

[93] *See, e.g.*, 29 C.F.R. § 1604.10(b) (1973) (providing that an employer's general disability policies "shall be applied to disability due to pregnancy or childbirth on the same terms and conditions as they are applied to other temporary disabilities").

[94] *See, e.g.*, Gonzales v. Carhart, 550 U.S. 124, 171–72 (2007) (Ginsburg, J., dissenting); United States v. Virginia, 518 U.S. 515, 532 (1996).

[95] *See generally* Neil S. Siegel, *"Equal Citizenship Stature": Justice Ginsburg's Constitutional Vision*, 43 NEW. ENG. L. REV. 799 (2009).

[96] For expressions of antisubordination understandings of equality, see Owen M. Fiss, *Groups and the Equal Protection Clause*, 5 PHIL. & PUB. AFF. 107, 151 (1976); Catharine A. MacKinnon, *Difference and Dominance: On Sex Discrimination, in* FEMINISM UNMODIFIED: DISCOURSES ON LIFE AND LAW 32, 38 (1987); Reva B. Siegel, *Equality Talk: Antisubordination and Anticlassification Values in Constitutional Struggles over* Brown, 117 HARV. L. REV. 1470, 1472–76 (2004); *see also* Jack M. Balkin & Reva B Siegel, *The American Civil Rights Tradition: Anticlassification or Antisubordination?*, 58 U. MIAMI L. REV. 9, 10 (2003); Jill Elaine Hasday, *The Principle and Practice of Women's "Full Citizenship": A Case Study of Sex-Segregated Public Education*, 101 MICH. L. REV. 755, 769–79 (2002).

[97] Brief for the Petitioner, *supra* note 1, at 34.

their childbearing capacity. Ginsburg was concerned with a practice harming a group.

In *Struck*, Ginsburg highlighted the forms of group disadvantage that discrimination can impose. Understanding the similarities between race discrimination and sex discrimination, she repeatedly related concerns about stereotyping and subordination. (In her 1970s advocacy, Ginsburg insisted that sex discrimination, like race discrimination, violated the antistereotyping principle: seemingly natural reasons for excluding women from public life actually rested on stereotypes that denied individuals the opportunity to compete and relegated women as a group to subordinate status.[98]) So, for instance, she emphasized in the brief that laws enforcing traditional sex stereotypes inflict harm because they reinforce "the subordinate position of women in our society and the second-class status our institutions historically have imposed upon them."[99]

More specifically, the *Struck* brief exemplifies three ways in which antisubordination values orient Ginsburg's thinking about sex equality.[100] First, she does not regard an antisubordination approach as an alternative to equality analysis. Rather, she regards antisubordination *as* equality—as equal standing and respect. She insists that sex discrimination exists even when a regulation is purportedly based on physical differences between the sexes, or "when its impact concentrates on a portion of the protected class, for example, married women, mothers, or pregnant women."[101] Her perspective deems constitutionally pertinent not only the existence of formal sex classifications or intentional discrimination, but also the effects and social meanings of governmental regulation of women. Those concerns define an antisubordination understanding of equality,[102] which guides determination of when and how equality values are implicated. As *Struck* illustrates, such guidance is critical in determining when sex differentiation implicates equality.

Second, the *Struck* brief illustrates how, in determining whether equality values are implicated, Ginsburg adopts an antisubordination perspective. She takes into consideration the standpoint of members of

---

[98]   For an account of the role Ginsburg's arguments played in the emergence of modern sex discrimination law, see generally Cary Franklin, *The Anti-Stereotyping Principle in Constitutional Sex Discrimination Law*, 85 N.Y.U. L. REV. 83 (2010).

[99]   Brief for the Petitioner, *supra* note 1, at 27; *see supra* text accompanying notes 65 and 67.

[100]   The antistereotyping principle as Ginsburg understood it is not co-extensive with all understandings of antisubordination commitments. For a recent argument that antistereotyping concerns are insufficient to combat the economic subordination of working-class women and men, see generally Deborah Dinner, *Beyond "Best Practices": Employment-Discrimination Law in the Neoliberal Era*, 92 IND. L.J. 1059 (2017).

[101]   Brief for the Petitioner, *supra* note 1, at 15.

[102]   For a classic focus on purposes, effects, and social meanings as decisive under equal protection analysis, see generally Charles L. Black Jr., *The Lawfulness of the Segregation Decisions*, 69 YALE L.J. 421 (1960).

historically excluded groups rather than reasoning from the perspective of members of included groups. The Court infamously adopted the perspective of included groups in *Plessy v. Ferguson* in 1896, when it endorsed the doctrine of "separate but equal,"[103] and in *Bradwell v. State of Illinois* in 1873, when it upheld the exclusion of women from the practice of law.[104] Justice Bradley wrote in *Bradwell* that "[t]he paramount destiny and mission of woman are to fulfil the noble and benign offices of wife and mother. This is the law of the Creator."[105] Ginsburg responds in her *Struck* brief that "the method of communication between the Creator and the jurist is never disclosed," and that " 'divine ordinance' has been a dominant theme in decisions justifying laws establishing sex-based classifications."[106] She instead continually presents the case from Captain Struck's point of view. She draws from the "petitioner's experience" to substantiate her assertion that "many women are capable of working effectively during pregnancy and require only a brief period of absence immediately before and after childbirth."[107] She underscores the devastating impact of the Air Force regulation on the careers of military women and its lack of justification apart from traditional stereotypes about how women are "supposed" to respond to a pregnancy.

Third, although Ginsburg's *Struck* brief stresses the equality dimension of discharge-for-pregnancy regulations,[108] she also advances a substantive due process claim in a way that reveals the link between her views on constitutionally protected equality and liberty.[109] (Feminists at the time understood *Struck* as both an equality and a liberty case, just as they understood *Roe v. Wade*,[110] decided the following year.[111]) In making

---

[103] 163 U.S. 537, 551 (1896) ("We consider the underlying fallacy of the plaintiff's argument to consist in the assumption that the enforced separation of the two races stamps the colored race with a badge of inferiority. If this be so, it is not by reason of anything found in the act, but solely because the colored race chooses to put that construction upon it.").

[104] 83 U.S. (16 Wall.) 130, 139 (1872).

[105] *Id.* at 141 (Bradley, J., concurring).

[106] Brief for the Petitioner, *supra* note 1, at 39.

[107] *Id.*

[108] *See Ginsburg Hearing, supra* note 90, at 206 ("The main emphasis was on her equality as a woman, vis-a-vis a man who was equally responsible for the conception."); *id.* ("I did think about it, first and foremost, as differential treatment of the woman, based on her sex.").

[109] *See id.* at 205 ("[I]t has never in my mind been an either/or choice, never one rather than the other; it has been both."); *id.* at 206 ("At no time did I regard it as an either/or, one pocket or the other issue."). Throughout her career, Ginsburg has also reasoned about abortion in equality as well as liberty frames. *See generally* Reva B. Siegel, *Equality and Choice: Sex Equality Perspectives on Reproductive Rights in the Work of Ruth Bader Ginsburg*, 25 COLUM. J. GENDER & L. 63 (2013).

[110] 410 U.S. 113 (1973).

[111] *See* Goodman et al., *supra* note 81, at 35 (discussing reproductive freedom as the right to decide whether to have children without state interference, and viewing *Struck* as about "coercion"). For an account of reproductive rights claims of the era, see Reva B. Siegel, *Sex Equality Arguments for Reproductive Rights: Their Critical Basis and Evolving Constitutional Expression*, 56 EMORY L.J. 815 (2007). "In these early briefs, liberty talk and equality talk were entangled as emanations of different constitutional clauses." *Id.* at 823.

the due process argument, Ginsburg continues to write in terms of "discrimination" and subordination[112] because she registers that laws intervening in major life decisions and enforcing status roles may simultaneously implicate equality and liberty.[113] For Ginsburg, it is less important to disentangle those commitments than it is to emphasize how they are intertwined.

In decades subsequent to *Struck*, however, some feminists criticized Ginsburg for having advocated a sex-blind formal equality in sex-discrimination cases; they portrayed her as having been exclusively and overly concerned with arbitrary sex-based differentiation[114]—in substantial part because she represented male plaintiffs in certain such cases.[115] Much of that criticism occurred during an era of backlash against perceived liberal decisions of the Warren and early Burger Courts, when an increasingly conservative Court was employing a formalist conception of classification to make equal protection doctrine blind to problems of disparate impact and hostile to affirmative action, in both sex and race cases.[116] In such an era, it was possible to (mis)construe Ginsburg's selection of male sex-discrimination plaintiffs as mirroring the formalist reasoning of the later Burger and Rehnquist Courts. Ginsburg's selection of a *pregnant* plaintiff to advance the equal protection claims of women, however, illustrates that she was no formalist. In *Struck* itself, Ginsburg explained that she was challenging laws that enforced traditional sex-role stereotypes because such laws subordinated women.[117] The stereotypes contested by her male plaintiffs (especially male caregivers) were likewise part of a system of gender roles

---

[112] *See, e.g.*, Brief for the Petitioner, *supra* note 1, at 52 ("The discriminatory treatment required by the challenged regulation . . . reflects the discredited notion that a woman who becomes pregnant is not fit for duty, but should be confined at home to await childbirth and thereafter devote herself to child care. Imposition of this outmoded standard upon petitioner unconstitutionally encroaches upon her right to privacy in the conduct of her personal life.").

[113] *See* Reva B. Siegel, *Dignity and the Politics of Protection: Abortion Restrictions under* Casey/Carhart, 117 YALE L.J. 1694, 1744–45 (2008) ("Concern that restrictions on women's liberty can communicate meanings about women's social standing lies at the heart of the sex discrimination cases, especially those cases invalidating laws that deny women autonomy to make decisions about their family roles.").

[114] *See, e.g.*, Judith Baer, *Advocate on the Court: Ruth Bader Ginsburg and the Limits of Formal Equality*, in REHNQUIST JUSTICE: UNDERSTANDING THE COURT DYNAMIC 216, 231 (Earl M. Maltz ed. 2003); David Cole, *Strategies of Difference: Litigating for Women's Rights in a Man's World*, 2 L. & INEQUALITY 33, 55 (1984).

[115] *See, e.g.*, Craig v. Boren, 429 U.S. 190 (1976); Weinberger v. Wiesenfeld, 420 U.S. 636 (1975); Moritz v. Comm'r, 469 F.2d 466 (10th Cir. 1972).

[116] For an account of those developments in race discrimination law, see generally Fiss, *supra* note 96; Siegel, *supra* note 96, at 1535–38. For an exploration of the implications in sex discrimination law, see Reva B. Siegel, *"The Rule of Love": Wife Beating as Prerogative and Privacy*, 105 YALE L.J. 2117, 2188–95 (1996) (showing how the Court's rejection of disparate impact claims in *Washington v. Davis*, 426 U.S. 229 (1976), and *Pers. Adm'r of Mass. v. Feeney*, 442 U.S. 256 (1979), shielded from equal protection scrutiny "facially neutral" practices (such as domestic violence policies) that have long played a role in subordinating women).

[117] *See supra* notes 65–67 and accompanying text (quoting Ginsburg's brief).

that subordinated women (and harmed men) by defining men as breadwinners and women as caregivers.[118]

WHY *STRUCK* MATTERS TODAY

The timing of the *Struck* brief is noteworthy. Ginsburg persuasively urged the Court to view pregnancy discrimination as sex discrimination, and to view sex discrimination as intertwined with women's autonomy to decide whether and when to bear children, at a time when the landscape of modern equal protection, sex discrimination doctrine and substantive due process law had yet to be worked out. Ginsburg talked about pregnancy discrimination in a way that tied pregnancy discrimination to women's equality, and women's equality to reproductive freedom,[119] before the Court split them apart in cases such as *Roe* and *Frontiero v. Richardson*[120] (involving an explicit sex-based distinction) in 1973, and *Geduldig v. Aiello* (involving pregnancy discrimination) the following year.[121] Unwilling to accept the submissions of Ginsburg and the women's movement, the Court made some fateful choices in those cases: to focus its sex equality jurisprudence on cases other than those involving pregnancy, and so to develop its sex equality jurisprudence in isolation from its contraception and abortion jurisprudence. Only by apprehending where the law was and where it was about to go when *Struck* was litigated can one fully appreciate the momentousness, the audacity, and the profundity of that brief—and the implications of the Court's taking a different path during the 1970s and 80s. In 1976, the Court held that equal protection, sex discrimination claims trigger heightened judicial scrutiny in a case involving young men who sought to purchase 3.2 percent beer.[122] Imagine how our understanding of constitutional sex discrimination and substantive due process doctrine might differ in important ways had the Court instead, or also, been prepared to recognize the equal protection claim of a pregnant Air Force captain who challenged a regulation requiring her either to have an abortion or to lose her military career.

In 1972, Ginsburg made a compelling argument that pregnancy discrimination is sex discrimination because of the social understandings about women that pregnancy discrimination reflects and the profound

---

[118] *See* Franklin, *supra* note 98, at 120–25. I recently had occasion to have dinner with Justice Ginsburg and Stephen Wiesenfeld, the plaintiff in *Weinberger v. Wiesenfeld* (cited *supra* note 115). In that case, the Court declared unconstitutional a provision of the Social Security Act that allowed a woman whose husband died to receive benefits based on his earnings but did not allow a man whose wife died to receive benefits based on her earnings. Ginsburg and Wiesenfeld have become close friends over the decades, which no doubt reflects her admiration for a man who was determined to raise his child as a single parent at a time when it was rare for fathers to do such a thing.

[119] *See generally* GREENHOUSE & SIEGEL, *supra* note 48 (reproducing feminist arguments for abortion rights from 1969 to 1973 that invoked privacy and equality and analyzed abortion regulation as part of the regulation of motherhood).

[120] 411 U.S. 677 (1973).

[121] 417 U.S. 484 (1974).

[122] *See* Craig v. Boren, 429 U.S. 190, 197 (1976).

limitations on their lives that it enforces. Although the Court eventually accepted much of Ginsburg's general vision of gender equality, it was slow to recognize pregnancy discrimination as sex discrimination.[123] The *Geduldig* Court in 1974 acknowledged—in a footnote that has seldom been read carefully—that discrimination against pregnant women might be animated by invidious discrimination against women, but it found the exclusion of pregnancy benefits from otherwise comprehensive disability insurance to be a rational method of saving taxpayers money.[124] In the 1970s, the Court did not seriously consider that pregnancy discrimination lay at the heart of the concerns animating the antistereotyping principle. The Court failed to apply the principle outside the context of express sex distinctions, even though feminist litigators argued that the antistereotyping principle applied to pregnancy. The Court did, however, yield to Congress's declaration that pregnancy discrimination can violate federal employment discrimination law, and it began enforcing the 1978 Pregnancy Discrimination Amendment (PDA) to Title VII of the Civil Rights Act of 1964.[125] After four decades of PDA litigation, Americans have come to view the claim that pregnancy discrimination is sex discrimination as one of fundamental—even constitutional—magnitude. The PDA is deeply entrenched.[126]

Nor did the Court in the 1970s carefully examine the relationship to which the *Struck* brief self-consciously pointed—between cases enforcing women's right to equal protection and decisions protecting their autonomy in deciding whether and when to bear children.[127] *Struck*, Ginsburg later wrote, "could have served as a bridge, linking reproductive choice to [sex discrimination]."[128] "[C]onfronted with Captain Struck's unwanted discharge," she continued, "might the Court have comprehended an argument, or at least glimpsed a reality, it later resisted—that disadvantageous treatment of a woman because of her pregnancy and reproductive choice is a paradigm case of discrimination

---

[123] Indeed, the Court self-consciously ducked that question in *Cleveland Board of Education v. LaFleur*, 414 U.S. 632 (1974), by turning an equal protection decision into a substantive due process decision.

[124] *See Geduldig*, 417 U.S. at 496–97 n.20.

[125] For a discussion, see Robert C. Post & Reva B. Siegel, *Legislative Constitutionalism and Section Five Power: Policentric Interpretation of the Family and Medical Leave Act*, 112 YALE L.J. 1943, 2042–43 (2003).

[126] The PDA responded to *Geduldig* and *General Electric Company v. Gilbert*, 429 U.S. 125, 136 (1976), which held that a disability benefit plan excluding disabilities related to pregnancy was not sex discrimination under Title VII. For discussion of the PDA's role in shaping popular and judicial understandings of sex discrimination, see Reva B. Siegel, *"You've Come a Long Way, Baby": Rehnquist's New Approach to Pregnancy Discrimination in Hibbs*, 58 STAN. L. REV. 1871, 1879–98 (2006).

[127] *See* Brief for the Petitioner, *supra* note 1, at 10; *id.* at 53–54 & n.55 (citing Roe v. Wade, 314 F. Supp. 1217 (N.D. Tex. 1970)). For Ginsburg's recent reemphasis on the link between constitutional equality and liberty in the area of reproductive rights, see Gonzales v. Carhart, 550 U.S. 124, 170–72, 184–86 (2007) (Ginsburg, J., dissenting) (citing constitutional sex equality cases as supporting the abortion right).

[128] RUTH BADER GINSBURG (WITH MARY HARTNETT & WENDY W. WILLIAMS), MY OWN WORDS 240 (2016) (reproducing Ruth Bader Ginsburg, *Speaking in a Judicial Voice*, 67 N.Y.U. L. REV. 1185 (1992)).

on the basis of sex?"[129] Ginsburg recently reflected that *Struck* "matters in the sense that what a woman does with her body is her business. It's not the business of the state. I think the case is significant because it says a woman has a choice either way. It's a woman's choice and not the government's."[130]

Ginsburg's hope that *Struck* "would be the first reproductive choice case"[131] went unfulfilled. And yet, through incremental changes that have been underrecognized, the Court has moved closer to Ginsburg's understanding of unconstitutional sex discrimination without entirely embracing it.[132] In equal protection and due process doctrines regarding pregnancy regulation, the Court has slowly internalized many of Ginsburg's concerns about the stereotyping faced by pregnant women like Captain Susan Struck. In *Nevada Department of Human Resources v. Hibbs*, the Court upheld the family-care leave provided by the Family and Medical Leave Act of 1993 (FMLA) as a valid exercise of Congress's power under Section Five of the Fourteenth Amendment to combat unconstitutional sex discrimination.[133] In so holding, the Court suggested—in line with Ginsburg's argument in *Struck*, and despite *Geduldig*—that pregnancy discrimination can constitute unconstitutional sex discrimination.[134] In *Planned Parenthood of Southeastern Pennsylvania v. Casey*, the Court emphasized the liberty of pregnant women (not their physicians, as it had in *Roe*) while emphasizing the sex-equality implications of abortion restrictions.[135] Most recently, in *Whole Woman's Health v. Hellerstedt*, the Court thwarted an attempted circumvention of *Casey* that repackaged an interest in protecting fetal life as an interest in protecting women's health.[136]

The antisubordination perspective that Ginsburg brought to bear in *Struck* would also shape her approach to equal protection as a Justice, including when speaking for the Court. For example, Ginsburg held for the Court in *United States v. Virginia (VMI)* that a military institute's male-only admissions policy violated equal protection, and she distinguished efforts to exclude women from efforts to include them by taking relevant differences into account.[137] More important than the debate over whether the Court applied "real" intermediate scrutiny or de

---

[129] *Id.* at 242.

[130] Ginsburg Interview, *supra* note 7.

[131] *Id.*

[132] For discussion of those developments from the perspective of legal doctrine, see generally Neil S. Siegel & Reva B. Siegel, *Pregnancy and Sex-Role Stereotyping: From Struck to Carhart*, 70 OHIO ST. L.J. 1095 (2009).

[133] 538 U.S. 721, 731 & n.5, 736 (2003).

[134] For discussion, *see generally* Siegel, *supra* note 126.

[135] 505 U.S. 833, 852, 856, 876, 897 (1992). For analysis of the equality reasoning in *Casey*, see generally Neil S. Siegel & Reva B. Siegel, *Equality Arguments for Abortion Rights*, 60 UCLA L. REV. DISCOURSE 160 (2013).

[136] 136 S. Ct. 2292 (2016).

[137] 518 U.S. 515, 533–34 (1996).

facto strict scrutiny in *VMI* is the analytical point that Ginsburg interpreted intermediate scrutiny as antisubordination: her account of that standard for the Court requires the judiciary to closely examine laws that classify on the basis of sex but allows the government to distinguish between men and women so long as "such classifications [are] not . . . used, as they once were, to create or perpetuate the legal, social, and economic inferiority of women."[138] Again writing for the Court in its most recent equal protection, sex discrimination decision, Ginsburg again invalidated a sex classification that subordinated women by reflecting and reinforcing traditional sex-role stereotypes.[139] So *Struck* is part-triumph, not just a missed opportunity, in that Ginsburg eventually leveraged her insights in that case to help forge constitutional law.

To be sure, other recent decisions are in serious tension with Ginsburg's understanding of the links between pregnancy discrimination and sex discrimination;[140] between sex discrimination and abortion restrictions;[141] and between sex classifications and women's subordination.[142] Should an increasingly conservative Court take a different path over the next several years, the story of *Struck v. Secretary of Defense* might serve as a reminder of the legal vulnerabilities and human costs of that path. It might also serve as a source of inspiration and hope for the future.

---

[138] *Id.* at 534 (citing Goesaert v. Cleary, 335 U.S. 464, 467 (1948)).

[139] *See* Sessions v. Morales-Santana, 137 S. Ct. 1678 (2017) (holding that equal protection principles prohibit a sex classification in federal immigration law that creates an exception for unwed U.S.-citizen mothers, but not for such fathers, to the physical-presence requirement for the transmission of U.S. citizenship to a child born abroad, but that only Congress may convert the exception into the main rule displacing other relevant provisions of the law).

[140] *See generally* Coleman v. Court of Appeals of Md., 132 S. Ct. 1327 (2012) (ignoring the links between pregnancy and sex-stereotyping in denying that Section Five authorized the FMLA's self-care provisions).

[141] *See* Gonzales v. Carhart, 550 U.S. 124 (2007) (rejecting a facial challenge to a federal ban on a controversial method of abortion).

[142] *See* Nguyen v. INS, 533 U.S. 53 (2001) (rejecting an equal protection challenge to a sex classification in federal immigration law that requires unwed U.S.-citizen fathers, but not unwed U.S.-citizen mothers, to prove parentage in order to convey citizenship to children born outside the United States).

3

Linda Greenhouse and Reva B. Siegel[*]

The Unfinished Story of *Roe v. Wade*

Roe v. Wade[1] is both a case and a symbol. It is the rare Supreme Court case that Americans know.[2] It holds a special place in constitutional law, remaining openly and intensely contested after nearly half a century despite continuing popular support.[3]

To those who support abortion rights, *Roe* demonstrates the Court's crucial role in protecting individual rights in the face of determined political opposition. For its critics, *Roe* represents the work of an "unelected" Court creating new constitutional rights; supposedly, by deciding matters properly left to democratic determination, the Court inflamed conflict over abortion and riled our politics.[4]

We explain the origins of the abortion right and conflicts over it differently. The story we tell is not simply a litigation history of a landmark case, but instead a story about the democratic foundations of our constitutional law. We start our account of the abortion conflict before

---

[*] Linda Greenhouse is the Joseph Goldstein Lecturer in Law at Yale Law School. Reva Siegel is the Nicholas deB. Katzenbach Professor at Yale Law School. For comments on the chapter, we thank Cary Franklin, Melissa Murray, Serena Mayeri, Robert Post, Jane Kamensky, and David Strauss. For excellent research assistance, we thank Dylan Cowit and Rachel Frank, and for invaluable library support we are indebted to Jason Eiseman and Julie Krishnaswami. We thank Karen Blumenthal for the historical records she shared with us.

[1] 410 U.S. 113 (1973).

[2] *See Supreme Court Survey—Agenda of Key Findings*, C-SPAN / PSB 27 (Aug. 2018), https://static.c-span.org/assets/documents/scotusSurvey/CSPAN%20PSB%202018% 20Supreme%20Court%20Survey%20Agenda%20of%20Key%20Findings%20FINAL%2008 %2028%2018.pdf (noting that, of the forty-seven percent of likely U.S. voters who could "name any cases decided by the U.S. Supreme Court," more than seventy-six percent referenced *Roe*).

[3] *See* Hannah Fingerhut, *About Seven-in-Ten Americans Oppose Overturning* Roe v. Wade, PEW RES. CENT. FACT TANK (Jan. 3, 2017), http://www.pewresearch.org/fact-tank/ 2017/01/03/about-seven-in-ten-americans-oppose-overturning-roe-v-wade/ (noting that, in 2016, sixty-nine percent of Americans said *Roe* "should not be completely overturned").

[4] *See* Cary Franklin, Roe *as We Know It*, 114 MICH. L. REV. 867, 867–71 (2016) (book review); Linda Greenhouse & Reva B. Siegel, *Before (and After)* Roe v. Wade: *New Questions About Backlash*, 120 YALE L.J. 2028, 2071–76 (2011), *reprinted in* LINDA GREENHOUSE & REVA B. SIEGEL, BEFORE ROE V. WADE: VOICES THAT SHAPED THE ABORTION DEBATE BEFORE THE SUPREME COURT'S RULING 263, 303–07 (2d ed. 2012), http://documents.law. yale.edu/sites/default/files/BeforeRoe2ndEd_1.pdf.

litigation begins. Conflict enters the picture well before the courts do, as people argue over the Constitution's meaning in their everyday lives. We recount how citizens who lacked power in any conventional sense were able over time to change the way the nation and its courts understood longstanding guarantees of liberty, of equality, and of life.

Roe itself, filed in a Dallas federal district court in March 1970, was one of many cases in the late 1960s and early 1970s that invoked the Constitution to challenge the century-old regime of criminal abortion statutes;[5] *Roe* just happened to be first in line on the Supreme Court's docket. These cases emerged from principled and heated dialogue among powerful social movements that initially did not even have courts in view. The story of *Roe v. Wade* is the story of conflict born in democratic politics that engendered the rights claims that the Court would ultimately recognize. The conflict continues to this day, even as advocates and their arguments have changed as few would have expected.

This framework offers a fresh context for reading *Roe*. Enlarging our perspective in this way allows us to recover claims for and against abortion rights to which the Court's opinion in *Roe* responded, as well as claims that the Court ignored—claims for women's equality and for protecting potential life that played an important role in reshaping the abortion right nearly twenty years later in *Planned Parenthood of Southeastern Pennsylvania v. Casey*.[6]

The account of *Roe*'s history this chapter offers can inform both normative and predictive debate about *Roe*'s future.

MOBILIZATION FOR REFORM

Abortion, at least in early pregnancy, was not a crime at the nation's founding.[7] But by the late nineteenth century, to deliberately terminate a pregnancy was a crime in every state except when necessary to save a woman's life.[8] Women turned to abortion nonetheless. By the mid-twentieth century, by some estimates, there were 1.2 million abortions a year, meaning that perhaps more than one of every four pregnancies ended in abortion.[9] Women of means could often find their way to a safe abortion, whether by traveling to countries where the procedure was legal

---

[5] On *Roe*, see Roe v. Wade, 314 F. Supp. 1217 (N.D. Tex. 1970). For other cases, see, for example, Crossen v. Breckenridge, 446 F.2d 833 (6th Cir. 1971); Doe v. Rampton, 366 F. Supp. 189 (D. Utah 1973); Abele v. Markle, 342 F. Supp. 800 (D. Conn. 1972), *vacated*, 410 U.S. 951 (1973); Corkey v. Edwards, 322 F. Supp. 1248 (W.D.N.C. 1971), *vacated*, 410 U.S. 950 (1973); Doe v. Scott, 310 F. Supp. 688 (N.D. Ill. 1970); People v. Belous, 458 P.2d 194 (Cal. 1969); State v. Munson, 201 N.W.2d 123 (S.D. 1972).

[6] 505 U.S. 833 (1992).

[7] JAMES C. MOHR, ABORTION IN AMERICA: THE ORIGINS AND EVOLUTION OF NATIONAL POLICY, at vii, 3 (1978); LESLIE J. REAGAN, WHEN ABORTION WAS A CRIME: WOMEN, MEDICINE, AND LAW IN THE UNITED STATES, 1867–1973, at 8 (1997).

[8] REAGAN, *supra* note 7, at 5.

[9] Mary Steichen Calderone, *Illegal Abortion as a Public Health Problem*, 50 AM. J. PUB. HEALTH 948, 950 (1960), *reprinted in* GREENHOUSE & SIEGEL, *supra* note 4, at 22, 23.

(Japan, England, and Sweden, by the 1960s)[10] or by referral to an underground network of doctors who provided safe abortions for a price.

But for women without the money or the network, terminating a pregnancy came at great risk, if the opportunity came at all.[11] In the 1930s, before the introduction of antibiotics, there were an estimated 10,000 abortion deaths a year, with thousands more women left permanently injured or rendered sterile from illegal and unsafe abortions.[12] The majority of these deaths occurred among women of color, even though they comprised a minority of the population.[13] As the years went by, there was little change in the racially disparate burden of illegal abortion. Only six percent of those who died from illegal abortions in New York City in the mid-1960s were white.[14] During this same period, black women were fourteen times more likely than white women to die from illegal abortion in Georgia.[15]

Alarmed public health doctors were among the first to call for reform. At a public health conference in 1959, Dr. Mary Steichen Calderone, the medical director of Planned Parenthood, delivered a paper entitled *Illegal Abortion as a Public Health Problem*.[16] The "frightening hush-hush" surrounding the subject, she argued, was "a symptom of a disease of our whole social body."[17] Calderone emphasized the inequities inflicted on poor women who had no access to doctors who would provide them a safe and legal abortion.[18]

In 1962, the American Law Institute (ALI), a prestigious group of lawyers, judges, and legal academics, proposed a modest but still pathbreaking reform as part of an ongoing project to modernize criminal law. Its proposal called for committees of doctors to authorize therapeutic abortions for women whose situations met certain approved indications. These included a pregnancy that resulted from rape or incest; that "would gravely impair the physical or mental health" of the woman; or would lead to a child born with a "grave physical or mental defect."[19]

---

[10]   GREENHOUSE & SIEGEL, *supra* note 4, at 3.

[11]   REAGAN, *supra* note 7, at 193.

[12]   FREDERICK J. TAUSSIG, ABORTION SPONTANEOUS AND INDUCED: MEDICAL AND SOCIAL ASPECTS 28 (1936).

[13]   *See* ABORTION IN THE UNITED STATES: A CONFERENCE SPONSORED BY THE PLANNED PARENTHOOD FEDERATION OF AMERICA, INC. AT ARDEN HOUSE AND THE NEW YORK ACADEMY OF MEDICINE 67–68 (Mary Steichen Calderone ed., 1958).

[14]   Harriet F. Pilpel, *The Abortion Crisis*, *in* THE CASE FOR LEGALIZED ABORTION NOW 97, 100–01 (Alan F. Guttmacher ed., 1967).

[15]   Loretta J. Ross, *African-American Women and Abortion: A Neglected History*, 3 J. HEALTH CARE FOR POOR & UNDERSERVED 274, 281 (1992).

[16]   Calderone, *supra* note 9, at 22–24.

[17]   *Id.* at 24.

[18]   *Id.* at 23.

[19]   MODEL PENAL CODE § 230.3 (AM. LAW INST., Proposed Official Draft 1962), *reprinted in* GREENHOUSE & SIEGEL, *supra* note 4, at 24, 25.

Notably, the ALI reform proposal, which a dozen states adopted from the late 1960s through 1970,[20] granted authority to doctors, not to women; the version Georgia enacted required a pregnant woman to persuade three doctors plus a three-member hospital committee that her pregnancy qualified for a legal abortion.[21] The American Medical Association, which had helped drive the nineteenth-century effort to criminalize abortion, adopted a new rule in 1970 that authorized its members to perform therapeutic abortions, but also instructed them not to engage in "mere acquiescence to the patient's demand."[22]

Other streams fed into a growing movement for reform. A 1968 best-selling book, *The Population Bomb,* warned that the earth was running out of resources.[23] While eugenicists once focused on controlling the birthrate among the nation's poor, mid-century environmentalists preached the virtues of separating sex and procreation and of limiting family size for the rich and poor alike.[24]

It was not until feminists joined the movement for decriminalization that woman-centered arguments for abortion reform emerged. Betty Friedan, the founder of the National Organization for Women, made such an argument in a fiery speech to an abortion-rights conference in Chicago in February 1969. The conference was sponsored by the Illinois Citizens for the Medical Control of Abortion,[25] a "staid" and "cautious" group whose founders were primarily concerned with "population and family-planning work."[26] Friedan presented the audience with a completely different rationale for reform: "[T]here is no freedom, no equality, no full human dignity and personhood possible for women until we assert and demand the control over our own bodies, over our own reproductive process."[27] Laws criminalizing abortion denied women the authority to shape their lives, Friedan argued. The repeal of criminal abortion laws would endow women with that practical and symbolic capacity: "Women are denigrated in this country, because women are not deciding the conditions of their own society and their own lives. Women are not taken

---

[20]   GENE BURNS, THE MORAL VETO: FRAMING CONTRACEPTION, ABORTION, AND CULTURAL PLURALISM IN THE UNITED STATES 185–86 (2005).

[21]   *See* MODEL PENAL CODE § 230.3, *supra* note 19, at 25; *see also* KRISTIN LUKER, ABORTION AND THE POLITICS OF MOTHERHOOD 55–57 (1984) (arguing that one of the primary goals of therapeutic abortion boards was to restrict access to abortions). For Georgia's multidoctor requirement, see Doe v. Bolton, 410 U.S. 179, 184 (1973).

[22]   *Resolution No. 44: Therapeutic Abortion,* 1970 AM. MED. ASS'N PROCEEDINGS OF HOUSE OF DELEGATES 221, 221, *reprinted in* GREENHOUSE & SIEGEL, *supra* note 4, at 25, 28–29.

[23]   PAUL R. EHRLICH, THE POPULATION BOMB 24–25 (1968).

[24]   *See, e.g.,* ZERO POPULATION GROWTH, INC., PROGRESS?, *reprinted in* GREENHOUSE & SIEGEL, *supra* note 4, at 55, 56–57.

[25]   GREENHOUSE & SIEGEL, *supra* note 4, at 277.

[26]   SUZANNE STAGGENBORG, THE PRO-CHOICE MOVEMENT: ORGANIZATION AND ACTIVISM IN THE ABORTION CONFLICT 16, 45, 53 (1991).

[27]   Betty Friedan, President, Nat'l Organization for Women, Abortion: A Woman's Civil Right (Feb. 1969), *reprinted in* GREENHOUSE & SIEGEL, *supra* note 4, at 38, 39.

seriously as people .... So this is the new name of the game on the question of abortion: that women's voices are heard."[28]

Feminists innovated forms of abortion protest designed to assert women's authority in domains where traditionally it had been denied. To challenge the conventions that consigned women to secrecy and shame about abortion, women shared their own abortion stories during public "speak-outs."[29] The Abortion Counseling Service of the Women's Liberation Movement, better known as Jane, organized to provide access to safe abortion—initially by identifying trustworthy physicians and then by teaching women to perform the procedure themselves.[30] By taking charge in this very practical—and civilly disobedient—way, activists sought to shift the locus of authority from government and doctors to women. The informational brochure Jane distributed asserted: "Only a woman who is pregnant can determine whether she has enough resources—economic, physical and emotional—at a given time to bear and rear a child. Yet at present the decision to bear the child or have an abortion is taken out of her hands by governmental bodies which can have only the slightest notion of the problems involved."[31]

Friedan was hardly the only voice that linked the right to abortion to women's empowerment. Frances Beal, a prominent African-American feminist, described the intersectional harms that abortion's criminalization inflicted on women of color.[32] Women in black and Puerto Rican communities lived in a kind of "double jeopardy": women of color were pressured to accept sterilization in exchange for welfare benefits, and also exposed to unsafe abortion when unready or unable to bear children. Beal emphasized that in 1969, "[n]early half of the child-bearing

---

[28] *Id.*

[29] For what may be the first abortion speak-out protesting the New York Legislature's failure to include women in its hearing on abortion reform, see Susan Brownmiller, *Everywoman's Abortions: "The Oppressor Is Man,"* VILL. VOICE, Mar. 27, 1969, at 1, *reprinted in* GREENHOUSE & SIEGEL, *supra* note 4, at 127, 128–30. On the hearing, which featured fourteen men and one nun on the list of speakers, see Edith Evans Asbury, *Women Break Up Abortion Hearing; Shouts for Repeal of Law Force Panel to Move*, N.Y. TIMES (Feb. 14, 1969), https://www.nytimes.com/1969/02/14/archives/women-break-up-abortion-hearing-shouts-for-repeal-of-law-force.html. On the aims of the feminist "Redstockings" in developing the speak-out technique, and its transatlantic spread, see ALICE ECHOLS, DARING TO BE BAD: RADICAL FEMINISM IN AMERICA, 1967–1975, at 142 (1989). Critically, the speak-out technique was shared among movements. *See* William N. Eskridge, Jr., *Challenging the Apartheid of the Closet: Establishing Conditions for Lesbian and Gay Intimacy, Nomos, and Citizenship, 1961–1981*, 25 HOFSTRA L. REV. 817, 824, 880 (1997) (discussing the use of speak-outs in the post-Stonewall gay rights movement).

[30] GREENHOUSE & SIEGEL, *supra* note 4, at 7.

[31] *Abortion, a Woman's Decision, a Woman's Right*, CWLU HERSTORY PROJECT, https://www.cwluherstory.org/jane-documents-articles/abortion-a-womans-decision-a-womans-right (reprinting "Jane's original informational pamphlet").

[32] Interview by Loretta J. Ross with Frances Beal, in Oakland, Cal., 28–29, 35–37 (Mar. 18, 2005), *in* VOICES OF FEMINISM ORAL HIST. PROJECT, https://www.smith.edu/libraries/libs/ssc/vof/transcripts/Beal.pdf.

deaths in New York City were attributed to abortion alone and out of these, 79% are among non-whites and Puerto Rican women."[33]

COUNTERMOBILIZATION: CONFLICT BEFORE *ROE*

As calls for reform spread from the medical and legal professions to popular movements, those who were committed to keeping abortion illegal began urgently to organize. The clergy of the Catholic Church played a leading role. In 1967, an ALI-style reform bill was pending in the New York Legislature that would have allowed a panel of doctors to determine whether a woman could have an abortion in cases of rape, incest, threat to her physical or mental health, or fetal abnormality. In response, priests in most of the state's 1,700 churches read a pastoral letter warning that the "right of innocent human beings to life is sacred."[34]

In that same year, the National Conference of Catholic Bishops, recognizing that reform was moving swiftly and that "more than half of all Catholics disagreed" with the official Church position, funded a "national educational campaign to provide institutional support for the right-to-life cause"; a year later, a young priest named Bishop James McHugh established the National Right to Life Committee (NRLC) to provide resources to oppose state-level legislative reform.[35]

During this period, the Catholic Church reaffirmed its view that the purpose of sex was to create new life within marriage, reiterating its prohibition on birth control.[36] But in the midst of a revolution in sexual mores and with American Catholics bitterly divided over whether to preserve the Church's ban on contraception,[37] the NRLC built the case for maintaining the criminalization of abortion in terms that made no reference to sex. Instead, the NRLC placed the fetus at the center of the argument, emphasizing its right to life within a constitutional and human rights framework.[38]

---

[33] FRANCES BEAL, BLACK WOMEN'S MANIFESTO: DOUBLE JEOPARDY: TO BE BLACK AND FEMALE (1969), *reprinted in* GREENHOUSE & SIEGEL, *supra* note 4, at 49, 52. For an account exploring the conflicting political pressures on women of color who faced population control measures as well as criminal abortion laws, see JENNIFER NELSON, WOMEN OF COLOR AND THE REPRODUCTIVE RIGHTS MOVEMENT (2003).

[34] George Dugan, *State's 8 Catholic Bishops Ask Fight on Abortion Bill: Pastoral Letter Read*, N.Y. TIMES (Feb. 13, 1967), http://query.nytimes.com/mem/archive/pdf?res=99 02E1DD103BE63ABC4B52DFB466838C679EDE.

[35] DANIEL K. WILLIAMS, DEFENDERS OF THE UNBORN: THE PRO-LIFE MOVEMENT BEFORE *ROE V. WADE* 88–89, 92, 94 (2016); *see also* GREENHOUSE & SIEGEL, *supra* note 4, at 295–97 & n.132.

[36] *See, e.g.*, PAUL VI, HUMANAE VITAE, ENCYCLICAL LETTER OF THE SUPREME PONTIFF PAUL VI (July 29, 1968), *reprinted in* GREENHOUSE & SIEGEL, *supra* note 4, at 73, 76.

[37] *See* GREENHOUSE & SIEGEL, *supra* note 4, at 74–75.

[38] *See* WILLIAMS, *supra* note 35, at 89–90. Emphasis on the fetus and its right to life may have obscured but did not eliminate Catholic views about the wrongs of nonprocreative sex, which found continuing expression in opposition to contraception, gay rights, and same-sex marriage. *See, e.g., Ministry to Persons with a Homosexual Inclination: Guidelines for Pastoral Care*, U.S. CONF. CATHOLIC BISHOPS 3–4 (Nov. 14, 2006), http://www.usccb.org/

Catholic opposition to abortion acquired new momentum under the leadership of Dr. John C. Willke. Willke, a family doctor, spent the 1960s traveling the country with his wife Barbara as Catholic sex and marriage counselors, opposing birth control and celebrating the virtues of saving sex for marriage and childbearing. In 1970, they enlisted in the antiabortion cause.[39] The next year, the Willkes self-published a pocket-sized book, *Handbook on Abortion*,[40] which sold 1.5 million copies in eighteen months.[41] The book was notable for two features. One was a graphic display of color photographs of fetuses.[42] The other, subtler but equally powerful, was its explicit appeal to "our pluralistic society,"[43] rooting opposition to abortion not in religious doctrine about the purposes of sex or the nature of life but instead in logic and medical science. *Handbook on Abortion* went through two dozen printings and was translated into many languages.[44]

To be sure, not all Catholics opposed decriminalization[45] and not everyone who opposed decriminalization was Catholic. But it was the Church leadership that led opposition to abortion reform, identifying that position so closely with Catholicism that Protestant churches—historically unwilling to join forces with the Catholic Church—largely stayed away.[46] (Surprisingly from today's perspective, in 1971 the National Association of Evangelicals and the Southern Baptist Convention adopted positions that accepted abortion in certain health-related circumstances.[47] In this period, evangelicals had little political

---

issues-and-action/human-life-and-dignity/homosexuality/upload/minstry-persons-homosexual-inclination-2006.pdf ("By its very nature, the sexual act finds its proper fulfillment in the marital bond . . . . There are a variety of acts, such as adultery, fornication, masturbation, and contraception, that violate the proper ends of human sexuality. Homosexual acts also violate the true purpose of sexuality.").

[39] *See* JOHN C. WILLKE ET AL., ABORTION AND THE PRO-LIFE MOVEMENT: AN INSIDE VIEW 32–33 (2014); Cynthia Gorney, *The Dispassion of John C. Willke*, WASH. POST (Apr. 22, 1990), https://www.washingtonpost.com/archive/lifestyle/magazine/1990/04/22/the-dispassion-of-john-c-willke/5d8be81a-7521-4986-b7c4-b052765349ac.

[40] J.C. WILLKE & BARBARA WILLKE, HANDBOOK ON ABORTION 145 (1971).

[41] GREENHOUSE & SIEGEL, *supra* note 4, at 99.

[42] Photographs of fetuses, *in* WILLKE & WILLKE, *supra* note 40, following p. 27.

[43] *Id.* at v.

[44] GREENHOUSE & SIEGEL, *supra* note 4, at 99.

[45] *See, e.g.*, George Gallup, *Abortion Seen Up to Woman, Doctor*, WASH. POST, Aug. 25, 1972, at A2, *reprinted in* GREENHOUSE & SIEGEL, *supra* note 4, at 208 ("Fifty-six per cent of Catholics believe[d] that abortion should be decided by a woman and her doctor . . . ."); *see also supra* note 35 and accompanying text (discussing the division of opinion among American Catholics in the early 1970s).

[46] *See* GREENHOUSE & SIEGEL, *supra* note 4, at 295–96 & n.132.

[47] Nat'l Ass'n of Evangelicals, *Statement on Abortion* (1971), *reprinted in* GREENHOUSE & SIEGEL, *supra* note 4, at 72, 73 (stating that abortion should be to available to safeguard the health or life of the woman, and after counseling, in cases of rape or incest); S. BAPTIST CONVENTION, RESOLUTION ON ABORTION (1971), *reprinted in* GREENHOUSE & SIEGEL, *supra* note 4, at 71, 72 (calling for legislation that would allow the possibility of abortion in cases of rape, incest, severe fetal deformity, and "carefully ascertained evidence of the likelihood of damage to the emotional, mental, and physical health of the mother").

engagement with abortion. Opposition to abortion was regarded as Catholic in origin and energy.[48])

The Catholic face of antiabortion activism had political implications that would grow exponentially in importance over the decade to come, offering new incentives for antiabortion advocacy. During the 1972 presidential campaign, leaders of the Republican Party—which to this point had supported liberalization of contraception and abortion—began to experiment with antiabortion advocacy in an effort to recruit Catholic voters away from their traditional allegiance to the Democratic Party.[49] An important figure was Kevin Phillips, a political strategist for the Nixon White House who made his name forecasting that the Republican Party could recruit white Southern Democrats to the GOP by appealing to race (the so-called "Southern Strategy").[50] Phillips was quick to recognize another source of new Republican voters: by adopting an antiabortion stance, Republicans might attract culturally conservative Catholic Democrats.[51]

Patrick Buchanan, another key Republican strategist, saw in the abortion conflict a chance to capture Catholic votes and much more. Working with Richard Nixon's presidential campaign, Buchanan identified new ways of attacking abortion that would tap into voters' unease with those who *supported* abortion—among them, the youth movements calling for liberalization of abortion laws as part of a broader progressive agenda for fundamental social transformation; movements then tying abortion to sexual revolution, civil rights, social justice, and an end to war; and, prominently, feminists emphasizing abortion's role in achieving women's equality in the home and workplace.[52] Buchanan was quick to appreciate that the growing conflict over abortion was not only about when life began but also involved wide-ranging questions of religion, sex, and sexuality—the topics at the heart of what he would later famously call the "cultural wars."[53] Americans were deeply divided about

---

[48]   GREENHOUSE & SIEGEL, *supra* note 4, at 263, 295–97 & n.132.

[49]   *See* WILLIAMS, *supra* note 35, at 188–89; *see also* GREENHOUSE & SIEGEL, *supra* note 4, at 286–87. Gallup polls of the era show that more Republicans than Democrats supported the decriminalization of abortion. *See infra* note 58 and accompanying text.

[50]   James Boyd, *Nixon's Southern Strategy: 'It's All in the Charts,'* N.Y. TIMES (May 17, 1970), http://www.nytimes.com/packages/html/books/phillips-southern.pdf.

[51]   Kevin Phillips, *How Nixon Will Win*, N.Y. TIMES (Aug. 6, 1972), http://www.ny times.com/1972/08/06/archives/how-nixon-will-win-a-republican-takes-to-the-soapbox-in-answer-to.html. *See generally* GREENHOUSE & SIEGEL, *supra* note 4, at 290.

[52]   GREENHOUSE & SIEGEL, *supra* note 4, at 286–92 (discussing strategies for Republicans to court Democratic voters devised by Phillips and Buchanan during the Nixon presidency; documenting how Buchanan urged President Nixon to attack abortion as a way of persuading Catholics and cultural conservatives long affiliated with the Democratic Party to vote for Republicans).

[53]   At the 1992 Republican National Convention, Buchanan warned that America was in the grips of a "cultural war" and denounced the "radical feminis[t] . . . agenda [that] Clinton & Clinton would impose on America: abortion on demand, a litmus test for the Supreme Court, homosexual rights, discrimination against religious schools, women in combat units. That's change, all right. But that's not the kind of change America needs." Patrick J. Buchanan, Address to the Republican National Convention in Houston (Aug. 17,

how to live together, and, as Buchanan understood, abortion was becoming a symbol of those deep divisions.

LEGISLATIVE CHANGE AND LEGISLATIVE LOCK-UP

As public attention to the abortion issue escalated, so did public support for reforming old criminal laws.[54] Between 1967 and 1970, a dozen states enacted laws that followed the ALI's model, permitting abortion—with multiple doctors' approval—for women whose situations met the stated criteria.[55] In 1970, Alaska, Hawaii, Washington, and New York went further to repeal their existing abortion prohibitions to permit women to terminate a pregnancy without restriction until a certain gestational age.[56]

By mid-1972, polls showed startlingly broad-based public appetite for reform of the nation's abortion laws. A Gallup poll published in August of that year showed that sixty-four percent of Americans—nearly two out of three—agreed that "abortion should be a matter for decision solely between a woman and her physician."[57] The responses showed little difference between men and women. Notably, a majority of Catholics (fifty-six percent) agreed with the statement. While a majority of both Republicans and Democrats also agreed, Republican support was notably higher (sixty-eight percent compared with fifty-nine percent).[58]

The momentum for reform seemed unstoppable, with state after state enacting legislation and poll numbers rising. But it all came to a halt after 1970. During the following two years, liberalization efforts failed across the country and no additional reform bills were enacted.[59] The New York Legislature, its members under intense pressure from the clergy of the Catholic Church, repealed the reform measure it had adopted two years earlier.[60] Only Governor Rockefeller's veto kept the reform law on the books.[61] In 1972, a closely watched Michigan referendum to liberalize abortion law failed.[62] This development was

---

1992), *in* AM. PRESIDENCY PROJECT, https://www.presidency.ucsb.edu/documents/address-the-republican-national-convention-houston.

[54]   *See* Judith Blake, *Abortion and Public Opinion: The 1960–1970 Decade*, 171 SCI. 540, 541 & tbl.1 (1971).

[55]   BURNS, *supra* note 20, at 177 tbl.5.1.

[56]   *Id.* at 178 tbl.5.3.

[57]   Gallup, *supra* note 45, at 208. This poll was in Justice Blackmun's files. *See* LINDA GREENHOUSE, BECOMING JUSTICE BLACKMUN: HARRY BLACKMUN'S SUPREME COURT JOURNEY 91 (2005).

[58]   Gallup, *supra* note 45, at 208. For an analysis of polling at the time of the decision showing somewhat weaker support for reform, see Neal Devins, *Rethinking Judicial Minimalism: Abortion Politics, Party Polarization, and the Consequences of Returning the Constitution to Elected Government*, 69 VAND. L. REV. 935, 948 (2016).

[59]   Corinna Barrett Lain, *Upside-Down Judicial Review*, 101 GEO. L.J. 113, 139 (2012).

[60]   GREENHOUSE & SIEGEL, *supra* note 4, at 281 n.69.

[61]   *Id.*

[62]   Robert N. Karrer, *The Formation of Michigan's Anti-Abortion Movement, 1967–1974*, 22 MICH. HIST. REV. 67, 95–98 (1996).

widely seen as a bellwether for the fate of the state-by-state legislative strategy.[63]

The shutdown of legislative reform in the face of overwhelming popular support illustrates the ability of a mobilized minority, committed to a single issue and institutionally funded and organized, to thwart reforms that have broad popular support.[64] In New York, for example, public support for the new abortion law stood at over sixty percent when the legislature repealed it, and support for liberalization in Michigan was fifty-nine percent when voters sent the reform referendum to defeat.[65] In frustration, and with reason to hope for a better outcome, advocates turned to the courts.

NEW CLAIMS ON THE CONSTITUTION

As the effort to secure legislative reform stalled, those in favor of abortion rights turned to other approaches and audiences. Might an appeal to the courts and to the Constitution succeed in changing the law governing abortion—and if so, on what grounds? Young lawyers—recent law school graduates, many of them women—began to make new claims, about a recent Supreme Court decision recognizing a right to privacy in reproductive decision-making,[66] and about the Constitution's guarantees of liberty and equality.

These early cases filed before *Roe* are striking as they express the constitutional injury of laws criminalizing abortion in a variety of ways— some that judges would take decades to recognize and others that judges do not recognize to this day. The cases illustrate popular dialogue about the meaning of the Constitution's guarantees, as citizens try to educate those in power about harms not shared equally across lines of sex, race, and class. Their voices likely played a role in leading judges to appreciate that laws criminalizing abortion inflicted constitutional injuries on women without necessarily persuading the judges of the precise constitutional character of those harms.

In fact, constitutional challenges to abortion statutes were already making their way through the courts, raised by doctors facing criminal prosecution for performing abortions.[67] In 1971, the U.S. Supreme Court reviewed the conviction of a doctor who argued that the health exception in the District of Columbia's abortion law was unconstitutionally vague because it left doctors uncertain whether an abortion would be legal or criminal. To avoid the constitutional question, the Court interpreted the law to give doctors latitude to use their ordinary professional judgment.[68]

---

[63]   *Id.*

[64]   *See* Lain, *supra* note 59, at 139–42.

[65]   *Id.* at 140–41.

[66]   Griswold v. Connecticut, 381 U.S. 479 (1965).

[67]   Risa L. Goluboff, *Dispatch from the Supreme Court's Archives: Vagrancy, Abortion, and What the Links Between Them Reveal About the History of Fundamental Rights*, 62 STAN. L. REV. 1361, 1379 (2010).

[68]   United States v. Vuitch, 402 U.S. 62, 71–72 (1971).

Two years earlier, in *People v. Belous*,[69] the California Supreme Court reversed a doctor's conviction on vagueness grounds. *Belous* drew national attention because the court went beyond vagueness to invoke, as a separate ground for reversing the doctor's conviction, the right to privacy first recognized by the U.S. Supreme Court four years earlier when it struck down a law criminalizing contraception in *Griswold v. Connecticut*.[70]

In invoking the right to privacy, the *Belous* court drew on a widely cited article by a recent law school graduate named Roy Lucas.[71] Lucas advocated directly challenging the constitutionality of criminal abortion statutes under the Fourteenth Amendment's rights of privacy and autonomy recognized in *Griswold*.[72]

Lucas had embarked on a quest that many others were soon to join: how to express intuitions about the injustice of abortion restrictions in constitutional law.[73] Spurred by the recent failure of a reform bill in the New York Legislature, reformers in October 1969 filed four separate lawsuits challenging the state's abortion ban.[74] Each lawsuit drew upon a model brief that Lucas had prepared, taking its arguments in different directions that reflected the interests of plaintiffs with distinct stakes in the abortion issue—doctors, ministers, an antipoverty organization, and a class of women arguing that the law violated their rights to privacy and equal protection.[75]

In this last case, *Abramowicz v. Lefkowitz*, Nancy Stearns of the Center for Constitutional Rights, along with other feminist lawyers, built upon the Lucas brief's emphasis on the right to privacy, offering new ways of expressing the constitutional injuries wrought by New York's criminal abortion law.[76] The Stearns brief appealed to equal protection and to the Eighth Amendment's prohibition of cruel and unusual punishments, as well as to a "right to life" that belonged to the *woman*.[77] These arguments

---

[69]   458 P.2d 194 (Cal. 1969).

[70]   *Id.* at 199 (citing *Griswold*, 381 U.S. at 485–86, 500). For an account of the *Griswold* decision, see Melissa Murray, *Sexual Liberty and Criminal Law Reform: The Story of* Griswold v. Connecticut, *in* REPRODUCTIVE RIGHTS AND JUSTICE STORIES 11 (Melissa Murray, Katherine Shaw & Reva B. Siegel eds., 2019).

[71]   458 P.2d at 201 n.10 (citing Roy Lucas, *Federal Constitutional Limitations on the Enforcement and Administration of State Abortion Statutes*, 46 N.C. L. REV. 730 (1968)).

[72]   Roy Lucas, *Federal Constitutional Limitations on the Enforcement and Administration of State Abortion Statutes*, 46 N.C. L. REV. 730, 755–56 (1968).

[73]   Lucas worked with, among others, Melvin Wulf, the legal director of the American Civil Liberties Union (ACLU), and Harriet Pilpel, an ACLU cooperating attorney and longtime advocate for the right to contraception and abortion. *See* LEIGH ANN WHEELER, HOW SEX BECAME A CIVIL LIBERTY 128–31 (2013).

[74]   GREENHOUSE & SIEGEL, *supra* note 4, at 140.

[75]   *See* Linda Greenhouse, *Constitutional Question: Is There a Right to Abortion?*, N.Y. TIMES, Jan. 25, 1970, *reprinted in* GREENHOUSE & SIEGEL, *supra* note 4, at 130, 134–36.

[76]   *See, e.g.*, Plaintiffs' Brief at 66, Abramowicz v. Lefkowitz, 305 F. Supp. 1030 (S.D.N.Y. 1969) (69 Civ. 4469).

[77]   *Id.* at 12, 35, 46.

all gave voice to feminist claims about the harms abortion bans inflicted on women that were not well expressed by the language of privacy in *Griswold*.

Stearns invited the courts to consider intersectional claims of class, race, and sex. At this time, the Supreme Court had not yet rejected class-based claims under the Equal Protection Clause, claims that at the time were being pressed in litigation across a variety of fronts.[78] Stearns was thus free to argue that abortion's criminalization violated equal protection by limiting safe abortion to women of means[79] and by inflicting disparate harms on poor women of color.[80]

Stearns also argued that criminal abortion laws discriminated on the basis of sex. She advanced this claim before the Court had held that sex discrimination violated equal protection—and on terms that the case law resists to this very day.[81] In the *Abramowicz* brief, Stearns and her colleagues argued that in forcing women to continue a pregnancy, criminal abortion laws violated equal protection by: (1) punishing the woman, but not the man, who engaged in sexual relations; and (2) relegating women to a society that expelled pregnant students, fired pregnant employees, and denied employment to women with children.[82] The brief further asserted that the abortion laws "are both a result and symbol of the unequal treatment of women" and reasoned that so long as "such a broad range of disabilities are permitted to attach to the status of pregnancy and motherhood, that status must be one of choice."[83]

Without case law to cite in support of these equal protection claims—and at a time when only one percent of Article III judges were women[84]—the feminist lawyers in *Abramowicz* invoked actual women as authority. The brief quoted plaintiffs' depositions and testimonies in ways that mirrored women's abortion speak-outs of the day.[85] The brief brought women's voices into the courtroom to show how laws criminalizing

---

[78] *See, e.g.*, San Antonio Indep. Sch. Dist. v. Rodriguez, 411 U.S. 1 (1973).

[79] *Cf.* Plaintiffs' Brief at 3, *Abramowicz*, 305 F. Supp. 1030 (69 Civ. 4469).

[80] Reva B. Siegel, Roe's *Roots: The Women's Rights Claims that Engendered* Roe, 90 B.U. L. REV. 1875, 1889 (2010) (citing equal protection wealth and race inequality claims in feminist challenges to criminal abortion laws in several states).

[81] In *Geduldig v. Aiello*, the Court famously rejected a claim that a California insurance program's refusal to include pregnancy as a disability subject to coverage constituted unconstitutional discrimination on the basis of sex. 417 U.S. 484 (1974). For a discussion of *Geduldig* and the Court's evolving analysis of the relationship between sex discrimination and pregnancy discrimination, see generally Neil S. Siegel & Reva B. Siegel, *Pregnancy and Sex Role Stereotyping: From* Struck *to* Carhart, 70 OHIO ST. L.J. 1095 (2009).

[82] Plaintiffs' Brief at 35–36, 37, *Abramowicz*, 305 F. Supp. 1030 (69 Civ. 4469).

[83] *Id.* at 40, 87.

[84] *Demography of Article III Judges, 1789–2015*, FED. JUDICIAL CTR., https://www.fjc.gov/history/exhibits/graphs-and-maps/gender (reporting that in 1970, seven of the 619 Article III judges—1.14%—were women).

[85] *See, e.g.*, Plaintiffs' Brief at 19, 21, *Abramowicz*, 305 F. Supp. 1030 (69 Civ. 4469).

abortion inflicted injuries that reflected and enforced inequalities of sex, race, and class.[86]

Nancy Stearns worked with movement lawyers to file similar suits with large, named groups of plaintiffs in Connecticut, New Jersey, Rhode Island, Massachusetts, and Pennsylvania.[87] The Connecticut case shows the same concern with intersecting forms of inequality. The pamphlet written to recruit plaintiffs challenged the ways criminal abortion laws and cultural forces together pressured women into bearing children they were not ready to have, while at the same time stigmatizing unwed motherhood and threatening sterilization and the loss of public benefits to poor women who bore children. "We are tired of being pressured to have children or not to have children. It's our decision," the pamphlet declared.[88]

Catherine Roraback, who had helped litigate *Griswold v. Connecticut*, and Nancy Stearns translated these movement claims into a life, liberty, and equality challenge to Connecticut's nineteenth-century abortion statute.[89] Ultimately, 1,700 women signed up as plaintiffs in the case that became known as *Women v. Connecticut*, or more formally, *Abele v. Markle*.[90] Litigation in the *Abele* case ultimately led to the invalidation of Connecticut's nineteenth-century abortion ban. The district court invoked principles of due process on which the Court in *Roe* would rely and principles of sex equality that would not inform the Court's abortion jurisprudence for decades. In its opinion, the district judge observed that in the century since Connecticut's ban on abortion had been enacted, there had been a transformation in the roles of women, citing due process precedent and the Nineteenth Amendment, Title VII of the 1964 Civil Rights Act, and *Reed v. Reed* (the first equal-protection sex discrimination case).[91]

---

[86] The New York lawsuits did not produce a court decision. They became moot early in 1970 when the New York Legislature, by a "dramatic last-minute switching of a single vote," repealed New York's criminal abortion law. *See* Bill Kovach, *Abortion Reform Is Voted by the Assembly, 76 to 73; Final Approval Expected*, N.Y. TIMES (Apr. 10, 1970), http://www.nytimes.com/1970/04/10/archives/abortion-reform-is-voted-by-the-assembly-76-to-73-final-approval.html.

[87] *See* Siegel, *supra* note 80, at 1886–87.

[88] GREENHOUSE & SIEGEL, *supra* note 4, at 169.

[89] Complaint for Declaratory Judgment, Injunction, & Other Appropriate Relief, Abele v. Markle, 342 F. Supp. 800 (D. Conn. 1972) (No. 14291).

[90] *Abele*, 342 F. Supp. 800; *Hearing on Abortion Before the J. Comm. on Pub. Health & Safety*, 1972 Leg., Spec. Sess., 18–23 (Conn. 1972) (statement of Catherine Roraback), *reprinted in* GREENHOUSE & SIEGEL, *supra* note 4, at 184, 186.

[91] *See Abele*, 342 F. Supp. at 802 & nn.8–9. The legislature reenacted the law, which was again struck down in an opinion that made the concept of fetal viability central to a balance between women's rights and the state's regulatory interests in abortion. *See* GREENHOUSE & SIEGEL, *supra* note 4, at 163–96 (collecting sources).

ROE V. WADE

"We never thought we were filing what would become *the* Supreme Court case," Sarah Weddington would write two decades later.[92] Only recently graduated from the University of Texas Law School when she helped launch the case that became *Roe v. Wade*, Weddington lacked the experience and movement connections of Nancy Stearns and Catherine Roraback.[93] In 1969, she was living in Austin when members of a local women's group approached her for help in providing birth control counseling for unmarried University of Texas students.[94] Abortion was not on the group's original agenda, but the issue soon arose as the women considered their potential legal liability for referring students to abortion providers.[95] The group asked Weddington to bring a federal lawsuit challenging the constitutionality of the Texas statute, which dated to 1854 and prohibited all abortions except those necessary to save a pregnant woman's life.[96]

Weddington agreed. Several years earlier, as a "scared" law student, Weddington and her boyfriend had traveled "to a dirty, dusty Mexican border town to have an abortion, fleeing the law that made abortion illegal in Texas" and spending all her money in the process.[97] Weddington accepted the invitation to challenge the law, in order to "help[ ] others avoid what we had gone through."[98]

Two years out of law school, Weddington had a legal research job but no experience practicing law.[99] Looking for help, she turned to her law school classmate, Linda Coffee, who had clerked for a federal district judge in Dallas, Judge Sarah T. Hughes, one of the first women appointed to the federal bench.[100] The plaintiffs the two women recruited included a married couple with medical reasons for avoiding pregnancy and an unmarried pregnant woman who for the purposes of the case was given the name Jane Roe. A doctor who was under indictment for performing an abortion later entered the case as an intervenor.[101]

---

[92]   SARAH WEDDINGTON, A QUESTION OF CHOICE 50 (40th anniversary ed. 2013).

[93]   For profiles of Nancy Stearns and Catherine Roraback, see Amy Kesselman, *Women Versus Connecticut: Conducting a Statewide Hearing on Abortion, in* ABORTION WARS: A HALF CENTURY OF STRUGGLE, 1950–2000, at 42, 43–44, 46–47 (Rickie Solinger ed., 1998).

[94]   DAVID J. GARROW, LIBERTY & SEXUALITY: THE RIGHT TO PRIVACY AND THE MAKING OF *ROE V. WADE* 390–93 (1994).

[95]   *Id.* at 391–93.

[96]   TEX. PENAL CODE ANN. §§ 1191–1196 (West 1972), *declared unconstitutional by* Roe v. Wade, 410 U.S. 113, 153 (1973); *see also* GARROW, *supra* note 94, at 395.

[97]   WEDDINGTON, *supra* note 92, at 13, 16.

[98]   *Id.* at 50–51.

[99]   *Id.* at 26, 51.

[100]   *Id.* at 53–54. Judge Hughes was the third woman appointed to an Article III court. *See Women as 'Way Pavers' in the Federal Judiciary*, U.S. COURTS (Feb. 26, 2015), http://www.uscourts.gov/news/2015/02/26/women-way-pavers-federal-judiciary.

[101]   GARROW, *supra* note 94, at 405, 433–34; WEDDINGTON, *supra* note 92, at 56–61. Weddington and Coffee soon thereafter amended both complaints to convert the cases into

In March 1970, Weddington and Coffee filed their three-page complaint in the United States District Court for the Northern District of Texas.[102] As a federal court challenge to the constitutionality of a state law, the case was referred to a special three-judge court, with direct appeal to the U.S. Supreme Court. The brief that Weddington and Coffee filed included a photocopy of portions of Roy Lucas's brief in the doctors' challenge to New York's criminal abortion statute.[103] The Weddington-Coffee brief questioned the state's interest in criminalizing abortion.[104] It argued that the Texas law was void for vagueness,[105] violated the right to privacy recognized in the Supreme Court's due process cases,[106] and discriminated against poor women.[107] The Weddington-Coffee brief incorporated the doctrinal privacy arguments that Roy Lucas had advanced in the New York litigation, but did not mention the movement equality concerns about sex and motherhood that Nancy Stearns and her colleagues were pressing as the reason for recognizing women's right to control their reproductive lives.

On June 17, 1970, the District Court, which included Judge Hughes, issued a per curiam opinion reasoning that the right to privacy announced in *Griswold* extended to decisions about abortion.[108] The court issued a declaratory judgment that the statute was unconstitutional but refused to enjoin its enforcement on the assumption that the state would conform its criminal prosecution to constitutional requirements.[109]

In the spring of 1971, the Supreme Court agreed to hear the appeals in both *Roe v. Wade* and *Doe v. Bolton*,[110] which declared unconstitutional Georgia's recent ALI-style reform statute. In the Texas case, Jane Roe's lawyers, with the assistance of Roy Lucas and Norman Dorsen, a prominent law professor and civil libertarian, focused their brief largely on the *Griswold*-anchored privacy objection to the state's abortion ban.[111] They raised a vagueness claim focusing on the law's harm to doctors and

---

class actions on behalf of all others similarly situated. *See* Roe v. Wade, 314 F. Supp. 1217, 1219 n.1 (N.D. Tex. 1970), *aff'd in part, rev'd in part*, 410 U.S. 113 (1973). A quarter of a century later, Norma McCorvey was converted to the antiabortion cause by the national director of Operation Rescue. *See* Reva B. Siegel, *The Right's Reasons: Constitutional Conflict and the Spread of Woman-Protective Antiabortion Argument*, 57 DUKE L.J. 1641, 1644–45 nn.12–14 (2008).

[102] Plaintiff's Original Complaint, *Roe*, 314 F. Supp. 1217 (Nos. 3-3690-B, 3-3691-C). *See generally* WEDDINGTON, *supra* note 92, at 64–65.

[103] Brief of Plaintiffs Jane Roe, John Doe, & Mary Doe at app., *Roe*, 314 F. Supp. 1217 (Nos. CA-3-3690, CA-3-3691); *see also* GARROW, *supra* note 94, at 438–39.

[104] Brief of Plaintiffs Jane Roe, John Doe, & Mary Doe at 7–9, *Roe*, 314 F. Supp. 1217 (Nos. CA-3-3690, CA-3-3691).

[105] *Id.* at 9–10.

[106] *Id.* at 13.

[107] *Id.* at 11–12.

[108] *Roe*, 314 F. Supp. at 1217, 1222.

[109] *Id.* at 1224 (quoting Dombrowski v. Pfister, 380 U.S. 479, 484–85 (1965)).

[110] 319 F. Supp. 1048, 1050, 1056–57 (N.D. Ga. 1970) (declaring unconstitutional GA. CODE ANN. § 26–1201 et seq. (1961)).

[111] Brief for Appellants at 91–94, Roe v. Wade, 410 U.S. 113 (1973) (No. 70-18).

argued that by criminalizing abortions, Texas was putting its female citizens at risk.[112]

In an amicus brief, Nancy Stearns voiced a variety of movement-informed equality arguments for the abortion right that were not included in the party brief. She maintained that denying women control over childbearing impoverished families. Her emphasis was on the gender bias of the law that deprived women of a choice over whether and when to become mothers.[113]

Texas incorporated into its brief a medical account of fetal development that the state asserted "establishes the humanity of the unborn child."[114] "We submit that the data not only shows [sic] the constitutionality of the Texas legislature's effort to save the unborn from indiscriminate extermination, *but in fact suggests a duty to do so*."[115] The state defended its law on the ground that the fetus has a right to life protected by the Due Process and Equal Protection Clauses of the Constitution.[116] The brief cited to numerous scientific sources[117] and, on the model of John Willke, included photographs of prenatal development.[118]

Justices Black and Harlan having unexpectedly retired at the beginning of the 1971 Term, only seven Justices sat for the arguments. Justice Blackmun, assigned by Chief Justice Burger to write the majority opinions striking down both the Texas and Georgia laws, focused his initial draft on the objections that the medical profession had been raising about criminal abortion laws: the laws were unconstitutionally vague and so exposed doctors to the risk of prosecution without notice.[119]

After Justices Powell and Rehnquist joined the Court in January 1972, the Justices decided to rehear the cases before a full bench. The new argument took place in October 1972—a fateful two years after the cases were filed. In the interim, as we have seen, popular support for decriminalization had surged and was still rising, while countermobilization was also mounting. In developments that would prove highly significant, Congress had voted to send the Equal Rights

---

[112] *Id.* at 125.

[113] Motion for Permission to File Brief & Brief Amicus Curiae on Behalf of New Women Lawyers, Women's Health & Abortion Project, Inc., National Abortion Action Coalition at 14, 26, 31, *Roe*, 410 U.S. 113 (Nos. 70-18, 70-40).

[114] Brief for Appellee at 31, *Roe*, 410 U.S. 113 (No. 70-18).

[115] *Id.*

[116] *Id.* at 56.

[117] *See, e.g., id.* at 32.

[118] *See, e.g., id.* at 35, 37, 39–40.

[119] Goluboff, *supra* note 67, at 1379.

Amendment (ERA) to the states for ratification[120] and a presidential campaign was underway.

Perhaps moved by the growing tide of lower court opinions striking down abortion prohibitions, as well as by poll results showing public support for abortion's decriminalization that crossed party lines and religious groups,[121] Justice Blackmun now approached his assignment with the confidence to base a new draft opinion not on the ground of vagueness but on a constitutional right, the right to privacy that the Court in *Griswold* had derived from the Ninth and Fourteenth Amendments.[122] Neither the state's arguments on behalf of the unborn nor concern about the welfare of pregnant women, he concluded, could outweigh a woman's fundamental right to terminate a pregnancy, at least in the early stages.[123]

In his opinion, Justice Blackmun identified the right to privacy as "founded in the Fourteenth Amendment's concept of personal liberty and restrictions upon state action."[124] It was, he said, "broad enough to encompass a woman's decision whether or not to terminate her pregnancy."[125] The majority reviewed the Court's due process precedents, going back to the early twentieth century, that protected intimate decision-making within and about family relations. These included *Meyer v. Nebraska*,[126] *Pierce v. Society of Sisters*,[127] *Griswold v. Connecticut*,[128] and *Loving v. Virginia*.[129]

Yet even as the Court recognized a woman's privacy interests in deciding whether to bear a child, it also recognized that the state had an interest in regulating abortion. The Court rejected Texas's claim that the unborn had a constitutionally protected right to life from conception,[130] concluding that a wide body of law demonstrated that "the word 'person,' as used in the Fourteenth Amendment, does not include the unborn."[131] Even so, Justice Blackmun reasoned, "[t]he pregnant woman cannot be

---

[120] MARJORIE J. SPRUILL, DIVIDED WE STAND: THE BATTLE OVER WOMEN'S RIGHTS AND FAMILY VALUES THAT POLARIZED AMERICAN POLITICS 31 (2017) (reporting votes in the House in 1971 and the Senate in 1972).

[121] *See* GREENHOUSE, *supra* note 57, at 91 (noting that Justice Blackmun had filed away a Gallup poll showing public opinion on abortion reform). For the Gallup poll results in Justice Blackmun's papers, see *supra* text accompanying notes 57–58.

[122] For Justice Blackmun's own outline of his reasons for his emergent view that the Texas law was unconstitutional, see GREENHOUSE, *supra* note 57, at 91–92.

[123] *Id.* at 95.

[124] Roe v. Wade, 410 U.S. 113, 153 (1973).

[125] *Id.*

[126] 262 U.S. 390 (1923).

[127] Pierce v. Soc'y of the Sisters of the Holy Names of Jesus & Mary, 268 U.S. 510 (1925).

[128] 381 U.S. 479 (1965).

[129] 388 U.S. 1 (1967).

[130] *Roe*, 410 U.S. at 156–58. For an overview of Texas's argument, see Brief for Appellee at 31–32, *Roe*, 410 U.S. 113 (No. 70-18).

[131] *Roe*, 410 U.S. at 157–58.

isolated in her privacy."[132] The state had "separate and distinct" regulatory interests in protecting pregnant women's health and in protecting potential life, interests that grew as a pregnancy progressed and eventually became "compelling."[133]

In creating this "trimester" framework, the *Roe* Court recognized a new state interest in regulating a pregnant woman to "protect[ ] the potentiality of human life."[134] The Court reasoned that this interest was outweighed by the woman's constitutionally protected right to decide whether to carry a pregnancy to term. Only at viability, when the fetus "presumably has the capability of meaningful life outside the mother's womb," did the state's interest in unborn life become compelling; "after viability," the state could "go so far as to proscribe abortion . . . except when it is necessary to preserve the life or health of the mother."[135]

The vote was 7–2. Justice Rehnquist dissented, focusing not on ethical questions about abortion but instead on jurisprudential questions about the appropriate role of courts in a constitutional democracy. He objected to the majority treating the right to privacy as a right worthy of judicial protection, arguing that the Court should have employed deferential rational basis review and that the trimester framework the Court adopted in its stead was "far more appropriate to a legislative judgment than to a judicial one."[136] He complained that "judicial legislation" of this kind repeated the errors of the Court's discredited decision in *Lochner*.[137]

Justice White, joined by Justice Rehnquist, made the point in harsher terms, emphasizing that under the Constitution the states retained authority to decide how to regulate abortion.[138] He was openly dismissive of the decision's solicitude for women's interests in controlling decisions about whether to become a mother and characterized the Court's framework in scathing terms: "During the period prior to the time the fetus becomes viable, the Constitution of the United States values the convenience, whim, or caprice of the pregnant woman more than the life or potential life of the fetus."[139]

Justice White's contemptuous account of women seeking abortion for "convenience, whim, or caprice" was largely unrebutted by the majority, which appealed to medical science for authority and often spoke as if doctors rather than women were the rights holders whom the Court was

---

[132] *Id.* at 159.

[133] *Id.* at 162–63.

[134] *Id.* at 162.

[135] *Id.* at 163–64.

[136] *Id.* at 173–74 (Rehnquist, J., dissenting).

[137] *Id.* at 174 (citing Lochner v. New York, 198 U.S. 45 (1905)).

[138] *Id.* at 221 (White, J., dissenting).

[139] *Id.*

empowering to make decisions on behalf of their female patients.[140] The majority did, for the first time, and perhaps in response to new rights claims, recognize reasons why a woman might seek to end a pregnancy.[141] But this passing discussion barely acknowledged the life-altering health harms or economic stakes of depriving women of control over the timing of motherhood, much less the assault on a woman's dignity of having others empowered to decide her life's course.

It is not surprising that the Court did not tie its analysis of the abortion right more closely to these considerations or, in recognizing the state's interest in protecting potential life, scrutinize more closely the state's reasons for compelling a woman to become a mother. *Roe* reached the Court at a moment of profound transition. After all, the Court was only on the verge of constructing a jurisprudence of women's rights—just days before handing down *Roe*, the Justices heard a young lawyer named Ruth Bader Ginsburg argue the landmark equal protection case *Frontiero v. Richardson*.[142]

FROM *ROE* TO *CASEY*: CONFLICT AND CONSTITUTIONAL CHANGE

The Court's decision consolidated strong public support for the abortion right. Two months after the Court decided *Roe*, a National Opinion Research Center survey "showed a remarkable liberalization of abortion attitudes on the part of all groups and subgroups of American society."[143] In February 1976, sixty-seven percent of those responding to a nationwide survey agreed with the statement: "[T]he right of a woman to have an abortion should be left entirely up to the woman and her doctor."[144]

Roe was greeted by criticism, though not the firestorm often imagined today.[145] (Strikingly, during the 1975 Senate confirmation hearing for John Paul Stevens, the first Supreme Court nominee since

---

[140] *See* Siegel, *supra* note 80, at 1897–1900; *see also* Nan D. Hunter, *Justice Blackmun, Abortion, and the Myth of Medical Independence*, 72 BROOK. L. REV. 147, 184–85 (2006).

[141] *See Roe*, 410 U.S. at 153 (citing the prospect of a "distressful life," physical or psychological harm, and mental health, among other reasons); *cf.* Siegel, *supra* note 80, at 1895–96 (discussing Stearns's view of the advocates' influence on the Court).

[142] 411 U.S. 677 (1973).

[143] William Ray Arney & William H. Trescher, *Trends in Attitudes Toward Abortion, 1972–1975*, 8 FAM. PLAN. PERSP. 117, 124 (1976). Arney and Trescher review post-*Roe* polling data and observe: "It is notable that the 1973 [National Opinion Research Center] survey, fielded just two months after the 1973 Supreme Court abortion decisions, showed a remarkable liberalization of abortion attitudes on the part of all groups and subgroups of American society . . . . Very little change occurred in the years following the decisions . . . ." *Id.* at 124. The authors further suggest that the Court's action may have had "an immediately legitimating effect on public opinion." *Id.*

[144] Sandra Stencel, *Abortion Politics, in* EDITORIAL RESEARCH REPORTS ON NATIONAL HEALTH ISSUES: TIMELY REPORTS TO KEEP JOURNALISTS, SCHOLARS AND THE PUBLIC ABREAST OF DEVELOPING ISSUES, EVENTS AND TRENDS 21, 36 (1977) (reporting on a *CBS News/New York Times* survey).

[145] *Cf.* Franklin, *supra* note 4, at 867–71.

Roe, there was not a single question about abortion.[146]) Abortion opponents continued their efforts, now seeking to amend the Constitution either by prohibiting abortion or by returning the abortion question to the states.[147] While those efforts failed, opponents were successful in cutting off state and federal funding for most abortions for poor women under the Medicaid program, restrictions that a series of Supreme Court decisions upheld.[148] The Court acquiesced in these funding decisions as consistent with the right recognized in *Roe*. It endorsed the government's "objective of protecting potential life" through "incentives that make childbirth a more attractive alternative than abortion"[149] for women who relied on government assistance for their medical care. Critics pointed out that the Court had interpreted *Roe* to expose poor women of color to the same health and reproductive inequalities they endured before *Roe*.[150]

In the decades after *Roe*, the abortion debate continued to change shape. In January 1973, few could have foreseen that the abortion right would become inextricably identified with the cause of women's equality, that the Republican Party would court voters by targeting for reversal a decision originally supported by five of six Republican-appointed Justices,[151] or that the party's strategists would find in abortion an issue that would prove capable of uniting Catholics and evangelicals, who had long mistrusted each other, in political coalition as Christians.[152]

The national ratification campaign for the ERA, which began just before the Court's decision in *Roe*,[153] helped widen debate from biology to the very structure and integrity of the American family. By 1977, Phyllis Schlafly was warning that the ERA would provide a new constitutional

---

[146] *Nomination of John Paul Stevens to Be a Justice of the Supreme Court: Hearing Before S. Comm. on the Judiciary*, 94th Cong. (1975), https://www.loc.gov/law/find/ nominations/stevens/hearing.pdf; *see also* Linda Greenhouse, *Justice John Paul Stevens as Abortion-Rights Strategist*, 43 U.C. DAVIS L. REV. 749, 751 (2010).

[147] H.R.J. Res. 261, 93d Cong. (1973). For a compilation and discussion of the proposed amendments, see *History of the Human Life Amendments*, HUM. LIFE AMEND., http://humanlifeamendment.com/index.php/history.

[148] Harris v. McRae, 448 U.S. 297 (1980); Maher v. Roe, 432 U.S. 464 (1977). For an account of the *McRae* decision, see Khiara M. Bridges, *Elision and Erasure: Race, Class, and Gender in* Harris v. McRae, *in* REPRODUCTIVE RIGHTS AND JUSTICE STORIES, *supra* note 70, at 117.

[149] *McRae*, 448 U.S. at 325.

[150] *See, e.g.*, Kristin Booth Glen, *Abortion in the Courts: A Laywoman's Historical Guide to the New Disaster Area*, 4 FEMINIST STUD. 1, 17–19 (1978); Linda Greenhouse, *Abortion Goes Before the Supreme Court Again*, N.Y. TIMES (Apr. 20, 1980), http://query.ny times.com/mem/archive/pdf?res=9805E6D71339E232A25753C2A9629C94619FD6CF.

[151] GREENHOUSE & SIEGEL, *supra* note 4, at 292–303; *see also Republican Party Platform of 1980* (1980), *in* AM. PRESIDENCY PROJECT, https://www.presidency.ucsb.edu/ documents/republican-party-platform-1980 (affirming the support of the Republican Party for "a constitutional amendment to restore protection of the right to life for unborn children" and calling for "the appointment of judges at all levels of the judiciary who respect traditional family values and the sanctity of innocent human life").

[152] GREENHOUSE & SIEGEL, *supra* note 4, at 294–99. On the debate over *Roe*'s role in polarization around abortion, see GREENHOUSE & SIEGEL, *supra* note 4.

[153] *Cf. supra* note 120 and accompanying text.

basis for abortion (and same-sex marriage).[154] A new "pro-family" politics emerged that embedded abortion in debates about family roles.[155] Defending the family and the unborn provided religious leaders an opportunity to reclaim a role for religion in the public square.[156]

Repeatedly the conflict over abortion converged on the Court, most fatefully in 1992 in *Planned Parenthood of Southeastern Pennsylvania v. Casey*,[157] a case involving a statute restricting abortion in conflict with the Court's post-*Roe* decisions.[158] When the case reached the Supreme Court, only Justice Blackmun remained of *Roe*'s seven-member majority—and a majority of Justices had been appointed by Presidents who openly sought *Roe*'s reversal.[159]

The Court that handed down *Casey* startled the nation by reaffirming—yet at the same time changing—*Roe*'s central holding. In writing *Casey*, no longer did the Court look outward, toward the authority of doctors or the science of pregnancy. It reached for a settlement between the contending forces within the Constitution itself.

Reasoning that the trimester framework, which only permitted the government to restrict abortion to protect potential life at the point of fetal viability, had "undervalue[d] the State's interest in [protecting] potential life,"[160] the Court allowed new restrictions on abortion before viability that its earlier decisions had prohibited. The Court replaced the trimester framework with a new "undue burden" standard that permitted the state to regulate abortion to protect unborn life from the beginning of pregnancy,[161] so long as the state protected life by means that respected

---

[154] SPRUILL, *supra* note 120, at 101–12; Reva B. Siegel, *Constitutional Culture, Social Movement Conflict and Constitutional Change: The Case of the De Facto ERA*, 94 CALIF. L. REV. 1323, 1389–93 (2006); *cf.* ROBERT O. SELF, ALL IN THE FAMILY: THE REALIGNMENT OF AMERICAN DEMOCRACY SINCE THE 1960S, at 296 (2012).

[155] MARY ZIEGLER, AFTER ROE: THE LOST HISTORY OF THE ABORTION DEBATE 14–15, 178–83 (2015).

[156] Sandra Salmans, *Christian Fundamentalists Press Own Campaign Within the G.O.P. Drive*, N.Y. TIMES (Aug. 17, 1984), http://www.nytimes.com/1984/08/17/us/christian-fundamentalists-press-own-campaign-within-the-gop-drive.html ("Fundamentalist Christians . . . emerged in 1980 as a new electoral force . . . . [T]heir agenda is uniformly family-oriented and conservative. It is against abortion [and] the proposed Federal equal rights amendment . . . ."); *see also, e.g.*, James M. Penning, *Pat Robertson and the GOP: 1988 and Beyond*, 55 SOC. RELIGION 327, 337 (1994).

[157] 505 U.S. 833 (1992). For an account of the *Casey* decision, see Serena Mayeri, *Undue-ing* Roe: *Constitutional Conflict and Political Polarization in* Planned Parenthood v. Casey, *in* REPRODUCTIVE RIGHTS AND JUSTICE STORIES, *supra* note 70, at 137.

[158] *See* Thornburgh v. Am. Coll. of Obstetricians & Gynecologists, 476 U.S. 747 (1986); City of Akron v. Akron Ctr. for Reprod. Health, Inc., 462 U.S. 416 (1983).

[159] *Cf.* Linda Greenhouse, *Changed Path for Court?; New Balance Is Held by 3 Cautious Justices*, N.Y. TIMES (June 26, 1992), http://www.nytimes.com/1992/06/26/us/changed-path-for-court-new-balance-is-held-by-3-cautious-justices.html ("In addition to Justice Powell, Justices William J. Brennan Jr. and Thurgood Marshall . . . have retired, as has Chief Justice Warren E. Burger. Justices Scalia, Kennedy, Souter and Thomas have all arrived . . . .").

[160] *Casey*, 505 U.S. at 873.

[161] *Id.* at 874, 878.

women's authority to decide whether to give birth.[162] In so holding, the Court created opportunities for opponents of abortion to enact restrictions on abortion that *Roe* itself never sanctioned, restrictions that were designed to transform the public's understanding of the morality and constitutionality of the practice.

Although *Casey* allowed states to enact abortion restrictions throughout pregnancy as *Roe* did not, it built upon *Roe*'s concerns with autonomy, speaking in the language of liberty, dignity, and equality.[163] Government could "*persuade*" a woman to carry her pregnancy to term,[164] but the "means chosen by the State to further the interest in potential life must be calculated to inform the woman's free choice, not hinder it."[165] The state could not prevent a woman from exercising a right the Court deemed essential to her ability "to participate equally in the economic and social life of the Nation."[166] Respect for the equal citizenship of women appears centrally in the opinion.[167] Nearly a generation later, voices barely acknowledged in *Roe* acquired primacy of place.

---

[162] *See* Linda Greenhouse & Reva B. Siegel, *Casey and the Clinic Closings: When "Protecting Health" Obstructs Choice*, 125 YALE L.J. 1428, 1431 (2016).

[163] *See, e.g., Casey*, 505 U.S. at 846–48, 851, 856.

[164] *Id.* at 878 (emphasis added).

[165] *Id.* at 877.

[166] *Id.* at 856.

[167] The joint opinion's account of a woman's constitutionally protected liberty to make decisions about bearing children is deeply informed by the Court's sex equality jurisprudence. *See id.* at 852 (observing that a woman's "suffering is too intimate and personal for the State to insist, without more, upon its own vision of the woman's role, however dominant that vision has been in the course of our history and our culture. The destiny of the woman must be shaped to a large extent on her own conception of her spiritual imperatives and her place in society"). Sex equality reasoning dominates the portions of the opinion striking down the spousal notice requirement—the only requirement in the Pennsylvania law that the Court invalidated. *See id.* at 895–98; *id.* at 898 ("A State may not give to a man the kind of dominion over his wife that parents exercise over their children."). The stare decisis section of the opinion similarly focuses on understandings about sexual and economic roles that have developed in reliance on the availability of abortion. *Id.* at 856 ("The ability of women to participate equally in the economic and social life of the Nation has been facilitated by their ability to control their reproductive lives.").

Justice Blackmun's concurrence also emphasized that "[a] State's restrictions on a woman's right to terminate her pregnancy . . . implicate constitutional guarantees of gender equality . . . . By restricting the right to terminate pregnancies, the State conscripts women's bodies into its service, forcing women to continue their pregnancies, suffer the pains of childbirth, and in most instances, provide years of maternal care. The State does not compensate women for their services; instead, it assumes that they owe this duty as a matter of course. This assumption—that women can simply be forced to accept the 'natural' status and incidents of motherhood—appears to rest upon a conception of women's role that has triggered the protection of the Equal Protection Clause." *Id.* at 928 (Blackmun, J., concurring). For an account of equality arguments concerning fetal-protective and woman-protective restrictions on abortion discussed in *Casey* and in Justice Ginsburg's dissent in *Gonzales v. Carhart*, 550 U.S. 124, 169, 172 (2007) (Ginsburg, J., dissenting) ("[L]egal challenges to undue restrictions on abortion procedures do not seek to vindicate some generalized notion of privacy; rather, they center on a woman's autonomy to determine her life's course, and thus to enjoy equal citizenship stature."), see Neil S. Siegel & Reva B. Siegel, *Equality Arguments for Abortion Rights*, 60 U.C.L.A. REV. DISC. 160 (2013). For a historical account of equality arguments advanced in *Casey*, see Mayeri, *supra* note 157.

As a matter of law, it is now *Casey* more than *Roe* that defines the reach of the abortion right.[168] Yet *Roe* continues to exert a powerful pull on the nation's politics—and its understanding of courts, rights, and constitutional law—conveying wildly different meanings to different audiences. At one and the same time, *Roe* is the site of practical political struggle and profound questions of principle. To some, it is the ultimate symbol of a court's usurpation of democratic prerogatives. To others, it sanctions the taking of unborn life. To still others, it stands for the dignity and empowerment of women—"a woman's autonomy to determine her life's course, and thus to enjoy equal citizenship stature."[169]

These are conflicts that law can shape—but cannot settle.

The debate continues to rage. As the Supreme Court's membership evolves, a Court that questioned the basis for the abortion right could decide cases along many paths—with implications for *Roe, Casey,* and more. But as we have seen, the Supreme Court is not the only actor and almost never has the final word on the questions that most deeply engage and define us. The debate over how the American public best understands the constitutional guarantees of liberty, equality, and life[170] will continue where our story began—in state legislatures and in state courts, in Congress, in social movements—and among the people themselves.

---

[168] *See* Whole Woman's Health v. Hellerstedt, 136 S. Ct. 2292, 2309 (2016) ("We begin with the [undue burden] standard, as described in *Casey*.").

[169] *Carhart,* 550 U.S. at 172 (Ginsburg, J., dissenting).

[170] *See* Reva B. Siegel, *ProChoiceLife: Asking Who Protects Life and How—And Why It Matters in Law and Politics,* 93 IND. L.J. 207 (2018).

4

Deborah Dinner*

Sex Equality and the U.S. Welfare Regime: The Story of *Geduldig v. Aiello*

In May of 1972, Sally Armendariz had a devastating accident. She was driving near her home in Gilroy, California, when another vehicle rear-ended her car. Armendariz suffered a miscarriage in her fourth month of pregnancy, and her doctor ordered her to stay home from work for three weeks. The loss of income could not have come at a worse time. Armendariz's husband had just become unemployed, and she was acting as the sole breadwinner for the couple and their eight-month-old son.[1]

Armendariz applied for assistance from California's temporary disability insurance program, meant to cushion economic hardships stemming from sickness or injury. The California Department of Human Resources denied Armendariz's claim, finding her disability ineligible because it related to pregnancy.[2] The program covered nearly every disability—and all disabilities experienced only by males—yet excluded "any injury or illness caused by or arising in connection with pregnancy . . . ."[3] The determination must have seemed a cruel irony to Armendariz. For the past ten years, she had paid one percent of her monthly salary into this social insurance program.[4] Yet at precisely the moment she most needed assistance for herself and her family, the state denied her help.

Armendariz's injuries may have stemmed from bad luck, but the fact that California failed to protect her was no accident. The exclusion of pregnancy from the state's temporary disability insurance program typified gender bias and hierarchy in the U.S. welfare regime, the term

---

*   Associate Professor, Emory University School of Law. The ideas in this essay are elaborated further in *The Sex Equality Dilemma: Work, Family, and Legal Change in Neoliberal America* (Cambridge University Press, Studies in Legal History Series, forthcoming 2020). I thank Serena Mayeri, Melissa Murray, Douglas NeJaime, Kate Shaw, and Reva Siegel for their helpful comments on this chapter and Matthew Demartini, Lucy Gauthier, and Lauren Weaver for their excellent research assistance.

1   FRED STREBEIGH, EQUAL: WOMEN RESHAPE AMERICAN LAW 81–82 (2009).

2   *Id.* at 82.

3   Aiello v. Hansen, 359 F. Supp. 792, 793 (N.D. Cal. 1973) (citing CAL. UNEMP. INS. CODE § 2626 (West 1973)). The program also disqualified persons institutionalized as dipsomaniacs, drug addicts, and sexual psychopaths. *Id.* at 794.

4   *Id.*

scholars use to describe the public and private benefits and regulations that support the reproduction and maintenance of the nation's populace.[5] In the late-nineteenth and early-twentieth centuries, policymakers' "gendered imagination" shaped their design of the liberal welfare state.[6] They subscribed to what historians later termed the family-wage ideal: the notion that the normative family was comprised of a male breadwinner, a female caregiver, and children.[7] Over the course of the twentieth century, both public social insurance programs—the government funded programs that administer statutorily defined benefits to pool social risks—and private fringe benefits—discretionary, employer-sponsored benefits for workers—evolved in ways that reinforced the family-wage ideal. A myriad of public and private benefits enabled white men and some men of color to assume the mantle of independence, a status that rested on both workingmen's ability to support their families and on their wives' unpaid domestic labor.[8] Breadwinning women were an anomaly within family-wage ideology; pregnant workers were anathema. As a result, the welfare regime failed to protect female wage earners against economic insecurity stemming from pregnancy and childbirth. In Armendariz's case, the state treated her as a mother, whose dependence should be resolved by the private family, rather than as a worker with dependents to support.

Not one to give up easily, Armendariz turned to the courts to combat the discrimination she faced. Armendariz was a tenacious daughter of a Mexican-American family that had worked for generations in California's farm fields. She was only the second person in her extended family to graduate from high school.[9] At the time of her miscarriage, she was working as a secretary at the Gilroy Office of California Rural Legal Assistance.[10] A sympathetic lawyer there put her in contact with Wendy Webster Williams, a fiery young feminist attorney who had just co-founded a law firm, Equal Rights Advocates, dedicated to finding legal solutions to gender inequality.

The litigation that ultimately reached the Supreme Court as *Geduldig v. Aiello* posed the question whether pregnancy discrimination

---

[5]   For an explanation of the hybrid, public-private character of the U.S. welfare regime, see JACOB S. HACKER, THE DIVIDED WELFARE STATE: THE BATTLE OVER PUBLIC AND PRIVATE SOCIAL BENEFITS IN THE UNITED STATES 12 (2012).

[6]   ALICE KESSLER-HARRIS, IN PURSUIT OF EQUITY: WOMEN, MEN, AND THE QUEST FOR ECONOMIC CITIZENSHIP IN 20TH-CENTURY AMERICA 5–6 (2001).

[7]   Ruth Milkman, *Editor's Preface* to 27 WOMEN, WORK, AND PROTEST: A CENTURY OF US WOMEN'S LABOR HISTORY, at xiii (Ruth Milkman ed., 2d. ed. 2013).

[8]   On the gendered dimensions of free-labor ideology, see generally ERIC FONER, RECONSTRUCTION: AMERICA'S UNFINISHED REVOLUTION, 1863–1877 (Henry Steele Commager & Richard B. Morris eds., 2d. ed. 2002); LAWRENCE B. GLICKMAN, A LIVING WAGE: AMERICAN WORKERS AND THE MAKING OF CONSUMER SOCIETY (1997); and AMY DRU STANLEY, FROM BONDAGE TO CONTRACT: WAGE LABOR, MARRIAGE, AND THE MARKET IN THE AGE OF SLAVE EMANCIPATION (1998).

[9]   STREBEIGH, *supra* note 1, at 82–83.

[10]   *Id.* at 83.

contravened constitutional sex equality imperatives.[11] The plaintiffs argued that the exclusion of pregnancy from California's otherwise comprehensive temporary disability insurance plan violated the Equal Protection Clause of the Fourteenth Amendment.[12] Their claim challenged the gender stereotypes that shaped the boundaries of the U.S. welfare regime: that women were marginal workers who would return to the home after childbirth; that women did not merit the income replacement extended to primary breadwinners; and that women could depend on wage-earning men to support them during pregnancy. If successful, their claim would also expand the scope of the welfare regime, requiring those states with disability insurance programs to provide equal coverage for pregnancy.

The story of *Geduldig v. Aiello* poses the crucially important question whether constitutional sex equality requires public responsibility for the costs of reproduction. This story begins with an account of the U.S. welfare regime's gendered origins, which simultaneously constructed women's secondary status in the labor market and private familial responsibility for reproduction. The story continues in the late 1960s and 1970s, analyzing feminist advocacy both to enforce Title VII of the Civil Rights Act of 1964, prohibiting sex discrimination in employment, and to win recognition for a constitutional right to sex equality under the Equal Protection Clause. Specifically, feminist attorneys and reformers drew an analogy between pregnancy and temporary disability as a means to secure the inclusion of pregnancy and childbirth within both the public and private dimensions of the welfare regime. In its 1974 decision in *Geduldig*, the U.S. Supreme Court momentarily halted this quest, in a ruling that limited the capacity for equal protection jurisprudence to realize either economic or reproductive justice for women. Not until the early twenty-first century would the Court recognize that pregnancy discrimination that reinforces gender stereotypes violates the Equal Protection Clause. Neither U.S. constitutional jurisprudence, nor the nation's political culture, however, has come fully to embrace the feminist claim that underpinned *Geduldig*: that sex equality requires the expansion of the welfare regime as well as the eradication of gender stereotypes. This asymmetry in the definition of sex equality has profound importance in an era of deepening economic inequality.

* * *

By the time of Armendariz's accident, the U.S. welfare regime had constructed reproduction as a private responsibility and, in so doing, excluded pregnant workers from its protections. The nation's first social insurance schemes—workmen's compensation and unemployment insurance—reinforced the family wage ideal. They emerged as a

---

[11]   417 U.S. 484 (1974). Because *Aiello v. Hansen* involved the constitutionality of a state statute, it was heard by a three-judge panel of a U.S. District Court with direct appeal to the U.S. Supreme Court. *Id.* at 486–87.

[12]   Aiello v. Hansen, 359 F. Supp. 792, 793 (N.D. Cal. 1973).

mechanism to help industrial male breadwinners support their families during periods of income loss.[13] By their very terms, these two programs excluded pregnancy. Workers' compensation provided income replacement for on-the-job injuries, excluding pregnancy as a condition perceived to arise in the home. Unemployment insurance supported those workers whom policymakers considered meritorious: men, who through no fault of their own found themselves without work and unable to provide for their family. Policymakers reasoned that by becoming pregnant, women essentially chose to render themselves incapable of working. Pregnant women were deemed to have left the workforce voluntarily even if their employers fired them because of their pregnancies. By the time that the Court would consider *Geduldig*, thirty-eight states disqualified pregnancy from unemployment insurance.[14]

Temporary disability insurance programs in five states (as well as Puerto Rico) similarly treated childbearing women as mothers rather than workers. Rhode Island had pioneered temporary disability insurance in 1943 in an effort to fill the gap between workmen's compensation and unemployment insurance, offering income security to workers who became sick or suffered non-workplace injuries.[15] While it had initially provided equal benefits for pregnancy,[16] the state ultimately capped the eligible period for pregnancy benefits at a shorter duration than other temporary disabilities.[17] In 1946, California enacted legislation creating its state temporary disability insurance fund;[18] New Jersey followed suit in 1948, New York in 1949, and Hawaii in 1969.[19] California, New York, and Hawaii wholly excluded pregnancy from coverage, and New Jersey provided lesser coverage for pregnancy than for other conditions. Several convergent trends made this exclusion appear natural: the costs of pregnancy-related benefits assumed social salience in light of gender stereotypes regarding women's marginal role in the workforce.[20] The hybrid, public-private character of social

---

[13]   *See* JOHN FABIAN WITT, THE ACCIDENTAL REPUBLIC: CRIPPLED WORKINGMEN, DESTITUTE WIDOWS, AND THE REMAKING OF AMERICAN LAW 33–42 (2004).

[14]   Elizabeth Duncan Koontz, *Childbirth and Child Rearing Leave: Job-Related Benefits*, 17 N.Y.L.F. 480, 486 (1971).

[15]   Rhode Island Cash Sickness Compensation Act, 1942 R.I. Acts & Resolves 168; *Sickness Benefit Measure Signed*, PROVIDENCE J., Apr. 30, 1942, at 22.

[16]   Koontz, *supra* note 14, at 485.

[17]   *Payment System Defended by UCB*, PROVIDENCE J., June 21, 1947, at 6; *Sickness Benefit Payments Pared: Limit of 15 Weeks for Pregnant Women Now in Effect*, PROVIDENCE J., July 26, 1946, at 19.

[18]   SHEILA B. KAMERMAN ET AL., MATERNITY POLICIES AND WORKING WOMEN 83 (1983).

[19]   *Id.* at 86, 90, 93.

[20]   *See, e.g.,* Selig Greenberg, *R.I. Cash Sickness Setup Facing Insolvency Threat*, PROVIDENCE J., Dec. 12, 1944, at 25 (commenting on the "precarious financial outlook" of the Cash Sickness Fund and the "drain" posed by "the large sums paid out for pregnancy" among other conditions); *see also Minutes of Hearing of December 15, 1948*, N.Y. State Joint Legis. Comm. on Labor and Indus. Conditions, 1948 Leg. 4–5 (1948) (arguing that temporary disability insurance would provide important security to the "breadwinner" who,

insurance mechanisms, furthermore, facilitated private employers' discrimination on the basis of pregnancy.[21]

The family-wage ideal shaped private employer policies and practices just as it did public social insurance. Employers excluded pregnancy from the fringe benefits meant to promote employee loyalty and retention. Pregnancy disability benefits, they reasoned, would constitute a wasted investment, functioning only as "a unique form of severance pay" because women did not return to the workforce following pregnancy.[22] By 1970, more than three-quarters of American workers had private health insurance for hospital and surgical care. Nearly forty percent excluded pregnancy-related coverage for employees and employees' female spouses.[23] By this time, too, almost two-thirds of wage-and-salary workers had access to temporary disability insurance, yet the majority of policies failed to offer coverage for pregnancy.[24] Employers did not only fail to enhance childbearing workers' economic security; they actively undermined it. Private companies as well as public employers such as school boards fired pregnant workers outright or routinely forced them to take mandatory, unpaid maternity leaves without any guarantee of job security.[25] Both social insurance programs and employment policies constructed childbearing women as dependents within the private family and as secondary participants in the labor market.

* * *

The plaintiffs in *Geduldig v. Aiello* endeavored to use antidiscrimination law as a tool to compel the inclusion of childbearing workers within the welfare regime's protections. To make the argument that California's temporary disability insurance violated the Equal Protection Clause, Wendy Williams argued, ". . . while pregnancy itself is *not* a disability, disabilities *caused* by pregnancy are similar to disabilities now compensated in all relevant respects."[26] The pregnancy disability paradigm originated several years prior in the advocacy of Catherine East, whom the far-more famous Betty Friedan later called the "midwife to the birth of the women's movement."[27] In the late 1960s, East was Executive Secretary to the Citizens' Advisory Council on the Status

---

lacking income and facing burdensome medical bills, would otherwise endure a "crushing" "blow to himself and to his dependents").

[21] N.J. COMM'N ON POST-WAR ECON. WELFARE, LEGISLATIVE MEMORANDUM, CASH SICKNESS BENEFITS: SUPPLEMENT TO THE FOURTH REPORT OF THE STATE COMMISSION ON POST-WAR ECONOMIC WELFARE, 171 Leg., at 8–12 (1947).

[22] Brief for Gen. Motors Corp. as Amicus Curiae at 13, Liberty Mut. Ins. v. Wetzel, 424 U.S. 737 (1975) (No. 74-1245).

[23] Koontz, *supra* note 14, at 491–92.

[24] *Id.* at 491.

[25] *Id.* at 490–91.

[26] Brief for Appellees at 25–26, Geduldig v. Aiello, 417 U.S. 484 (1974) (No. 73-640).

[27] *East, Catherine Shipe, 1916–1996. Papers of Catherine Shipe East, 1941–1995: A Finding Aid*, HARV. U. LIBR. (https://hollisarchives.lib.harvard.edu/repositories/8/resources/6895, last visited February 1, 2019).

of Women (CACSW), a federal commission that performed research and issued reports and recommendations on women's issues.[28] East initiated a study of how state laws and employer polices regulated pregnancy, publishing her findings under the byline of the Director of the Women's Bureau in the U.S. Department of Labor, Elizabeth Koontz. "Contrary to popular belief," the article lamented, "the state laws singling out maternity for special treatment in employment all are exclusionary or restrictive."[29] The female capacity for pregnancy had long served as the rationalization for social policy limiting women's work hours and regulating the conditions of women's labor. Yet East and her fellow reformers had found that when it came to pregnancy, itself, the gendered rhetoric of protection rang hollow. East's influential report drew attention to the precarity of pregnant workers—at once breadwinners and mothers—within the U.S. welfare regime.

There was no predetermined legal solution to the question of how best to meet the needs of pregnant workers. Conceptualizing their economic insecurity as a problem of discrimination was contingent rather than inevitable. Indeed, the temporary disability paradigm for pregnancy, which the plaintiffs and their lawyers pursued in *Aiello*, represented a departure from postwar feminist advocacy. Throughout the 1940s and 1950s, many feminists—especially those rooted in the labor movement—had advocated for the expansion of public and private benefits for childbearing women workers. This earlier advocacy premised the claim to benefits not on any antidiscrimination rights but rather on working women's needs and the social importance of pregnancy. Yet gender ideologies rooted in the family-wage ideal and rising hostility to the New Deal welfare state proved insurmountable obstacles.[30] The defeat of feminists' earlier efforts to realize maternity-related entitlements pushed them to find new legal tools. The rise of sex equality as a legal ideal—the enactment of Title VII of the Civil Rights Act of 1964 prohibiting discrimination in employment because of sex as well as race, color, national origin, and religion; Congress's passage of the Equal Rights Amendment in 1971; and the nascent legal campaign for sex equality under the Fourteenth Amendment—pulled them.

A comparison of two key position papers issued by the CACSW illustrates the sea change in feminist advocacy. In 1967, the CACSW issued a report stating: "[T]o provide substantial equality of treatment of both sexes, there must be special recognition of absence due to

---

[28]   *Id.* For an account of the Citizens' Advisory Council, see CYNTHIA HARRISON, ON ACCOUNT OF SEX: THE POLITICS OF WOMEN'S ISSUES, 1945–1968, 152–54, 178–80, 306 (1988).

[29]   Koontz, *supra* note 14, at 482.

[30]   DOROTHY SUE COBBLE, THE OTHER WOMEN'S MOVEMENT: WORKPLACE JUSTICE AND SOCIAL RIGHTS IN MODERN AMERICA 127–32 (2004).

pregnancy."[31] *Substantial* equality, the Council asserted in 1966, could not be achieved via formal equality—same treatment of similarly situated individuals—but rather required a recognition of reproductive sex difference, with pregnancy subject to 'special' recognition. In 1970, the CACSW performed an abrupt turnaround, issuing a report stating: "Childbirth and complications of pregnancy are, for all job-related purposes, temporary disabilities and should be treated as such under any health insurance, temporary disability insurance, or sick leave plan of an employer, union, or fraternal society."[32] The temporary disability paradigm represented a new strategy for realizing economic security for pregnant workers, based on an antidiscrimination right rather than on an independent claim to a social-welfare entitlement.

The temporary disability paradigm for pregnancy offered three ideological and strategic advantages for feminist legal reformers. First, the temporary disability paradigm affirmed that a woman's pregnancy leave would rest on an individual determination of physical capacity, rather than on a generalization about women as a class. It thereby challenged the widespread practice of imposing mandatory maternity leaves, which effectively amounted to termination of pregnant women. It also gave women greater control over the timing and duration of leave.

Second, the temporary disability paradigm reflected feminists' effort to enshrine within law an emerging distinction between biological "sex" and the social construction of "gender." By 1970, feminist advocates began to consider their earlier goal of maternity leave flawed because it entrenched a cultural association between pregnancy and early infant care. While biology fixed childbearing as a female function, women's primary responsibility for childrearing was malleable. CACSW Chair Jacqueline Gutwillig explained: "The subject of child rearing we felt was a separate topic that required separate treatment as both men and women have the responsibility to rear children."[33] Feminist reformers hoped that by disaggregating pregnancy from childrearing leave, they might ultimately encourage a more equitable distribution of caregiving labor within the family.

Third, the temporary disability paradigm would mandate the inclusion of pregnancy within employment-related benefits, while also obscuring the costs of such inclusion. Antidiscrimination law could force both states and employers to provide health insurance and income replacement for pregnancy on an equal basis with other temporary disabilities. Yet assimilating pregnancy to a sex-neutral benefit category already in existence—that of temporary disability—would make the costs

---

[31]   INTERDEPARTMENTAL COMM. ON THE STATUS OF WOMEN & CITIZENS' ADVISORY COUNCIL ON THE STATUS OF WOMEN, REPORT ON PROGRESS IN 1966 ON THE STATUS OF WOMEN 46 (1967).

[32]   CITIZENS' ADVISORY COUNCIL ON THE STATUS OF WOMEN, JOB-RELATED MATERNITY BENEFITS 1 (1970).

[33]   CITIZENS' ADVISORY COUNCIL ON THE STATUS OF WOMEN, WOMEN IN 1971 app. D at 54 (1972).

of pregnancy-related benefits less visible. Reformers argued that such subterfuge was especially important to avoid employment discrimination in a hybrid welfare regime in which employers paid for much of the costs of pregnancy disability benefits.[34] Feminist advocates hoped classifying pregnancy as a temporary disability would provide income replacement for childbearing workers, without discouraging employers from hiring women.

While posing multiple advantages, the temporary disability paradigm also represented feminists' adaptation to the legal and political constraints they faced. The temporary disability paradigm created a sharp legal divide that severed pregnancy and childbirth from early infant care, in ways at odds with many women's experiences. Embracing this paradigm also meant setting aside the goal of childrearing leave, leaving it for a future political battle.[35]

The Equal Employment Opportunity Commission (EEOC)—the administrative agency responsible for enforcing Title VII—did not immediately embrace the temporary disability paradigm. In the late 1960s, when the meaning of the sex provision of Title VII was still unclear,[36] the EEOC took the position that pregnancy was "a condition peculiar to the female sex" that should not be equated with "sickness."[37] Sonia Pressman, an attorney in the Legislative Division of the General Counsel's Office, encouraged the EEOC to issue guidelines interpreting Title VII to require employers to grant women six weeks' pregnancy leave.[38] Another EEOC staff attorney, Susan Deller Ross, was more attentive to the limits as well as the potential of an antidiscrimination statute. She thought the courts would decline to follow any EEOC regulation based on Pressman's proposal; an antidiscrimination statute granted comparative rights and not affirmative entitlements.[39] Ross learned of the temporary disability paradigm from Catherine East, who drew her attention to the CACSW's spanking-new 1970 report. Deller

---

[34]   *Id.* at 22.

[35]   Memorandum from Catherine East on Sex Discrimination as a Growing Problem for Management (on file with Schlesinger Library, Radcliffe Institute, Harvard University, Catherine East Papers, box 4, folder 29) (explaining that the CACSW had not yet "taken up the subject of child rearing [leave]" and might advocate for sex-neutral leave in the future).

[36]   For a discussion of the multiple interpretations of sex equality under Title VII, in the early years following the creation of the EEOC, see KATHERINE TURK, EQUALITY ON TRIAL: GENDER AND RIGHTS IN THE MODERN AMERICAN WORKPLACE 12–42 (2016).

[37]   11/22/67 386IIIE 6-8-7139 (loose sheet), (on file with Schlesinger Library, Radcliffe Institute, Harvard University, Sonia Pressman Fuentes Papers, box 3, folder 2).

[38]   STREBEIGH, *supra* note 1, at 116; Sonia Pressman Fuentes, Comments for the "The Pregnancy Discrimination Act: The Statutory and Historical Context" Panel at the Yale Journal of Law and Feminism Symposium, Respecting Expecting: The 30th Anniversary of the PDA (Nov. 7, 2008) (transcript on file with author); Skype Interview with Sonia Pressman Fuentes (former attorney, U.S. EEOC, Office of General Counsel) (Aug. 18, 2016).

[39]   Interview with Susan Deller Ross, Dir. & Professor, Int'l Women's Human Rights Clinic at Georgetown Univ. Law Ctr., in Wash., D.C. (Dec. 2008).

Ross "bought into it very fast and very easily."[40] In her view, the paradigm held considerable promise: It affirmed pregnant women's rights to continue to work if they were able to do so; required equal treatment of pregnancy under health and disability benefits; and did not create a sex-specific entitlement. Antidiscrimination law promised to be a potent and yet imperfect tool for providing for realizing childbearing women's economic autonomy and security within the liberal welfare regime.

* * *

Wendy Williams took up that tool readily; her personal and professional background had prepared her for a fight against pregnancy discrimination. As a law student at the University of California, Berkeley, Williams had founded the Boalt Hall Women's Association, at a time when women comprised only ten percent of the class. After graduating, Williams had clerked for California Supreme Court Justice Raymond J. Peters.[41] She played a pivotal role in drafting the opinion in *Sail'er Inn, Inc. v. Kirby*, the nation's first decision striking down a state law as unconstitutional sex discrimination.[42] Within weeks of the decision, Williams headed east to Yale Law School for a conference on the teaching of "Women and the Law" organized by a group of female students. There, Williams and two Boalt Hall students, Mary Dunlap and Nancy Davis, began dreaming up a women's legal organization—the firm that ultimately would litigate *Geduldig v. Aiello*.[43]

Williams had initially hoped that the litigation on behalf of Sally Armendariz would stay in the California state court system, where *Sail'er Inn* offered a promising precedent. The California Supreme Court had granted heightened scrutiny to sex, reasoning that women, like racial minorities, suffered stigma and discrimination based on an identity characteristic that bore no relation to their ability to contribute to society.[44] Williams feared her clients would lose in the U.S. Supreme Court, which had not yet applied heightened scrutiny to sex. The Supreme Court had only once held that a law discriminated on the basis of sex in violation of the Equal Protection Clause, in the 1971 case of *Reed v. Reed,* striking down a state's preference for male estate administrators. The Court, however, had declined to grant heightened scrutiny to sex, as then-attorney Ruth Bader Ginsburg had urged in her plaintiffs' brief. Instead, the Court had applied only rational basis review, which required merely a rational relationship between a state law and the legitimate state interest it served. To Williams' chagrin, a procedural motion by

---

[40]   *Id.*

[41]   Interview with Wendy W. Williams, Professor Emerita, Georgetown Univ. Law Ctr., in Wash., D.C. (Dec. 16, 2008).

[42]   The case struck down a state law that prohibited bars from hiring women as bartenders. Sail'er Inn, Inc. v. Kirby, 485 P.2d 529, 531 (Cal. 1971) (en banc). For an account of Williams' role, see NANCY WOLOCH, A CLASS BY HERSELF: PROTECTIVE LAWS FOR WOMEN WORKERS, 1890s–1990s, at 240 (2015).

[43]   Interview with Wendy W. Williams, *supra* note 41.

[44]   *Sail'er Inn*, 485 P.2d at 539–41.

California placed the litigation in federal district court where, when consolidated with another case, it assumed the name *Aiello v. Hansen*.[45] The decision of the U.S. District Court for the Northern District of California was, however, a pleasant surprise. The majority did not apply heightened scrutiny. But it held that pregnancy-related disability did not substantially differ from other, covered temporary disabilities in any manner relevant to the program's purpose: mitigating individuals' economic hardship during periods of disability-induced unemployment.[46]

The district court ruling for the plaintiffs in June 1973 panicked state officials. Dwight M. Geduldig, the director of the California Department of Human Resources warned that extending temporary disability benefits to pregnancy would cost $120 million per year beyond the program's annual $375 million in expenditures. He anticipated that the program would "bust," going insolvent within the year, if the California legislature did not increase the employer payroll tax that funded it.[47] Feminist advocates would later contest these projections, arguing that they were premised on gender stereotypes regarding women's birth rates and the time they required for childbearing leave. Undoubtedly, however, inclusion of pregnancy would increase the costs of the temporary disability insurance program. The stage was set for the Supreme Court to answer a vexing question: did constitutional sex equality require redrawing the boundaries of the welfare state?

Only a few months later, in the fall of 1973, the Supreme Court heard oral arguments in its first case involving pregnancy discrimination.[48] The case, *LaFleur v. Cleveland Board of Education*, concerned a school board policy dating to the early 1950s, which forced pregnant women to take maternity leave without any guarantee of job security in the fourth or fifth month of their pregnancies.[49] On the day of the oral argument, Justice Blackmun wrote a memo noting that equal protection would provide an "easier" and "cleaner" basis for the decision than due process. Yet Justice Blackmun did not think that the mandatory maternity regulations constituted sex discrimination. From his perspective, the maternity rules distinguished not between male and female teachers but "between those who are disqualified to teach for reasons of pregnancy and

---

[45] Aiello v. Hansen, 359 F. Supp. 792 (N.D. Cal. 1973).

[46] *Id.* at 797–801.

[47] *Disability Payment on Pregnancy Held Peril to Coast Plan*, N.Y. TIMES, June 3, 1973, at L27.

[48] The Court had actually agreed to hear an earlier pregnancy discrimination case, *Struck v. United States*, *see* Neil S. Siegel, *The Pregnant Captain, the Notorious REG, and the Vision of RBG: The Story of* Struck v. Secretary of Defense, *in* REPRODUCTIVE RIGHTS AND JUSTICE STORIES 33 (Melissa Murray, Katherine Shaw & Reva B. Siegel eds., 2019), but after the Air Force changed its policy the Court remanded the case to the Ninth Circuit for a consideration of the issue of mootness, and thus never considered the case on the merits.

[49] Transcript of Deposition of Dr. Mark C. Schinnerer, LaFleur, 326 F. Supp. 1208 (Nos. C 71-292, C 71-333) (on file with the Western Reserve Historical Society, Women's Law Fund, box 23, folder 15).

those who are disqualified for other medically indicated reasons."[50] Equal protection mandated that the school boards treat pregnancy the same as other medical disabilities, granting leave according to the facts of each individual's case.[51] According to Justice Blackmun's conference notes, all the Justices with the possible exception of Justice Thurgood Marshall agreed with him that the *LaFleur* case did not concern sex discrimination; Justice Marshall thought that sex equality might be at stake.[52] The Sixth Circuit decision had struck down the Cleveland Board of Education's mandatory maternity leave as a violation of equal protection. The Board's policy imposed an employment restriction on pregnant teachers but not on male teachers who experienced a range of disabilities, without any legitimate state interest for such a sex-based classification.[53]

Notwithstanding the Sixth Circuit's decision, the Supreme Court's upcoming docket provided an incentive to avoid interpreting *LaFleur* as a sex equality case. The month before deciding *LaFleur*, the Justices had accepted an appeal from the U.S. District Court for the Northern District of California in *Geduldig v. Aiello*.[54] That case would pose a more robust challenge to the gendered structure of the liberal welfare state than did *LaFleur*. The *LaFleur* litigation pitted principles of individual freedom, anti-stereotyping, and reproductive autonomy against bureaucratic authority, paternalistic conceptions of pregnancy, and patriarchal opposition to maternal employment. In contrast to *Geduldig*, *LaFleur* did not pose a redistributive challenge that would require redesigning the welfare regime. The sex equality claim in *LaFleur* aligned with an emerging interest in antidiscrimination law as a mechanism to rationalize labor markets. As the state of California and business interests insisted, *Geduldig* not only challenged gender stereotypes but also implicated an affirmative claim on state resources. Recognizing pregnancy discrimination as a violation of equal protection in *LaFleur*, therefore, would pose a larger threat down the road.

To feminists' chagrin, if not their complete surprise, the Court failed to decide *LaFleur* under the Equal Protection Clause. Instead, the five-Justice majority held that the challenged regulations violated the Due Process Clause of the Fourteenth Amendment "because they employ[ed] irrebuttable presumptions that unduly penalize a female teacher for deciding to bear a child."[55] By deciding the case under the much-maligned doctrine of "irrebuttable presumptions," the Court evaded the question whether pregnancy discrimination might violate equal protection doctrine. Jane Picker, the lawyer who had litigated the *LaFleur* case,

---

[50]   Memorandum from Harry A. Blackmun to the Conference (Oct. 15, 1973) (on file with Harry A. Blackmun Papers, Library of Congress, Box 175, folder).

[51]   *Id.*

[52]   *Id.*

[53]   LaFleur v. Cleveland Board of Education, 465 F.2d 1184, 1188–89 (6th Cir. 1972).

[54]   Geduldig v. Aiello, 414 U.S. 1110 (1974) (noting probable jurisdiction and setting the case for oral argument).

[55]   Cleveland Bd. of Educ. v. LaFleur, 414 U.S. 632, 648 (1974).

predicted that in deciding *Geduldig* the Court would "not be able to escape the issue [of sex classifications under the Equal Protection Clause] as readily . . . ."[56] The question that loomed could not be more fundamental: did constitutional sex equality mandate the inclusion of pregnancy and childbirth within the liberal welfare regime?

Business trade associations and the state of California answered with a resounding, "no." Although *Geduldig* concerned a challenge to a state insurance program,[57] its outcome would directly affect private employers' fringe-benefit plans. The California law allowed employers to offer private disability insurance plans as an alternative to the state-administered Unemployment Compensation Disability Fund. To gain approval of a "voluntary plan," an employer had to show that it offered benefits that exceeded those offered under the state plan.[58] Therefore, if the Court held that equal protection required the state plan to include coverage for pregnancy, then employers would also have to provide such coverage. In addition, business as well as civil rights groups recognized that a ruling under the Equal Protection Clause would have significant consequences for legal standards under Title VII.[59] The U.S. Chamber of Commerce and California business-trade associations and employers— the Merchants and Manufacturers Association, the Federated Employers of the Bay Area, Southern California Edison Company, Union Oil Company of California, and Pacific Mutual Life Insurance Company— submitted amici curiae briefs defending the pregnancy exclusion.[60]

As explicit appeals to gender stereotypes lost their political potency and legal validity, business groups and the state of California devised new strategic arguments to oppose pregnancy disability benefits. These market conservatives articulated a conception of sex equality that deployed liberal ideals—anti-stereotyping and reproductive privacy—to

---

[56] Letter from Jane M. Picker, Women's Law Fund, to Ronald S. Longhofer, Assoc. Editor, Mich. Law Review (Feb. 13, 1974) (on file with the Western Reserve Historical Society); *see also* Letter from Ronald Longhofer, Assoc. Editor, Mich. Law Review, to Lewis R. Katz, Professor of Law, Case W. Reserve Univ. (on file with the Western Reserve Historical Society) (requesting Katz's reaction to the use of the "conclusive presumptions" doctrine in LaFleur).

[57] The question before the Supreme Court was whether the exclusion of routine pregnancy from California's temporary disability insurance program violated the Equal Protection Clause. Soon after the district court ruling in *Aiello*, California had modified its disability insurance program to offer coverage for an "abnormal pregnancy with involuntary complications." *Geduldig*, 417 U.S. at 490–91, 490 n.15 (discussing amendments to CAL. UNEMP. INS. CODE § 2626). As a result, plaintiffs Carolyn Aiello, Sally Armendariz and Elizabeth Johnson became entitled to benefits; plaintiff Jacqueline Jaramillo's claim remained before the Court because her disability stemmed from normal pregnancy and childbirth. *Id.* at 490–92.

[58] Brief of Merchs. & Mfrs. Ass'n et al. as Amici Curiae at 2–4, *Geduldig*, 417 U.S. 484 (No. 73-640) [hereinafter Merchants Brief, Geduldig].

[59] Brief of the U.S. EEOC as Amicus Curiae at 1–2, *Geduldig*, 417 U.S. 484 (No. 78-640); Brief of Int'l Union of Elec., Radio, and Mach. Workers, AFL-CIO-CLC as Amicus Curiae at 1–3, *Geduldig*, 417 U.S. 484 (No. 78-640) [hereinafter IUE Brief, Geduldig].

[60] Merchants Brief, Geduldig, *supra* note 58, at 2; Brief for the Chamber of Commerce of the United States of America in Support of the Appellant at 4–5, *Geduldig*, 417 U.S. 484 (No. 73-640).

preserve the costs of reproduction as a private responsibility. To oppose the plaintiffs' claim in *Geduldig*, California needed to argue that state classification on the basis of pregnancy did not constitute sex discrimination. To this end, the state's brief appealed to feminist rhetoric asserting women's individual freedom and autonomy. The brief read: "[P]regnancy [is not] the *sine qua non* of being a woman. . . . [A] large part of woman's struggle for equality involves gaining social acceptance for roles alternative to childbearing and childrearing."[61] The brief thus appropriated a distinction between biological sex and the social construction of gender, which feminists had articulated, to oppose rather than to advance substantive gender equality.

Assuming the Court agreed that a pregnancy-based classification did not discriminate because of sex, California would still need to persuade the Court that the pregnancy exclusion should survive rational basis review. To this end, the state sought to show that pregnancy was not a temporary disability. California argued: "Pregnancy is neither an illness nor an injury but is a normal biological function. . . . [I]t is voluntary and subject to planning."[62] The defendants and amici cited the Supreme Court's landmark decisions legalizing birth control and abortion as evidence. The Court's opinion in *Roe v. Wade*, they argued, had made pregnancy truly volitional.[63] Because legal liberalism had rendered pregnancy a private choice, California argued, women and not the state should bear the economic costs of pregnancy and childbirth. Market conservatives thus fused free-market principles with libertarian conceptions of reproductive autonomy in an effort to preserve private familial responsibility for the economic costs of pregnancy and childbirth.

The Court's decision in *Geduldig* held that the exclusion of pregnancy from California's temporary disability insurance program did not violate the Equal Protection Clause. Justice Potter Stewart wrote the majority opinion, joined by Chief Justice Burger and Justices White, Blackmun, Powell, and Rehnquist. The Court rejected the plaintiffs' claim that the pregnancy-based exclusion discriminated on the basis of sex, reasoning that "[t]here is no risk from which men are protected and women are not."[64] In removing "pregnancy . . . from the list of compensable disabilities," California's program merely divided the state's workers into "pregnant women and nonpregnant persons."[65] While only women comprised the first group, both men and women comprised the second group accruing the program's benefits.[66] The ease of this legal formalism ironically resulted, in part, from legal advances in

---

[61]   Reply Brief for Appellant at 2, *Geduldig*, 417 U.S. 484 (No. 73-640).

[62]   *Id.* at 13.

[63]   Brief for Appellant at 19 & n.23, *Geduldig*, 417 U.S. 484 (No. 73-640).

[64]   *Geduldig*, 417 U.S. at 496–97.

[65]   *Id.* at 496–97 n.20.

[66]   *Id.*

reproductive rights and from evolving social norms that gave women greater freedom not to become mothers.

The Court's opinion had evaluated California's disability insurance program from an allegedly sex-neutral vantage—the list of disabilities covered for both males and females as well as the value of the total benefits that accrued to each sex. Yet this vantage was implicitly based on the male bodies that formed the archetype for the liberal welfare state's subject, bodies that did not experience pregnancy. By contrast, Justice William Brennan's dissent in *Geduldig* evaluated the question of discrimination from the perspective of women's embodied needs. Instead of evaluating the percentage of the total benefits paid by California that accrued to each sex, as the majority did, Justice Brennan's dissent examined the state's coverage of the disabilities experienced by each sex. Brennan reasoned that the pregnancy exclusion represented a sex-based classification because "a limitation is imposed upon the disabilities for which women workers may recover, while men receive full compensation for all disabilities suffered, including those that affect only or primarily their sex . . . ."[67]

Geduldig formed part of a several-year trend on the Burger Court to cut off the expansion of constitutional rights at the border of the U.S. welfare regime. Having dispatched with the sex-discrimination argument, the majority conducted a rational basis review of the pregnancy exclusion. Citing recent decisions that rejected equal protection challenges to social welfare regulations, the majority opinion concluded that the California legislature had broad discretion to design the state's temporary disability insurance program, so long as the distinctions drawn by the program were rational.[68] Thus, California had authority to set appropriate benefit levels, select the risks to be insured, and determine the employee contribution rate necessary to maintain the program's solvency.[69] The rhetoric of scarcity pervaded the majority's opinion, and the Court's deference to the state legislature reflected its concerns about the burden that the plaintiff's claim would place on the public fisc.

* * *

In deciding *Geduldig* under the Equal Protection Clause, the Court was likely also looking ahead to a potential case concerning sex discrimination standards under Title VII. Only two months prior, the U.S. District Court for the Eastern District of Virginia had ruled in favor of the plaintiffs in *Gilbert v. General Electric Co.*[70] *Gilbert* originated when more than 300 women members of Local 161 of the International Union of Electrical Workers (IUE) in Salem, Virginia, filed pregnancy

---

[67]   *Geduldig*, 417 U.S. at 501 (Brennan, J., dissenting).
[68]   *Id.* at 494–95 (majority opinion).
[69]   *Id.* at 494.
[70]   Gilbert v. Gen. Elec. Co., 375 F. Supp. 367 (E.D. Va. 1974).

discrimination grievances with the EEOC.[71] The workers experienced pregnancy discrimination as an affront to their identities as mothers as well as workers.[72] They also understood that employers' bias regarding pregnancy and motherhood lay at the core of a host of discriminatory practices ranging from unequal pay to failure to promote.[73] In the *Gilbert* litigation, the IUE and amici argued that the exclusion of pregnancy from General Electric Company's temporary disability insurance plan violated Title VII of the Civil Rights Act of 1964.[74] At a moment of fluidity between constitutional and statutory definitions of sex equality, the Justices likely anticipated that the Supreme Court's ruling under the Equal Protection Clause in *Geduldig* would affect lower courts' interpretation of employers' duties under Title VII.

Just two years after its *Geduldig* decision, in December 1976, the Court ruled for the defendant in *Gilbert*. In rejecting the plaintiffs' claim, the Court imported a cramped interpretation of sex equality from the constitutional to the statutory context.[75] The same six Justices who had formed the majority in *Geduldig* did so again in the *Gilbert* decision.[76] Writing for the majority, Justice Rehnquist held that the logic of *Geduldig*—that classifications on the basis of pregnancy did not discriminate on the basis of sex—also applied under Title VII.[77] The Court also concluded that the plaintiffs, as in *Geduldig*, had failed to show that the exclusion of pregnancy served as a pretext for invidious discrimination.[78] Pregnancy's significant differences "from the typical covered disease or disability," namely its voluntary character, made its exclusion rational.[79]

Geduldig and *Gilbert* together brought into sharp relief the difficulty of convincing courts that economic justice was a critical component of sex

---

[71] *Discrimination on the Basis of Pregnancy, 1977: Hearing on S. 995 Before the Subcomm. on Labor of the S. Comm. on Human Resources*, 95th Cong. 301 (1977) [hereinafter *S. 995 Hearings*] (statement of Ruth Weyand, Associate General Counsel, International Union of Electrical, Radio, & Machine Workers).

[72] Susan M. Hartmann, The Other Feminists: Activists in the Liberal Establishment 43–44 (1998).

[73] *See S. 995 Hearings, supra* note 71, at 300 (statement of Ruth Weyand, Associate General Counsel, International Union of Electrical, Radio, & Machine Workers) ("[W]omen . . . feel that ending discrimination because of pregnancy is the key to promotion and wages.").

[74] Brief of Commonwealth of Mass. et al. as Amici Curiae, at 5–6, Liberty Mut. Ins. v. Wetzel, 424 U.S. 737 (1976) (No. 74-1245).

[75] *See* Gen. Elec. Co. v. Gilbert, 429 U.S. 125 (1976) (holding that private disability benefits do not violate Title VII where they do not cover pregnancy-related disabilities).

[76] The Court heard oral argument in Gilbert twice. In the 1975 term, Justice Blackmun had sat out on the arguments and the Court deadlocked on the case 4–4. In 1976, Justice Blackmun participated when the Court heard the case on re-argument and placed his vote on the side of the defendants. Harry A. Blackmun, Conference Notes on Gen. Elec. Co. v. Gilbert (Jan. 21, 1976) (on file with Harry A. Blackmun Papers, Library of Congress, Box 238, Case No. 74-1589).

[77] *Gilbert*, 429 U.S. at 127, 135–36.

[78] *Id.* at 136.

[79] *Id.*

equality. Mary Ann Dunlap of Equal Rights Advocates—the firm that had litigated *Geduldig*—excoriated the Court for the hollowness of its sex equality jurisprudence: "the Supreme Court has selected only those forms of sex discrimination . . . that are cheap and easy to remedy, involving symbolic rights as opposed to economic ones . . . ."[80] Following this setback, feminists turned once more to the legislative arena to pursue a vision of sex equality that challenged the fundamental terms of the public-private welfare regime.

In the wake of *Gilbert*, feminist, labor, and civil rights activists launched a campaign for legislation that would override the decision. Their unified advocacy overcame opposition from business trade associations that argued Congress should not impose responsibility upon employers to "subsidiz[e] parenthood."[81] In addition, advocacy by some anti-abortion activists, who believed that support for pregnant workers would encourage women to bring their children to term, contributed to the passage of the Pregnancy Discrimination Act (PDA) of 1978.[82] The Act codifies the temporary disability paradigm that Catherine East had advocated, Wendy Webster Williams had litigated, and the IUE's female membership had asserted. The PDA amends Title VII by defining "sex" under the statute to include "pregnancy, childbirth, or related medical conditions."[83] The PDA thus renders unlawful (in the absence of an employer's affirmative defense) both disparate treatment on the basis of pregnancy and facially neutral employment practices that have a disparate impact on pregnant women.

Yet the imprint of both market and social conservatism limits the PDA's ability to realize economic security for childbearing women. In a concession to anti-abortion activists, the PDA exempts employers from the obligation to provide health insurance coverage for abortion, except in the case of medical complications arising from an abortion or when carrying the fetus to term would endanger a woman's life.[84] In addition, the PDA represents the shift in feminist advocacy, in the context of backlash from business and market conservatives against the welfare state, from a universal social-welfare entitlement to an antidiscrimination right. Judicial ambivalence about the redistributive scope of the PDA's mandate persists in contemporary doctrinal controversies. Employers are not obligated to accommodate pregnant workers—to give a pregnant cashier a chair, for example, or a pregnant warehouse worker a light-duty job that does not involve lifting heavy

---

[80] Mary C. Dunlap, Summary of Memorandum Concerning Implications of General Electric Co. v. Gilbert, 45 U.S.L.W. 4031 (12/7/76) for Sex Discrimination Litigation at 1 (Dec. 10, 1976) (on file with the Schlesinger Library, Radcliffe Institute, Harvard University, Catherine East Papers, box 10, folder 14).

[81] *S. 995 Hearings, supra* note 71, at 94.

[82] Deborah Dinner, *Strange Bedfellows at Work: Neomaternalism in the Making of Sex Discrimination Law*, 91 WASH. U. L. REV. 453, 496–503 (2014).

[83] *See* 42 U.S.C. § 2000e(k) (2012).

[84] *Id.*

boxes—unless an employer extends light-duty to other temporarily disabled workers and the failure to do the same for pregnancy acts as a pretext for discrimination.[85] Courts are widely hostile to pregnancy-related disparate-impact claims, even as they recognize the formal availability of this theory of liability under the PDA.[86] Thus, conservative jurisprudence often reduces women's rights under the PDA to a comparative right to receive the same treatment as other temporarily disabled workers, even as more expansive interpretations of the statute exist that would broaden its ability to advance women's economic security.

The PDA's limitations are especially significant in an era of rising income inequality and increasingly precarious forms of work. The number of states offering temporary disability insurance programs has not expanded from the five that had implemented such programs by 1969. Private employers have cut back on discretionary fringe benefits in the late twentieth century. The capacity for the PDA to protect pregnant workers diverges along class lines. Professional women are more likely to work for employers who offer relatively generous disability and health insurance benefits; in these workplaces, the imperative of equal treatment for pregnancy offers access to substantive protections. Low-income women are more likely to work in contingent and precarious jobs without even minimal benefits; equal treatment of pregnancy is a "hollow promise" for these workers.[87] The U.S. welfare regime provided a fragile foundation on which to rest an antidiscrimination right to childbearing women's economic security, one that has morphed and constricted in recent decades.

* * *

Despite the partial repudiation of the logic of *Geduldig* by Congress' enactment of the PDA, this now-infamous decision continued through the late twentieth century to act as a firewall severing state regulation of pregnancy from sex equality under the U.S. Constitution. The Court's jurisprudence departed starkly from the claims made by the grassroots women's movement, which argued that the legal regulation of pregnancy was at the core of both women's equality and liberty.[88] Over the course of the 1970s, however, the Court effaced these claims in its *Geduldig* ruling

---

[85]   *See* Young v. United Parcel Serv., Inc. 135 S. Ct. 1338, 1354 (2015) (holding that the failure to assign a pregnant employee to light duty so as to accommodate her partial incapacity might constitute a prima facie case of sex discrimination where the employer offered such accommodations to other employees).

[86]   *See* Dinner, *supra* note 82, at 523–24.

[87]   *See* Catherine Albiston & Lindsey Trimble O'Connor, *Just Leave*, 39 HARV. J.L. & GENDER 1, 1 (2016).

[88]   Reva B. Siegel, Roe's Roots: *The Women's Rights Claims that Engendered* Roe, 90 B.U. L. REV. 1875, 1881–83 (2010) (analyzing feminists' claims that access to birth control and abortion was essential to challenging women's subordination).

as well as in subsequent decisions that upheld the exclusion of non-therapeutic abortions from Medicaid coverage.[89]

To the welcome surprise of feminists, in 2003 the Court issued an opinion that began to break down the boundaries between reproduction and constitutional equality. In *Nevada Department of Human Resources v. Hibbs*, a state employee alleged that Nevada had denied him family leave in violation of the Family and Medical Leave Act of 1993 (FMLA) and sued for damages. Nevada asserted sovereign immunity as a defense. Relevant precedent held that Congress could authorize private damage suits against nonconsenting states only when legislating to enforce the Reconstruction Amendments. Accordingly, the question the Court needed to decide in *Hibbs* was whether the family-leave provision of the FMLA represented a valid exercise of Section Five of the Fourteenth Amendment.[90] Precedent required that these provisions be "congruent and proportional" to a pattern of constitutional violations in the states.[91]

Hibbs presented vexing constitutional dilemmas about the definition of sex equality under the Equal Protection Clause and the scope of Congress' Section Five power. Congress had amassed evidence that states had discriminated when they provided family leave to female but not male employees and when they offered women maternity leaves that extended beyond a period of physical disability for childbirth to include time for infant care.[92] In conceptualizing this behavior as a violation of Section One of the Fourteenth Amendment, the Court determined that states violated equal protection when they acted to enforce gender stereotypes and not only when they acted with an intent to harm women. As Professor Siegel shows, *Hibbs* answered the question that *Geduldig* left open: When is pregnancy discrimination unconstitutional? In a footnote, the *Geduldig* majority had buried an oblique suggestion that the exclusion of pregnancy from a legislative scheme might violate equal protection when it functioned as a pretext for sex discrimination.[93] *Hibbs* turned this forgotten footnote into a clarion note that resounds across constitutional jurisprudence. The case stands for the proposition that states violate the Equal Protection Clause when they regulate pregnancy and parenting in ways that reinforce gender stereotypes.[94]

Hibbs also took partial steps toward answering a second question at the heart of *Geduldig*. To what extent might gender equality require social welfare entitlements? Congress had fashioned in the FMLA a remedy far more capacious than a mere prohibition on sex discrimination

---

[89]   *Id.* at 1901–02 (first citing Geduldig v. Aiello, 417 U.S. 484 (1974); then citing Maher v. Roe, 432 U.S. 464 (1976); and then citing Harris v. McRae, 448 U.S. 297 (1980)).

[90]   538 U.S. 721, 738–40 (2003).

[91]   *See* Robert C. Post, *Foreword: Fashioning the Legal Constitution: Culture, Courts, and Law*, 117 HARV. L. REV. 4, 13–19 (2003) (discussing the doctrinal dilemma in *Hibbs*).

[92]   Reva B. Siegel, *You've Come a Long Way, Baby: Rehnquist's New Approach to Pregnancy Discrimination in* Hibbs, 58 STAN. L. REV. 1871, 1885, 1889–92 (2006).

[93]   417 U.S. at n.20.

[94]   *Id.* at 1892–93.

in the provision of family and medical leave; it had mandated an affirmative entitlement to twelve weeks' family leave. In upholding the FMLA's family-leave provision, the Court gave an extremely wide berth to Congress to respond to the harms of gender inequality in creative and robust ways. The Court went so far as to suggest that an affirmative entitlement to family leave remedied the disparate impact that the lack of state leave had on women.[95] *Hibbs* stands for the proposition that Congress has the power to remedy gender inequality not only by including pregnancy, female breadwinners, and male caregivers within existing social-insurance programs but by creating new entitlements. The decision does not mandate such entitlements, however; nor should it. As Professor Lawrence Sager long ago recognized, the realization of this under-enforced constitutional value is the responsibility of Congress and, we might add, state legislatures and state and federal administrative agencies.[96]

As a nation, we have not yet come fully to recognize the welfarist as well as the anti-stereotyping dimensions of sex equality. Our constitutional jurisprudence requires that the state not treat men as breadwinners and women as caregivers. In large part, however, this jurisprudence allows policies and employment practices that perpetuate private, familial responsibility for reproduction and caregiving. The failure of employers, states, and the federal government to socialize the costs and burdens of reproduction has a disproportionate burden on working-class women and men, who are least able to resist exploitation in the workplace and who lack the resources to commodify care. *Geduldig's* influence, while lightening in constitutional jurisprudence, continues to cast a dark shadow over the working lives of men and women who lack adequate leave, who work hours that are alternately too long or too unpredictable, and who struggle to care at home while earning a decent livelihood.

---

[95]   *Hibbs*, 538 U.S. at 738 (holding that Congress was within its Section Five powers in enacting an affirmative leave entitlement because the absence of any leave policy "would exclude far more women than men from the workplace"); *see also* Samuel R. Bagenstos, Nevada Department of Human Resources v. Hibbs: *Universalism and Reproductive Justice, in* REPRODUCTIVE RIGHTS AND JUSTICE STORIES 183 (Melissa Murray, Katherine Shaw & Reva B. Siegel eds., 2019).

[96]   *See generally* Lawrence Gene Sager, *Fair Measure: The Legal Status of Underenforced Constitutional Norms*, 91 HARV. L. REV. 1212 (1978).

5

Maya Manian*

Coerced Sterilization of Mexican-American Women: The Story of *Madrigal v. Quilligan*

In 1973, twenty-three-year-old Consuelo Hermosillo arrived at the Los Angeles County USC Medical Center in the midst of labor. In an effort to persuade her to sign a consent form for sterilization, medical staff claimed that she was "high risk" and could die from another pregnancy.[1] While she endured labor pains and waited for a cesarean section to be performed, a nurse told Hermosillo that her cesarean surgery would not proceed until she consented in writing to a tubal ligation.[2] Fearing that her baby might die if she did not consent and unable to stand the pain any longer, Hermosillo signed the consent form.[3] She was so upset about signing the form that she "said a bad word."[4] Years later, Hermosillo described herself as "a bird who wants to fly and has had its wings cut."[5]

Hermosillo's experience was not anomalous. After a whistleblower leaked evidence of rampant sterilization abuse at the Los Angeles County USC Medical Center, nine other women joined Hermosillo in a lawsuit alleging that medical personnel systematically coerced Mexican-

---

* Professor of Law, University of San Francisco School of Law. I am grateful to the editors for including me in this volume. For helpful comments, I thank Khiara Bridges, Serena Mayeri, Melissa Murray, Douglas NeJaime, Kate Shaw, Reva Siegel, Cilla Smith, and participants at the University of San Francisco Law School Faculty Scholarship Workshop and SMU Dedman Law School Faculty Forum. Thanks to Amy Wright for her excellent services as research librarian.

[1] Appellants' Brief at 18, Madrigal v. Quilligan, 639 F.2d 789 (9th Cir. 1981) (No. 78-3187) (unpublished table opinion) (on file with the Stanford University Libraries Department of Special Collections, M0673, Mexican American Legal Defense and Educational Fund Records, RG#5, Series 2: Litigation Files, 1968–1982, Box 946, Folder 11) [hereinafter Appellants' Brief].

[2] A tubal ligation—colloquially known as having one's "tubes tied"—involves closing a woman's fallopian tubes in order to prevent future pregnancies. *See Tubal Ligation*, U.S. NAT'L LIBRARY OF MEDICINE, NAT'L INST. OF HEALTH: MEDLINE PLUS (Oct. 9, 2014), http://www.nlm.nih.gov/medlineplus/ency/article/002913.htm.

[3] Appellants' Brief, *supra* note 1, at 18–19.

[4] *Id.* at 19.

[5] Trial Transcript at 19, Madrigal v. Quilligan, No. CV 75-2057-JWC (C.D. Cal. June 30, 1978) (on file with the Stanford University Libraries Department of Special Collections, M0673, Mexican American Legal Defense and Educational Fund Records, RG#5, Series 2: Litigation Files, 1968–1982, Box 946, Folder 5).

American women into submitting to sterilization under similar circumstances. The resulting case, *Madrigal v. Quilligan,* dramatically altered public consciousness and public policy on coerced sterilization.

COERCED STERILIZATION IN THE UNITED STATES

The long history of coerced sterilization in the United States has been well documented. Scholars have shown that both public and private actors targeted the poor, the disabled, and racial minorities, particularly minority women, for coercive sterilization.[6] In *Buck v. Bell*, the U.S. Supreme Court legitimized early twentieth century eugenic sterilization practices with Oliver Wendell Holmes' notorious declaration: "Three generations of imbeciles are enough."[7] It was not until Nazi Germany adopted American eugenic theory and practice that public opinion about eugenics ultimately shifted in the United States.[8] The counter-movement against eugenic sterilization culminated in the U.S. Supreme Court's 1942 decision in *Skinner v. Oklahoma.*[9] Although *Skinner* did not explicitly overrule *Buck v. Bell*, it rejected *eugenic* sterilization as a valid state goal and recognized that procreation "involves one of the basic civil rights of man."[10]

Yet *Skinner* did not lead to the end of forced sterilization in the United States. Although support for eugenics-based sterilization laws waned, new justifications for coerced sterilization arose. Following World War II, concerns about population control, immigration, and welfare costs emerged as new rationales for targeting marginalized populations for sterilization. As historian Virginia Espino argues, in the 1960s, federal family planning funding ushered in a new era of neo-eugenics in which medical personnel would obtain signed consent forms using coercion tactics aimed at poor patients, especially women of color.[11] Thus, the influx of federal family planning funds in the 1960s and 1970s both increased access to reproductive health care and increased abusive sterilization practices.[12] Poor women simultaneously benefited from affordable means of fertility control and were subject to coerced fertility control.[13]

---

[6]   *See generally* Paul A. Lombardo, THREE GENERATIONS, NO IMBECILES: EUGENICS, THE SUPREME COURT, AND BUCK V. BELL (2008).

[7]   274 U.S. 200, 207 (1927).

[8]   *See* VICTORIA F. NOURSE, IN RECKLESS HANDS: SKINNER V. OKLAHOMA AND THE NEAR TRIUMPH OF AMERICAN EUGENICS 129–31 (2008).

[9]   316 U.S. 535 (1942).

[10]   *Skinner*, 316 U.S. at 541. Critically, however, the *Skinner* court explicitly linked procreative rights to marital arrangements.

[11]   Virginia Espino, *Women Sterilized as They Give Birth: Forced Sterilization and the Chicana Resistance in the 1970s, in* LAS OBRERAS: CHICANA POLITICS OF WORK AND FAMILY 65–82 (Vicki Ruiz & Chon Moriega eds., 2000).

[12]   *See* Lisa C. Ikemoto, *Infertile by Force and Federal Complicity: The Story of* Relf v. Weinberger, *in* WOMEN AND THE LAW STORIES 189–191 (Elizabeth M. Schneider & Stephanie M. Wildman eds., 2011).

[13]   *See* Johanna Schoen, CHOICE & COERCION: BIRTH CONTROL, STERILIZATION, AND ABORTION IN PUBLIC HEALTH AND WELFARE 3 (2005) (describing the "double-edged

Women of color were particularly at risk for sterilization abuse, with each geographic region of the United States having its own disfavored group.[14] A 1970 National Fertility Study found that twenty percent of all married black women and roughly the same percentage of all Chicana women had been sterilized; over thirty-five percent of women of childbearing age in Puerto Rico had been sterilized.[15] In California, Mexican-American women were the group most prominently targeted for sterilization.[16] California had an especially checkered history of compulsory sterilization. In 1909, it became the third state to adopt laws authorizing the sterilization of the "feeble-minded."[17] In her history of eugenics in the United States, Alexandra Minna Stern found that California accounted for one third of the sixty thousand nonconsensual sterilizations performed nationwide in the early twentieth century.[18] Stern discovered that long before the allegations of sterilization abuse in *Madrigal v. Quilligan*, a disproportionate number of patients with Spanish surnames suffered forced sterilization at California institutions.[19] As she explains, ideological notions of Mexican-American women as hyper-fertile often drove these eugenic sterilization practices.[20] Sociologist Elena Gutierrez argues that coerced sterilization of Mexican-origin women in 1970s California resulted from a perfect storm of post-World War II fears about population growth combined with historic racial prejudices against Mexican Americans, as well as a huge influx of federal dollars for family planning.[21] Thus, *Madrigal v. Quilligan* is not only a story about coerced sterilization in the 1970s era, but should also be viewed as "an important link on a longer chain of eugenics and reproductive injustice in California that reaches back to the 1900s and forward to the twenty-first century."[22]

---

application of reproductive technologies" which "could extend reproductive control to women, or they could be used to control women's reproduction.").

[14]   *See* Ikemoto, *supra* note 12, at 196 (noting that sterilization abuse was occurring around the country in the 1960s and 1970s with African American, Chicana, Native American, Puerto Rican, and poor white women all targeted depending on the region).

[15]   *See* ANGELA DAVIS, WOMEN, RACE, AND CLASS 219 (1981).

[16]   In this chapter, I use the terms Mexican American, Mexican origin, or Chicana/o interchangeably.

[17]   Buck v. Bell, 274 U.S. 200, 205 (1927).

[18]   *See* Alexandra Minna Stern, *Sterilized in the Name of Public Health: Race, Immigration, and Reproductive Control in Modern California*, 95 AMER. J. PUB. HEALTH 1128, 1128 (2005); ALEXANDRA MINNA STERN, EUGENIC NATION: FAULTS AND FRONTIERS OF BETTER BREEDING IN MODERN AMERICAN 99–110 (2005).

[19]   *See id.* at 109–110.

[20]   *See id.* at 110.

[21]   *See* ELENA R. GUTIERREZ, FERTILE MATTERS: THE POLITICS OF MEXICAN-ORIGIN WOMEN'S REPRODUCTION 2–13; 29–54 (2008).

[22]   *See* STERN, EUGENIC NATION, *supra* note 18, at 223 (noting that *Madrigal* is most often viewed as an illustration of incidents of forced sterilization in the 1960s and 1970s rather than as a crucial "link" in the long history of coerced sterilization).

THE MADRIGAL TEN

The Los Angeles County USC Medical Center ("Medical Center")—famous in the 1970s as the setting for the soap opera *General Hospital*[23]—operated an overwhelmingly busy maternity ward serving largely low-income and immigrant populations. Dr. Bernard "Buddy" Rosenfeld, a young resident working at the Medical Center in the early 1970s, blew the whistle on widespread sterilization abuse on the maternity ward. Rosenfeld believed that women of Mexican origin were being sterilized without their knowledge or consent. Determined to bring these abuses to light, he surreptitiously copied medical records for hundreds of sterilizations at the Medical Center. After his shifts, he spent hours typing letters to journalists, civil rights groups, and government officials in the hopes of spurring legal action.[24] Rosenfeld later estimated that while he was at the Medical Center, "between 20 to 30 percent of the doctors pushed sterilization on women who either did not understand what was happening to them or who had not been given the facts regarding their options."[25]

Eventually, Rosenfeld's efforts paid off. Twenty-six-year-old Antonia Hernández, a recent UCLA law school graduate, and twenty-nine-year-old Charles Nabarrete, both Mexican-American attorneys at the nearby Model Cities Center for Law and Justice, took on the case.[26] Hernández grew up on the east side of Los Angeles in a predominantly Mexican-American community.[27] Hernández and Nabarrete joined with the Chicana feminist organization Comisión Feminil to mount a class action lawsuit against the U.S. Department of Health, Education, and Welfare (HEW), the California State Department of Health, and the individual doctors who had performed or supervised the sterilizations, including the head of the obstetrics department, Dr. Edward J. Quilligan.[28] Hernández followed up on the medical files that Rosenfeld provided, tracking down

---

[23]   *See Los Angeles County + USC Medical Center*, L.A. Conservancy, https://www.la conservancy.org/locations/los-angeles-countyusc-medical-center (last visited Mar. 1, 2018).

[24]   *See* Renee Tajima-Peña, *"Más Bebés?": An Investigation of the Sterilization of Mexican-American Women at Los Angeles County-USC Medical Center During the 1960s and 70s*, THE SCHOLAR AND FEMINIST ONLINE, (Summer 2013), available at: http://sfonline. barnard.edu/life-un-ltd-feminism-bioscience-race/mas-bebes-an-investigation-of-the-sterilization-of-mexican-american-women-at-los-angeles-county-usc-medical-center-during-the-1960s-and-70s/, at 2; *see also* Marcela Valdes, *When Doctors Took 'Family Planning' Into Their Own Hands*, N.Y. TIMES MAG. (Feb. 1, 2016), http://www.nytimes.com/ 2016/02/01/magazine/when-doctors-took-family-planning-into-their-own-hands.html.

[25]   *See* Carlos G. Velez-Ibanez, *The Nonconsenting Sterilization of Mexican Women in Los Angeles: Issues of Psychocultural Rupture and Legal Redress in Paternalistic Behavioral Environments, in* TWICE A MINORITY: MEXICAN AMERICAN WOMEN 239 (Margarita B. Melville ed., 1980) (citation omitted).

[26]   A third lawyer, Georgina Torres-Rizk, also worked on the case until just before the trial for money damages. *See* GUTIERREZ, *supra* note 21, at 45 n.60.

[27]   *See* Tajima-Peña, *supra* note 24, at 2.

[28]   The federal district court eventually denied class certification, but proceeded with the injunctive relief and damages claims for the ten named plaintiffs. *See* Appellants' Brief, *supra* note 1, at 1.

the women listed in the medical records all over the east side of Los Angeles. As Hernández later recounted:

> I must have interviewed a hundred women . . . . [a]nd then I had the difficult job of saying to many of the women, 'Do you know you were sterilized?' It was a very painful process. And some of them knew, but they all had the misconception that their tubes were tied but could be untied.[29]

Gloria Molina, who led the Comisión Feminil at the time, assisted the attorneys by offering her organization as a class plaintiff in the case.[30] Hernandez faced the challenging task of finding and convincing individual women to become lead plaintiffs in the lawsuit. Many of the women felt deep shame over what happened to them and feared going public with such a private matter. At first, Consuelo Hermosillo wanted nothing to do with a public court case. She and her husband did not even discuss the coerced sterilization with each other, much less with anyone else. Hermosillo joined the suit as a plaintiff only after seeing the evidence that Rosenfeld gathered. Without telling her husband or children, she secretly rode the bus alone to the courthouse in the hope that the case would protect other women from what she had suffered.[31]

Ultimately, the lawyers convinced ten women to file a lawsuit: Guadalupe Acosta, Estella Benavides, Maria Figueroa, Rebecca Figueroa, Consuelo Hermosillo, Georgina Hernández, Maria Hurtado, Dolores Madrigal, Helena Orozco, and Jovita Rivera. None of the women were receiving federal welfare benefits at the time, but all were eligible for medical assistance at the federally-funded Medical Center.[32] The "Madrigal Ten" alleged that doctors at the Medical Center coercively sterilized each of them between June 1971 and March 1974. Their suit sought injunctive relief to strengthen federal and state policies on informed consent to sterilization, as well as money damages for the injuries the women suffered.[33] The Madrigal Ten's stories exposed common patterns in the ways Medical Center staff coerced Mexican-American women into undergoing sterilization procedures. All of the ten cases involved women whose primary language was Spanish and who had undergone a tubal ligation after childbirth by cesarean section. Nurses and physicians used multiple tactics to exploit the fact that the women had limited English language skills and were seeking medical care for childbirth.

---

[29] GUTIERREZ, *supra* note 21, at 35–36.
[30] *See* Letter from Judge Michael L. Stern, August 29, 2018 (on file with author).
[31] *See* Valdes, *supra* note 24.
[32] GUTIERREZ, *supra* note 21, at 43–44.
[33] Complaint at 1–2, Madrigal v. Quilligan, No. CV-75-2057 (C.D. Cal. June 30, 1978) (on file with the Stanford University Libraries Department of Special Collections, M0673, Mexican American Legal Defense and Educational Fund Records, RG#5, Series 2: Litigation Files, 1968–1982, Box 945, Folder 3) [hereinafter Complaint].

First, all of the women were approached for consent to sterilization while in the midst of labor—some after being heavily medicated—and were pressured into signing English language consent forms that they could not understand. Maria Hurtado arrived at the Medical Center for a routine checkup that turned into an emergency cesarean delivery. Hurtado was given a consent form to sign without any explanation while she was medicated for labor pains. She signed the forms believing that she was consenting to the cesarean surgery. She underwent a tubal ligation following the delivery of her child, but did not learn that she was irreversibly sterilized until six weeks later when she appeared for a routine follow up appointment.[34] Similarly, Rebecca Figueroa arrived at the Medical Center for an emergency cesarean delivery due to blood loss.[35] Just before being taken to the operating room, she signed two English language consent forms that she could not read, also believing that she was consenting to cesarean surgery.[36]

Second, many of the women faced multiple requests by various Medical Center staff to submit to sterilization. Medical Center personnel repeatedly approached and urged Helena Orozco to consent to sterilization. Orozco refused on the ground that she preferred to use birth control pills, as she had done in planning for her current pregnancy.[37] Weak and confused from sharp labor pains, Orozco was crying when she finally capitulated and signed the sterilization consent form in order to stop the Medical Center staff's relentless entreaties.[38] Orozco later explained: "I just wanted them to leave me alone, sign the papers and get it over with . . . . I was in pain on the table when they were asking me all those questions."[39] Georgina Hernández arrived at the hospital bleeding and experiencing labor pains.[40] Medical Center staff pressed her to consent to sterilization at the time of her admission, but she refused. As her labor progressed, the doctors informed her that a cesarean delivery was necessary. Despite her documented refusal, while in labor and about to undergo an emergency cesarean section, the doctor again asked her about having her "tubes tied."[41] Hernández alleged that the doctor told her that Mexican people were very poor and cautioned her not to have any more children because she could not provide financial support for

---

[34] *Id.* at 9; Appellants' Brief, *supra* note 1, at 20. *See also* Antonia Hernández, *Chicanas and the Issue of Involuntary Sterilization: Reforms Needed to Protect Informed Consent,* 3 CHICANO L. REV. 3, 4–9 (1976) (summarizing plaintiffs' affidavits).

[35] Complaint, *supra* note 33, at 13.

[36] Appellants' Brief, *supra* note 1, at 20.

[37] Complaint, *supra* note 33, at 10.

[38] *Id.* at 11; Appellants' Brief, *supra* note 1, at 18.

[39] GUTIERREZ, *supra* note 21, at 42.

[40] Complaint, *supra* note 33, at 12; *see also* Madrigal v. Quilligan, No. CV 75-2057-JWC at 14–15 (C.D. Cal. June 30, 1978) (on file with the Stanford University Libraries Department of Special Collections, M0673, Mexican American Legal Defense and Educational Fund Records, RG#5, Series 2: Litigation Files, 1968–1982, Box 945, Folder 2) [hereinafter Opinion].

[41] Opinion, *supra* note 40, at 15.

them.[42] She again refused and only signed a consent for the cesarean operation. Shortly before going inside the operating room, the doctor asserted that Hernández agreed to be sterilized and noted her consent in her file.[43] Hernández later recalled: "And this lady came, I don't remember seeing her face, I just remember her voice telling me, 'Mijita, you better sign those papers or your baby could probably die here.' "[44] Hernández only learned that she had been permanently sterilized three weeks later at her post-delivery examination.[45]

Third, in addition to being repeatedly presented with English language sterilization consent forms in the midst of labor pains, many of the women lacked accurate information about the need for and consequences of a tubal ligation. Dolores Madrigal was admitted to the Medical Center for delivery of her second child. She rebuffed multiple suggestions by the nurse and physician that she submit to sterilization. Under the severe pain of labor, and after overhearing the nurse tell her husband that she would die if she had another child, Madrigal signed the consent form out of fear, even though she could not read its contents. Like many of the women, Madrigal also believed the procedure was reversible—that if her tubes were *tied* they could be *untied*.[46] Estella Benavides was similarly pressured into signing a consent form during labor based on the assertion that another pregnancy would kill her. Afraid for her life and fearing to leave her children without her support, she signed the consent form.[47] Benavides subsequently explained that in her pain she was not thinking about whether the operation would render her permanently sterile: "[I was] not thinking of anything since the doctors had told me that they were protecting me. The only thing I was thinking about was about my girls . . . ."[48] In an effort to persuade them to consent to sterilization, several of the women were also falsely told that California does not permit more than three cesarean sections to be performed on a woman.[49]

Finally, some of the women never even signed a consent form for sterilization. Instead, the physician waived consent based on asserted exigent circumstances. Maria Figueroa was approached while groggy from anesthesia in the delivery room. Figueroa stated that the doctor was "after me, after me" to consent.[50] Finally, in order to silence the doctor's insistence, Figueroa agreed to a tubal ligation if the baby was a boy. The physician delivered a baby girl, but nevertheless proceeded to sterilize Figueroa. Figueroa never signed any forms indicating her consent to a

[42] *Id.*
[43] *See id.*
[44] Tajima-Peña, *supra* note 24, at 1.
[45] Complaint, *supra* note 33, at 12.
[46] *Id.* at 8.
[47] *Id.* at 13.
[48] Appellants' Brief, *supra* note 1, at 19.
[49] *Id.* at 14–15.
[50] *Id.* at 16.

sterilization.[51] Guadalupe Acosta's child was born dead. She was also sterilized after her cesarean surgery, and did not learn of her sterilization until more than two months later when she returned to the Medical Center to request birth control pills. Acosta never signed a consent form for sterilization.[52] While still anesthetized from the birth of her child by cesarean, the physician asked Jovita Rivera whether she wanted sterilization.[53] She alleged that the physician told her she should be sterilized because her children would be a burden on the government.[54] Rivera had only a cloudy recollection of the events in the operating room, but thought the procedure was reversible. The physician asserted that Rivera verbally consented to the procedure, but she never signed a consent form. Neither the physician nor any other staff informed Rivera that she would be irreversibly sterilized.[55]

THE LITIGATION AND THE CHICANA FEMINIST MOVEMENT

The Madrigal Ten filed their lawsuit in June 1975 and launched their pursuit of injunctive relief to toughen federal and state policies surrounding informed consent to sterilization. In their legal filings on behalf of the women, Hernández and Nabarrete argued that the lack of appropriate Spanish language consent forms and other safeguards to protect against coerced sterilization resulted in violations of the women's constitutional right to procreate.[56] In particular, the women's attorneys relied on *Roe v. Wade* to argue that the U.S. Constitution protects a woman's decision to bear a child.[57] At that time, only two years after the *Roe* decision, the dominant narrative around reproductive rights concerned abortion rights. The Madrigal Ten's lawyers sought a broader conception of reproductive rights—one that encompassed the right to choose an abortion *and* the right to give birth. The lawyers brought the still-nascent framework of reproductive justice to bear on the case, incorporating concerns about discrimination along intersectional lines of gender, race, poverty, and immigration status—all issues at play in the *Madrigal* case.[58]

---

[51] Complaint, *supra* note 33, at 10; Appellants' Brief, *supra* note 1, at 17 (noting that the physician in fact attempted to have the consent formed signed *after* the sterilization procedure had been performed).

[52] Complaint, *supra* note 33, at 11; Appellants' Brief, *supra* note 1, at 21–23 (explaining that Acosta was at no point asked to consent to tubal ligation).

[53] Appellants' Brief, *supra* note 1, at 11.

[54] Complaint, *supra* note 33, at 9.

[55] *Id.*

[56] Complaint, *supra* note 33, at 1–3. The Complaint did not assert claims for violation of the tort law doctrine of informed consent.

[57] 410 U.S. 113 (1973); Complaint, *supra* note 33, at 17 (also relying on Griswold v. Connecticut, 381 U.S. 479 (1965) and Skinner v. Oklahoma, 316 U.S. 535 (1942)).

[58] *See* Dorothy Roberts, *Reproductive Justice, Not Just Rights*, DISSENT MAG. (Fall 2015), *available at* https://www.dissentmagazine.org/article/reproductive-justice-not-just-rights (" '[R]eproductive justice' . . . [is] a framework that includes not only a woman's right not to have a child, but also the right to have children and to raise them with dignity in

*The First Phase—Feminist Movement Tensions
over Strengthening Sterilization Regulations*

The first phase of the *Madrigal* litigation—focusing on injunctive relief that would strengthen sterilization consent policies—resulted in victory for the women.[59] However, the Chicana activists working on the *Madrigal* matter did not confine their efforts to secure stronger sterilization policies to litigation. Instead, they used multiple strategies to achieve their policy goals. They lobbied for legislative reform and engaged in public education, including generating widespread media attention for their cause.[60]

Critically, the *Madrigal* case galvanized Chicana feminist activism in ways that highlighted tensions between mainstream white feminists and women of color. In the 1960s and 1970s, white feminist groups focusing on reproductive rights emphasized the right *not* to become a parent, but women of color during this same time period began fighting for a broader conception of reproductive justice.[61] While white feminist activists argued for unimpeded access to sterilization, contraception, and abortion, women of color sought to expand the discussion of reproductive rights to include their concerns about abusive practices designed to restrict racial minority women's reproduction.[62] Historically, birth control activists like Margaret Sanger often cast access to contraception as a form of "negative eugenics" that would allow those in power to control the birth rates of "less desirable classes," particularly communities of color.[63]

In 1977, as part of the *Madrigal* litigation, when Chicana feminist groups pushed the California Department of Health to require a waiting period prior to sterilization procedures, white feminist groups resisted. Comisión Feminil attempted to sway the California chapter of the National Organization for Women (NOW) to support sterilization waiting periods, but to no avail. NOW was concerned that waiting periods would be used to deny sterilizations to women who wanted them.[64] Board members from Comisión Feminil presented information about the Madrigal Ten to the NOW board, yet NOW never modified its stance:

---

safe, healthy, and supportive environments. This framework repositioned reproductive rights in a political context of intersecting race, gender, and class oppressions.").

[59]   *See* GUTIERREZ, *supra* note 21, at 50.

[60]   *Id.* at 95, 98–99.

[61]   *See* JENNIFER NELSON, WOMEN OF COLOR AND THE REPRODUCTIVE RIGHTS MOVEMENT 4–5 (2003); *see* Khiara M. Bridges, *Elision and Erasure: Race, Class, and Gender in* Harris v. McRae, *in* REPRODUCTIVE RIGHTS AND JUSTICE STORIES 117, 120–121 (Melissa Murray, Katherine Shaw & Reva B. Siegel eds., 2019) (describing anti-sterilization abuse activism of CARASA, the Committee for Abortion Rights and Against Sterilization Abuse).

[62]   *See* DOROTHY ROBERTS, KILLING THE BLACK BODY: RACE, REPRODUCTION AND THE MEANING OF LIBERTY 57–103 (1999).

[63]   *Id.* at 74–75; *see also* DAVIS, *supra* note 15, at 212–215 (describing Margaret Sanger and the American Birth Control League's approval of the eugenics movement).

[64]   GUTIERREZ, *supra* note 21, at 104.

> We [Comisión Feminil] were trying to get support of the other
> women's organizations, feminist organizations, and I think we
> were also a little surprised that the support we just assumed
> would be there because we were all struggling for women's
> rights wasn't there . . . . We found quickly that NOW was the
> group that said, "No, when we go in and want sterilization
> procedures, we don't want to wait 48 hours, we want it on
> demand." But . . . [w]omen were being sterilized without their
> consent, consent forms being shoved in front of them in the
> middle of labor, in English, a language they didn't understand
> and read, and they [NOW] were just totally against that process
> [of waiting periods].[65]

Despite resistance from white feminist groups, Chicana feminists
organized against "sterilization abuse"—a term coined by women of color
fighting lax sterilization regulations—won policy changes at both the
federal and state levels through both litigation and lobbying efforts.[66]
Ultimately, the *Madrigal* trial judge, U.S. District Judge E. Avery Crary,
granted a preliminary injunction against the California Department of
Health. He ordered state health officials to rewrite Spanish language
sterilization consent forms to a sixth grade educational level.[67] The
Medical Center's own hospital study found that 45% of its Mexican-
American patients read at a sixth-grade level, yet the sterilization
consent forms at the time were written at a twelfth-grade reading level.[68]
Later, state regulations were amended to add a seventy-two hour waiting
period prior to sterilization procedures, in large part based on input from
Chicana feminist groups working on the *Madrigal* case.[69]

In the midst of the *Madrigal* litigation, the U.S. Department of
Health, Education and Welfare (HEW) issued new guidelines requiring
hospitals receiving federal funds to have bilingual consent forms and a
monitoring program to ensure compliance with the new regulations.[70] At
the time, HEW paid for approximately 100,000 to 150,000 sterilizations
of low income women each year. Another infamous 1970s sterilization
abuse case—*Relf v. Weinberger*—prompted changes in the HEW
sterilization regulations.[71] *Relf* involved the forced sterilization of two
African-American sisters, only twelve and fourteen years old, who were
sterilized by a federally-funded family planning clinic in Alabama. Mrs.
Relf signed an "X" on a consent form she could not read, discovering too

---

[65]   *Id.* at 104–05.

[66]   *Id.* at 94–108.

[67]   *See* Robert Rawitch, *State Enjoined in Sterilization Suit Filed by Women*, L.A.
TIMES, Oct. 7, 1975, at B1.

[68]   *See id.*

[69]   *See* GUTIERREZ, *supra* note 21, at 106–08 (describing how the lobbying and public
education efforts of the Chicana feminist activists helped shape the new sterilization
regulations).

[70]   *See* Rawitch, *supra* note 67.

[71]   Relf v. Weinberger, 372 F. Supp. 1196 (D.D.C. 1974).

late that she had inadvertently "consented" to the permanent sterilization of her daughters Mary Alice and Minnie Relf.[72] According to the Southern Poverty Law Center, which filed the *Relf* lawsuit, poor women "were forced to agree to be sterilized when doctors threatened to terminate their welfare benefits unless they consented to the procedures."[73] The *Relf* plaintiffs asserted that by funding sterilization without sufficient regulations to protect patient autonomy, the federal government had effectively authorized coerced sterilization. The trial judge in *Relf*, Judge Gerhard Gesell, concluded that "an indefinite number of poor people have been improperly coerced into accepting a sterilization operation."[74] As in *Madrigal*, Judge Gesell found that patients seeking medical care for childbirth were frequently targets for coerced sterilization. For example, he noted in the opinion that one woman "was actually refused medical assistance by her attending physician unless she submitted to a tubal ligation after the birth."[75] In 1978, HEW promulgated even more stringent regulations that finally resolved the *Relf* litigation.[76]

In October 1976, Judge Crary signed off on a settlement agreement between the *Madrigal* plaintiffs and the California Department of Health, approving California's enhanced sterilization consent requirements.[77] After winning the preliminary injunction against California, Nabarrete declared that except for the question of financial damages, "we've won everything we asked for."[78] Ultimately, the litigation pursued by the Madrigal Ten and the Relf sisters helped to spur more demanding procedures for consent to sterilization at the federal and state levels.[79]

The Second Phase—Compensation for the Madrigal Ten

Judge Crary's rulings granting the women's claims for injunctive relief ultimately resolved all of the legal issues except for the question of financial compensation for the ten named plaintiffs. When Judge Crary died in April 1978, the damages phase of the *Madrigal* case was transferred to U.S. District Court Judge Jesse W. Curtis, who scheduled

---

[72] *See* Ikemoto, *supra* note 12, at 179–206.

[73] Valdes, *supra* note 24.

[74] *Relf*, 372 F. Supp. at 1199.

[75] *Id.*

[76] Ikemoto, *supra* note 12, at 201.

[77] Stipulation for Judgment Between Plaintiffs and Defendants Obledo and Lackner, No. CV 75-2057 (C.D. Cal. June 30, 1978) (on file with the Stanford University Libraries Department of Special Collections, M0673, Mexican American Legal Defense and Educational Fund Records, RG#5, Series 2: Litigation Files, 1968–1982, Box 944, Folder 8).

[78] Rawitch, *supra* note 67.

[79] *See Hospitals Challenge Sterilization Rules*, L.A. TIMES, Feb. 9, 1977, at E20A (noting that the *Madrigal* and *Relf* cases prompted California to enact legislation requiring a fourteen-day waiting period before sterilization on patients paying with private insurance as well as with Medicaid).

testimony on the damages trial to begin May 30, 1978.[80] Judge Curtis, a seventy-year-old Nixon appointee, lived aboard his yacht in the upscale Newport Beach area.[81] The judge and the defendants' lawyers, who hailed from a prestigious Beverly Hills law firm and were "the best that money could buy," presented a stark cultural contrast to the Mexican-American lawyers and their clients.[82]

At the trial, each woman testified in Spanish about the circumstances surrounding her sterilization. In presenting their testimony to the court, Hernández and Nabarrete argued that together, the women's stories demonstrated a systemic practice of doctors coercing sterilization of Mexican-American women for "social reasons."[83] Hernández asserted that the doctors forced laboring Mexican-American women to have tubal ligations, based on the doctors' beliefs that sterilization would remedy overpopulation of racial groups who "tended toward having large families."[84]

Karen Benker's testimony was critical to Hernández' claim that racial discrimination motivated coercive practices at the Medical Center. At the time, Benker was a medical student and a firsthand witness to what was happening on the maternity ward. She testified about what she viewed as the Medical Center's concerted effort to reduce the birth rate of racial minorities. In her testimony, she recounted her first day of orientation on the obstetrics ward, when she met Dr. Quilligan in the hallway. She recalled Dr. Quilligan explaining that the department had recently received a federal grant "to show how low we can cut the birth rate of the Negro and Mexican populations in Los Angeles County."[85] She described an entrenched system of abusive practices animated by the stereotype of Mexican-American women as hyper-fertile. On the stand, Benker detailed the coercive practices she witnessed at the Medical Center almost daily:

> The doctor would hold a syringe in front of the mother who was in labor pain and ask her if she wanted a pain killer; while the woman was in the throes of a contraction the doctor would say, 'Do you want the pain killer? Then sign the papers. Do you want

---

[80]   *See* Narda Zacchino, *Trial Hears Handwriting Expert: Sterilized Women Were 'Troubled,' Court Told*, L.A. TIMES, June 15, 1978, at B30. The plaintiffs were denied their request for a jury trial for technical reasons; thus the case proceeded as a bench trial. *See* Brief Amici Curiae of the Reproductive Freedom Project of the ACLU Foundation and the ACLU Foundation of Southern California at 21–24 (on file with the Stanford University Libraries Department of Special Collections, M0673, Mexican American Legal Defense and Educational Fund Records, RG#5, Series 2: Litigation Files, 1968–1982, Box 946, Folder 11).

[81]   *See* Velez-Ibanez, *supra* note 25, at 244.

[82]   *See id.* at 242–44.

[83]   GUTIERREZ, *supra* note 21, at 1.

[84]   *See id.* at 45.

[85]   *Id.* at 45.

the pain to stop? Do you want to have to go through this again? Sign the papers.'[86]

Reacting to Benker's testimony, Judge Curtis dismissed as irrelevant the doctors' social motivations for pressuring racial minority women to undergo sterilization:

> I do not think it is surprising that you might find a doctor who believes that people who are inclined to have big families shouldn't, and particularly for good medical reasons, undertakes to persuade a person not to have a large family. And if that person agrees and is willing to be sterilized, then I cannot see anything wrong with the doctor having suggested it or having convinced the patient . . . . What I want to know here is: To what extent the doctors had overridden the wishes of the patients, if they had. And if they have in some instances, what is their medical justification for doing it?[87]

In addition to Benker, Hernández and Nabarrete called a number of expert witnesses on behalf of the Madrigal Ten. Dr. Don Sloan, a New York gynecologist-obstetrician, testified that a woman in advanced labor could not give informed consent for a sterilization operation under those stressful circumstances.[88] In contrast to what Judge Curtis later claimed in his opinion, the lawyers were not arguing that a laboring woman could *never* consent to surgery. Rather, they emphasized that given the overall context—including the stress of active labor, language barriers, and lack of prior information about the procedure—the physicians in *Madrigal* failed to take adequate care to ensure their patients had actually consented.[89] A handwriting expert also testified about his comparison of the women's signatures on forms signed shortly after they were admitted with signatures on their sterilization consent forms signed later. He found a dramatic change in the handwriting, indicating that the women were troubled or in pain when they signed the consent to sterilization.[90]

The most controversial expert testimony came from Carlos Velez-Ibanez, a cultural anthropologist hired as a consultant to the trial team. Velez-Ibanez testified as to the harms caused by the coerced sterilizations—and particularly, the emotional strain that sterilization had wrought in the lives of the Madrigal Ten.[91] After conducting a field study with the women, Velez-Ibanez found deteriorated relationships

---

[86]   *Id.* at 41.

[87]   *Id.* at 46–47.

[88]   *See* Narda Zacchino, *10 Women Will Appeal Ruling on Sterilization*, L.A. TIMES, July 8, 1978, at A26.

[89]   *See* Reply-Brief of Plaintiffs-Appellants at 7–8, Madrigal v. Quilligan, 639 F.2d 789 (9th Cir. 1981) (No. 78-3187) (unpublished table opinion) (on file with the Stanford University Libraries Department of Special Collections, M0673, Mexican American Legal Defense and Educational Fund Records, RG#5, Series 2: Litigation Files, 1968–1982, Box 945, Folder 4).

[90]   *See* Zacchino, *supra* note 80.

[91]   *See* Velez-Ibanez, *supra* note 25, at 244–45 (describing the trial proceedings).

between the women and their husbands in most of the cases, as well as increased aggression and dysfunction between the women and their children. Most of the women did not share the fact of their coerced sterilization with family or friends and often withdrew from important social relations because of shame over their lack of fertility.[92] Velez-Ibanez presented his findings to the court, describing the pain endured by the women: "For each woman her sense of continuity with the past had been fractured, her sense of self-worth had been shattered, self-blame had been internalized, and a new social identity of impotence had been generated. . . . The final effect was acute depression."[93] As a cultural anthropologist, Velez-Ibanez aimed to explain the significance of fertility in the plaintiffs' culture, and to show that the Madrigal Ten's coerced sterilization caused "severe psychocultural and social results even beyond those expected of other women in the United States."[94] Judge Curtis initially considered excluding Velez-Ibanez' testimony. According to Velez-Ibanez, Curtis remarked from the bench that he did not see how an anthropologist's testimony would bear on damages because, "We all know that Mexicans love their families."[95]

In an unpublished opinion, Curtis ruled against the Madrigal Ten. Curtis failed to see how the case as a whole exposed a broader pattern of abuse at the Medical Center based on gender, race, and class. Instead, Curtis viewed the case as ten distinct random occurrences. The opinion recited each woman's story *seriatim*, concluding in each case that the attending physician had a "bona fide" or "good faith" belief that the patient consented based simply on a signed consent form or other medical documentation.[96] Curtis disregarded the high-pressure circumstances under which each woman's consent was obtained. In the opinion, Curtis also adopted a disdainful tone towards Hernández and Nabarrete's primary legal argument that the hospital had specifically targeted Mexican-American women's reproduction, rejecting outright the idea of a "concerted plan by hospital attendants and doctors to push them, as members of a low socio-economic group . . . to consent to sterilization in order to accomplish some sinister, invidious, social purpose."[97]

Strikingly, Curtis' opinion did not dispute much of the extensive evidence of abuse presented by Hernández and Nabarrete at trial. Nevertheless, Curtis concluded that the women's fundamental rights to procreate were not violated. Curtis credited the physicians' testimony that, generally speaking, they would not perform a sterilization procedure on a patient without her consent. Instead of questioning whether the coercive circumstances by which consent was obtained

---

[92] *See id.* at 241–42.

[93] *Id.* at 242.

[94] *Id.* at 235.

[95] *Id.* at 244.

[96] Opinion, *supra* note 40, at 9–18.

[97] *Id.* at 3.

undermined the validity of the consent forms, Curtis found satisfactory the physicians' testimony that it was their "custom and practice" to only perform sterilization procedures when "certain in their own mind that the patient understood the nature of the operation and was requesting the procedure."[98]

For example, in discussing Dolores Madrigal's sterilization, Curtis acknowledged that Madrigal refused the staff's urging to submit to sterilization several times prior to the operation.[99] Curtis credited Madrigal's account that, while she was in the midst of labor pains and after she had already indicated that she did not want a tubal ligation, the Medical Center staff called in her husband to consent to her sterilization. The opinion also affirmed that Madrigal overheard an interpreter telling her husband that she might die in the event of a future pregnancy. Finally, Curtis noted that hospital staff then told Madrigal that her husband had agreed to the operation and again insisted that she sign the consent form.[100] Despite these coercive conditions, Curtis concluded that the physician who performed the surgery properly relied on the signed form to support his "bona fide belief that Mrs. Madrigal had given her informed and voluntary consent, and that his belief was reasonable."[101] Curtis' analysis of each woman's story follows this same line of reasoning, accepting each physician's claim of a "custom and practice" of relying on documentation for consent.[102]

Curtis summarized the case as "essentially the result of a breakdown in communications between the patients and the doctors."[103] He recognized that the women's ability to understand and speak English was "limited," but nevertheless found it sufficient that the physicians had acquired enough familiarity with Spanish "to get by."[104] The opinion stressed that even with the availability of interpreters, "misunderstandings are bound to occur."[105] Yet Curtis never recognized that, given the great likelihood of misinformation in these circumstances, clinicians should bear the burden of ensuring effective informed consent, especially with the fundamental right to procreate at stake. Instead, Curtis placed the burden of communicating consent on the patients, rather than on the physicians performing the sterilization:

> There is no doubt that these women have suffered severe emotional and physical stress because of these operations. One can sympathize with them for their inability to communicate clearly, but one can hardly blame the doctors for relying on

---

[98]   *Id.* at 8.

[99]   *Id.* at 9.

[100] *See id.*

[101] *Id.* at 10.

[102] *Id.* at 9–18.

[103] *Id.* at 6.

[104] *Id.*

[105] *Id.*

these indicia of consent which appeared to be unequivocal on their face and which are in constant use in the Medical Center.[106]

In an inversion of its intended purpose, Curtis treated the sterilization consent form as a shield against physician liability rather than as a means to protect patient autonomy.[107]

Finally, Curtis dismissed the testimony of Carlos Velez-Ibanez regarding the harmful impact of coerced sterilization on the women, and, in fact, used that testimony to undermine the women's claims. Curtis noted that Velez-Ibanez needed a significant amount of time to conduct his study, which found that reproductive capacity was particularly important to women from small rural communities in Mexico. Curtis then asserted that "the staff of a busy metropolitan hospital which has neither the time nor the staff to make such esoteric studies would be unaware of these atypical cultural traits."[108] As Velez-Ibanez later commented, "it is ironic that the very evidence used to illustrate the damages done to the social and cultural systems of these women was, in fact, partially used by the court to rationalize a decision against them."[109]

Judge Curtis' analysis in *Madrigal* contrasts sharply with Judge Gesell's decision in the *Relf* case. Curtis' crabbed conception of consent defined voluntary consent to sterilization as a mere formality—as long as *some* indicia of consent was documented, clinicians need not ensure that voluntary consent actually existed in substance. In comparison, Judge Gesell emphasized that true consent must be "voluntary in the full sense of that term."[110] Noting that "[e]ven its dictionary definition assumes an exercise of free will and clearly precludes the existence of coercion," Gesell emphasized that "when important human rights are at stake, [voluntary consent] entails a requirement that the individual have at his disposal the information necessary to make his decision and the mental competence to appreciate the significance of that information."[111] Stressing that "[t]he dividing line between family planning and eugenics is murky," Gesell demanded more stringent sterilization consent procedures precisely to prevent express or implied threats by doctors and other family planning staff.[112] Curtis imposed no such legal requirements on the Medical Center physicians, relieving them of any obligation to refrain from relying upon sterilization consent forms obtained through coercive practices. Further, Curtis' decision in *Madrigal* was unpublished. Importantly, unpublished opinions cannot be cited—indeed,

---

[106] *Id.* at 19.

[107] *See* REBECCA KLUCHIN, FIT TO BE TIED: STERILIZATION AND REPRODUCTIVE RIGHTS IN AMERICA, 1950–1980 160–161, 171–72 (2009) (noting that Curtis' opinion failed to grapple with modern standards of informed consent in medical practice).

[108] Opinion, *supra* note 40, at 7.

[109] Velez-Ibanez, *supra* note 25, at 242.

[110] *Relf,* 372 F. Supp. at 1201.

[111] *Id.* at 1202 (citations omitted).

[112] *See id.* at 1204.

they may not even be broadly accessible.[113] On this account, by denying the women any relief in an unpublished opinion, Curtis also silenced the Madrigal Ten's stories, suppressing any legal recognition of the harms that the women endured.[114]

STERILIZATION ABUSE REDUX

Despite their loss in the damages phase of the litigation, the Madrigal Ten were instrumental in achieving significant law reform. In addition to serving as the catalyst for California's strengthened regulations for ensuring voluntary consent to sterilization, the *Madrigal* litigation also inspired the anti-sterilization abuse movement in California and helped to shape Chicana feminism in the 1970s. In 2003, California finally apologized for its history of coercive sterilization, although it did not award victims any reparations.[115]

The story of the Madrigal Ten still resonates today. The threat of sterilization abuse continues to loom for vulnerable populations, particularly poor women and women of color. Only ten years after California's official apology for abusive sterilization practices, an independent investigation found that the state's prison system had sterilized almost one hundred and fifty female inmates—most of whom were low-income women and women of color—without proper approval.[116] Echoing the plaintiffs in *Madrigal*, a number of the women prisoners stated that, although they had signed consent forms, they had done so under extreme pressure and without full information about the procedure and its ramifications.[117] Clinician attitudes towards coercive sterilization also appears to have changed little in this context. The California prison physician defending the prisoner sterilizations used poverty as a justification for the unlawful procedures: "Over a 10-year period, [the cost of sterilizing the prisoners] isn't a huge amount of money . . . compared to what you save in welfare paying for these unwanted children—as they procreated more."[118]

---

[113] Indeed, outside of archival records, only an excerpt of Curtis' opinion in *Madrigal* is publicly available.

[114] *See* Melissa Murray & Kristin Luker, CASES ON REPRODUCTIVE RIGHTS AND JUSTICE 882–889 (2015). The Ninth Circuit Court of Appeal also denied the women's request for redress in an unpublished table opinion. Madrigal v. Quilligan, 639 F.2d 789 (9th Cir. 1981) (No. 78-3187) (unpublished table opinion) (on file with the Stanford University Libraries Department of Special Collections, M0673, Mexican American Legal Defense and Educational Fund Records, RG#5, Series 2: Litigation Files, 1968–1982, Box 945, Folder 4).

[115] *See* Carl Ingram, *State Issues Apology for Policy Sterilization*, L.A. TIMES, March 12, 2003 at B1; Alexandra Minna Stern et al., *California's Sterilization Survivors: An Estimate and Call for Redress*, 107 AMER. J. PUB. HEALTH 50, 53 (2017) (noting that North Carolina and Virginia provided redress to compulsory sterilization survivors and urging California to follow suit).

[116] *See* Corey G. Johnson, *Female Inmates Sterilized in California Prisons Without Approval*, THE CTR. FOR INVESTIGATIVE REPORTING (July 7, 2013), https://www.revealnews.org/article-legacy/female-inmates-sterilized-in-california-prisons-without-approval/.

[117] *See* Patrick McGreevy & Phil Willon, *Female Inmate Surgery Broke Law*, L.A. TIMES, July 14, 2013, at A4.

[118] Johnson, *supra* note 116.

As new reproductive technologies advance, the tension between access and abuse that *Madrigal* highlights continues to resurface. For example, in recent years medical and family planning professionals have been enthusiastically promoting long-acting reversible contraception ("LARC").[119] LARCs, such as intrauterine devices, generally require a medical provider for both insertion and removal. As Dorothy Roberts has noted, [major media and scientific publications have published articles "recommending increased use of provider-controlled long-acting contraceptives among low-income populations in order to reduce poverty, high school drop-out rates, and Medicaid costs."[120] Reproductive justice advocates fear that unchecked enthusiasm for LARCs might lead once again to coercive reproductive control over vulnerable women.[121] Of course, because LARCs and sterilization offer effective fertility control, many women would also benefit from greater access to these technologies.[122] Yet reproductive technologies continue to present both promise and peril. Since ideology often drives the use of these technologies, the risk remains that efforts to increase access will also increase abuse, particularly on marginalized populations.[123]

THE MADRIGAL TEN REVISITED

Almost forty years after *Madrigal v. Quilligan*, historian Virginia Espino found the surviving plaintiffs and convinced them to tell their story to the documentary filmmaker Renee Tajima-Peña.[124] The defendant doctors, some of whom give their side of the story in the

---

[119] The American College of Obstetricians and Gynecologists (ACOG) recommends that physicians "incorporate immediate postpartum LARC into their practices." *See* AM. COLL. OF OBSTETRICIANS AND GYNECOLOGISTS, COMMITTEE OPINION NO. 670: IMMEDIATE POSTPARTUM LONG-ACTING REVERSIBLE CONTRACEPTION (Aug. 2016), available at https://www.acog.org/clinical-guidance-and-publications/committee-opinions/committee-on-obstetric-practice/immediate-postpartum-long-acting-reversible-contraception.

[120] Roberts, *supra* note 58. Others have noted that some programs offer free LARC insertion, but provide no coverage for the cost of removal. *See* Michelle H. Moniz, Kayte Spector-Bagdady, Michele Heisler, & Lisa Hope Harris, *Inpatient Postpartum Long-Acting Reversible Contraception: Care That Promotes Reproductive Justice*, 130 OBSTETRICS & GYNECOLOGY 783 (2017).

[121] *See, e.g.*, Jenny A. Higgins, *Celebration Meets Caution: Long Acting Reversible Contraception (LARC)'s Boons, Potential Busts, and the Benefits of a Reproductive Justice Approach*, 89 CONTRACEPTION 237, 239 (2014); Anu Manchikanti Gomez, Liza Fuentes & Amy Allina, *Women or LARC First? Reproductive Autonomy and the Promotion of Long-Acting Reversible Contraceptive Methods*, 46 PERSPECTIVES ON SEXUAL & REPRODUCTIVE HEALTH 171, 171, 173 (2014).

[122] *See* Sonya Borrero, Nikki Zite, Joseph E. Potter & James Trussell, *Medicaid Policy on Sterilization—Anachronistic or Still Relevant?*, 370 NEW ENG. J. MED. 102, 102 (2014); *see also* Lisa H. Harris & Taida Wolfe, *Stratified Reproduction, Family Planning Care and The Double Edge of History*, 26 CURRENT OPINION IN OBSTETRICS & GYNECOLOGY 539, 539–40 (2014) (noting a growing consensus that sterilization consent regulations should be revisited to allow for easier access but cautioning that the history of coerced sterilization must be taken into account).

[123] Ikemoto, *supra* note 12, at 204 (noting that the *Relf* case also involved the coercive imposition of Depo Provera shots and intrauterine devices on poor patients and that "surgical sterilization is not unique in its potential for use as a social control.").

[124] *See* NO MÁS BEBÉS (NO MORE BABIES) (Moon Canyon Films 2015), *available at* http://www.pbs.org/independentlens/films/no-mas-bebes/.

documentary film *No Más Bebés*, continue to maintain their innocence. The women maintain that they never consented to irreversible sterilization.

Espino and Tajima-Peña found, unsurprisingly, that the involuntary sterilizations were devastating for many of the women. Maria Figueroa's marriage deteriorated after she was sterilized; she later attempted suicide.[125] Guadalupe Acosta died in 2003 following a series of tragic events. Acosta's first child had been taken away from her and the baby delivered at the Medical Center died at birth. After her partner learned of her sterilization, he abandoned Acosta and their two surviving children.[126] Helena Orozco's son Joseph blames his mother's coerced sterilization for a "downhill slope" in his family's life: "First they sterilized her under duress, trying to lie, and then they go to court with many of them thinking they might make this right, and then all of a sudden the doctors get away with what they did . . . . Her life turned for the worse."[127]

The lawyers and physicians who advocated for the Madrigal Ten went on to prominence in their continued fight for civil rights. Antonia Hernández became the president of the Mexican American Legal Defense and Educational Fund and later the CEO of the California Community Foundation. Gloria Molina became the first Chicana elected to the Los Angeles City Council.[128] Buddy Rosenfeld, whose risky detective work as a young resident brought these sterilization abuses to light, practices as a gynecologist in Texas. His specialty is reversing tubal ligations. Rosenfeld and his wife also run an abortion clinic in Houston. As he explained to a journalist: "I'm still involved in reproductive rights. It's the same thing."[129]

Despite the trauma of the coerced sterilizations, some of the women also managed to rebuild their lives. Consuelo Hermosillo, who was only twenty-three years old when she was sterilized, became a successful chef. Her son, who owns multiple restaurants in the Los Angeles area, discovered what happened to his mother only after reading about the case in a college Chicano studies class.[130] In the documentary film about the case, Hermosillo listens to an old recording made by the trial team. In the recording, she describes a recurring dream of bringing a newborn baby boy to Mexico, but she will not show her miracle baby to any of the friends

---

[125] *See* Diana Gonzalez, *Forced Sterilizations: A Long and Sordid History*, ACLU OF S. CAL. (May 18, 2016), https://www.aclusocal.org/en/news/forced-sterilizations-long-and-sordid-history.

[126] *See* Claudia Dreifus, *A Group of Mexican Immigrant Women Were Sterilized Without Their Consent. Can A New Film Bring Justice Where the Courts Failed?*, THE NATION (Jan. 27, 2016), http://www.thenation.com/article/a-group-of-mexican-immigrant-women-were-sterilized-without-their-consent-can-a-new-film-bring-justice-where-the-courts-failed/.

[127] GUTIERREZ, *supra* note 21, at 124.

[128] *See* Valdes, *supra* note 24.

[129] *See* Dreifus, *supra* note 126.

[130] *See id.*

and family who want to see him. Looking back forty years later, Hermosillo's feelings of loss still remain: "It's like when you bury somebody . . . . You're always going to carry it in your head."[131]

---

[131] David Montgomery, *Sterilized Against Their Will in a Los Angeles Hospital: Latinas Tell the Story in a New Film*, WASH. POST (Jan. 10, 2016), https://www.washington post.com/news/arts-and-entertainment/wp/2016/01/10/sterilized-against-their-will-in-a-los-angeles-hospital-latinas-tell-the-story-in-a-new-film/?utm_term=.8a549bc46396.

6

Khiara M. Bridges*

Elision and Erasure: Race, Class, and Gender in *Harris v. McRae*

On June 30, 1980, the Supreme Court decided *Harris v. McRae*,[1] rejecting First and Fifth Amendment challenges to the Hyde Amendment. The Court held that the Hyde Amendment—a funding restriction which, in the version that was challenged in the case, prohibited the use of federal Medicaid funds for abortions except where the pregnancy is a product of rape or incest or "where the life of the mother would be endangered if the fetus were carried to term . . ."[2]—does not violate the rights of the indigent women who rely upon Medicaid, the federally-funded health coverage program, for their basic healthcare. Accordingly, if a poor woman's pregnancy will not kill her, but will "only" cause severe physical or psychological harm, the Hyde Amendment mandates that federal funding for an abortion must be denied. This is true even though the government continues to pay the medical costs associated with carrying the pregnancy to term.[3]

In upholding the Hyde Amendment, the Court reasoned that while its decision in *Roe v. Wade*[4] held that the government may not place obstacles in front of an individual seeking to terminate a pregnancy before fetal viability, the withdrawal of federal funding for abortions did

---

* Professor of Law and Professor of Anthropology, Boston University. Thanks to Chelsea Tejada and Kristina Fried for amazing research assistance. Thanks as well to Brian Flaherty in the BU Law Library for fantastic research support.

1 Harris v. McRae, 448 U.S. 297 (1980).

2 *Id.* at 302 (quoting the Hyde Amendment, H.R.J. Res. 440, 96th Cong., 93 Stat. 923 § 109 (1979)). The breadth of the Hyde Amendment has changed over the years. While the current version contains a rape and incest exception, other versions have not made such allowances. *See Harris*, 448 U.S. at 302–03 (noting that the Hyde Amendment that was in effect for the fiscal year 1977 did not make an exception for rape or incest). Further, while the current version allows Medicaid funding for the termination of a pregnancy that endangers a woman's life, other versions were broader. *See id.* at 303 (noting that the Hyde Amendment that was "applicable for most of fiscal year 1978, and all of fiscal year 1979 . . . had an additional exception for 'instances where severe and long-lasting physical health damage to the mother would result if the pregnancy were carried to term when so determined by two physicians' ").

3 *Id.* at 303.

4 Roe v. Wade, 410 U.S. 113 (1973).

not represent such an obstacle. Rather, the Court asserted, it was indigence that impeded the poor woman's ability to terminate a pregnancy. On this account, the Hyde Amendment was merely a refusal to remove an impediment that the state did not create, and thus represented no infringement on the abortion right.

The Hyde Amendment and its legitimation in *McRae* had the effect of eliminating the availability of federal funds to an estimated 250,000 to 300,000 Medicaid-reliant women seeking abortions; only 2,000 women were expected to continue to qualify for federal Medicaid funding in Hyde's wake.[5]

Today, many understand that because people of color disproportionately bear the burden of poverty in this country, restrictions on Medicaid funds for abortion services disproportionately impact women of color. They comprehend that the Hyde Amendment coerces large numbers of women of color into motherhood, and that at the same time, it compels large numbers of women of color to resort to desperate measures to terminate unwanted pregnancies. Thus, many appreciate that the question of Medicaid funding for abortions—like the question of public benefits more generally—is a racially salient one. Consequently, many might be surprised to find that the majority opinion in *Harris v. McRae* makes absolutely no mention of race. Indeed, it makes no mention of gender, and it makes little mention of class—wholly effacing the fact that *poor women* of *color* bear the brunt of the Hyde Amendment. With these omissions in mind, this essay re-centers issues of race, class, and gender in the story of *Harris v. McRae* while also explaining why these elements were absent from the Court's opinion. By excavating these critical elements, the essay provides a more complete understanding of the case and its place in the broader debate over abortion access and reproductive rights and justice.

RESPONDING TO *ROE*

McRae's story begins with *Roe v. Wade*. Immediately after the Court handed down *Roe*, abortion opponents sprang into action, determined to overturn the decision or, in the alternative, dramatically limit its impact.[6] To this end, in April 1976, Senator Jesse Helms of North Carolina made a motion for the full Senate to consider a constitutional amendment providing that "[w]ith respect to the right of life guaranteed in this Constitution, every human being, subject to the jurisdiction of the United States, or of any State, shall be deemed, from the moment of fertilization, to be a person and entitled to the right of life."[7] This constitutional

---

[5]   Linda Greenhouse, *Limit on Abortions Paid with Medicaid Upheld by Justices*, N.Y. TIMES, July 1, 1980, at A1.

[6]   MARY ZIEGLER, AFTER *ROE*: THE LOST HISTORY OF THE ABORTION DEBATE 38 (2015) (noting that the decision "help[ed] pro-lifers clarify their legal priorities" and spurred them to "mobiliz[e] to amend the Constitution and ban all abortions").

[7]   *Human Life Amendment Highlights: United States Congress (1973–2003)*, *Human Life Amendment*, HUMAN LIFE ACTION (Feb. 6, 2004), https://www.humanlifeaction.org/sites/default/files/HLAhghlts.pdf.

amendment, alongside similar amendments that were proposed in subsequent years, were clearly intended to overturn *Roe*. They were all defeated, however.[8] These losses prompted abortion opponents, whose commitment to *Roe*'s demise was unwavering, to try another approach.[9]

In September 1976, Representative Henry John Hyde of Illinois introduced the amendment that would come to bear his name as part of an annual appropriations bill. He made clear that his proposal to eliminate federal funding for abortions under the Medicaid program was a stopgap measure, intended to prevent abortions in the absence of a constitutional amendment that would prohibit them entirely. When introducing the language to the House, Hyde explained:

> Yesterday, remarks were made that it is unfortunate to burden an appropriations bill with complex issues, such as busing, abortion, and the like. I certainly agree that it is very unfortunate. The problem is that there is no other vehicle that reaches this floor in which these complex issues can be involved. Constitutional amendments which prohibit abortions stay languishing in subcommittee, much less committee, and so the only vehicle where the Members may work their will, unfortunately, is an appropriation bill. I regret that. I certainly would like to prevent, if I could legally, anybody having an abortion, a rich woman, a middle-class woman, or a poor woman. Unfortunately, the only vehicle available is the HEW Medicaid bill.[10]

While Hyde expressed regret to his House colleagues about introducing such a contentious issue into an appropriations bill, he later spoke about his efforts in self-congratulatory terms. As he explained to a Maryland audience, "[Representative] Bauman got me aside one day and said this bill was coming up that appropriated all sorts of money for abortions and wouldn't it be a nice idea if we could just sneak an amendment in there that would halt this nefarious practice.... I might add that [Representative Bauman] drafted the amendment and we waited and handed it up and the next thing I knew I was in the well addressing my colleagues on behalf of the right to life."[11]

THE HYDE AMENDMENT'S VICTIMS

It was clear to many that the burdens of the Hyde Amendment would disproportionately fall upon women of color, who are overrepresented

---

[8]   *Id.*

[9]   In addition to the Hyde Amendment, other efforts to limit *Roe* included measures that would "prohibit the use of foreign assistance funds to finance abortions; . . . limit participation of legal-service attorneys in abortion litigation; . . . prohibit Federal financing for Peace Corps volunteers seeking abortions; . . . [and] prevent the United States Civil Rights Commission from studying the issue." Helen Epstein, *Abortion: An Issue That Won't Go Away*, N.Y. TIMES, Mar. 30, 1980, at SM111.

[10]   123 CONG. REC. 19,700 (1977) (statement of Rep. Hyde).

[11]   McRae v. Califano, 491 F. Supp. 630, 644 (E.D.N.Y. 1980).

among the nation's indigent. (Indeed, the named plaintiff in *McRae*, Cora McRae, was a black woman who filed a lawsuit after she was informed that Medicaid would not pay for her medically necessary abortion.[12]) Because of the Hyde Amendment's racial impact, many opponents of the funding restriction articulated their disapproval of the measure in the language of race. One important activist group that challenged the restriction in racial terms was the Committee for Abortion Rights and Against Sterilization Abuse ("CARASA"). Most CARASA members were socialist feminists whose activism focused on issues of reproductive justice because they understood the relationship between economic oppression, reproductive control, and women's subordination.[13] Although class was the lens through which CARASA tended to view women's disadvantage, its members had no trouble seeing the Hyde Amendment's racial implications. And what they saw was an antinatalist effort to force women of color to submit to sterilizations.

Since 1970, the federal government has covered the cost of sterilizations for poor women under Title X.[14] CARASA argued that if the Hyde Amendment rendered abortions unavailable to indigent women, while sterilizations remained accessible under Title X, desperate women would choose to be sterilized to avoid unwanted pregnancies. As CARASA explained:

> The abortion cutbacks will mean increased sterilization abuse because federally funded abortions are no longer an option for poor women. Since birth control is never 100% effective, sterilizations become the only funded alternative to bearing unwanted children. . . . Both the Hyde Amendment and forced sterilization are illegitimate interferences with a woman's right

---

[12]   Some news outlets reported that Cora McRae suffered from "varicose veins and blood clots," which made the abortion that she sought a medically indicated one. *See Chronology on Abortion Issue*, N.Y. TIMES, July 1, 1980, at B8. Interestingly, other news outlets did not mention her medical condition and suggested that she sought an abortion for nontherapeutic reasons. *See* John P. MacKenzie, *Ban on Federal Abortion Aid Rejected*, WASH. POST, Oct. 23, 1976, at A3 (stating that Cora McRae sought an abortion because "she was separated from her husband and could not work to support her 4-year-old daughter unless she could terminate the pregnancy"); *see* Janis Johnson, *Judges Block Ban on Abortion Funds: Judges Block New Ban on Medicaid Abortions*, WASH. POST, Oct. 2, 1976, at A1, A7 ("The woman, Cora McRae, said in an affidavit that she is separated from her husband, has a 4-year-old daughter, and could not work to support her unless she had an abortion."). While McRae's actual circumstances are unknown, it is notable that some mainstream news outlets suggested that she was not being completely truthful about the "real" reason she sought an abortion. We might wonder why these outlets felt comfortable implying that she—a poor, black woman—was being deceitful.

[13]   JENNIFER NELSON, WOMEN OF COLOR AND THE REPRODUCTIVE RIGHTS MOVEMENT 134 (2003).

[14]   In its original version, Title X did not enumerate which types of family planning services it would cover. Family Planning Services and Population Research Act of 1970, H.R. 19318, 91st Cong. (1970). Although not specifically mentioned, Title X funded sterilizations for poor women soon after its passage. *See* Sheila M. Rothman, *Funding Sterilization and Abortion for the Poor*, N.Y. TIMES, Feb. 22, 1975, at 27. In 1978, a regulation was enacted specifying that these sterilizations could only be done with the consent of a mentally competent individual who is at least 21 years old. 42 C.F.R. § 50.203 (1978).

to choose whether or not to bear children. To limit a woman's reproductive choices is sexist; to promote sterilizations in Black, Hispanic and Native American communities is racist.[15]

Faye Wattleton, the first black president of the Planned Parenthood Federation of America, also challenged the Hyde Amendment in racial terms. Wattleton, who had worked as a nurse during much of her early career, became active in the fight for abortion rights because she witnessed the brutality that the inability to access safe, legal abortion inflicted on communities of color. Wattleton recalled caring for a girl who died after she attempted to self-abort: "One of the cases I remember in Harlem was a really beautiful 17-year-old girl. She and her mother had decided to induce an abortion by inserting a Lysol douche into her uterus. It killed her."[16] It was Wattleton's experience working with poor people of color that prompted her vigorous objections to the Hyde Amendment. As she recalled, " 'The Hyde Amendment incensed me. . . . You see, my whole experience with abortion had been with women who were not affluent. The women who came to my hospitals under less than dignified circumstances were not affluent. That girl in Harlem Hospital who died was not affluent. So what I saw occurring seemed to me a throwback to the pre-1973 days.' "[17]

Judge John Francis Dooling of the Eastern District of New York, whose decision striking down the Hyde Amendment was appealed to the Supreme Court and ultimately culminated in the *McRae* decision, also recognized that the funding restriction would operate in racially unjust ways. He observed that, due to poverty, poor women suffered from more health problems than their wealthier counterparts, making the indigent more likely to require medically necessary abortions. He then acknowledged the racial geography of this increased need: "The markedly higher health risk of poor women is almost certainly indirectly reflected in the circumstance that maternal mortality per 100,000 live births, as reported in the Vital Statistics of the United States for 1968, 1971, 1973 and 1975, was three times as frequent among black women as among others; maternal deaths from toxemia were four times more frequent among black women than among others."[18]

Indeed, it was quite clear to Judge Dooling that the question of whether Medicaid funds would be available to the poor woman seeking an abortion, and the question of whether that woman would be able to

---

[15]   NELSON, *supra* note 13, at 155.

[16]   Epstein, *supra* note 9.

[17]   *Id.*

[18]   McRae v. Califano, 491 F. Supp. 630, 669 (E.D.N.Y. 1980). Interestingly, racial disparities in maternal mortality rates have remained the same in the three decades that have passed since Judge Dooling wrote his opinion. Black women are still three to four times more likely than white women to die from pregnancy-related causes. *See* Linda Villarosa, *Why America's Black Mothers and Babies Are in a Life-or-Death Crisis*, N.Y. TIMES (Apr. 11, 2018), https://www.nytimes.com/2018/04/11/magazine/black-mothers-babies-death-maternal-mortality.html.

terminate her pregnancy safely and legally, were questions of *racial justice*. He cited a CDC study showing that "minority group women accounted for a disproportionate number of the deaths following illegal abortions, which suggested a need to provide better and more widely available legal abortion services especially for those women who are at high risk of seeking illegal abortions. Any actions which impede their access to legal abortion may increase the risk of death."[19]

Representative Hyde himself seemed to recognize the racial implications of the funding restriction that he proposed. When he introduced the amendment on the House floor, he elaborated its pro-life ethos, asserting "[a] life is a life. The life of a ghetto kid is just as important as the life of a rich person."[20] Hyde's reference to the "ghetto kid" likely was as much a nod to the restriction's racial effects as it was a reference to its impact on the poor. Still, even if Hyde did not appreciate the amendment's likely impact on women of color, many of his House colleagues were quick to surface these concerns. In a statement on the House floor, Representative Yvonne Brathwaite Burke, the first member of Congress to give birth while in office and to be granted a maternity leave,[21] forcefully denounced the proposed amendment because of its impact on the black community:

> [T]his really should be called the forced childbearing amendment. And who is forced? I want to tell the Members why overwhelmingly large numbers of blacks are concerned. We are concerned because we do not believe that young girls should be forced to have children. . . . We also regret the fact that those children do not have a chance to get adopted, because there are no adoptive homes available for little black girls and boys who are born in poverty. They remain in foster homes if they are lucky.[22]

Representative Louis Stokes of Ohio also introduced into the record the black and brown women who would be forced into childbearing—or maimed in the attempt to avoid childbearing—by the Hyde Amendment. As he explained, "I have watched the poor in this society, the majority of whom are black and who need these services, be segregated out once again and segmented into a special class in America. . . . Today by adopting this Hyde amendment we will have once again made minorities and the poor separate and unequal."[23]

It was likely because a number of congresspersons denounced the proposed amendment in racial terms that Representative Robert Dornan,

---

[19]   *McRae*, 491 F. Supp. at 656–57.

[20]   123 CONG. REC. 19,700 (1977) (statement of Rep. Hyde).

[21]   *BURKE, Yvonne Brathwaite*, HISTORY, ART & ARCHIVES: U.S. HOUSE OF REPRESENTATIVES, https://history.house.gov/People/Detail?id=7693#biography (last visited Nov. 17, 2018).

[22]   123 CONG. REC. 19,709 (1977) (statement of Rep. Burke).

[23]   *Id.* at 19,712 (statement of Rep. Stokes).

a proponent of the amendment, felt compelled to *defend* it in racial terms on the House floor:

> I say to some of the black Members here, they are kidding themselves if they think this is not an issue that is fed by racism on the proabortion side. I have heard many rock-ribbed Republicans brag about how fiscally conservative they are and then tell me that I was an idiot on the abortion issue. When I asked why, they whisper, "Because we have to hold down them, we have to stop the population growth." To them, population growth means blacks, Puerto Ricans, or other Latins . . . .[24]

The congressional debates make clear that individuals on both sides of the issue understood that the Hyde Amendment profoundly implicated race. And yet, although the *McRae* litigation occurred at a time when white feminists and racial justice activists were joining forces to challenge laws and policies that, like the Hyde Amendment, harmed both white women and people of color,[25] the white feminist lawyers who challenged the Hyde Amendment did not marshal the restriction's racial impacts to challenge its constitutionality. Indeed, rooting their challenge to the Hyde Amendment's constitutionality in the First and Fourteenth Amendments, they failed to mention the racial implications of the law at all.[26]

To be sure, these omissions were not inadvertent. As the next section explains, jurisprudential shifts in equal protection law informed the lawyers' decision to minimize race, class, and gender in their arguments. Essentially, by 1980, the Court's equal protection jurisprudence made it extraordinarily difficult to prevail in claims sounding in race—as well as poverty and sex. This jurisprudence deprived the lawyers challenging the Hyde Amendment of the ability to use this language to describe the injury that the restriction imposed.

THE BURGER COURT AND THE EVOLVING LANDSCAPE OF EQUAL PROTECTION LAW

As *McRae* made its way through the courts, the litigators charged with challenging the Hyde Amendment faced formidable opposition.

---

[24]   *Id.* at 19,704 (statement of Rep. Dornan).

[25]   SERENA MAYERI, REASONING FROM RACE: FEMINISM, RACE, AND THE CIVIL RIGHTS REVOLUTION 188 (2014) ("[T]he struggles over abortion funding and affirmative action in employment aligned the interests of feminists with those of poor women and people of color in ways that previous Court cases had not. The result was an increasingly robust coalition that operated in spite of the separation of race and sex in legal doctrine.").

[26]   Specifically, they argued that the Hyde Amendment violated the free exercise clause, inasmuch as it prevented women who would be guided to abortion on religious grounds from practicing their religion; the establishment clause, inasmuch as the Catholic church was heavily involved in organizing and leading the effort to get the Hyde Amendment in its most restrictive form passed; the due process clause, inasmuch as the funding restriction infringed the abortion right found in *Roe*; and the equal protection clause, inasmuch as the law discriminated against the class of indigent women who required medically necessary abortions. *See* Brief of Appellees at 137–85, Harris v. McRae, 448 U.S. 297 (1980) (No. 79-1268), 1980 WL 339642, at *109–85.

Among those defending the Hyde Amendment in the Supreme Court was a new voice in the pro-life movement: Americans United for Life ("AUL").[27]

In addition to AUL, the lawyers challenging the Hyde Amendment faced an inhospitable doctrinal landscape. This doctrinal landscape largely explains why the *McRae* litigators—who included the Center for Constitutional Rights lawyers Rhonda Copelon and Nancy Stearns, ACLU Reproductive Freedom Project director Janet Benshoof, New York University Law School professor Sylvia Law, and several others—failed to challenge the Hyde Amendment as a racially discriminatory measure. These lawyers made no mention of race in their challenge to the Hyde Amendment because the Burger Court's precedents counseled strongly against it. Specifically, the Court's 1976 decision in *Washington v. Davis*[28] held that courts cannot use heightened scrutiny to review laws that have racially disparate effects absent a showing of discriminatory intent. While *Davis* left open the possibility that intent might be proved in a number of ways—including by looking at the foreseeable impact of a law—subsequent cases shut down these evidentiary pathways.[29] Namely, two years after *Davis*, in *Personnel Administrator v. Feeney*,[30] the Court defined discriminatory intent as taking a course of action " 'because of,' not merely 'in spite of' " its racial effects.[31] *Davis*, as narrowed by *Feeney*, made the Hyde Amendment's disparate impact on women of color virtually irrelevant, as the funding restriction was facially neutral and there was no evidence that it was intended to harm people of color. Recognizing that arguing that the Hyde Amendment ran afoul of the Constitution's prohibition against racial discrimination was unlikely to be successful, the lawyers avoided framing their arguments in racial terms.

The Court's precedents not only prompted the *McRae* litigators to minimize the Hyde Amendment's disproportionate impact on persons of color. Precedent also discouraged them from highlighting that the amendment's victims were *poor*. In a series of earlier cases, the Court effectively sidelined socioeconomic status as a trait that, like race or gender, would trigger heightened judicial scrutiny. In 1970, the Court decided *Dandridge v. Williams*, which upheld a Maryland law that limited the size of Aid to Families with Dependent Children grants such that families with seven or more persons would not receive grants that met their statutorily determined standard of need. The Court acknowledged that the funding scheme, which concerned "the most basic

---

[27]   Although AUL was in its infancy in 1980, it has since evolved into an influential pro-life organization. *Accomplishments: AUL's Proven Track Record of Success*, AMS. UNITED FOR LIFE, https://aul.org/what-we-do/achievements/ (last visited January 26, 2019).

[28]   Washington v. Davis, 426 U.S. 229 (1976).

[29]   Reva B. Siegel, *The Supreme Court 2012 Term—Foreword: Equality Divided*, 127 HARV. L. REV. 1, 16–9 (2013).

[30]   Pers. Adm'r of Mass. v. Feeney, 442 U.S. 256 (1979).

[31]   *Id.* at 279.

needs of impoverished human beings," undeniably harmed the poor.[32] Nevertheless, because the Court conceptualized the statute as one that fell in the "area of economics and social welfare,"[33] it held the funding scheme constitutional under deferential rational basis review. As a result of *Dandridge* and its progeny, the *McRae* litigators confronted a jurisprudential landscape that made the Hyde Amendment's " 'blatant[ ] discriminat[ion]' against the poor"[34] constitutionally insignificant. As such, Copelon and her team were well-advised to avoid arguing that the funding restriction violated the equal protection clause because it discriminated against the poor. Nor was it prudent to construct a claim around Faye Wattleton's view that "as long as abortion *is* legal in this country, poor people should have the same access as the rich."[35]

Similarly, the *McRae* litigators faced precedent that rendered the Hyde Amendment's impact on *women* equally insignificant. In 1974, the Court held in *Geduldig v. Aiello* that discrimination on the basis of pregnancy was not sex discrimination[36]—despite the Court having proceeded from the assumption that only women can get pregnant.[37] In order for Copelon and her team to argue that the Hyde Amendment discriminated on the basis of sex because it discriminated against women seeking abortions, they would have had to convince the Court that *Geduldig* had been incorrectly decided. Ultimately, they decided that the more prudent strategy was to avoid "arguing that the Supreme Court had been wrong in the pregnancy discrimination cases" and to show instead "how decided cases supported the[ir] claims."[38]

In many ways, the tragedy of *Harris v. McRae* was a tragedy of timing. A series of cases decided just ten years before *McRae* made it infinitely more difficult for the Court to hear—and for the Constitution to reflect—facts about race, class and gender. In a very short period of time, the constitutional landscape had been dramatically altered. Had *McRae* reached the Court just ten years earlier, the opinion likely would have read very differently—even if the Court had reached the same conclusion and upheld the Hyde Amendment. However, by the time the Court heard *McRae* in 1980, the Court's prior precedents had foreclosed avenues that

---

[32]   Dandridge v. Williams, 397 U.S. 471, 485 (1970).

[33]   *Id.*

[34]   Rhonda Copelon & Sylvia Law, *"Nearly Allied to Her Right to Be"—Medicaid Funding for Abortion: The Story of* Harris v. McRae, *in* WOMEN AND THE LAW STORIES 208, 218 (Elizabeth Schneider & Stephanie Wildman eds., 2010).

[35]   Epstein, *supra* note 9.

[36]   Geduldig v. Aiello, 417 U.S. 484 (1974).

[37]   It is unlikely that in 1974, the Court had been presented with arguments that people other than women—specifically transgender men or nonbinary people—are able to become pregnant. Thus, the Court that decided *Geduldig* conceptualized "women" as the only class of people who could become pregnant and "men" as the class of people who could not become pregnant. Despite this understanding, the Court nevertheless held that because some women do not become pregnant, discrimination against pregnant people is not sex-based discrimination. *Id.*

[38]   Copelon & Law, *supra* note 34, at 222.

would have made claims rooted in race, class, and gender more obviously cognizable.

The politics swirling around the Equal Rights Amendment ("ERA"), and the effort to ratify it, also dissuaded Copelon and her team from arguing that the Hyde Amendment was sex discrimination prohibited by the equal protection clause. Many proponents of the ERA were wary of arguing that restrictions on abortion and abortion funding amounted to sex discrimination because they worried that support for the ERA—and the votes to ratify it—would be undermined (especially among more moderate legislators) if there was any established link between abortion rights and equal protection.

This fear was certainly justified, as "more than half the public support for the ERA came from people who opposed abortion on demand."[39] If the equal protection clause was shown to ensure abortion access and abortion funding, then there would be little hope that the ERA—which many assumed would be a more powerful protector of women's rights than the equal protection clause—would gain the support of more moderate legislators and their constituents who, despite their interest in greater constitutional protections for women, did not support robust abortion rights. In the end, Eleanor Smeal, then-president of the National Organization for Women, which had spent much time and effort trying to get the ERA passed and ratified, convinced the *McRae* litigators not to argue the unconstitutionality of the Hyde Amendment on equal protection grounds.[40] As such, the politics of ERA ratification, together with the hostile precedent that the Court had established in earlier decisions, led the *McRae* litigators to downplay that the Medicaid funding restriction harmed *women*.

Although the legal landscape presented serious challenges that prompted the *McRae* litigators to avoid arguments sounding in race, class, and gender, other groups, in their amicus briefs, were less constrained. The Association of Legal Aid Attorneys of the City of New York (ALAA) submitted a brief, which several other organizations, including CARASA, signed, arguing that the Hyde Amendment amounted to "invidious discrimination" against poor and minority women. Focusing on the disjunction between the prohibition on federal funding for abortion and Title X's subsidization of sterilization, ALAA argued that such sterilizations were coercive, as they could not be voluntarily chosen in a milieu in which abortion was not federally subsidized. Inasmuch as the Hyde Amendment compelled this result, ALAA concluded that it "invidiously discriminates against poor and

---

[39]   JANE J. MANSBRIDGE, WHY WE LOST THE ERA 127 (Univ. Chi. Press 7th prtg. ed.1986).

[40]   *Id.* at 125 ("[I]n Washington, against some resistance, Eleanor Smeal persuaded the feminist lawyers in the federal abortion funding case not to make this [equal protection] argument. In this way Smeal hoped to keep the ERA and abortion funding separate.").

minority women and deprives them of their constitutional rights to privacy, liberty and equal protection."[41]

Thus, although concerns about race, class, and gender drove much of the debate about Medicaid funding for abortion, precedent (and politics) counseled those who challenged the Hyde Amendment to downplay or ignore these elements in their legal arguments. And in its opinion, the Court also elided these issues. But even as the majority avoided discussion of race, class, and gender, other members of the Court were keen to note the amendment's impact on marginalized constituencies. In a vigorous dissent, Justice Thurgood Marshall noted that the amendment's burden would be felt disproportionately by "members of minority races" who "obtain abortions at nearly double the rate of whites."[42] Marshall argued that something more than the rational basis review that the majority used to uphold the law was warranted because the Hyde Amendment, which he described as "designed to deprive poor and minority women of the constitutional right to choose abortion," would have a "devastating impact on the lives of minority racial groups."[43]

Adhering to precedent not only minimized arguments rooted in race, class, and gender, it also minimized the lived experiences of those most affected by the Hyde Amendment, including Cora McRae and the plaintiffs in a companion case, *Williams v. Zbaraz*.

RACE, CLASS, AND GENDER IN *WILLIAMS V. ZBARAZ*

Among those who had a first-hand understanding of the Hyde Amendment's effects on poor communities of color was David Zbaraz, a Jewish OB/GYN and the named plaintiff in *Williams v. Zbaraz*.[44] Zbaraz was one of "two physicians who perform[ed] medically necessary abortions for indigent women"[45] who lodged a Fourteenth Amendment challenge against an Illinois funding scheme that mirrored the Hyde Amendment. *Williams* ultimately held that just as the Hyde Amendment did not violate the Fifth Amendment, the Illinois law did not run afoul of the Fourteenth Amendment.

Zbaraz defied the stereotype of abortion providers as obstetricians who have a purely clinical view of abortion. He described it as a " 'nasty dirty, yukky thing.' "[46] He denied that an abortion was just like any other medical procedure, asking " 'Have you ever seen one[?] . . . I don't care what anyone says, it is not a tonsillectomy, not just any old medical procedure. It's terminating a potential human life.' "[47] Nevertheless, he

---

[41]   Brief of The Association of Legal Aid Attorneys et. al. as Amici Curiae at 15, Harris v. McRae, 448 U.S. 297 (1980) (No. 79-1268), 1980 WL 339659, at *15.

[42]   Harris v. McRae, 448 U.S. 297, 343 (1980) (Marshall, J., dissenting).

[43]   *Id.* at 344.

[44]   Williams v. Zbaraz, 448 U.S. 358 (1980).

[45]   *Id.* at 361.

[46]   Fred Barbash, *Abortionist: Doctor Joins Suit for Right to Do Operation He Hates*, WASH. POST, Mar. 3, 1980, at A1.

[47]   *Id.*

performed abortions—and fought for the right of indigent persons to access safe, legal abortions—because he realized that the failure to ensure such access would harm poor women of color most of all.

Zbaraz completed his residency at Michael Reese Hospital on the south side of Chicago. During his residency, in the days before *Roe* protected the right to abortion for those with the ability to pay, Zbaraz recalled " 'seeing one, two or three 13- or 14-year-old girls coming in every Saturday night with 104-degree temperatures and puss pouring out of their uteruses, victims of septic abortions. The infection would shoot through their bodies and cause shock or death. The kids would die or lose their uteruses.' "[48] After *Roe* was decided, Zbaraz continued to see a fair share of patients who needed medical care following unsafe abortions that were performed at sites that offered more "affordable" services. In order to ensure that these places would not "become the only choice for poor women," he established a clinic in Michael Reese that performed abortions for indigent people.[49] " 'These patients were in need, and I was one hell of an abortionist,' he repeated."[50] Zbaraz was moved to get involved in the challenge to the Hyde Amendment and the analogous Illinois law because, in effect, " 'They outlawed abortions for poor women,' " and in so doing, portended a "return to the Saturday nights of his residency" and " 'the carnage on the streets.' "[51]

Interestingly, Zbaraz's adversary in the litigation was Jasper F. Williams, a black OB/GYN who supported the Illinois abortion funding restriction. A physician who headed the obstetrics clinic at St. Bernard Hospital in Chicago, Williams was also an entrepreneur and an amateur pilot. He founded a number of lucrative businesses, including a black-owned broadcasting company named Seaway Communications, a medical center called the Williams Clinic that served the black community, and a black-owned bank named Seaway National Bank. Indeed, at the time of his death at age 67—when the twin-engine Comanche airplane that he was piloting back to Chicago after a vacation in the Bahamas and Florida crashed into an Indiana cornfield[52]—Seaway National Bank was the largest black-owned bank in the country.[53]

Williams was well aware that indigent people of color received poor quality healthcare in Chicago, and he led a number of efforts to remedy the disparity. During his stint as president of the National Medical Association, the oldest and largest organization of black physicians, Williams called for an investigation into all of the patient deaths that

---

[48] *Id.*

[49] *Id.*

[50] *Id.*

[51] *Id.*

[52] Kenan Heise, *Dr. Jasper Williams; Founded Clinic*, CHI. TRIBUNE, Apr. 17, 1985, at A6.

[53] Glenn Fowler, *Dr. Jasper F. Williams Killed*, N.Y. TIMES, Apr. 17, 1985, at D27.

occurred shortly after admission to Chicago-area hospitals.[54] The incident that prompted Williams's call for action was the death of Lena Fulwiley, a 15-year-old black girl who went to Cook County Hospital—a large public hospital that served the poor community that surrounded it— complaining of abdominal pains. The two white doctors who examined her diagnosed her with a venereal disease, gave her a shot of penicillin, and sent her home. She died shortly thereafter when her appendix burst. An autopsy failed to show that she had a venereal disease. In a letter to the Commissioner of Health, Williams spoke about Fulwiley as well as another person who was " 'turned away from County with a ruptured aneurysm . . . who died the following day after being referred back to County by a private physician.' "[55] Williams argued that these cases and " 'several other instances . . . support the claims of cursory, inadequate care where Negroes are concerned.' "[56] Williams wrote that while the poverty of these victims of medical neglect partly explained the poor quality of healthcare that they received, their race was likely also a factor. He argued that while "the poor in general are frequently mishandled at County, . . . the Negro poor are at an even greater disadvantage simply because of their color."[57]

Williams's work to improve the healthcare provided to indigent people of color in Chicago extended to other arenas. In an op-ed in the *Chicago Defender*, a weekly newspaper with a primarily black readership that focused on issues affecting the black community, Williams warned about the dangers of receiving medical care from individuals who were not licensed to practice medicine:

> The person who is ill would do well to insure the type of treatment he is about to receive when seeking the care of a doctor by inquiring before treatment is begun if the "doctor" is a licensed physician and surgeon. . . . This will help save the millions of dollars lost each year and to prevent the serious injury and frequent death which results when unscrupulous persons seek to prescribe medicine. There is no bargain basement in care for the sick. There is only a basement, and it is damp, dark and dirty.[58]

Williams's background and advocacy might have led him to oppose the Hyde Amendment and to support Medicaid funding for indigent abortions. He clearly understood that poor people of color were likely to receive inferior medical care, and he surely was aware that indigent women of color seeking abortions were uniquely vulnerable to this risk. He also likely recognized that, in the absence of Medicaid funding, poor

[54] Betty Washington, *NMA Asks Hospital Probe*, CHI. DAILY DEFENDER, Nov. 13, 1967, at 6.

[55] *Id.*

[56] *Id.*

[57] *Id.*

[58] Jasper F. Williams, *Here's to Health*, CHI. DEFENDER, June 9, 1962, at 8.

black women who wanted and needed to terminate their pregnancies might turn to the "damp, dark, and dirty" basement of back alley abortions performed by "unscrupulous persons."[59] Like Zbaraz, Williams might have become a champion of Medicaid funding for abortion because of an awareness of the "serious injury and frequent death"[60] that result when safe, legal abortions are not accessible.

Instead, Williams joined the *Zbaraz* litigation to defend Illinois's version of the Hyde Amendment, prioritizing the fetus's potential life over the life, health, and safety of indigent women. His reasons for doing so were complicated. On the one hand, there was his simple belief that life begins at conception, which he elaborated in congressional testimony in support of an antiabortion bill.[61] Perhaps Williams's belief that life begins at conception led him to his conviction, described during a different hearing before a congressional committee, that "the number of medical cases in which abortion is an indicated and appropriate part of the treatment is practically nil."[62] As he explained:

> Since 1953, I have never seen a patient who died because she needed an abortion and it could not be performed. I have seen patients die with sickle-cell disease. Aborting them would not have helped. Those patients could have been treated a little bit better by the prevention of pregnancy; but once they were pregnant, not aborting them did not make the situation worse. The same is true of congestive heart failure. . . . Open heart surgery is performed on pregnant patients. Doctors now have the tools and the knowledge with which to work so that they can handle almost any disease a patient might have, whether that patient is pregnant or not, and without interrupting the pregnancy.[63]

On the other hand, Williams's opposition to Medicaid funding for abortion—and abortion, more generally—may have stemmed from his belief that abortion in the black community was part of a genocidal plot. In different congressional testimony, which was reported in an article in the *Washington Post*, Williams proposed that a concern with the growing number of black people receiving welfare assistance explained the broad availability of abortion in black communities:

> Because of the large number [of abortions] being performed on blacks, I have the feeling that there are ulterior motives

---

[59] *Id.*

[60] *Id.*

[61] Bill Peterson, *Geneticist Warns Abortion Ban Would Outlaw IUDs*, WASH. POST, Apr. 25, 1981, at A3.

[62] *Constitutional Amendments Relating to Abortion: Hearings on S.J. Res. 17, S.J. Res. 18, S.J. Res. 19, and S.J. Res. 110 Before the Subcomm. on the Constitution of the S. Comm. on the Judiciary*, 97th Cong. 267 (1981) (statement of Jasper Williams, Jr., M.D., past president, National Medical Association).

[63] *Id.* at 268.

involved. I am not certain that it is because you are interested in the welfare of the black woman or whether you are just tired of the increased public aid rolls, that the black woman increases by having more and more illegitimate babies. . . . If you look at that side of the question, then it looks like genocide.[64]

Williams was not alone in his view that abortion was part of a larger effort to decimate the black community. The *Chicago Defender* conducted a poll in 1971 in which close to *two-thirds* of the respondents reported fearing that state-funded abortions threatened the black community with genocide.[65] Some—including the Reverend Jesse Jackson—went so far as to oppose the use of *contraception* among black women out of a concern that a reduction in their fertility would mean a reduction in black people's political power. Although Jackson later supported contraception and abortion—including Medicaid-funded abortion—he was once fiercely opposed to any mechanism that suppressed black birthrates. As he explained:

> You have to recognize that the American group that has been subjected to as much harassment as our community has is suspect of any programs that would have the effect of either reducing or leveling off our population growth. Virtually all the security we have is in the number of children we produce. . . . We don't want birth control; we want blacks so we will have power.[66]

Despite these fears, many persons of color who were staunchly committed to black empowerment and racial justice were strong supporters of access to contraception and abortion. Their position was informed by the understanding that linking black liberation to black reproduction meant that black *women* would, quite literally, bear the burdens of elevating the race. The view that black women ought to be able to control their fertility—whether that entailed becoming a mother or avoiding motherhood—was also informed by the recognition that individuals resort to dangerous measures when they are denied such control. On this account, limiting abortion access in the name of black liberation could force poor black women to resort to unsafe abortion practices. As one activist concluded, "the Black brother's argument against legal, safe abortion is, in itself, genocidal, killing off Black women in the name of the fetus."[67] Essentially, many activists who supported abortion rights and

---

[64]   *Id.; Ghetto Doctor Likens Abortion to Genocide*, WASH. POST, Oct. 20, 1981, at A14.

[65]   Frances Beal, *Black Women's Manifesto; Double Jeopardy; To Be Black and Female, in* BEFORE ROE V. WADE: VOICES THAT SHAPED THE ABORTION DEBATE BEFORE THE SUPREME COURT'S RULING 49 (Linda Greenhouse & Reva Siegel eds., 2010).

[66]   *Id.*

[67]   Bev Cole, *Black Women and the Motherhood Myth, in* BEFORE ROE V. WADE, *supra* note 65, at 53. Whatever Williams's reasons for opposing abortion, his efforts to reduce and eliminate abortion access continued after his death. Alongside Eugene Diamond, a pediatrician in Illinois, Williams attempted to intervene as a defendant in a challenge to an Illinois law that criminalized abortion under certain circumstances. If his motion to intervene as a defendant was denied, Williams sought to be appointed as "guardian ad litem

access responded to the "abortion is black genocide" argument by observing that the prospect of genocide lay on both sides of the equation. If the availability of abortion is genocidal because black fetuses will be killed, the unavailability of abortion also threatens genocide because of the lengths to which desperate black women will go to terminate an unwanted pregnancy.

In essence, it was not at all uncommon for individuals to consider race, class, and gender when arriving at their decisions to support or oppose abortion generally, or Medicaid funding for abortion specifically. Nevertheless, these considerations were completely effaced in the Court's decision to uphold the constitutionality of the Hyde Amendment.

THE CONTINUED STRUGGLE AGAINST
THE HYDE AMENDMENT

The fight for Medicaid funding for abortion did not end with the Court's decision in *McRae*. Reeling from the Supreme Court defeat, many activists took the struggle to the states and fought for the right to Medicaid funding for abortion under state constitutions—sometimes under state ERAs. They occasionally won. For example, in *Doe v. Maher*, decided in 1986, the Connecticut Superior Court considered the legality of the state's version of the Hyde Amendment under the state constitution.[68] Noting that "*McRae* and *Zbaraz* are not controlling," the court rejected *McRae*'s reasoning in its entirety.[69] Critically, the court noted that under the challenged funding restriction, Connecticut would cover the expenses associated with childbirth while denying those associated with abortion. Further, the restriction would result in the state covering the cost of all medically necessary healthcare, "save one— the medically necessary abortion."[70] Concluding that such a funding choice was not at all neutral, the court held that the restriction violated the right to privacy protected in the Connecticut constitution. Additionally, the court found that inasmuch as the restriction discriminated against pregnancy, a condition that is "unique to women,"[71] it was impermissible sex discrimination that ran afoul of the state's Equal Rights Amendment.

---

for unborn children subject to abortion." Diamond v. Charles, 476 U.S. 54, 57 n.4 (1985). Williams died before his motion made it all the way to the Supreme Court, where it ultimately was denied due to his lack of a "judicially cognizable interest" in the challenged statute. *Id.* at 56.

[68]   Doe v. Maher, 515 A.2d 134 (Conn. Super. Ct. 1986).

[69]   *Id.* at 429, 437. Also quite remarkably, the Connecticut court opinion includes the brutality that Medicaid funding restrictions inflict—brutality that was excised from the Court's rather sterile opinion in *McRae*. The Connecticut court dedicates space to telling the stories of the people who stood to be maimed by Medicaid funding restrictions, including a "thirteen year old girl who began vomiting five times a day, and developed an acute state of depression which was characterized by frequent crying spells and which interfered with her progress at school" and "a woman whose fetus could not survive outside of the womb because it had anencephaly." *Id.* at 434–35.

[70]   *Id.* at 430.

[71]   *Id.* at 444.

Of course, litigators and activists who challenged Medicaid funding restrictions under state constitutions lost, too—as they did in Pennsylvania, with a lower court stating that "[i]t is true, of course, that the decision of the United State Supreme Court in [*McRae*] is not binding on us in a case involving the Pennsylvania Constitution, but our courts have consistently held that, *for purposes of equal protection claims*, the content of our Constitution is not significantly different from that of the Federal Constitution."[72] The Pennsylvania Supreme Court ultimately held that the funding restriction was consistent with the state's constitution.[73]

At times, victories in the fight against the Hyde Amendment in the states have been achieved outside of constitutional litigation. Activists in Illinois—the home of Representative Hyde, David Zbaraz, and Jasper Williams—won one such victory in late 2017 when, after a concerted grassroots campaign, they convinced the Republican governor to sign a bill that funds both medically necessary and nontherapeutic abortions through the state's Medicaid program.[74]

As of October 1, 2018, thirty-two states and the District Columbia follow the Hyde Amendment and fund under the state Medicaid program only abortions for pregnancies that are life endangering or are the result of rape or incest.[75] (South Dakota only funds abortions for pregnancies that pose a threat to the individual's life, making no rape or incest exception.) Eighteen states go beyond the Hyde Amendment and fund medically necessary abortions, with thirteen states doing so as a result of a court victory.[76]

* * *

Almost forty years later, *McRae* is a case of great historic significance. It marked AUL's debut on the national scene in its defense of the Hyde Amendment in the litigation.[77] Emboldened by its victory in *McRae*, AUL pressed its fight to limit abortion access in various arenas. AUL was not the only abortion opponent emboldened by *McRae*. After *McRae* was decided, Representative Hyde declared that the decision was

---

[72]   Fischer v. Pennsylvania Department of Public Welfare, 444 A.2d. 774, 777–78 (Pa. Commw. Ct. 1982).

[73]   Fischer v. Department of Public Welfare, 502 A.2d. 114, 121 (Pa. 1985).

[74]   Chris Kenning, *Illinois Republican Governor Signs Controversial Abortion Bill*, REUTERS (Sep. 28, 2017, 7:16 PM), https://www.reuters.com/article/us-illinois-abortion/illinois-republican-governor-signs-controversial-abortion-bill-idUSKCN1C33F5.

[75]   *State Funding of Abortion Under Medicaid*, GUTTMACHER INST., https://www.guttmacher.org/state-policy/explore/state-funding-abortion-under-medicaid (last updated Oct. 1, 2018).

[76]   *Id.*

[77]   *Accomplishments: AUL's Proven Track Record of Success*, AM. UNITED FOR LIFE, https://aul.org/what-we-do/achievements/ (last visited January 26, 2019). *See* Cary Franklin, *Whole Woman's Health v. Hellerstedt and What It Means to Protect Women*, in REPRODUCTIVE RIGHTS AND JUSTICE STORIES 223 (Melissa Murray, Katherine Shaw & Reva B. Siegel eds., 2019).

encouragement to those struggling to outlaw abortion,[78] and John Willke of the National Right to Life Committee declared that he took *McRae* as an invitation to " 'redouble our efforts to restore legal protections to all human beings from the time of fertilization.' "[79] Certainly, *McRae* cannot be understood without acknowledging the anti-abortion energies that it stoked and legitimated.

McRae is also significant because the decision to uphold the Hyde Amendment now has effects beyond the indigent.[80] The Affordable Care Act ("ACA") has broadened the reach of the Hyde Amendment well beyond Medicaid. Under the ACA, individuals with incomes that exceed Medicaid limits, but do not exceed 400 percent of the federal poverty level, receive federal subsidies that they can use to purchase private health insurance on health insurance exchanges.[81] However, the ACA makes clear that these federal subsidies cannot be used to purchase insurance coverage for abortion services. Indeed, in an executive order, President Obama reiterated that the restrictions that the Hyde Amendment imposes on individuals with public insurance—the restrictions that the Court legitimated in *McRae*—would now be imposed on individuals with *private insurance* if their private insurance was purchased with the assistance of federal monies.[82] In this way, the Hyde Amendment now reaches beyond the realm of public insurance, affecting more than just the poor.

Finally, *McRae* is significant because it marks a return to the pre-*Roe* days. Wealthier women have always been able to access safe abortion in this country—even prior to the Court's decision in *Roe*. As historian David Garrow notes, before *Roe* was decided, "there were hundreds upon hundreds of doctors in this country who secretly performed abortions for women whom they knew and who could pay."[83] However, these doctors were inaccessible to poor women, who had neither the money to purchase

---

[78]   *Q&A: The Court's Abortion Ruling*, Bos. GLOBE, July 1, 1980, at 1.

[79]   *Id.*

[80]   *See* Douglas NeJaime & Reva B. Siegel, *Conscience Wars: Complicity-Based Conscience Claims in Religion and Politics*, 124 YALE L.J. 2516, 2540–42 (2015) (discussing other legislation that regulates objections to abortion by focusing on money transfers through insurance programs).

[81]   26 U.S.C. § 36B (2011).

[82]   Exec. Order No. 13,535, 75 Fed. Reg. 15,599 (Mar. 29, 2010). The ACA delegates to the Department of Health and Human Services (HHS) the authority to make regulations on segregating public funds (which cannot be used to purchase abortion coverage) from private funds (which can be used to purchase the same). 42 U.S.C. § 18023(b)(2)(C) (2010); *see also, e.g.*, Patient Protection and Affordable Care Act, HHS Notice of Benefit and Payment Parameters for 2016, 80 Fed. Reg. 10,749, 10,840 (Apr. 28, 2015). Thus, the ability of persons to purchase from an exchange a private insurance plan that offers abortion coverage turns on the willingness of politicians to believe that private and public funds have actually been segregated. *See* Paige Winfield Cunningham, *Planned Parenthood Defunded for One Year Under GOP Health Bill*, WASH. POST (May 4, 2017), https://www.washington post.com/news/powerpost/wp/2017/05/04/planned-parenthood-defunded-for-one-year-under -gop-health-bill/?utm_term=.95000865a31e.

[83]   David J. Garrow, *Abortion Before and After* Roe v. Wade: *A Historical Perspective*, 62 ALB. L. REV. 833, 834 (1999).

the services that the doctors offered nor the connections that would enable poor women to find them. Before *Roe*, poor women were forced to either carry their pregnancies to term or to attempt to terminate their pregnancies under unsafe conditions. The inability of the Medicaid-dependent poor to rely on public health insurance to cover the cost of their abortions marks a return to the past. Just as in the days that preceded *Roe*, wealthier women now can purchase the safe abortion services that they want and need in the market; their indigent counterparts, who are disproportionately persons of color, are either forced into motherhood or forced to risk their lives and health in the attempt to avoid the same.[84] This is an atavism that Judge Dooling acknowledged in his decision to strike down the Hyde Amendment. He observed that in the face of Medicaid funding restrictions, "the difference noted in the period before the changes in state laws, and before *Roe v. Wade* and *Doe v. Bolton*, between the treatment accorded the indigent and those with the means to pay for medical care appears to be resumed."[85] In essence, as long as the Hyde Amendment remains good law, we will live in the past.

---

[84] Leslie J. Reagan, When Abortion Was a Crime: Women, Medicine, and the Law in the United States, 1867–1973, at 137 (1998) (A study in the 1930's found "[a]ccess to physician-induced abortions and reliance upon self-induced methods for abortion varied greatly by class and race. Most affluent white women went to physicians for [illegal] abortions, while poor women and black women self-induced them.").

[85] McRae v. Califano, 491 F. Supp. 630, 689 (E.D.N.Y. 1980).

7

Serena Mayeri*

Undue-ing *Roe*: Constitutional Conflict and Political Polarization in *Planned Parenthood v. Casey*

Planned Parenthood of Southeastern Pennsylvania v. Casey[1] is "the most important abortion decision you may never have heard about,"[2] and not only because it has governed state regulation of pregnancy terminations longer than *Roe v. Wade*[3] ever did. When it was decided in June 1992, *Casey* seemed most important for what it did *not* do: overturn *Roe*. In the quarter century since the Court's surprise decision upholding *Roe*'s "core" but replacing its controversial "trimester" framework with the protean "undue burden" standard, activists, scholars, lawyers, litigants, judges, and ordinary citizens have debated and shaped *Casey*'s significance—not only for reproductive rights and justice, but also for social movement activism, the constitutional meanings of equality and liberty, partisan electoral strategy, and the centrality of judicial appointments to American politics.

In this regard, *Casey* is not simply a sequel to *Roe v. Wade*; it is a story about how constitutional law is made. Acting on cherished beliefs about constitutional principle, social movement activists on both sides of the abortion debate worked to shape the Constitution's meaning—in courts of law, but also in legislatures, in the streets, and in the court of public opinion. They strategized, lobbied, and litigated; they engaged in

* Professor of Law and History, University of Pennsylvania Law School. Special thanks are due to the editors of this volume, Reva Siegel, Melissa Murray, and Kate Shaw, for their invaluable guidance. I am also grateful for the insights of fellow participants in the Law Stories Convening on Reproductive Rights and Justice at Yale, for Seth Kreimer's expert input and feedback, and for helpful conversations and correspondence with Mary Ziegler. For assistance in gathering sources, I thank Shachar Gannot, Patricia Jerjian, and Emily Prifogle; Alvin Dong of the Biddle Law Library at Penn Law; archivists at the Barnard College Archives and Princeton's Mudd Library; and Patrick Kerwin and his colleagues at the Library of Congress. All errors are my own.

1   505 U.S. 833 (1992).

2   Nina Martin, *The Supreme Court Decision that Made a Mess of Abortion Rights*, MOTHER JONES (Feb. 29, 2016), https://www.motherjones.com/politics/2016/02/supreme-court-decision-mess-abortion-rights/.

3   410 U.S. 113 (1973).

electoral politics and direct action; they fought with energy and urgency born of deep conviction.

Advocacy for and against abortion rights informed the Supreme Court's decision in *Casey*, shaping the decision's paradoxical result. On the one hand, the ruling provided a more powerful constitutional foundation for abortion rights, foregrounding the claims to women's equal citizenship long emphasized by feminists.[4] On the other, *Casey* honored the state's interest in potential life, and by green-lighting a wider range of abortion regulations, allowed anti-abortion activists and legislators to limit abortion access in the name of protecting women. For feminist advocates of reproductive justice, *Casey*'s invocation of women's equality has fallen short of its promise, given the deleterious consequences of post-*Casey* abortion regulations for poor and low-income women's access to reproductive health care. For the conservative legal movement, *Casey* symbolizes the paramount importance of securing judicial appointees committed to its tenets. As conservatives' efforts reshape the Court succeed, the lessons learned from the *Casey* conflict continue to sculpt the contours of constitutional law and politics today.

"A CHILL WIND BLOWS"

After *Roe*, abortion opponents put reproductive rights and justice advocates on the defensive, employing various strategies to undermine or reverse the Court's decision. Between 1973 and 1980, abortion foes focused primarily on two campaigns: one for a Human Life Amendment that would enshrine fetal rights in the federal constitution by declaring that life begins at conception; and another for restrictions on public funding for abortion care. The Supreme Court upheld state and federal funding bans in *Maher v. Roe*[5] and *Harris v. McRae*,[6] but efforts to shepherd a Human Life Amendment through Congress stalled. The Court struck down most abortion regulations that came before it: under *Roe*'s strict scrutiny standard, states could not prohibit abortion or enact fetal protective restrictions before the third trimester.[7] Dissenters from *Roe* and its progeny believed that courts should not consider abortion a fundamental right, but rather should defer to legislative judgments about abortion and uphold regulations with a "rational basis."[8]

Unable to enact a constitutional amendment to proscribe abortion, and frustrated with their limited success in the courts, abortion opponents reassessed their strategy of pushing for *Roe*'s immediate reversal. The legislation and litigation that culminated in *Planned*

---

[4]   Linda Greenhouse & Reva B. Siegel, *The Unfinished Story of* Roe v. Wade, *in* REPRODUCTIVE RIGHTS AND JUSTICE STORIES 53 (Melissa Murray, Katherine Shaw & Reva B. Siegel eds., 2019).

[5]   432 U.S. 464 (1977).

[6]   448 U.S. 297 (1980).

[7]   *See, e.g.*, Belotti v. Baird, 443 U.S. 622 (1979); Planned Parenthood of Central Mo. v. Danforth, 428 U.S. 52 (1976).

[8]   *See, e.g.*, Roe v. Wade, 410 U.S. 113, 172–75 (Rehnquist, J., dissenting).

Parenthood v. Casey reflected the rise of an incremental approach pioneered by Americans United for Life (AUL). The AUL Legal Defense Fund sought to emulate the NAACP Legal Defense Fund's successful midcentury campaign to dismantle racial segregation one case at a time.[9] Rather than challenge *Roe* directly, AUL strategists counseled the passage of "carefully drafted statutes" (often drawn from AUL's own model legislation) that would extend the government's regulatory power without provoking the ire of pro-choice judges or prematurely presenting to the Court a complete prohibition on abortion.[10] Anti-abortion incrementalists understood that courts and the American public did not yet accept the premise that abortion at any stage of pregnancy was murder and should be outlawed. Activists would continue to press this absolutist argument outside of court; in the meantime, they could substantially reduce abortions by placing increasingly onerous barriers in the way of women seeking to end a pregnancy.[11]

The Pennsylvania Abortion Control Act of 1982 epitomized this new incrementalism. The Act was the brainchild of antiabortion crusader Stephen Freind, a thirty-something state lawmaker and author of a semiautobiographical 1987 novel called *God's Children* about a firebrand pro-life politician who, like Freind, was a Catholic, chain-smoking former FBI agent who believed that abortion was murder.[12] His proposed state statute borrowed from the AUL's model legislation. The product of secretive negotiations between Freind's team of antiabortion state legislators and Republican Governor Richard Thornburgh, the 1982 Act included a twenty-four-hour waiting period; a parental consent requirement for minors; a requirement that second-trimester abortions be performed in a hospital, with a second physician present to save the life of the fetus if possible; and a ban on the funding of abortions by state employee health plans.[13]

A devoted cadre of health care providers, lobbyists, and lawyers stood ready to challenge abortion restrictions.[14] Morgan Plant, a lobbyist for Planned Parenthood, walked the halls of the state capitol in Harrisburg, buttonholing legislators. Plant's job wasn't easy; as she later

---

[9]   *See, e.g.,* Richard S. Myers, *Prolife Litigation and the American Civil Liberties Tradition, in* ABORTION AND THE CONSTITUTION: REVERSING *ROE V. WADE* THROUGH THE COURTS 23 (Dennis J. Horan et al. eds., 1987); Victor G. Rosenblum & Thomas J. Marzen, *Strategies for Reversing* Roe v. Wade *Through the Courts, in id.* at 195.

[10]   *See* Rosenblum & Marzen, *supra* note 9.

[11]   On the rise of incrementalism, see MARY ZIEGLER, AFTER ROE: THE LOST HISTORY OF THE ABORTION DEBATE, CHAP. 2 (2015).

[12]   STEPHEN F. FREIND, GOD'S CHILDREN (1987).

[13]   Thornburgh had vetoed an earlier version of the bill that he believed was unconstitutional. *See* Gov. Dick Thornburgh to the Honorable, the Senate of the Commonwealth of Pennsylvania, Dec. 23, 1981 (ACLU Records, Box 5124, Folder Penn. PP Law, Mudd Library, Princeton University) [hereinafter ACLU Records].

[14]   On obstacles facing abortion law reformers in Pennsylvania state politics, see Rosemary Nossif, *Pennsylvania: The Impact of Party Organization and Religious Lobbying, in* ABORTION POLITICS IN AMERICAN STATES ch. 1 (Mary C. Segers & Timothy A. Byrnes eds., 1995).

told a reporter, "Anti-abortion bills move through the Pennsylvania Legislature like hot knives through butter."[15] Kathryn "Kitty" Kolbert, a Temple Law alumna who had begun her career as a legal aid lawyer in the late 1970s, soon found herself at the center of almost every abortion case in the Pennsylvania courts as an attorney at Philadelphia's Women's Law Project (WLP), where she partnered with other lawyers including Tom Zemaitis of the law firm Pepper Hamilton; Seth Kreimer, a University of Pennsylvania law professor active in the ACLU; and eventually with Linda Wharton, a Rutgers law graduate who later became WLP's managing attorney.[16]

For the moment, pro-choice advocates seemed to have the law on their side. But Ronald Reagan's election to the presidency augured changes in the constitutional landscape. Reagan, who as Governor of California had supported abortion law reform, campaigned for President on a pledge to roll back abortion rights, affirmative action, and welfare benefits. He enjoyed crucial support from religious conservatives: "I know you can't endorse me, but I want you to know that I endorse you," he famously declared to a group of Christian leaders in 1980.[17]

President Reagan's first Supreme Court nominee, Arizona judge and former state legislator Sandra Day O'Connor, who had once supported the ERA, dismayed those who hoped for a more solidly "pro-life" nominee.[18] But in a 1983 case reviewing abortion restrictions enacted by the City of Akron, Ohio, Justice O'Connor wrote a dissent calling *Roe*'s trimester framework "unworkable." She contended that courts should strike down abortion regulations only when they imposed an "undue burden" on women's decision whether to terminate a pregnancy.[19] In 1986, when the Supreme Court ruled Freind's Pennsylvania statute unconstitutional in *American College of Obstetricians and Gynecologists v. Thornburgh*,[20] Justice O'Connor again championed the undue burden standard in dissent. *Roe*'s author, Justice Harry A. Blackmun, wrote for the majority: "The States are not free, under the guise of protecting maternal health or potential life, to intimidate women into continuing pregnancies."[21] Justice O'Connor, however, did not agree that the law constituted intimidation. In her view, the Pennsylvania regulations did

---

[15] Quoted in Michael DeCourcy Hinds, *Pennsylvania Under Abortion Spotlight*, N.Y. TIMES, Sept. 20, 1989, at A16.

[16] *See* Cynthia Gorney, *Endgame*, WASH. POST (Feb. 23, 1992), https://www. washingtonpost.com/archive/lifestyle/magazine/1992/02/23/endgame/125da2a0-5886-41ce-9cad-13144b44cffa/.

[17] George Skelton, *Reagan Gains with Some Evangelicals*, L.A. TIMES, Sept. 17, 1980, at B4.

[18] *See* SERENA MAYERI, REASONING FROM RACE: FEMINISM, LAW, AND THE CIVIL RIGHTS REVOLUTION 208 (2011).

[19] City of Akron v. Akron Ctr. Reproductive Health, 462 U.S. 416, 463–65 (1983) (O'Connor, J., dissenting).

[20] 476 U.S. 747 (1986).

[21] *Id.* at 759–62.

not impose a sufficiently heavy burden on women to warrant invalidation.[22]

The Court's composition began to shift less than a week after the 5–4 *Thornburgh* decision, when Chief Justice Warren E. Burger announced his retirement; President Reagan nominated Antonin Scalia to replace Burger and elevated William H. Rehnquist to Chief Justice. When swing Justice Lewis F. Powell, Jr., retired the following year, Reagan's first choice replacement was conservative Yale law professor and D.C. Circuit Judge Robert Bork. Bork's nomination horrified pro-choice advocates and their allies. An originalist, Bork had attacked the very foundation of the constitutional right to privacy, calling *Griswold v. Connecticut*[23] "unprincipled." Because of his stance on *Griswold*, as well as his other controversial positions on civil rights and liberties, opponents characterized Bork as "outside the mainstream," scuttling his nomination.[24] After a second unsuccessful nomination, Reagan's third choice, Ninth Circuit Judge Anthony M. Kennedy, won unanimous confirmation following a hearing in which he affirmed his support for *Griswold*.[25] Unlike Bork, who had called *Roe* "an unconstitutional . . . [,] . . . serious and wholly unjustifiable usurpation of state legislative authority,"[26] Kennedy's views on abortion were unknown.[27]

Sensing an opening, Friend soon reintroduced an anti-abortion bill in the Pennsylvania legislature.[28] This time, his negotiating partner was Governor Robert P. Casey, Sr., a prominent Democrat who opposed abortion but believed pro-life advocates should support "child and maternal health programs," "education," "rape counseling and support services," and other policies "born of the recognition that our moral responsibility to mothers and children does not end at birth."[29] Instead, legislators settled on informed consent, parental consent, and funding restriction provisions that Governor Casey signed into law in March 1988.[30] The *Pittsburgh Post-Gazette* described a "weary-looking" Morgan Plant decrying a "94 percent male" legislature for a "long and expensive

---

[22]   *Id.* at 827–28 (O'Connor, J., dissenting).

[23]   381 U.S. 479 (1965).

[24]   Reva B. Siegel, *How Conflict Entrenched the Right to Privacy*, 124 YALE L.J.F. 316, 320–21 (2015); *see also* DAVID GARROW, LIBERTY AND SEXUALITY: THE RIGHT TO PRIVACY AND THE MAKING OF *ROE V. WADE* 671 (1994).

[25]   Al Kamen, *Kennedy Confirmed, 97–0*, WASH. POST, Feb. 4, 1988, at A1.

[26]   LINDA GREENHOUSE, BECOMING JUSTICE BLACKMUN 188 (2005).

[27]   *See, e.g.*, Stuart Taylor, *Judge Kennedy: Tilting Right but Not Far*, N.Y. TIMES, Nov. 15, 1987, at A1.

[28]   Harry Stoffer, *Bill to Restore Curbs on Abortions Passed, Sent to Casey*, PITTSBURGH POST-GAZETTE, Dec. 3, 1987, at 9.

[29]   Robert P. Casey, *Why Casey Vetoed the Anti-Abortion Bill*, PHILA. INQUIRER, Dec. 20, 1987, at 77.

[30]   Michael Blood, *Casey Signs Abortion Bill; Test Planned*, PITTSBURGH POST-GAZETTE, Mar. 26, 1988, at 1.

tradition . . . of passing unconstitutional anti-abortion legislation which is then litigated unsuccessfully at great expense to the taxpayers."[31]

Pro-choice organizations immediately mounted a class-action challenge to the new statute.[32] In April, Federal District Court Judge Daniel Huyett III issued a temporary restraining order and then preliminary injunctions blocking most of its provisions.[33] Meanwhile, antiabortion activists stepped up protests at abortion clinics, facing fines and jail time for contempt of court.[34] Operation Rescue, founded in 1986 to vindicate the slogan, "If you believe abortion is murder, act like it's murder," achieved national fame in the summer of 1988 when demonstrations during the Democratic National Convention led to thousands of arrests.[35] George H.W. Bush's decisive victory over Michael Dukakis in the 1988 presidential election heartened abortion opponents.[36] Pro-choice activists worried that clinic blockades, funding prohibitions, antiabortion violence, and a provider shortage endangered access more than ever before.[37]

When *Webster v. Reproductive Health Services*[38] reached the Supreme Court in 1989, Justice Blackmun "expected the worst."[39] The Missouri law challenged in *Webster* banned public employees and publicly owned hospitals and clinics from providing abortions; required women to obtain prenatal tests to determine fetal viability if a physician dated the pregnancy at twenty weeks or beyond; and included a preamble declaring that human life began at conception.[40] With a record-setting seventy-eight amicus briefs, and the Solicitor General requesting that *Roe* be overruled,[41] Chief Justice Rehnquist drafted a majority opinion acknowledging that the regulations could be upheld without "revisiting *Roe*," but he "proceeded to do precisely that."[42] The majority (including Justice Kennedy) upheld the restrictions, but to the palpable outrage of concurring Justice Scalia, Justice O'Connor resisted the call to confront

---

[31]   Quoted in Harry Stoffer, *Bill to Restore Curbs on Abortions Passed, Sent to Casey*, PITTSBURGH POST-GAZETTE, Dec. 3, 1987, at 9.

[32]   Joseph A. Slobodzian, *2 Class-Action Lawsuits Are Filed in Bid to Stop State Abortion Law*, PHILA. INQUIRER, Apr. 19, 1988, at 5-B.

[33]   Joseph Slobodzian, *Judge Blocks Implementation of Abortion-Control Law*, PHILA. INQUIRER, Apr. 19, 1988, at 1-B.

[34]   Susan Caba, *Jail Terms: A New Tactic for Anti-Abortion Protests*, PHILA. INQUIRER, July 4, 1988, at 9.

[35]   Ronald Smothers, *Atlanta Protests Prove Magnet for Abortion Foes*, N.Y. TIMES, Aug. 13, 1988, at 6.

[36]   GARROW, *supra* note 24, at 673.

[37]   *Id.* at 682–83.

[38]   492 U.S. 490 (1989).

[39]   GREENHOUSE, *supra* note 26, at 190.

[40]   *Id.*

[41]   GARROW, *supra* note 24, at 674.

[42]   GREENHOUSE, *supra* note 26, at 191.

Roe directly.[43] Nevertheless, Justice Blackmun wrote, "the signs are evident and very ominous, and a chill wind blows."[44]

THE "SCARIEST FEELING"

The *Webster* decision invited a new wave of abortion-restrictive legislation across the nation.[45] Pennsylvania's leading antiabortion activists met at the Harrisburg Holiday Inn in September 1989 to strategize.[46] Pro-Life Federation Director Denise Neary described the "scariest feeling . . . right after *Webster*. It was like the eyes of the nation were upon us . . . . [W]e were going to fail the whole movement if we didn't come through."[47] The forty-year-old Neary was a "veteran pragmatist," willing to accept slow regulatory suffocation as a substitute for outright abolition. As another activist put it, "Until we get a human life [constitutional] amendment, we have to fight a holding action, a guerilla war, to make abortions as difficult as possible to obtain."[48]

In 1989, Freind introduced more legislation, including a requirement that married women seeking an abortion notify their husbands.[49] The spread of such requirements alarmed pro-choice advocates. But they also presented an opportunity to advance equality-based arguments that many feminists believed provided a more compelling moral, legal, and historical foundation for abortion rights than privacy and due process. In February 1990, Kolbert outlined a strategy for challenging the spousal notification provision under the federal Equal Protection Clause and state Equal Rights Amendments, to "insure that men and women will have a right to equally participate within society, and to avoid simplistic, outdated assumptions about the roles of men and women."[50]

Meanwhile, anti-abortion protests raged outside Pittsburgh's Women's Health Services. Reverend John Guest and his fellow activists hoped "to persuade women not to have abortions." Director Sue Roselle insisted that more than a thousand demonstrators chanting and praying outside did not disrupt the clinic's regular Saturday routine: "We had a

---

[43] *Id.* at 193.

[44] Webster v. Reprod. Health Servs., 492 U.S. 490 (1989).

[45] *See* ABORTION POLITICS IN AMERICAN STATES, *supra* note 14, at xvii (noting that 351 abortion bills were introduced in the year after *Webster*); *see also* GARROW, *supra* note 24, at 680–81 (noting that overall, *Webster* galvanized pro-choice support but Pennsylvania's "antiabortion consensus was not shaken").

[46] Gorney, *supra* note 16.

[47] *Id.*

[48] *Id.* On Neary, see also ZIEGLER, *supra* note 11, at 39.

[49] The bill also included a prohibition on terminations after twenty-four weeks and a ban on abortions for reasons of sex-selection. Albert J. Neri, *Abortion Controls Approved*, PITTSBURGH POST-GAZETTE, Oct. 25, 1989, at 1.

[50] Kathryn Kolbert & Simon Heller, ACLU Reproductive Freedom Project, to ACLU Affiliates and Other Interested Parties, Re: Husband Notification Provisions (Feb. 22, 1990), at 13–14 (Kathryn Kolbert Papers, Box 16, Barnard College Archives) [hereinafter Kolbert Papers]. Several courts had already held abortion restrictions unconstitutional under state sex equality and privacy provisions. *See, e.g.*, Doe v. Maher, 40 Conn. Supp. 394 (Conn. Super. Ct. 1986).

full schedule and we did 53 abortions," using "alternate entrances" and escorts for patients.[51] But with momentum on Guest's side, abortion rights supporters faced a dilemma: challenge the Pennsylvania law and risk decimating *Roe*, or let the law go into effect. As Freind said, "We're in a no-loss situation. They are in a no-win situation."[52]

Tracking anti-abortion legislation had become nearly a full-time job.[53] Guam's ban, passed in March 1990, caught advocates on both sides off-guard. Anita Arriola, a thirty-two-year-old pro-choice lawyer whose mother, Guam Senator and Catholic lay leader Elizabeth Arriola, authored the restrictive law, alerted ACLU Reproductive Rights Project Director Janet Benshoof. Benshoof called the statute's surprise unanimous passage, under threat of excommunication by Guam's Catholic Archbishop, "Pearl Harbor for women."[54] She rushed to the airport and flew 8,000 miles in an unsuccessful attempt to persuade Guam's governor to veto the bill.[55]

In June, another set of Supreme Court rulings on parental notification further raised the stakes. Pro-lifers declared victory but needed one more Justice to overturn *Roe*, given Justice O'Connor's hesitation about one of the restrictions—a two-parent notice requirement.[56] When liberal Justice William J. Brennan, Jr. suffered a stroke and retired suddenly in July, *Roe*'s fate looked more precarious than ever.

In August 1990, a four-day trial tested the constitutionality of the Pennsylvania regulations. Both sides expected Judge Huyett—the Nixon appointee, World War II veteran, and former chair of the Berks County Republican Party who had struck down the 1982 Act—to rule for the plaintiffs; their goal was to build a detailed factual record.[57] Given the dearth of abortion providers, especially in rural areas, a 24-hour waiting period would delay many procedures by as much as two weeks, testified Sylvia Stengle, head of the Allentown Women's Clinic, one of the named plaintiff organizations. Plaintiff Dr. Thomas Allen, an obstetrician/

---

[51]   Linda Wilson Fuoco, *No Arrests as Abortion Issue Draws 1,200 Protesters*, PITTSBURGH POST-GAZETTE, Feb. 19, 1990, at 6.

[52]   *Judge Limits Pennsylvania Abortion Law*, CHI. TRIB., Jan. 12, 1990, at D11.

[53]   Gorney, *supra* note 16.

[54]   Jane Gross, *Guam Approves Bill Posing a Challenge to Abortion Ruling*, N.Y. TIMES (Mar. 16, 1990), http://www.nytimes.com/1990/03/16/us/guam-approves-bill-posing-a-challenge-to-abortion-ruling.html.

[55]   United Press Int'l, *ACLU Official Pleads Not Guilty to Abortion Counseling* (Mar. 21, 1990), https://www.upi.com/Archives/1990/03/21/ACLU-official-pleads-not-guilty-to-abortion-counseling/2998637995600/; Dan Balz, *Guam Surprises Abortion Activists*, WASH. POST (Mar. 24, 1990), https://www.washingtonpost.com/archive/politics/1990/03/24/guam-surprises-abortion-activists/baa34434-7f08-44a8-b463-ffb30c90b524/?utm_term=.c24e7cfd b848.

[56]   Ohio v. Akron Ctr. for Reprod. Health, 497 U.S. 502 (1990); Hodgson v. Minnesota, 497 U.S. 417 (1990).

[57]   Ron Devlin, *Quiet Reading Court Becomes Battlefield of Pa. Abortion Law*, MORNING CALL (Allentown, Pa.) (Aug. 5, 1990), http://articles.mcall.com/1990-08-05/news/2 759048_1_abortion-law-huyett-abortion-providers.

gynecologist who had helped to establish Pittsburgh's "first free-standing abortion clinic," testified to the adverse psychological effects and the "substantial increase in the risk of death" or complications from postponed abortions.[58] The plaintiffs argued that the waiting period "demean[ed]" women by suggesting they could not "make a rational decision without being forced to wait some prescribed period."[59] The true intent behind the provision, attorney Tom Zemaitis insisted, was "to keep women tied up long enough [that] they'll change their minds."[60]

Reproductive rights advocates also attacked parental consent provisions in and out of court. *No Way Out: Young, Pregnant, and Trapped by the Law*, a 1991 ACLU pamphlet and one of the *Casey* plaintiffs' many exhibits, recounted the death of seventeen-year-old Becky Bell from a "botched illegal abortion," obtained because she feared "disappointing" her parents.[61] The pamphlet described life-threatening methods to which teenagers resorted, such as ingesting toxic chemicals, inserting knitting needles, and taking dangerous drugs.[62] Parental physical and sexual abuse, drug addiction, and emotional instability prevented many girls from notifying their parents or triggered hostile or violent reactions when they did.[63] Thirteen-year-old Spring Adams of Oregon, for example, pregnant because of her father's sexual assault, managed to arrange an abortion six hours away in Portland only to be shot dead by her father while she lay sleeping.[64]

Pennsylvania's husband notification requirement seemed most constitutionally vulnerable. Psychologist Lenore Walker testified that domestic violence survivors would face insuperable obstacles to invoking statutory exemptions. Women were "most likely to be murdered when attempting to report abuse or to leave an abusive relationship."[65] Many wives who had nonconsensual marital sex did not define their experiences as rape, much less report the assaults to unreceptive authorities.[66] "Forcing a battered woman to notify her husband is like giving him a hammer to just beat her," Walker declared.[67] One survivor, Joan Dillon,

---

[58]   Planned Parenthood of Se. Pa. v. Casey, 744 F. Supp. 1323, 1352 (E.D. Pa. 1990) (citing Trial Testimony of Dr. Allen, Vol. I, at 88).

[59]   Trial Transcript, Day 4, Planned Parenthood of Se. Pa. v. Casey, at 21, ACLU Records, Box 5184, Folder: Trial Transcript [hereinafter "*Casey* Trial Transcript"]

[60]   *Id.*

[61]   ACLU Reproductive Freedom Project, No Way Out: Young, Pregnant, and Trapped by the Law (Kolbert Papers, Box 16).

[62]   *Id.*

[63]   *Id.*

[64]   *Id.*

[65]   Brief Amicus Curiae of the Pennsylvania Coalition Against Domestic Violence, et al, Planned Parenthood v. Casey, Third Circuit, at 8–9 (Kolbert Papers, Box 6) [hereinafter Third Circuit Brief of Pennsylvania Coalition].

[66]   *Id.* at 6.

[67]   Brief for Petitioners and Cross-Respondents, Planned Parenthood of Se. Pa. v. Casey, 505 U.S. 833 (1992) (Nos. 91-744, 91-902), 1992 U.S. S. Ct. Briefs LEXIS 288, at *21, (quoting Joint Appendix, *Casey*, at 228); Associated Press, *Spouse Notification of Abortion Challenged in State Law*, PITTSBURGH POST-GAZETTE, Aug. 1, 1990, at 4.

testified that when she finally managed to leave her severely abusive husband, police rebuffed several calls for help. Once, after seeking enforcement of a protective order, Dillon was told, "[C]all me when you're dead, honey."[68] Nor did the exemptions cover psychological abuse, threats to harm or abscond with a woman's children, or withdrawal of financial support.[69]

Judge Huyett's ruling for the plaintiffs weeks later candidly acknowledged the tenuous nature of the constitutional rights his decision vindicated. "Individuals can no longer feel as secure with the protections provided by the judiciary . . . . [A] woman's privacy rights and individual autonomy may soon be subjected to the vicissitudes of the legislative process."[70] Indeed, hearings on President Bush's nomination of David H. Souter to replace Justice Brennan were only weeks away.

Then, in October 1991, another unwelcome surprise for abortion rights supporters: A Third Circuit panel upheld all but the spousal notification provision. Parsing recent caselaw at length, Judge Walter Stapleton concluded that the undue burden standard Justice O'Connor first articulated in her *Akron* dissent had effectively replaced the strict scrutiny required by *Roe*.[71] Bush-appointed Judge Samuel Alito wrote a separate opinion endorsing the spousal notification provision's constitutionality. As a rising star in the Reagan administration, Alito had counseled then-Solicitor General Rex Lee on how best to use an amicus brief in *Thornburgh* to exploit "this opportunity to advance . . . the eventual overruling of *Roe v. Wade* and, in the meantime, [to] mitigat[e] its effects."[72] In 1985, "no one seriously believe[d]" the demise of *Roe* was imminent.[73] Not so, six years and four Justices later.

Judge Alito interpreted Justice O'Connor's undue burden standard to require not merely "a heavy impact on a few women" but "a broader inhibiting effect."[74] While "the plight of any women, no matter how few, who may suffer physical abuse or other harm" was "a matter of grave concern," the statute contained adequate exceptions. Moreover, Judge Alito wrote, the plaintiffs had not shown that spousal notification would

---

    [68]   Third Circuit Brief of Pennsylvania Coalition, *supra* note 65, at 14.

    [69]   *Id.* at 14–16.

    [70]   Planned Parenthood of Se. Pa. v. Casey, 744 F. Supp. 1323, 1397 (E.D. Pa. 1990), *aff'd in part, rev'd in part*, 947 F.2d 682 (3d Cir. 1991), *aff'd in part, rev'd in part*, 505 U.S. 833 (1992).

    [71]   Judge Stapleton's clerks at the time included Brett Kavanaugh. *See* Linda Greenhouse, *A Kavanaugh Signal on Abortion?* N.Y. TIMES (July 18, 2018), https://www.ny times.com/2018/07/18/opinion/abortion-kavanaugh-trump-supreme-court.html.

    [72]   Memorandum from Samuel Alito to the Solicitor General, Re: Thornburgh v. American College of Obstetricians and Gynecologists 8 (May 30, 1985) (National Archives and Records Administration, Record Group 60, Department of Justice, Files of the Assistant Attorney General, Charles Cooper, 1981–1985, Accession #060-89-216, Box 20, Folder: Thornburgh v. American College of Obstetricians & Gynecologists).

    [73]   *Id.*

    [74]   *Casey*, 947 F.2d at 721 (Alito, J., concurring in part and dissenting in part), *aff'd in part, rev'd in part*, 505 U.S. 833.

impose a greater burden on women than parental notice requirements the Court had approved.[75] Therefore, he believed, the applicable standard was rational basis review, a relatively lenient standard that required only that a law be reasonably related to a legitimate government interest. Legislators, Judge Alito wrote, "could have rationally believed that some married women are initially inclined to obtain an abortion without their husbands' knowledge because of perceived problems—such as economic constraints, future plans, or the husbands' previously expressed opposition—that may be obviated by discussion."[76] Criticism of Judge Alito's abortion writings followed him to his Supreme Court confirmation hearings fifteen years later. In the meantime, Judge Alito embodied the potential of conservative judicial appointments to reshape constitutional law.[77]

NARAL executive director Kate Michelman called the Third Circuit decision in *Casey* "shocking" and a harbinger of *Roe*'s demise. Though they agreed on little else, Pennsylvania Pro-Life Federation's Denise Neary concurred that "*Roe v. Wade* is doomed."[78] Days earlier, the Senate had confirmed Clarence Thomas as Justice Thurgood Marshall's replacement; of the *Roe* majority, only Justice Blackmun remained on the Court.[79] Kolbert heard of the Third Circuit's decision while speaking to a group of college students in Massachusetts about abortion rights organizing. Kolbert appeared "drawn and visibly shaken" as she "abandoned her prepared speech . . . , gazed at a roomful of students who were still in diapers in 1973 and wondered how to explain that some judges . . . had just pronounced *Roe v. Wade* dead."[80] This, Kolbert declared, "is as bad as it gets."[81]

Galvanized by a memorandum that Kolbert sent via overnight mail, Pennsylvania's leading pro-choice advocates and clinic directors converged on Philadelphia to strategize. The options were uniformly grim. They could decline to appeal, allowing the regulations to take effect and ceding the fight to other challengers. They could request a rehearing en banc before the entire Third Circuit, a "delaying tactic" at best.[82] Or, they could appeal directly to the U.S. Supreme Court, a move that would catapult the Pennsylvania case to the "front of the pipeline," already clogged with at least seven different cases vying for the dubious honor of

---

[75]   *Id.* at 723–24.

[76]   *Id.* at 726.

[77]   *See, e.g.,* Emily Bazelon, *Alito v. O'Connor: How the Nominee Tried to Restrict* Roe, SLATE (Oct. 31, 2005), http://www.slate.com/articles/news_and_politics/jurisprudence/2005/10/alito_v_oconnor.html.

[78]   Michael deCourcy Hinds, *Appeals Court Upholds Limits for Abortions,* N.Y. TIMES (Oct. 22, 1991), http://www.nytimes.com/1991/10/22/us/appeals-court-upholds-limits-for-abortions.html.

[79]   GREENHOUSE, *supra* note 26, at 199.

[80]   Gorney, *supra* note 16.

[81]   *Id.*

[82]   *Id.*

"plac[ing] *Roe*'s neck squarely on the chopping block."[83] After an anguished discussion, Planned Parenthood lobbyist Morgan Plant "cast her vote for immediate appeal to the U.S. Supreme Court."[84] As Kolbert explained: "It's a question of what you have to lose that you haven't already lost."[85]

"A KIND OF HEROISM IN TRYING"

The pro-choice movement's strategy was incredibly "audacious."[86] All but certain of *Roe*'s demise, leaders preferred a clean evisceration to an incremental death by a thousand cuts. Rescinding abortion rights, they reasoned, would galvanize women to take political and electoral action; delaying the inevitable would only enable Bush's reelection and more conservative judicial appointments. Whereas Pennsylvania argued that the Court need not revisit *Roe* to uphold the regulations, pro-choice advocates framed the "question presented" in *Casey* in the starkest terms possible: "Has the Supreme Court overruled *Roe v. Wade*, holding that a woman's right to choose abortion is a fundamental right protected by the United States Constitution?"[87]

Inside Justice Blackmun's chambers, initial reactions to the *Casey* petition for certiorari were mixed as the clerks weighed the costs and benefits of voting to hear the appeal. As clerk Molly McUsic wrote in January 1992, *Roe*'s death might not be inevitable. Justices Rehnquist or White could retire; Bush could lose the election or appoint a moderate. On the other hand, "Perhaps the Court has done all it can do," and "the only way" was "for women to take control of their own destiny" and win through political activism "rights that are rooted in the necessary popular support."[88] McUsic worried "that women may still be far too disenfranchised, abused, and disempowered to claim their most basic right to physical integrity. But if so . . . this Court is powerless to stop it."[89] At first, clerk Jeffrey Meyer believed that "the benefits to the women who will be helped by delaying [*Roe*'s demise] along with the chance that Roe might be preserved" counseled delay.[90] Ultimately, though, Justice Blackmun's clerks unanimously recommended he vote to hear *Casey*.[91]

---

[83]   *Id.* (quoting Planned Parenthood's Roger Evans).

[84]   *Id.*

[85]   Joseph Slobodzian & Wanda Motley, *Pa. to Appeal Abortion Decision*, PHILA. INQUIRER, Oct. 23, 1991, at B1.

[86]   *See* JEFFREY TOOBIN, THE NINE 8 (2008).

[87]   Petition for a Writ of Certiorari, Planned Parenthood v. Casey, 505 U.S. 833 (1992) (Nos. 91-744, 91-902); *see also* Memorandum to Ira from Loren and Phil, Re: Casey Campaign (Dec. 23, 1991) (Kolbert Papers, Box 1) (describing strategy).

[88]   Molly McUsic, Attachment, at 8 (Jan. 4, 1992) (Harry A. Blackmun Papers, Box 604, Folder 4, Library of Congress) [hereinafter Blackmun Papers].

[89]   *Id.*

[90]   *Id.* at 51.

[91]   Steff to Mr. Justice (Jan. 10, 1992) (Blackmun Papers, Box 604, Folder 4). For more, see GREENHOUSE, *supra* note 26, at 201–02.

Seasoned observers admired Kolbert's tenacious oral argument. Journalist Lyle Denniston wrote, "No victories come from arguing lost causes, even historic ones . . . but there is a kind of heroism in trying."[92] Kolbert sought to "raise the stakes significantly" by arguing that Pennsylvania's position endangered the very right to privacy itself.[93] State attorney general Ernest Preate struggled to address Justice O'Connor's probing questions about the spousal notification provision.[94] The Bush Administration challenged *Roe* head-on:[95] The National Right to Life Committee praised Solicitor General Kenneth Starr for insisting that "a State's interest in protecting fetal life throughout pregnancy," not merely post-viability, "outweighs a woman's liberty interest in an abortion."[96]

The Justices' early deliberations in *Casey* confirmed abortion rights supporters' worst fears. On May 27, Chief Justice Rehnquist circulated a draft majority opinion that reduced "women's interest in having an abortion" to "a form of liberty protected by the Due Process Clause" but subject to state regulation constrained only by rational basis review.[97] "One cannot ignore the fact that a woman is not isolated in her pregnancy, and that the decision to abort necessarily involves the destruction of a fetus,"[98] Chief Justice Rehnquist wrote. No "deeply rooted tradition of relatively unrestricted abortion in our history" supported a due process fundamental right warranting the application of strict scrutiny.[99] It seemed inevitable that Justice Blackmun would dissent; his early draft lamented that Rehnquist "would have women sit shiv'ah—the Court having overruled *Roe*, all that remains is the unveiling of the headstone. Meanwhile, with a wink and a nod, States would be on notice to do as they please."[100]

"AT LEAST PART OF WHAT I SAY SHOULD COME AS WELCOME NEWS"

Two days later, a handwritten note from Justice Kennedy arrived in Justice Blackmun's chambers. "I need to see you," Justice Kennedy wrote, "as soon as you have a few free moments. I want to tell you about some developments in Planned Parenthood v. Casey, and at least part of what

---

[92] Lyle Denniston, *The Judicial Politics of Abortion*, AM. LAW., June 1992, at 95.

[93] *Id.*

[94] *Id.* at 96.

[95] *See* Brief for Respondents at 205, Planned Parenthood of Se. Pa. v. Casey, 505 U.S. 833 (1992) (Nos. 91-744, 91-902).

[96] David G. Savage, *Abortion Issue Argued Before Supreme Court*, L.A. TIMES, Apr. 23, 1992, at A1; Brief of the United States as Amicus Curiae Supporting Respondents at 28, *Casey*, 505 U.S. 833 (Nos. 91-744, 91-902).

[97] Chief Justice William H. Rehnquist, First Draft of Opinion for the Court, Planned Parenthood v. Casey, No. 91-744, May 27, 1992, at 12 (Blackmun Papers, Box 602, Folder 1).

[98] *Id.* at 10.

[99] *Id.* at 11.

[100] Justice Harry A. Blackmun, Changes to Second Draft of Concurring/Dissenting Opinion in Casey, at 18, No. 91-744 (Blackmun Papers, Box 601, Folder 7).

I say should come as welcome news."[101] Justice Kennedy had met privately with Justices O'Connor and Souter to craft a joint opinion that embraced a middle ground between overruling and endorsing *Roe*. The opinion rejected *Roe*'s trimester framework and strict scrutiny in favor of an "undue burden" standard, but reaffirmed the "essential holding" recognizing the abortion right as central to women's liberty, autonomy, and equality. In contrast to *Thornburgh*, the joint opinion upheld all of the Pennsylvania regulations except for the spousal notification requirement.

Justice Blackmun's law clerk Stephanie Dangel initially felt "somewhat ambivalent": the joint opinion was "admir[able]" but "does not go as [far] as it should." Dangel worried the ruling might "remov[e] abortion from the political agenda just long enough to ensure the re-election of Pres. Bush and the appointment of another nominee from whom the Far Right will be sure to exact a promise to overrule *Roe*."[102] She advised Justice Blackmun to use his separate writing to praise the joint opinion and "give the undue burden standard . . . as much *bite* as possible."[103] Dangel also drafted a closing paragraph signaling that though *Roe* was safe—barely—for now, abortion rights still hung in the electoral balance. "You are the person American women look to in order to find out what is really happening in this case," Dangel advised. When Justice John Paul Stevens counseled Justice Blackmun to remove the final paragraph, Dangel dissuaded him: "I can't help but fear," she wrote, "that without that last paragraph women are going to think they can rest easy."[104]

Meanwhile, Justice Stevens negotiated revisions to the joint opinion that would allow him and Justice Blackmun to join as much of it as practicable. Justice Stevens's own opinion explained why he believed the requirements upheld by the majority—informed consent, parental consent, and waiting periods—imposed an undue burden.[105] He also considered including a section resting abortion rights more explicitly on the Equal Protection Clause.[106] Feminists from Catharine MacKinnon to Ruth Bader Ginsburg had long criticized *Roe* for emphasizing privacy and physicians' prerogatives over women's equality and autonomy.[107] The *Casey* plaintiffs emphasized how the law "perpetuates the pernicious stereotype that women are subordinate within marriage and incapable of

---

[101] Tony to Harry, May 24, 1992 (Blackmun Papers, Box 601, Folder 6).

[102] Steff to Mr. Justice, June 16, 1992, at 1 (Blackmun Papers, Box 602, Folder 4).

[103] *Id.* at 1–2.

[104] GREENHOUSE, *supra* note 26, at 206.

[105] Planned Parenthood of Se. Pa. v. Casey, 505 U.S. 833, 914–22 (1992) (Stevens, J., concurring in part and dissenting in part).

[106] On Justice Stevens's deliberations, see BILL BARNHART & GENE SCHLICKMAN, JOHN PAUL STEVENS: AN INDEPENDENT LIFE 239–43 (2010).

[107] *See, e.g.*, Ruth Bader Ginsburg, *Some Thoughts on Autonomy and Equality in Relation to* Roe v. Wade, 63 N.C. L. REV. 375 (1985); Sylvia A. Law, *Rethinking Sex and the Constitution*, 132 U. PA. L. REV. 955 (1984); Catharine MacKinnon, *Reflections on Sex Equality Under Law*, 100 YALE L.J. 1281 (1991).

making independent moral decisions"[108] and harkened "back to the days when 'the female [was] destined solely for the home and rearing of the family and only the male for the marketplace and the world of ideas.' "[109] Several briefs cited law professor Reva Siegel's 1992 article *Reasoning from the Body*, which uncovered how nineteenth-century abortion restrictions reflected not only the professionalization of medicine and concern for fetal life but also a powerful ideological imperative to confine women to their proper roles as wives and mothers and to preserve white racial dominance—in contravention of modern equal protection law.[110] *Casey* seemed to Dangel "like the perfect case" to advance an "equal protection basis for the abortion right." In another pending case, *Bray v. Alexandria Women's Health Clinic*, Justice Stevens had drafted an opinion explaining why antiabortion protesters who blocked women's access to clinics acted from gender-based animus in violation of a statute prohibiting conspiracies to deprive individuals of their constitutional rights.[111] Justice Stevens's "scholarly opinion" in *Bray* made him "the logical person" to elaborate the equal protection rationale.[112]

To Dangel's frustration, Justice Stevens did not take this approach, but his partial concurrence, as well as Justice Blackmun's partial concurrence and the joint opinion all invoked sex equality principles that were mostly absent in previous abortion rulings. To wit, the joint opinion's stare decisis section emphasized how "[a]n entire generation has come of age free to assume *Roe*'s concept of liberty in defining the capacity of women to act in society, and to make reproductive decisions."[113] And "[t]he ability of women to participate equally in the economic and social life of the Nation has been facilitated by their ability to control their reproductive lives."[114]

The plaintiffs' careful work in building a trial court record also bore fruit. The Justices recited the district court's extensive factual findings on the devastating scourge of domestic violence.[115] Rejecting state and spousal paternalism, the joint opinion distinguished adult women from minors and from men who conceived children.[116] Whereas children "will often not realize that their parents have their best interests at heart," justifying parental consent requirements, "[w]e cannot adopt a parallel

[108] Brief for Petitioners and Cross Respondents, Planned Parenthood of Se. Pa. v. Casey, 505 U.S. 833 (1992) (Nos. 91-744, 91-902), 1992 U.S. S. Ct. Briefs LEXIS 288, at *37.

[109] Brief for Petitioners and Cross-Respondents, *Casey*, 505 U.S. 833 (1992) (Nos. 91-744, 91-902), 1992 U.S. S. Ct. Briefs LEXIS 288, at *66 (quoting Stanton v. Stanton, 421 U.S. 7, 14–15 (1975)).

[110] Reva B. Siegel, *Reasoning from the Body: An Historical Perspective on Abortion Regulation and Questions of Equal Protection*, 44 STAN. L. REV. 261 (1992).

[111] 506 U.S. 263 (1993).

[112] Steff to Mr. Justice, June 18, 1992, at 1 (Blackmun Papers, Box 602, Folder 4).

[113] Planned Parenthood of Se. Pa. v. Casey, 505 U.S. 833, 860 (1992).

[114] *Id.* at 856.

[115] *Id.* at 887–91.

[116] *Id.* at 895, 896.

assumption about adult women."[117] While fathers eventually developed an equal interest to mothers in parenting their children, "[b]efore birth . . . state regulation with respect to the child a woman is carrying will have a far greater impact on the mother's liberty than on the father's."[118]

The joint opinion explicitly rejected the "common law" view of women as subservient wives and mothers subject to their husbands' authority. Depriving women of "full and independent legal status" was "no longer consistent with our understanding of the family, the individual, or the Constitution."[119] To force a woman to notify her husband would "empower him with [a] troubling degree of authority over his wife;" he had "no enforceable right to require a wife to advise him before she exercises her personal choices."[120] Spousal notification, in sum, was "repugnant to our present understanding of marriage and of the nature of the rights secured by the Constitution. Women do not lose their constitutionally protected liberty when they marry."[121]

Justices Stevens and Blackmun's partial concurrences underscored the joint opinion's solicitude for women's equality as well as liberty interests. Justice Stevens declared *Roe* "an integral part of a correct understanding of both the concept of liberty and the basic equality of men and women."[122] Justice Blackmun emphasized that "[b]ecause motherhood has a dramatic impact on a woman's educational prospects, employment opportunities, and self-determination, restrictive abortion laws deprive her of basic control over her life."[123] Abortion regulations "implicate constitutional guarantees of gender equality . . . . By restricting the right to terminate pregnancies, the State conscripts women's bodies into its service . . . . [The] assumption . . . that women can simply be forced to accept the 'natural' status and incidents of motherhood . . . appears to rest upon a conception of women's role that has triggered the protection of the Equal Protection Clause."[124]

Chief Justice Rehnquist excoriated the joint opinion for honoring stare decisis only in the breach, inventing an undue burden standard "largely out of whole cloth."[125] *Roe*, he wrote, "stands as a sort of judicial Potemkin Village . . . a monument to the importance of adhering to precedent. But behind the façade" was "an entirely new method of

---

[117] *Id.* at 898.

[118] *Id.* at 896.

[119] *Id.* at 897.

[120] *Id.* at 898.

[121] *Id.*

[122] *Id.* at 912 (Stevens, J., concurring in part and dissenting in part).

[123] *Id.* at 928 (Blackmun, J., concurring in part, concurring in the judgment in part, and dissenting in part).

[124] *Id.* Justice Blackmun's opinion cited an emerging understanding within the legal academy that abortion rights rested upon equality as well liberty and privacy. *See id.* at 928 n. 4 (citing the works of Professors Reva Siegel, Catharine MacKinnon, Laurence Tribe, and Cass Sunstein).

[125] *Id.* at 964–65 (Rehnquist, C.J., concurring in part and dissenting in part).

analysis."[126] Justice Scalia minced even fewer words. "[T]he best the Court can do to explain how . . . the word 'liberty' *must* be thought to include the right to destroy human fetuses is to rattle off a collection of adjectives that simply decorate a value judgment and conceal a political choice."[127] Far from "resolv[ing] the deeply divisive issue of abortion," Justice Scalia insisted, *Roe* "destroyed the compromises of the past" and "rendered compromise impossible for the future."[128] The joint opinion opened, "Liberty finds no refuge in a jurisprudence of doubt." Justice Scalia retorted, "Reason finds no refuge in this jurisprudence of confusion."[129] And he recoiled from the notion that social movement activism—"political pressure"—should affect "objective" questions of constitutional law. He concluded: "We should get out of this area, where we have no right to be, and where we do neither ourselves nor the country any good by remaining."[130]

On the final day of the Term, June 29, 1992, the Justices spoke from the bench to announce their opinions to a rapt courtroom.[131] From Sarah Weddington, the feminist lawyer who had argued *Roe*, to the ultraconservative Robert Bork, activists voiced "unhappiness" with the decision.[132] By "split[ting] the difference," pro-choice advocates worried, the Court had defused a potent political weapon and bolstered Bush's reelection chances.[133] Abortion opponents lamented *Casey* as "The Dred Scott of Our Time."[134] Kate Michelman of NARAL declared it "a disaster" and Kolbert agreed with *Roe*-opposing *Wall Street Journal* editorialists that the ruling would lead to "endless litigation"[135] and "full employment for lawyers."[136]

Leading commentators, however, hailed *Casey* as a "landmark" ruling. Journalist Linda Greenhouse praised its "tightly reasoned framework . . . in some respects . . . clearer and stronger than *Roe* itself."[137] Constitutional expert Laurence Tribe lauded the decision as

---

[126] *Id.* at 966.

[127] *Id.* at 983 (Scalia, J., dissenting in part).

[128] *Id.* at 995.

[129] *Id.* at 992–93.

[130] *Id.* at 1002.

[131] David G. Savage, *High Court Affirms Right to Abortion but Allows Some Restrictions by States*, L.A. TIMES, June 30, 1992, at A1.

[132] Robert H. Bork, *Again, a Struggle for the Soul of the Court*, N.Y. TIMES, July 8, 1992, at A19.

[133] Marshall Ingwerson & Clara Germani, *Supreme Court Treads in Middle on Abortion*, CHR. SCI. MON., July 1, 1992, at 1.

[134] Nat Hentoff, *Lifeless Reasoning by the Court*, WASH. POST, July 7, 1992; Richard John Neuhaus, *The Dred Scott of Our Time*, WALL ST. J., July 2, 1992, at A8.

[135] Editorial, *The Sun Still Rises*, WALL ST. J., June 30, 1992, at A16.

[136] Tamar Lewin, *Long Battles over Abortion are Seen: One Party Sees 'Full Employment for Lawyers' for a Long Time*, N.Y. TIMES, June 30, 1992, at A18.

[137] Linda Greenhouse, *A Telling Court Opinion; The Ruling's Words Are About Abortion, But They Reveal Much About the Authors*, N.Y. TIMES (July 1, 1992), http://www.nytimes.com/1992/07/01/us/supreme-court-telling-court-opinion-ruling-s-words-are-about-abortion-but-they.html.

"put[ting] the right to abortion on a firmer jurisprudential foundation than ever before."[138] Historian David Garrow went even further, suggesting that *Casey* "almost certainly guarantees that the central core of [*Roe*] will never again be in any significant danger."[139] He declared, "Many difficult pro-choice struggles remain ahead, but the biggest battle is now indeed over."[140]

The months after *Casey* were "a low point in the history of the pro-life movement."[141] The election of Bill Clinton to the presidency heralded a "change in climate" for abortion, as the new administration reversed many Reagan- and Bush-era policies.[142] Election postmortems credited abortion with widening the "gender gap" that helped propel Clinton to victory.[143] "It's Abortion, Stupid," wrote one political scientist, referencing the Clinton campaign mantra about the primacy of economic issues.[144] The electoral outlook for the pro-life movement seemed bleak: "The central concern at the June 1993 NRLC convention was how to keep the Republican Party . . . in the fight against abortion."[145] When *Roe* dissenter Justice Byron White announced his retirement in March 1993, Clinton nominated Ruth Bader Ginsburg, the "Thurgood Marshall" of women's rights.[146] Former Reagan Solicitor General Rex Lee declared *Roe* safe, even before the Senate confirmed Stephen Breyer to replace the retiring Justice Blackmun the following summer.[147] The Freedom of Access to Clinic Entrances Act of 1994 undermined antiabortion blockades and enhanced penalties for perpetrators of clinic violence.[148] But although abortion opponents had lost several battles, the war was far from over.

"TWO STEPS FORWARD, ONE STEP BACK"

In 2003, activists, lawyers, and scholars gathered in Philadelphia for a symposium commemorating *Roe*'s thirtieth anniversary. Kitty Kolbert's contribution, "Two Steps Forward and One Step Back," invoked Justice

---

[138] *Id.*

[139] David Garrow, *A Landmark Decision*, DISSENT (Fall 1992), https://www.dissent magazine.org/article/a-landmark-decision.

[140] *Id.*

[141] Martin, *supra* note 2.

[142] Amy Goldstein & Richard Morin, *Thousands Voice Opposition in 20th March for Life*, WASH. POST, Jan. 23, 1993, at A1.

[143] Michael X. Delli Carpini & Esther R. Fuchs, *The Year of the Woman? Candidates, Voters, and the 1992 Elections*, 108 POL. SCI. Q. 29 (1993).

[144] Alan I. Abramowitz, *It's Abortion, Stupid: Policy Voting in the 1992 Presidential Election*, 57 J. POL. 176 (1995).

[145] James Kelly, *Beyond Compromise:* Casey, Common Ground, and the Pro-Life Movement, *in* ABORTION POLITICS IN AMERICAN STATES, *supra* note 14, at 193.

[146] William J. Clinton, Remarks Announcing the Nomination of Ruth Bader Ginsburg To Be a Supreme Court Associate Justice, June 14, 1993, https://www.presidency.ucsb.edu/ documents/remarks-announcing-the-nomination-ruth-bader-ginsburg-be-supreme-court-associate-justice.

[147] David G. Savage, *Supreme Court's Byron White Will Step Down After 31 Years*, L.A. TIMES, Mar. 20, 1993, at A1.

[148] 18 U.S.C. § 248 (2012).

Blackmun's assessment of abortion rights' trajectory.[149] Despite activists' dire predictions, *Casey* had changed little, in Kolbert's view. Abortion rights supporters faced wave after wave of restrictive state legislation. Under Republican congressional control, federal efforts to ban so-called "partial birth" abortion flourished.[150] In 2006, pro-choice lawyers' assessment of the undue burden standard's implementation was cautiously optimistic.[151] By 2012, *Casey*'s twentieth anniversary, however, Kolbert and Linda Wharton sounded a grimmer note: *Casey*'s "partial victory" enabled "a plethora of burdensome abortion restrictions," including "onerous licensing and regulatory schemes" (known as Targeted Regulation of Abortion Providers (TRAP) laws) and "unrelenting antiabortion harassment and violence" that drove clinics out of business, leaving eighty percent of American counties without any abortion provider.[152] Fueled by an antiabortion political resurgence, these laws, mounting costs, and courts' lax enforcement of the undue burden standard "increasingly threaten[ed] to make abortion unavailable to America's most vulnerable women"[153] and "emboldened attacks on a wide range of reproductive freedoms, including birth control, that were unimaginable" before *Casey*.[154]

On *Casey*'s twentieth birthday, antiabortion law professor Michael Stokes Paulsen called it "the greatest judicial atrocity in American history."[155] But pro-life views of *Casey*'s impact on abortion regulation aligned with Kolbert's. Michael J. New, an antiabortion economist, wrote in 2017 of *Casey*'s "silver lining": since 1992, state restrictions had multiplied, abortion rates declined, pro-choice Republican politicians virtually disappeared, a majority of Americans called themselves "pro-life," and young adults—once the most pro-choice demographic—were now the group most likely to oppose legal abortion.[156]

Pro-choice and feminist assessments of *Casey*'s constitutional legacy are mixed. Advocates praise the joint opinion's recognition of the equality harms caused by abortion regulations and by intimate partner violence.[157] For those who championed the Equal Protection Clause as a

---

[149] Kathryn Kolbert, *Two Steps Forward and One Step Back*, 6 U. PA. J. CONST. L. 686 (2004).

[150] *Id.* at 688.

[151] Linda J. Wharton, Susan Frietsche, & Kathryn Kolbert, *Preserving the Core of Roe: Reflections on* Planned Parenthood v. Casey, 18 YALE J.L. & FEM. 317 (2006).

[152] Linda J. Wharton & Kathryn Kolbert, *Preserving* Roe v. Wade . . . *When You Win Only Half the Loaf*, 24 STAN. L. & POL'Y REV. 143, 157–58 (2013).

[153] *Id.* at 145.

[154] *Id.*

[155] Michael Stokes Paulsen, Planned Parenthood v. Casey *at Twenty: The Worst Constitutional Decision of All Time*, WITHERSPOON INST.: PUB. DISCOURSE (June 29, 2012), http://www.thepublicdiscourse.com/2012/06/5772/.

[156] Michael J. New, Casey *at 25: Pro-Life Progress Despite a Judicial Setback*, NAT'L REV. (June 29, 2017), http://www.nationalreview.com/article/449104/planned-parenthood-vs-casey-25-years-later-abortion-has-declined.

[157] *See, e.g.*, ELIZABETH SCHNEIDER, BATTERED WOMEN AND FEMINIST LAWMAKING 3–4 (2000).

superior foundation for abortion rights, *Casey*'s sex equality language gestured toward such a reconstitution. Some cautiously embrace how *Casey*, despite its shortcomings, articulated conceptions of dignity and equality that incorporated values on both sides in the abortion debate.[158] Feminist critics lamented that *Casey* barely acknowledged how restrictive laws harmed poor women of color marginalized by race, class, region, and immigration status. Professor Lisa Pruitt, for example, stressed how legal barriers to abortion devastated impoverished women living in rural communities or Native American reservations miles from the nearest provider.[159] On this view, *Casey* paid lip service to sex equality while reducing access to reproductive health services for women who bore the brunt of racial and economic injustice in an increasingly unequal society.[160]

Casey's sex equality language proved generative not only for progressives but also for pro-life advocates, who relied on it to revitalize "woman-protective" rationales for abortion regulation.[161] In the 1970s, pro-life feminists had prized women's ability to become parents without sacrificing their own lives and career ambitions; they worried that economic constraints, coercive employers and sexual partners, unequal responsibility for family care, and sex discrimination all conspired to make the choice to terminate a pregnancy no choice at all.[162] Antiabortion feminists therefore championed laws against pregnancy discrimination in the workplace,[163] generous social welfare provisions for women and children, and other progressive policies designed to enable women to choose motherhood.[164]

As the antiabortion movement aligned with the New Right and sidelined feminist activists and arguments,[165] woman-protective arguments emerged from a worldview that envisioned motherhood as the site of women's highest fulfillment and abortion as deeply injurious, producing pathologies such as "Post Abortion Syndrome."[166] By the early 1990s, pro-life strategists concluded that a sole focus on unborn children

---

[158] *See, e.g.*, Linda Greenhouse & Reva B. Siegel, Casey *and the Clinic Closings: When 'Protecting Health' Obstructs Choice*, 125 YALE L.J. 1428, 1479 (2016).

[159] Lisa R. Pruitt, Planned Parenthood of Southeastern Pennsylvania v. Casey, *in* FEMINIST JUDGMENTS: REWRITTEN OPINIONS OF THE UNITED STATES SUPREME COURT (Kathryn M. Stanchi et al. eds., 2016).

[160] *See, e.g.*, Akiba Solomon, *The Personal is Political: That's the Challenge:* Roe v. Wade *and a Black Nationalist Womanist Writer*, DISSENT (Winter 2013), https://www.dissentmagazine.org/article/the-personal-is-political-thats-the-challenge-roe-v-wade-and-a-black-nationalist-womanist-writer-2.

[161] Reva B. Siegel, *The Right's Reasons: Constitutional Conflict and the Spread of Woman-Protective Anti-Abortion Argument*, 57 DUKE L.J. 1641 (2008).

[162] *See* ZIEGLER, *supra* note 11.

[163] *See* Deborah Dinner, *Strange Bedfellows at Work: Neomaternalism in the Making of Sex Discrimination Law*, 91 WASH. U. L. REV. 453 (2014).

[164] ZIEGLER, *supra* note 11; Ziegler, *Women's Rights on the Right: The History and Stakes of Modern Pro-Life Feminism*, 28 BERKELEY J. GENDER L. & JUST. 232 (2013).

[165] *See id.*

[166] *See* Siegel, *The Right's Reasons*, *supra* note 161.

and traditional family values failed to attract new adherents, requiring a rhetorical turn that "fus[ed] feminist and gender-conventional claims about women" in a "pro-woman" strategy.[167] *Casey*'s invitation to states to regulate abortion in the interest of maternal health throughout pregnancy and the joint opinion's focus on sex equality both reinforced this shift, galvanizing the AUL to "educat[e] legislators and judges about abortion's harms to women."[168] The woman-protective strategy reached its apotheosis in *Gonzales v. Carhart*, when Justice Kennedy wrote for a 5–4 majority upholding the Federal Partial Birth Abortion Act: "Respect for human life finds an ultimate expression in the bond of love the mother has for her child . . . . [I]t seems unexceptionable to conclude some women come to regret their choice to abort the infant life they once created and sustained," causing "[s]evere depression and loss of esteem."[169]

Casey's infusion of sex equality into the constitutional law of abortion found new life in Justice Ginsburg's fiery *Carhart* dissent. Calling post-abortion regret an "anti-abortion shibboleth," Justice Ginsburg wrote that the majority's "way of thinking reflects ancient notions about women's place in the family and under the Constitution . . . that have long since been discredited," citing a litany of constitutional sex equality cases.[170] Abortion opponents took notice, warning against testing an abortion ban in the Supreme Court for fear Justice Kennedy would embrace Justice Ginsburg's equal protection analysis.[171]

Casey's constitutional legacy extends beyond abortion. *Casey*'s themes of dignity and bodily integrity resurfaced in cases involving the right to die.[172] In gay rights cases, Justice Kennedy built upon *Casey*'s synthesis of due process and equal protection, liberty and equality, its approach to history, and even its coyness about the appropriate level of judicial scrutiny applicable to such regulations.[173] In *Lawrence v. Texas*, Justice Kennedy used *Casey* to overturn *Bowers v. Hardwick*,[174] the 1986 decision upholding Texas's anti-sodomy law, suggesting that *Casey*'s expansive interpretation of due process could not be reconciled with *Bowers*'s narrow definition of individual rights.[175] *Casey* also laid

---

[167] *Id.; see also* Reva B. Siegel, *Abortion and the Woman Question: Forty Years of Debate*, 89 IND. L.J. 1365 (2014) (quoting David Reardon, Jack Willkie, and Frederica Mathewes-Green).

[168] *Americans United For Life: Defending Life in Law Since 1971*, AM. UNITED FOR LIFE, http://www.aul.org/about-aul/history/ (describing how this strategy emerged post-*Casey*).

[169] 550 U.S. 124, 159 (2007).

[170] *Id.* at 185 (Ginsburg, J., dissenting).

[171] Siegel, *supra* note 167, at 1379.

[172] *See, e.g.*, Washington v. Glucksberg, 521 U.S. 702 (1997).

[173] *See, e.g.*, Obergefell v. Hodges, 135 S. Ct. 2071 (2015); United States v. Windsor, 133 S. Ct. 2675 (2013); Lawrence v. Texas, 539 U.S. 558 (2003); Romer v. Evans, 517 U.S. 620 (1996); Cary C. Franklin, *Marrying Liberty and Equality: The New Jurisprudence of Gay Rights*, 100 VA. L. REV. 817 (2014); Kenji Yoshino, *The New Equal Protection*, 124 HARV. L. REV. 747 (2011).

[174] Bowers v. Hardwick, 478 U.S. 186 (1986).

[175] *Lawrence*, 539 U.S. at 558 (overruling *Bowers*, 478 U.S. 186).

groundwork for *Obergefell v. Hodges*, which used a history of inequality and injustice to justify rather than circumscribe constitutional freedoms.[176]

Further, *Casey* imparted foundational lessons about electoral politics and judicial appointments. For pro-choice advocates, *Casey* confirmed the importance of mobilizing voters and the danger that an ambivalent, partial affirmation of *Roe* would "lull [women] into complacency."[177] *Casey* was Exhibit A in the conservative case for "no more Souters" and for judicial appointees committed to overruling *Roe*. The conservative legal movement cultivated a highly credentialed judicial "farm team" through the Federalist Society;[178] by the end of the George W. Bush administration, handpicked conservative appointees, including Samuel Alito and John G. Roberts, Jr. on the Supreme Court, pervaded the federal judiciary. President Barack Obama matched Bush's judicial appointments in numbers,[179] but Republican obstruction prevented him from filling *Casey* dissenter Justice Scalia's seat after his sudden death in February 2016.

With a landmark abortion case before the Court and a Clinton on the ballot,[180] observers noticed uncanny "political parallels" between 1992 and 2016.[181] In late June, in *Whole Woman's Health v. Hellerstedt*, a 5–3 majority reaffirmed *Casey*'s holding and strengthened the undue burden standard.[182] Some saw abortion as a but-for cause, albeit one of many, for Donald Trump's victory in November: white evangelical women might have been disgusted by Trump's braggadocio about sexually assaulting women, but they kept their eyes on the Supreme Court prize.[183] Whatever role voters' antiabortion commitments played in Trump's victory, no one disputed that the Right succeeded in impressing upon conservative voters the importance of electing a President who would appoint reliably pro-life Justices.[184] And the conservative legal movement tethered abortion to a

---

[176] *Obergefell*, 135 S. Ct. at 584; *see also Lawrence*, 539 U.S. at 558.

[177] Wharton & Kolbert, *supra* note 152, at 145.

[178] Laurence Baum & Neal Devins, *Federalist Court*, SLATE (Jan. 31, 2017), http://www.slate.com/articles/news_and_politics/jurisprudence/2017/01/how_the_federalist_society_became_the_de_facto_selector_of_republican_supreme.html.

[179] *See id.*

[180] Not to mention a pro-life Democrat named Bob Casey in the Pennsylvania governor's office.

[181] Martin, *supra* note 2.

[182] 136 S. Ct. 2292 (2016).

[183] *See, e.g.*, Olga Khazan, *Why Christians Overwhelmingly Backed Trump*, ATLANTIC (Nov. 9, 2016), https://www.theatlantic.com/health/archive/2016/11/why-women-and-christians-backed-trump/507176/; Elizabeth Dias, *'I Pray for Him Daily.' Why Socially Conservative Women Stand By Trump*, TIME (Feb. 20, 2018), http://time.com/5166765/donald-trump-evangelicals-religion-women/.

[184] *See, e.g.*, Ed Stetzer, *Searching for Gorsuch: For Many Evangelicals, "It's the Supreme Court, Stupid,"* CHRISTIANITY TODAY (Jan. 31, 2017), https://www.christianity today.com/edstetzer/2017/january/gorsuch-many-evangelicals-supreme-court-stupid.html.

wide-ranging agenda with devastating implications for nearly every progressive legal reform of the preceding several decades.[185]

President Trump moved quickly to fill Justice Scalia's empty seat, choosing from a Federalist Society-approved list of potential nominees.[186] The Senate confirmed Neil Gorsuch to the Court in April 2017. In the first eighteen months of Trump's administration, twenty-two judges joined the federal courts of appeals.[187] In June 2018, twenty-six years after he co-authored *Casey*, Justice Kennedy announced his retirement. After contentious hearings marked by intense partisan disagreement even before allegations of sexual assault and alcohol abuse emerged, the Senate confirmed Brett M. Kavanaugh to the Court in October 2018 by a narrow 50–48 margin.[188] Senator Susan Collins, Republican of Maine, insisted to the end that Justice Kavanaugh had secured her decisive vote by assuring her that he considered *Roe* "settled law."[189] In reality, the question was when and how, not if, what remained of the abortion right announced in *Roe* would meet its demise.[190] Opponents of abortion had learned the political lessons of *Casey* too well to countenance a nominee whose vote to undermine abortion rights—through dramatic or gradual means—was anything less than a virtual certainty.

---

[185] *See* Serena Mayeri, *How Abortion Rights Will Die a Death by 1,000 Cuts*, N.Y. TIMES (Aug. 30, 2018), https://www.nytimes.com/2018/08/30/opinion/brett-kavanaugh-abortion-rights-roe-casey.html.

[186] Jess Bravin, *White House Narrows List for Supreme Court Nomination*, WALL ST. J. (June 28, 2018), https://www.wsj.com/articles/no-surprises-expected-in-trumps-next-supreme-court-pick-1530229181.

[187] John Gramlich, *With Another Supreme Court Pick, Trump is Leaving His Mark on Higher Federal Courts*, Pew Research Center (July 16, 2018), http://www.pewresearch.org/fact-tank/2018/07/16/with-another-supreme-court-pick-trump-is-leaving-his-mark-on-higher-federal-courts/.

[188] Sheryl Gay Stolberg, *Kavanaugh is Sworn In After Close Confirmation Vote in Senate*, N.Y. TIMES (Oct. 6, 2018), https://www.nytimes.com/2018/10/06/us/politics/brett-kavanaugh-supreme-court.html.

[189] *See* Abigail Abrams, *Here's Sen. Susan Collins' Full Speech About Voting to Confirm Kavanaugh*, TIME (Oct. 5, 2018), http://time.com/5417444/susan-collins-kavanaugh-vote-transcript/; Elise Viebeck & Gabriel Pogrund, *Sen. Susan Collins Says Kavanaugh Sees* Roe v. Wade *as 'Settled Law'*, WASH. POST (Aug, 21, 2018), https://www.washingtonpost.com/powerpost/sen-susan-collins-said-kavanaugh-sees-roe-v-wade-as-settled-law/2018/08/21/214ae5dc-a54c-11e8-8fac-12e98c13528d_story.html?utm_term=.32c8717fe877.

[190] *See, e.g.*, Testimony of Melissa Murray, Professor of Law, New York University School of Law, Before the Committee on the Judiciary, U.S. Senate, Hearing on the Nomination of Judge Brett Kavanaugh to the Supreme Court of the United States (September 7, 2018), https://www.judiciary.senate.gov/imo/media/doc/Murray%20Testimony.pdf; Nancy Gertner, *Brett Kavanaugh's Record Makes His Antiabortion Stance Clear*, BOSTON GLOBE (Aug. 13, 2018), https://www.bostonglobe.com/opinion/2018/08/12/brett-kavanaugh-record-makes-his-antiabortion-stance-clear/6dA1RJGzXjcgAI5Wn2jTDL/story.html.

8

Priscilla A. Ocen*

Pregnant While Black: The Story of *Ferguson v. City of Charleston*

INTRODUCTION

*"I can't do what I want
to do with my own body because I am the wrong
sex the wrong age the wrong skin."*

– June Jordan, "A Poem About My Rights"

On August 4, 1991, Crystal Ferguson, a 31-year-old poor, pregnant, black woman, was admitted to the Medical University of South Carolina ("MUSC"),[1] a public hospital in the City of Charleston and the only medical center within fifty miles that served indigent populations.[2] She was in distress. Six weeks before she was due to have her third child, Ferguson suffered an abruptio placentae, a potentially life threatening complication. Ferguson was immediately scheduled for a cesarean surgery and delivered a healthy baby.[3] Nurse Shirley Brown, the head case manager of the MUSC obstetrics clinic where Ferguson received care, however, suspected that Ferguson's complication was caused by cocaine use and ordered a drug test.[4] The drug test was conducted without a warrant and without Ferguson's consent, pursuant to a policy developed by the hospital in collaboration with local police and

---

*   Professor of Law, Loyola Law School. Many thanks to Ira Chasnoff, Susan Dunn, Lynn Paltrow and Priscilla Smith for sharing their insights and experience with this important case. I am grateful to Melissa Murray, Kate Shaw and Kimberlé Crenshaw for their helpful feedback. This chapter is dedicated to the memory of Crystal Ferguson.

1   *See* Joint Appendix at 459–60, Ferguson v. City of Charleston, 532 U.S. 67 (2001) (No. 99-936).

2   Barry Siegel, *In the Name of the Children: Get Treatment or Go to Jail, One South Carolina Hospital Tells Drug-Abusing Pregnant Women. Now It Faces a Lawsuit and a Civil-Rights Investigation*, L.A. TIMES (Aug. 7, 1994), http://articles.latimes.com/1994-08-07/magazine/tm-24470_1_south-carolina-hospital.

3   Joint Appendix, *supra* note 1, at 456, 463.

4   Second Amended Class Action Complaint at 39–40, Ferguson v. City of Charleston, No. 2-93-2624-2 (D.S.C. Oct. 5, 1993).

prosecutors.[5] The test came back positive.[6] Ferguson was subsequently arrested and charged with felony child abuse.[7] The charges were later dismissed.[8]

In October of 1993, Ferguson filed suit in the Federal District Court of South Carolina, alleging that the drug testing policy violated her right to equal protection, procreation, and to be free from unreasonable searches and seizures as guaranteed by the Fourth Amendment.[9] After suffering a series of losses before lower federal courts, Ferguson successfully petitioned the United States Supreme Court for review. The petition, however, was limited to a narrow question: "whether a state hospital's performance of a diagnostic test to obtain evidence of a patient's criminal conduct for law enforcement purposes is an unreasonable search if the patient has not consented to the procedure."[10] In *Ferguson v. City of Charleston*, the Court answered this question in the affirmative, declaring that the hospital's warrantless drug testing policy violated the Fourth Amendment.[11]

The standard story of *Ferguson v. City of Charleston* emphasizes the ways in which Fourth Amendment doctrine vindicated the privacy rights of pregnant women. At first blush, Ferguson's story presents a classic Fourth Amendment calculation: how to balance a personal interest in privacy against the bureaucratic needs of the state. This chapter troubles that standard account. Instead, this chapter suggests that the story of *Ferguson* is about a fundamental contradiction: the simultaneous hypervisibility and invisibility of poor pregnant black women in law. Although poor pregnant black women are hypervisible targets for multiple forms of state regulation and punishment, the intersectional subordination they experience renders them invisible to traditional legal frameworks that purport to provide protection.

In the case of Crystal Ferguson, her identity as a poor black woman who sought to carry a pregnancy to term, despite her cocaine addiction, made her a hypervisible target of both the racialized war on drugs and efforts by conservative activists to undermine *Roe v. Wade* through the stubborn insistence that a fetus's right to life ought to trump a woman's right to privacy and reproductive autonomy.

The story of *Ferguson v. City of Charleston* also reveals, however, the ways in which law failed to recognize the intersectional dynamics that

---

[5]   *Id.* at 23–24; *see also* Joint Appendix, *supra* note 1, at 1284–1312 (showing memorandums between the hospital and law enforcement to develop the Interagency Policy).

[6]   *Id.* at 41.

[7]   *Id.* at 43.

[8]   David W. MacDougall, *Cocaine Counts Against Pregnant Women Modified*, THE POST & COURIER, May 4, 1993.

[9]   Ferguson v. City of Charleston, 308 F.3d 380, 393 (4th Cir. 2002).

[10]   Ferguson v. City of Charleston, 532 U.S. 67, 69–70 (2001).

[11]   *Id.* at 86.

made Ferguson and other pregnant black women vulnerable to criminalization and state regulation of their reproductive lives. Indeed, throughout the proceedings, federal courts rejected the expansive articulations of reproductive autonomy and equal protection offered by Ferguson and her attorneys. Because she sought to carry a pregnancy to term, Ferguson's injury was not cognizable in a reproductive rights framework grounded in abortion and contraception. Because she was targeted by a facially neutral drug testing policy, her claims of racial discrimination were dismissed. While the involvement of law enforcement in the policy that resulted in her arrest provided Ferguson with a Fourth Amendment avenue of relief, the Court's decision in *Ferguson* only limited *how* the state went about punishing women for drug use during pregnancy without resolving the question of whether they *could* punish women for maternal drug use. As a result of this omission, women across the country—who are disproportionately black—continue to be prosecuted for allegedly endangering fetal life during pregnancy.

In the end, the story of *Ferguson* highlights the need for a capacious vision of reproductive justice, one that can contest the limitations of existing constitutional jurisprudence and in so doing protect the interests of poor black women who are among the most vulnerable to state regulation of their bodies and their reproductive choices.

THE STORY OF CRYSTAL FERGUSON

Born in 1961, Crystal Ferguson grew up in a poor Charleston neighborhood.[12] She survived neglect and abuse. "My childhood was lousy," she once remarked.[13] Growing up, she witnessed her family members struggle with alcoholism.[14] When she was twelve years old, she was sexually assaulted by a relative.[15] Overwhelmed by misplaced shame, she explained, "I never reported it to the police and it made me feel very low, like a whore."[16] For a time, Ferguson was placed in foster care. Likely influenced by the trauma she experienced at home, she began using cocaine,[17] a problem with which she would struggle for decades to come, particularly when "crack cocaine"—a cheap form of cocaine—began to saturate the streets of poor black communities in the 1980s.[18]

---

[12]   Telephone Interview with Lynn Paltrow, Executive Director, Nat'l Advocates for Pregnant Women (Oct. 31, 2017).

[13]   Diane Taylor, *Mothers in Chains*, GUARDIAN (Apr. 7, 2001), https://www.the guardian.com/theobserver/2001/apr/08/life1.lifemagazine1.

[14]   *Id.*

[15]   *Id.*

[16]   *Id.*

[17]   *See* Joint Appendix, *supra* note 1, at 456–59.

[18]   Charisse Jones, *Crack and Punishment: Is Race the Issue?*, N.Y. TIMES (Oct. 28, 1995), https://www.nytimes.com/1995/10/28/us/crack-and-punishment-is-race-the-issue. html ("Crack, which emerged in the mid-1980s, had been deemed a new drug plague, blamed for escalating gang violence and for a surge in the number of neglected children flooding the child welfare system. . . . Although Federal statistics find that half of crack users are white,

At 31, Ferguson lived with her two children in a small mobile home in a poor, racially segregated Charleston neighborhood.[19] "My home environment, I had a lot of problems," she would later admit.[20] She worked a series of low-wage jobs to make ends meet, including at a dry cleaners.[21] In 1990, however, she was unemployed.[22] Ferguson struggled to find work in an environment where the jobless rate for blacks was nearly three times the jobless rate for whites.[23] Instead, she relied on food stamps and unemployment benefits to provide for herself and her children.[24] Her financial problems compounded when she learned that her husband, who also struggled with drug use, was stealing from her.[25] In the midst of her own troubles, Ferguson was also caring for her mother, who was suffering from a terminal illness.[26]

Despite these challenges, Ferguson worked tirelessly to build a happy life for herself and her children. She was a loving mother, frequently taking her children to parks and libraries.[27] She wanted her children to have a better life than she did.[28] Moreover, Ferguson tried to inspire her children through her Christian faith, frequently quoting scripture and singing gospel around the house.[29] When Ferguson learned she was pregnant with her third child, she was both anxious and excited. Wanting to ensure that she had a healthy pregnancy, Ferguson sought prenatal care at the North Area Health Department (NAHD) in Charleston, where she could receive publicly subsidized treatment.[30]

Ferguson attended her weekly prenatal appointments and followed her doctor's recommendations.[31] But she still struggled with cocaine use, for which she could not afford treatment. Importantly, there were no outpatient treatment facilities for pregnant women in Charleston even if she could have paid.[32] Left with few viable options, she tried to manage

---

the sale and use of the substance, a cheaper form of cocaine, is often concentrated in poor, urban, minority communities, experts say.").

[19] Siegel, *supra* note 2; Taylor, *supra* note 13; Telephone Interview with Lynn Paltrow, *supra* note 12.

[20] Joint Appendix, *supra* note 1, at 457.

[21] Telephone Interview with Lynn Paltrow, *supra* note 12.

[22] *See* Joint Appendix, *supra* note 1, at 458–59.

[23] *See* STACEY PATTON, THE STATE OF RACIAL DISPARITIES IN CHARLESTON COUNTY, SOUTH CAROLINA 2000–2015 12 (2017) (describing racial disparities in the unemployment rate in the 1980s, when the unemployment rate was 3.7 percent for whites and 10.9 percent for whites).

[24] Joint Appendix, *supra* note 1, at 458.

[25] *Id.* at 458–59.

[26] *See id.* at 475.

[27] Taylor, *supra* note 13.

[28] *Id.*

[29] *Id.*

[30] Second Amended Class Action Complaint, *supra* note 4, at 38.

[31] *See* Joint Appendix, *supra* note 1, at 473.

[32] *Id.* at 457, 601–02.

her cocaine problem on her own, but failed.[33] When asked about her drug use by the medical staff at NAHD, she told them the truth, "I confessed that I was using [cocaine] and I needed help."[34] Having heard that the MUSC had programs that could help pregnant women with substance abuse problems, she asked NAHD for a referral to the MUSC for further treatment.[35] What Ferguson could not have known then is that the referral to MUSC would place her squarely at the center of looming debates about the race, reproductive rights, and the constitutionality of criminalizing poor women for drug use during pregnancy.

PREGNANT WHILE BLACK: THE INTERSECTION OF ANTI-CHOICE POLITICS AND THE WAR ON DRUGS IN THE LIVES OF POOR BLACK WOMEN

In the mid-1980s, two seemingly distinct political and social dynamics intersected, creating the conditions for the criminalization of pregnant women: the war on drugs and the fetal rights movement. In 1986, the war on drugs reached a fevered pitch, as state and federal governments ratcheted up criminal enforcement and penalties for drug possession and distribution—particularly for crack cocaine.[36] For example, President Ronald Reagan won congressional approval of the 1986 Anti-Drug Abuse Act, which notoriously established harsh mandatory minimum sentences, and created a 100:1 disparity between crack and powder cocaine, causing prison populations to rise to unprecedented levels and producing significant racial disparities.[37] At the same time, conservatives advanced efforts to undermine the abortion right guaranteed by *Roe v. Wade* through the recognition of fetal personhood.[38] In 1973, the same year that *Roe* was decided, the Human Life Amendment, a proposed constitutional amendment giving fetuses legal rights, was introduced in Congress.[39] While the amendment ultimately failed, it opened the floodgates for similar legislation at the state level.[40] These two happenings violently collided in the lives of poor black women when the news media began to publish stories about "crack babies," infants exposed to cocaine in utero, thus triggering debates about

---

[33]   *See id.* at 457–59.

[34]   *Id.* at 456.

[35]   *Id.* at 456–57.

[36]   *See, e.g.,* MICHELLE ALEXANDER, THE NEW JIM CROW: MASS INCARCERATION IN THE AGE OF COLORBLINDNESS 51–58 (2012).

[37]   *Id.* at 53.

[38]   *See, e.g.,* Clarke D. Forsythe, *The Blackmun Myth*, NAT'L REV. (Sept. 16, 2009), https://www.nationalreview.com/2009/09/blackmun-myth-clarke-d-forsythe/ (outlining the various attempts by conservative activists to use fetal personhood to undermine *Roe v. Wade*).

[39]   Robert N. Lynch, *The National Committee for a Human Life Amendment, Inc.: Its Goals and Origins*, 20 CATH. LAW. 303, 306 (1974); *see also* H.R.J. Res. 261, 93rd Cong. (1973) ("Neither the United States nor any State shall deprive any human being, from the moment of conception, of life without due process of law; nor deny to any human being, from the moment of conception, within its jurisdiction, the equal protection of the laws.").

[40]   *See* Elizabeth L. Thompson, *The Criminalization of Maternal Conduct During Pregnancy: A Decisionmaking Model for Lawyers*, 64 IND. L. J. 357, 359–62 (1989).

whether and to what extent the state should step in to protect fetuses from the "irresponsible choices" of their mothers.[41]

Initially, little was known about the impact of maternal cocaine use on fetal development. Then, in the mid-1980s, Dr. Ira Chasnoff, a leading neonatologist and president of the National Association for Perinatal Addictions and Research, published studies suggesting that cocaine use during pregnancy was associated with a number of negative fetal outcomes, including stillbirth, low birth weight, irritability, and premature births.[42] Building on this work, Chasnoff went on to publish additional studies finding that 11 percent of the pregnant women at 36 public hospitals tested positive for illicit drugs or alcohol.[43] The study was limited: it examined only a handful of hospitals, reported only exposure to rather than harm caused by substance use, and documented all forms of illicit drugs and alcohol. Nevertheless, news reports extrapolated those findings, focusing only on cocaine, suggesting that if similar patterns existed across the country, approximately 375,000 babies each year would be irreparably harmed by cocaine exposure.[44]

The studies generated a great deal of press, and soon the public was saturated with images of premature, underweight, jittery black babies who could not be consoled by human touch. Breathless news accounts declared that "[t]he inner-city crack epidemic is now giving birth to the newest horror: a bio-underclass, a generation of physically damaged cocaine babies whose biological inferiority is stamped at birth."[45] Stories with alarming headlines such as "A Time Bomb in Cocaine Babies"[46] and "Disaster In Making: Crack Babies Start to Grow Up," declared that cocaine exposed babies were likely to be saddled with lifelong mental and emotional deficits that could lead to criminality and permanent dependency on the welfare system.[47]

Amid the crack baby media frenzy, additional medical studies suggested that symptoms associated with maternal cocaine use were more likely caused by other factors, such as poverty or lack of access to prenatal care. Other studies found that cocaine use during pregnancy did

---

[41]   *See* Jean Davidson, *Pregnant Addicts: Drug Babies Push Issue of Fetal Rights*, L.A. TIMES (Apr. 25, 1989), http://articles.latimes.com/1989-04-25/news/mn-1784_1_ pregnant-addicts-child-abuse-drug-babies-push-issue.

[42]   Ira J. Chasnoff, et al., *Cocaine Use in Pregnancy*, 313 NEW ENG. J. MED. 666, 668–69 (1985); Ira J. Chasnoff, et al., *Temporal Patterns of Cocaine Use in Pregnancy: Perinatal Outcome*, 261 J. AMER. MED. ASS'N 1741, 1742–44 (1989).

[43]   Jane E. Brody, *Widespread Abuse of Drugs by Pregnant Women Is Found*, N.Y. TIMES (Aug. 30, 1988), https://www.nytimes.com/1988/08/30/us/widespread-abuse-of-drugs-by-pregnant-women-is-found.html.

[44]   LAURA E. GÓMEZ, MISCONCEIVING MOTHERS: LEGISLATORS, PROSECUTORS AND THE POLITICS OF PRENATAL DRUG EXPOSURE 22 (1997).

[45]   Charles Krauthammer, *Children of Cocaine*, WASH. POST, July 30, 1989, at C7.

[46]   *See* Courtland Milloy, *A Time Bomb in Cocaine Babies*, WASH. POST (Sept. 17, 1989), https://www.washingtonpost.com/archive/local/1989/09/17/a-time-bomb-in-cocaine-babies/634afdf8-3c4c-499c-9fc8-8a1dbe4058cf/?utm_term=.00bf8d8f52ec.

[47]   *See* Martha Shirk, *Disaster in Making: Crack Babies Start to Grow Up*, ST. LOUIS POST-DISPATCH, Sept. 18, 1990, at A1.

not necessarily lead to fetal harm.[48] Collectively, the literature on the long-term prospects of children who were exposed to cocaine in utero was, at best, unclear.[49] Indeed, Dr. Chasnoff himself condemned the hysterical media coverage of his work as overly simplistic, noting that his comments were taken out of context and his work extended to reach conclusions that were not supported by the data.[50] Nevertheless, the "crack baby" meme continued to spread and, as Laura Gómez notes, "[b]y 1990, at the end of the first generation of medical studies on prenatal cocaine exposure and the peak of news media coverage of 'crack babies,' the American public had a strong conviction that prenatal drug exposure constituted a new and important social problem."[51]

In many ways, the media attention and public response to crack babies was shaped by the perceived culprit: poor black women.[52] Indeed, news reports regarding substance abuse during pregnancy disproportionately focused on black women and cocaine,[53] despite the fact that drug use during pregnancy is extremely low[54] and relatively equivalent across racial groups.[55] As Dorothy Roberts notes, the crack baby narrative traded on "the historical devaluation of black ... mothers." [56] The caricature of the irresponsible and selfish crack mother fit neatly with preexisting stereotypes of black women as "[i]nnately biologically flawed by hypersexuality."[57] As failed and incompetent mothers, black women—not broader structural inequalities produced by discrimination in the realms of housing, employment, education, and health—were blamed for social problems, including negative fetal outcomes.[58] Framed as such, suppression of black motherhood through arrests and criminal prosecution supplanted strategies for addressing the

---

[48]   See, e.g., GEO. WASH. UNIV. CTR. FOR HEALTH POLICY RES., AN ANALYSIS OF RESOURCES TO AID DRUG EXPOSED INFANTS AND THEIR FAMILIES 12–13 (1993).

[49]   See Wendy Chavkin, Cocaine and Pregnancy—Time to Look at the Evidence, 285 J. AMER. MED. ASS'N 1626 (2001); Deborah A. Frank, et al., Growth, Development, and Behavior in Early Childhood Following Prenatal Cocaine Exposure, 285 J. AMER. MED. ASS'N 1613 (2001).

[50]   Telephone Interview with Ira Chasnoff (Jan. 29, 2018).

[51]   GÓMEZ, supra note 44, at 25.

[52]   SHELLY GEHSHAN, S. REGIONAL PROJECT ON INFANT MORTALITY, A STEP TOWARD RECOVERY: IMPROVING ACCESS TO SUBSTANCE ABUSE TREATMENT FOR PREGNANT AND PARENTING WOMEN: RESULTS FROM A REGIONAL STUDY 1 (1993); Leslie Brody, Another Chance: For the Sake of Her Two Children Mother Turns Her Back on Crack, ST. PETERSBURG TIMES, Dec. 23, 1988, at A6.

[53]   See Kristen W. Springer, The Race and Class Privilege of Motherhood: The New York Times Presentations of Pregnant Drug-Using Women, 25 SOC. F. 476, 478–80 (2010).

[54]   Id. at 479.

[55]   Id. at 490.

[56]   Dorothy E. Roberts, Punishing Drug Addicts Who Have Babies: Women of Color, Equality, and the Right of Privacy, 104 HARV. L. REV. 1419, 1423 (1991).

[57]   RICKIE SOLINGER, WAKE UP LITTLE SUSIE: SINGLE PREGNANCY AND RACE BEFORE ROE V. WADE 43 (1992).

[58]   See Patricia Hill Collins, Black Women and Motherhood, in MOTHERHOOD AND SPACE 149 (Sarah Hardy & Caroline Wiedmer eds., 2005); Roberts, supra note 56, at 1436.

broader structural dynamics that limited the life chances of black women and their children.[59]

In the wake of hyperbolic accounts of crack babies, the criminal justice system emerged as a potent tool to regulate black motherhood, as prosecutors began to disproportionately charge black women for drug use during pregnancy. Prosecutors alleged that women who used drugs during pregnancy harmed fetal life, and therefore state intervention was necessary to protect fetal rights.[60] Prosecutors charged women with crimes ranging from child abuse to second-degree murder under the dubious theory that the terms "child" or "person" as used in penal codes extended to fetuses.[61] In spite of the weakness of the legal authority for such an interpretation,[62] prosecutors in twenty-four states used the fetal health rationale to justify the arrest and prosecution of approximately two hundred women, more than half of whom were black, for drug use during pregnancy.[63] South Carolina, however, accounted for an outsized number of arrests, as prosecutors partnered with the staff at MUSC to drug test and arrest pregnant women.[64] Indeed, by the end of the 1980s, MUSC was ground zero for the criminalization of pregnant women.

THE BIRTH OF THE INTERAGENCY POLICY AT MUSC

In 1988, Nurse Shirley Brown, the head case manager at the MUSC obstetrics clinic, was increasingly concerned about cocaine use among pregnant women who received care at the clinic. Nurse Brown had read news accounts of "crack babies" and studies suggesting that cocaine increased the risk of negative fetal outcomes.[65] Brown increasingly observed newborns in the obstetrics clinic manifesting symptoms associated with in utero cocaine exposure.[66] She wanted to do something about it. Although there were rumors among staff that she looked down upon the "mixing of the races"[67] and believed that "cocaine was a problem in the Black community and something should be put in the water to sterilize these women,"[68] Brown obtained the support of her supervisor

---

[59]   See, e.g., Roberts, *supra* note 56, at 1436–44.

[60]   See Lynn M. Paltrow & Jeanne Flavin, *Arrests of and Forced Interventions on Pregnant Women in the United States, 1973–2005: Implications for Women's Legal Status and Public Health*, 38 J. HEALTH POL. POL'Y & L. 299, 322 (2013).

[61]   GOMEZ, *supra* note 44, at 63–64.

[62]   See Paltrow & Flavin, *supra* note 60, at 299–301.

[63]   *Id.* at 309–10, 315–17; *see also* Lisa C. Ikemoto, *The Code of the Perfect Pregnancy: At the Intersection of the Ideology of the Ideology of Motherhood, the Practice of Defaulting Science, and the Interventionist Mindset of the Law*, 53 OHIO ST. L.J. 1205, 1268 (1992).

[64]   See LYNN M. PALTROW, REPROD. FREEDOM PROJECT, CRIMINAL PROSECUTIONS AGAINST PREGNANT WOMEN: NATIONAL UPDATE AND OVERVIEW 3 (1992) (finding that "[a] disproportionate number of these cases come from just two states, Florida and South Carolina, and are concentrated in two counties in each of those states").

[65]   Joint Appendix, *supra* note 1, at 155; Siegel, *supra* note 2.

[66]   Siegel, *supra* note 2.

[67]   Taylor, *supra* note 13.

[68]   Letter from Wyndi Anderson, Director, S.C. Advocs. for Pregnant Women, to Kwesi Mfume, President & CEO, NAACP (Jan. 30, 2000) (on file with author); *see also* Joint Appendix, *supra* note 1, at 1192–93.

for a collaboration with local law enforcement after hearing a radio program describing Charleston County Solicitor Charles Condon's efforts to prosecute pregnant drug users.[69]

Charles Condon, a 41-year-old white man, was an ambitious politician and an aggressive prosecutor. At the time, Condon was running as a Republican for state Attorney General,[70] touting his tough on crime record and highlighting his bona fides as an anti-abortion advocate.[71] When representatives from MUSC contacted Condon, he quickly convened a meeting regarding an "Interagency Policy on cocaine abuse during pregnancy."[72] Meeting attendees, including representatives from the hospital and local law enforcement agencies, discussed a policy that would facilitate the arrest and prosecution of women who used cocaine during pregnancy.[73] Attendees agreed that pregnant women would be prosecuted for cocaine use on the theory that the words "child" as used in the state's child neglect statute[74] and "person" in state law punishing the delivery of drugs to a person under eighteen years of age[75] included fetal life, notwithstanding the fact that no state court had ever interpreted those statutes in such a manner.[76] Pursuant to the Interagency Policy, patients were to be tested for cocaine use at the discretion of medical staff when they met certain criteria established by members of the Interagency team.[77] Police were to be informed of any positive results.[78] According to Condon, the Interagency Policy was necessary because the women could not be trusted to do what was best for themselves or their children, asserting that "unless you have sanctions in place, unless you understand the basic irresponsibility of these drug-addicted women, it won't work."[79] The policy did not, however, require the hospital to obtain the consent of patients prior to conducting the drug test for law enforcement purposes.

---

[69]   Joint Appendix, *supra* note 1, at 73–74; *see also* Edgar O. Horger III, et al., *Cocaine in Pregnancy: Confronting the Crisis*, 86 J.S.C. MED. ASS'N 527, 530 (1990).

[70]   Siegel, *supra* note 2.

[71]   Rick Bragg, *Defender of God, South and Unborn*, N.Y. TIMES, (Jan. 13, 1998), https://www.nytimes.com/1998/01/13/us/defender-of-god-south-and-unborn.html.

[72]   Second Amended Class Action Complaint, *supra* note 4, at 11.

[73]   *Id.*

[74]   S.C. CODE 1976 § 63–5–70 (West 2008).

[75]   *Id.* § 44–53–440 (West 2008).

[76]   MacDougall, *supra* note 8 (noting that South Carolina lower courts had ruled that fetuses were not "children" under state law and the question of whether a fetus was a "person" under state law was unresolved).

[77]   According to the policy, drug tests could be ordered at the discretion of medical staff if one of the following nine criteria were met: no prenatal care; late prenatal care; incomplete prenatal care; abruptio placentae; intrauterine fetal death; preterm labor; intrauterine growth retardation; previously known drug or alcohol abuse; congenital abnormalities). *See* Joint Appendix, *supra* note 1, at 1309.

[78]   Ferguson v. City of Charleston, 121 S. Ct. 1281, 1285 (2001).

[79]   Charles Condon, *Clinton's Cocaine Babies*, HOOVER INSTITUTION (April 1, 1995), https://www.hoover.org/research/clintons-cocaine-babies.

The initial policy took a zero-tolerance approach: if a urine drug screen returned positive, women were to be immediately arrested.[80] The policy was later amended to include an "amnesty provision" that enabled women to receive counseling and an opportunity to avoid arrest if they went to an in-patient drug treatment program.[81] All parties agreed that the involvement of law enforcement and the threat of arrest "provided the necessary 'leverage' to make the [treatment p]olicy effective."[82]

The Interagency Policy, however, only applied to maternal cocaine use. Although Condon was aware that maternal alcohol and tobacco use also represented a threat to fetal health, he chose not to prosecute women for using those substances while pregnant.[83] Prosecuting poor black crack cocaine users came with no political cost; indeed, Condon surmised that he could gain politically by targeting black "crack mothers" while simultaneously burnishing his credentials as an anti-abortion politician:

> [T]here's not enough political will to move after pregnant women who use alcohol or cigarettes. There is, though, a political basis for this interagency program. Leaders can take a position against crack. Our legal system reflects our cultural mores. That's our system. That's the real world. . . .[84]

OBJECTIONS TO THE INTERAGENCY POLICY FROM A LEADING NEONATOLOGIST

After the Interagency Policy was drafted, Condon sent a copy to Chasnoff to tout what Charleston was doing about maternal cocaine abuse.[85] "I was absolutely horrified," Chasnoff would later remark.[86] Chasnoff shared several concerns about the policy with Condon. First, Chasnoff explained that the policy was "loaded with racial bias."[87] Second, Chasnoff noted the screening criteria adopted by the Interagency Taskforce, particularly those related to prenatal care and stillbirth, were more indicative of the endemic poverty confronted by black women in Charleston than cocaine use.[88] Lastly, Chasnoff argued that punishing women for drug use during pregnancy was counterproductive.[89] He

---

[80] *Id.*

[81] Joint Appendix, *supra* note 1, at 1308.

[82] Brief of Respondents, Ferguson v. City of Charleston, 532 U.S. 67 (2001) (No. 99-936), 2000 WL 1341474, at *8.

[83] Joint Appendix, *supra* note 1, at 300–02; Siegel, *supra* note 2.

[84] Siegel, *supra* note 2.

[85] Joint Appendix, *supra* note 1, at 280–82; Telephone Interview with Ira Chasnoff, *supra* note 50.

[86] Telephone Interview with Ira Chasnoff, *supra* note 50.

[87] *Id.*

[88] *Id.; see also* David C. Lewis, et al., Open Letter to Media, *Physicians, Scientists to Media: Stop Using the Term "Crack Baby"*, (Feb. 25, 2004), *available at* http://www.come-over.to/FAS/CrackBabyTerm.htm.

[89] Telephone Interview with Ira Chasnoff, *supra* note 50.

argued that the threat of criminal punishment would scare women away from the prenatal care they need to ensure healthy pregnancies.[90]

Notwithstanding Chasnoff's admonitions, Condon chose to push forward with the Interagency Policy rather than direct resources toward treatment. Indeed, others involved in the creation and implementation of the policy, including Charleston Police Chief Greenberg, publicly opposed the construction of a drug treatment facility that could accommodate pregnant women and their children in Charleston.[91]

THE IMPLEMENTATION OF THE INTERAGENCY POLICY

The Interagency Policy went into effect in October 1989 and, although it formally applied to the entire hospital, as a practical matter it was enforced exclusively against indigent women who received care through the obstetrics clinic.[92] Between 1989 and 1994, approximately 200 women tested positive for cocaine use during pregnancy and 30 were subject to arrest.[93] Women like Sandra Powell were taken out of the hospital in handcuffs while bleeding from vaginal deliveries or just after cesarean surgery.[94] Women like Theresa Joseph were pressured into being sterilized by MUSC staff.[95] One woman, Lori Griffin, was held in a local jail for three weeks after testing positive during a prenatal visit, with little access to adequate care and nutrition while incarcerated.[96] As Chasnoff predicted, the policy had a racially disparate effect, as black women constituted 90 percent of the women who tested positive for cocaine and 29 of the 30 women arrested under the policy.[97] Crystal Ferguson was one of those women.

On August 4, 1991, Ferguson was admitted to MUSC and delivered a healthy baby girl via cesarean section. She named her Annika, a derivative of the Hebrew word for "grace."[98] Little grace, however, was extended to Ferguson when her drug screen was positive for cocaine for the second time in a test conducted pursuant to the Interagency Policy. One doctor told her that Annika "would never be an A student."[99] Another doctor called her "no good" and suggested that, instead of having Annika, she should have had her "tubes tied."[100] Ferguson was scared; she did not

---

90   *Id.*

91   *See* Siegel, *supra* note 2.

92   Brief for Petitioners, Ferguson v. City of Charleston, 532 U.S. 67 (2001) (No. 99-936), 2000 WL 728149, at *12–13.

93   *Id.*

94   *Id.* at *8, *10–11.

95   *Id.* at *13, n.10.

96   *Id.* at *7.

97   *See id.* at *12–13.

98   *See* TERESEA NORMAN, WORLD OF BABY NAMES loc. 2076 (2003) (ebook). Ferguson's daughter's full name was Virginia Daisy Annika Ferguson. *See Crystal Ferguson Obituary*, POST & COURIER, http://www.legacy.com/obituaries/charleston/obituary.aspx?n=crystal-ferguson&pid=88684787 (last visited Dec. 9, 2018).

99   Taylor, *supra* note 13.

100 *Id.*

want to go to jail and she did not want lose her child. To avoid both, Ferguson found an outpatient center where she could undergo treatment.[101]

Although Ferguson agreed to go to treatment, her case was nevertheless forwarded to the County Solicitor's office for further action. Approximately eight days after her release from the hospital and mere hours before she was scheduled to start her first day of outpatient treatment, Ferguson was arrested and charged with "knowingly, willfully and unlawfully consuming" cocaine and "endanger[ing] the life, health and welfare of her unborn child."[102] She faced ten years in prison for her first criminal offense.[103] Following her arrest, she sat in a small, filthy jail cell for approximately 11 hours before being released on bail.[104]

FIGHTING BACK: CHALLENGING THE INTERAGENCY POLICY

Lynn Paltrow first got word about the arrests at MUSC while attending a conference in Florida. Two social workers told Paltrow that there was a "horrible white nurse who is targeting black pregnant patients, you have to do something about it."[105] At the time, Paltrow, a then-31-year-old white woman, was a staff attorney at the Center for Reproductive Rights and Policy in New York.[106] Although she began her career litigating for abortion rights, she had spent a number of years challenging the criminalization of women for behavior during pregnancy. She began litigating cases on behalf of pregnant women after becoming disillusioned with the mainstream reproductive rights movement's focus on choice, abortion, and contraception. In her estimation, the mainstream reproductive rights choice-based agenda was largely organized around the experiences of white, middle-class women, a perspective which obscured the structural constraints placed upon marginalized women's ability to make meaningful reproductive decisions.[107] Moreover, she knew from defending against "virtually all of the most critical early prosecutions of pregnant substance abusers"[108] that pregnancy—or the right to procreate—was as much a site of government control of women's bodies as abortion, particularly for poor black women whose reproduction has long been viewed as a social problem in need of correction rather than

---

[101] *Id.*

[102] Second Amended Class Action Complaint, *supra* note 4, at 42–43.

[103] Joint Appendix, *supra* note 1, at 465–66. Ferguson was charged with distributing drugs to a person under the age of eighteen, a felony which carries a maximum penalty of ten years of imprisonment. *See* S.C. CODE 1976 § 44–53–440 (West 2008).

[104] Joint Appendix, *supra* note 1, at 464–65.

[105] Telephone Interview with Lynn Paltrow, *supra* note 12.

[106] *Id.*

[107] *See* Lynn M. Paltrow, *The War on Drugs and the War on Abortion: Some Initial Thoughts on the Connections, Intersections and Effects*, 28 S.U. L. REV. 201, 227–30 (2001).

[108] Siegel, *supra* note 2.

a human right to be protected.[109] When she looked into the allegations at MUSC, it was clear that this is precisely what was happening: the childbearing of poor black women was deemed a social problem which the state sought to restrict through criminal punishment.

Given the important interests at stake and the vulnerable women targeted by the policy, Paltrow decided to pursue a legal challenge.[110] In order to do so, however, she needed plaintiffs. Eventually, she received a call from Ted Phillips, a defense attorney based out of Charleston; Phillips indicated that two of his clients, Crystal Ferguson and Theresa Joseph, wanted to pursue legal action against the hospital.[111] Paltrow quickly jumped into action, securing the assistance of local attorney Susan Dunn.[112] Together, they successfully challenged the charges against Ferguson and Joseph.[113] Soon thereafter, eight other women, all but one of whom were black, agreed to join the lawsuit.[114]

THE COMPLAINT: CENTERING RACE AND PRIVACY

Having identified plaintiffs, Paltrow next had to frame the legal injury caused by the Interagency Policy. This was no easy task. The women targeted by law enforcement were poor, black, and drug users. Moreover, the women were not being punished because they sought to terminate a pregnancy, but rather because they chose to carry their pregnancies to term.[115] As such, the issues confronting her clients did not neatly square with existing constitutional or statutory law or the dominant advocacy strategies centered on abortion.[116] Instead, Paltrow

---

[109] Lynn Paltrow, Keynote Speech at the University of Washington School of Law Gates Public Service Law Speaker Series, Why I stopped defending abortion and started defending pregnant women (Mar. 7, 2011) *available at* https://www.law.washington.edu/multimedia/2011/gpsllynnpaltrow/transcript.pdf.

[110] Paltrow also filed complaints with the Civil Rights Division of the United States Department of Health and Human Services, alleging racial discrimination. *See* Philip J. Hilts, *Hospital Put on Probation Over Tests on Poor Women*, N.Y. TIMES (Oct. 5, 1994), https://www.nytimes.com/1994/10/05/us/hospital-put-on-probation-over-tests-on-poor-women.html. Based on a paper published by Edgar Horger and Nurse Brown, Paltrow also filed a complaint with National Institute of Health, alleging that the hospital was engaging in a social experiment regarding the effect of the threat of arrest of pregnant drug users. National Institute for Health agreed and threatened to withdraw federal funding. While the lawsuit was pending, MUSC agreed to terminate the program in exchange for the preservation of its federal grants. Telephone Interview with Lynn Paltrow, *supra* note 12.

[111] Telephone Interview with Lynn Paltrow, Executive Director, Nat'l Advocates for Pregnant Women (Sept. 27, 2017); Press Release, Nat'l Advocates for Pregnant Women, Some Reflections on An American Hero: Ted Phillips (Feb. 2005) (on file with author).

[112] Telephone Interview with Lynn Paltrow, *supra* note 12.

[113] *See* MacDougall, *supra* note 8; Telephone Interview with Lynn Paltrow, *supra* note 12.

[114] Telephone Interview with Lynn Paltrow, *supra* note 111.

[115] *Id.*

[116] *See* Kimberlé Crenshaw, *Demarginalizing the Intersection of Race and Sex: A Black Feminist Critique of Antidiscrimination Doctrine, Feminist Theory and Antiracist Politics*, 1989 U. CHI. LEGAL F. 139, 150–52 (1989) (discussing how a single-issue framework further marginalizes those who are unable to fit neatly within that framework).

would need to craft a set of legal claims as intersectional as the harms experienced by Ferguson and others.

The Right to Procreate

For Paltrow, at bottom, the case involved the right to procreate and parent, a right that was largely underdeveloped in constitutional jurisprudence.[117] In particular, she argued that these cases invoked "the constitutional right to privacy that guarantees all women, even those with addiction problems, the right to decide, without coercion, whether or not to have a child."[118] Given the dearth of precedent on the rights of pregnant women, mainstream feminists and reproductive rights advocates often framed the issue of state intervention during a pregnancy as conflict between fetal and maternal rights.[119] Relying on the Court's rejection of fetal personhood in *Roe v. Wade*,[120] advocates argued that fetuses do not have rights independent of their mothers. As such, they argued, state efforts to regulate maternal behavior in order to protect independent fetal rights were unconstitutional, as they undermined women's constitutionally protected right to bodily integrity and reproductive autonomy.[121] In addition, advocates often cited the Supreme Court's decision in *Cleveland Board of Education v. LaFleur*,[122] striking down a mandatory leave policy for pregnant teachers, for the principle that if "the state may not force a woman to bear a child against her will, it may not act to penalize her for deciding to bear a child."[123] In her first opportunity to litigate the scope of the right to procreate in federal court, Paltrow drew upon these arguments, alleging that "by adopting, implementing and maintaining the Interagency Policy, [the defendants] have infringed on plaintiffs right to make reproductive choices by punishing birth by women with substance abuse problems."[124]

The Right to Equal Protection of the Laws

While state efforts to burden women's right to procreate was at the core of the claim against MUSC and the City of Charleston, Paltrow recognized that anti-black bias animated the punitive response to maternal drug use. Indeed, as Dorothy Roberts has observed, black

---

[117] At the time Paltrow was developing the complaint, the Supreme Court had decided a few cases regarding the substantive right to procreate. *See, e.g.*, Skinner v. Oklahoma, 316 U.S. 535 (1942); Cleveland School Board v. LaFleur, 414 U.S. 632 (1974).

[118] Lynn M. Paltrow, *Winning Strategies: Defending the Rights of Pregnant Women*, 17 CHAMPION 19, 20 (1993).

[119] See Janet Gallagher, *Prenatal Invasions & Interventions: What's Wrong with Fetal Rights*, 10 HARV. WOMEN'S L.J. 9, 12–14 (1987); *Maternal Rights and Fetal Wrongs: The Case Against the Criminalization of "Fetal Abuse"*, 101 HARV. L. REV. 994, 997–98 (1988).

[120] Roe v. Wade, 410 U.S. 113, 162 (1973) ("In short, the unborn have never been recognized in the law as persons in the whole sense.").

[121] *See, e.g.*, Paltrow, *Winning Strategies, supra* note 118.

[122] 414 U.S. 632 (1976).

[123] *See, e.g.*, Dawn E. Johnson, *The Creation of Fetal Rights: Conflicts with Women's Constitutional Rights to Liberty, Privacy and Equal Protection*, 95 YALE L.J. 599, 618 (1986).

[124] Second Amended Class Action Complaint, *supra* note 4, at 82.

women are disproportionately "punished because the combination of their poverty, race, and drug addiction is seen to make them unworthy of procreating."[125] In order to address the race and class dynamics at the heart of the punitive response to maternal drug use, the complaint echoed Roberts' call to develop a "constitutional theory that acknowledges the complementary and overlapping qualities of the Constitution's guarantees of equality and privacy."[126] Although it would be difficult to establish that intentional discrimination motivated the development of the Interagency Policy as required by the Supreme Court in *Washington v. Davis*,[127] Paltrow alleged in the complaint that the plaintiffs were subject to discrimination in violation of the Fourteenth Amendment.[128] In particular, the complaint alleged that while the Interagency Policy was facially neutral, it was in fact undergirded by racial animus toward black women. Paltrow also alleged that the policy disproportionately impacted black women in violation of Title VI of the Civil Rights Act of 1964.[129]

The Right to (Informational) Privacy

Lastly, Paltrow was attentive to the ways in which the abrogation of her clients' decisional privacy—the choice to procreate—was facilitated by the assault on their informational privacy—the ability to keep personal information out of the hands of the government.[130] Indeed, state actors have long used black women's private information as a means to undermine their substantive rights. For example, state welfare programs routinely condition the receipt of state aid on the waiver of privacy rights within the home and with regard to personal information.[131] Such private information, once obtained, often serves as the basis for a host of punitive state interventions that impact black women's decisional rights, such as the initiation of child removal proceedings by social service agencies, which could result in the termination of parental rights.[132] Similarly, in the case of Crystal Ferguson, her arrest, and subsequent loss of liberty, would not have been possible without the pervasive forms of surveillance, testing and reporting conducted by MUSC staff in concert with police and prosecutors. Given this dynamic, Paltrow contested the violation of Ferguson's right to informational privacy, alleging that the Interagency Policy "subjected plaintiffs to drug testing without consent and without a valid search warrant, and subjected them to criminal prosecution and the

---

[125] Roberts, *supra* note 56, at 1472.

[126] *Id.* at 1471.

[127] 426 U.S. 229 (1976).

[128] *See* Deborah J. Krauss, *Regulating Women's Bodies: The Adverse Effect of Fetal Rights Theory on Childbirth Decisions and Women of Color*, 26 HARV. C.R.-C.L. L. REV. 523, 545–46 (1991).

[129] Second Amended Class Action Complaint, *supra* note 4, at 86.

[130] *Id.* at 82–84.

[131] *See, e.g.*, KHIARA M. BRIDGES, REPRODUCING RACE: AN ETHNOGRAPHY OF PREGNANCY AS A SITE OF RACIALIZATION 41–44 (2011); Kaaryn Gustafson, *The Criminalization of Poverty*, 99 J. CRIM. L. & CRIMINOLOGY 643, 697–98 (2009).

[132] *See, e.g.*, DOROTHY ROBERTS, SHATTERED BONDS: THE COLOR OF CHILD WELFARE 38–40 (2001).

threat of criminal prosecution based on drug tests performed on plaintiffs" in violation of the Fourth Amendment. Importantly, in pressing this Fourth Amendment claim, Paltrow acknowledged the ways in which emergent patters of racial profiling and criminalization were used to undermine black women's reproductive autonomy.

THE TRIAL

On October 5, 1993, Paltrow filed an 87-page complaint summarizing the legal injuries experienced by Ferguson and others with the United States District Court for the District of South Carolina.[133] The case was assigned to U.S. District Judge C. Weston Houck, a judge who famously ruled in *Faulkner v. Jones* that the Citadel, the Military Academy of South Carolina, unconstitutionally barred enrollment of largely white female candidates in violation of the Fourteenth Amendment's equal protection clause.[134] Paltrow was initially hopeful that, given his decision in *Faulkner*, Judge Houck would be receptive to the plaintiffs' framing of reproductive privacy and anti-discrimination law. Such hopes, however, were quickly dashed when Judge Houck refused to issue a preliminary injunction to halt the operation of the Interagency Policy, instead finding that halting the program would cause irreparable harm to fetal life.[135] With this ruling, the plaintiffs were quickly confronted the reality of a federal judiciary hostile to claims-making by black women, particularly in the realms of reproductive rights and anti-discrimination.

In a series of rulings, Judge Houck dismissed the plaintiffs' procreation and Title VI claims, narrowly applying Supreme Court doctrine. First, Houck rejected the notion that the drug testing and arrest protocol burdened the plaintiffs' right to procreation by punishing them for choosing to carry a pregnancy to term despite a drug addiction.[136] "I just don't see it," Judge Houck remarked, "no one was nor does the record reflect that anyone was threatened with sterilization or arrest."[137] In reaching this conclusion, Houck dramatically limited to the right to procreate to instances where the state intervention physically prevents procreation, essentially rendering the right to procreate a nullity except in the case of forced sterilization.

In a separate written order, Houck dismissed the plaintiffs' Title VI claim, finding that the plaintiffs did not demonstrate that "a facially neutral practice has a disproportionate adverse effect on a group protected by Title VI."[138] Instead, Judge Houck concluded that "[n]one of

---

[133] Second Amended Class Action Complaint, *supra* note 4.

[134] Faulkner v. Jones, 858 F. Supp. 552, 566 (D.S.C. 1994); *see also* Schuyler Kropf, *Federal Judge Charles Weston Houck dies; opened door for women* in The Citadel, POST & COURIER (July 19, 2017), https://www.postandcourier.com/news/federal-judge-charles-weston-houck-dies-opened-door-for-women/article_fb9a0f28-6ccd-11e7-9c85-a714033ecdf4.html.

[135] Siegel, *supra* note 2.

[136] *See* Joint Appendix, *supra* note 1, at 1414–15.

[137] *Id.* at 1366, 1396.

[138] Ferguson v. City of Charleston, 186 F.3d 469, 480, 482 (4th Cir. 1999).

the challenged practices, procedures, or courses of action of the defendants have an adverse discriminatory effect on the plaintiffs."[139] Paltrow was shocked by the ruling. "We thought [the race discrimination claim] was a slam dunk based on disproportionate impact. The judge's decision demonstrated to me how unlikely it is to get justice under the existing legal structure, particularly for black women."[140] Indeed, the plaintiffs did not fare much better with the jury.

From November 20, 1996 through December 19, 1996, nearly seven years after the development of the Interagency Policy, the plaintiffs presented their remaining Fourth and Fourteenth Amendment claims to the jury. Paltrow and her legal team presented testimony from Ferguson and other women regarding the degrading experiences at MUSC and the fact that they did not consent to drug testing for law enforcement purposes.[141] The jury heard from expert witnesses such as Ira Chasnoff, who testified that the policy was ineffective and the criteria for urine testing did not make sense from a medical perspective.[142] Expert witnesses were called to explain how the policy targeted black women. The plaintiffs also elicited testimony from Nurse Brown confirming her disdain for interracial relationships and her belief that cocaine abusing black women should be sterilized.[143]

The largely white jury, however, rejected the plaintiffs' evidence, instead finding that the policy did not violate either the Fourth or the Fourteenth Amendment.[144]

THE APPEAL

Ferguson vowed to continue her fight for justice, appealing the jury's verdict to the United States Court of Appeals for the Fourth Circuit. Priscilla Smith, an experienced appellate attorney with the Center for Reproductive Rights, took over the case on appeal while Paltrow assisted with the amicus strategy.[145] Although relatively new to the case, Smith faced a similar quandary: how to articulate the harm inflicted upon her black women clients given existing constitutional law regarding anti-discrimination and reproductive autonomy? After reviewing the trial record, and noting the difficulties with presenting robust procreation and equal protection claims, Smith decided to focus the appeal on the Fourth Amendment and Title VI violations.[146]

The Fourth Circuit, however, did not address the issue of whether the plaintiffs consented to drug testing at MUSC for law enforcement

---

[139] Joint Appendix, *supra* note 1, at 1413.

[140] Telephone Interview with Lynn Paltrow, *supra* note 12.

[141] *See generally* Joint Appendix, *supra* note 1.

[142] *See id.* at 281, 285–86.

[143] *Id.* at 209; *see also id.* at 1192–93.

[144] *Id.* at 1320–21.

[145] Telephone Interview with Lynn Paltrow, *supra* note 12; Telephone Interview with Priscilla Smith (Nov. 15, 2017).

[146] Telephone Interview with Priscilla Smith, *supra* note 145.

purposes, instead finding that the searches constituted a "special need" that does not require a warrant or individualized suspicion.[147] Under the "special need" doctrine, "where a Fourth Amendment intrusion serves special governmental needs, beyond the normal need for law enforcement, it is necessary to balance the individual's privacy expectations against the Government's interests to determine whether it is impractical to require a warrant or some level of individualized suspicion in the particular context."[148] Applying this test, the panel found that even if the drug testing was not authorized by a warrant or patient consent, maternal drug use "created a special need beyond normal law enforcement goals" that excused the failure to comply with the traditional demands of the Fourth Amendment.[149] The Fourth Circuit also rejected Ferguson's Title VI racial discrimination claim.[150]

PETITIONING THE UNITED STATES
SUPREME COURT FOR REVIEW

Concerned that the Fourth Circuit's decision would result in the proliferation of punitive drug testing programs, more arrests, and further threats to women's reproductive autonomy, the plaintiffs sought review of the Fourth Circuit's application of the "special needs" warrant exception by the Supreme Court.[151] Although race was at the center of the development and implementation of the drug testing program, Smith ultimately decided to forego review of the race discrimination claims, because the legal team feared antagonizing the justices given the Court's overall hostility to racial discrimination claims.[152] Ultimately, the Supreme Court granted review of the Fourth Circuit's application of the "special needs" exception and oral argument was set for October 4, 2000.[153]

FERGUSON V. CITY OF CHARLESTON
BEFORE THE SUPREME COURT

On the morning of oral argument, Priscilla Smith was nervous. She had several appellate oral arguments under her belt, but this was her first before the Supreme Court.[154] She was also aware that Crystal Ferguson and the other plaintiffs were watching her. She wanted to make them proud. She confidently began her argument, asserting that:

> This case involves pregnant women who sought medical care at
> a public hospital and who then were searched by their doctors
> for evidence of crimes and arrested, seven of them right out of

---

[147] Ferguson v. City of Charleston, 186 F.3d 469, 479 (4th Cir. 1999).

[148] *Id.* at 486 (quoting Nat'l Treasury Emp. Union v. Von Raab, 489 U.S. 656, 665–66 (1989)) (emphasis omitted).

[149] *Id.* at 479.

[150] Ferguson v. City of Charleston, 186 F.3d 469, 482 (4th Cir. 1999).

[151] Telephone Interview with Priscilla Smith, *supra* note 145.

[152] *Id.*

[153] Ferguson v. City of Charleston, 532 U.S. 67, 67 (2001).

[154] Telephone Interview with Priscilla Smith, *supra* note 145.

their hospital beds. The special needs exception does not apply
to this case to excuse the lack of warrants . . . .[155]

The Justices quickly interjected, posing questions about the precise
nature of the urine testing protocol and its relationship to overall law
enforcement objectives.[156]

In their briefs, the plaintiffs attempted to frame the question of
privacy around race, contending that a finding that the testing protocol
constituted a special need could result in greater state regulation of
women's bodies, thus undermining the substantive rights to bodily
integrity and reproductive autonomy, with racially disparate results.[157]
The Court, however, seemed disinterested in such arguments, as the
Justices made no mention of race or reproductive autonomy during the
oral argument. Rather, the Justices focused their attention on the extent
of law enforcement involvement in the development and implementation
of the Interagency Policy, the medical basis for the testing criteria and
whether the threat of arrest actually advanced fetal interests,
particularly after a birth.[158] For example, Justice O'Connor focused on
whether the drug testing was conducted as a routine matter or whether
it was based on a discretionary set of criteria,[159] while Justices Kennedy
and Souter's questions examined whether the hospital could disclose to
third parties information about drug use that was discovered as part of
basic medical care.[160]

On March 21, 2001, the Court ruled in favor of Ferguson in a 6–3
decision.[161] The majority opinion, written by Justice Stevens, began by
carefully describing the facts of the case. The Court did not, however,
mention the race of the petitioners, signaling the colorblind Fourth
Amendment analysis the Court would employ as it struck down MUSC's
drug testing program.

In rejecting the "special needs" doctrine, the Court found that the
women's privacy interests outweighed whatever special needs
purportedly justified the drug testing program. In particular, the Court
found that the intrusion into the women's privacy was far more
significant than the minimal intrusions in prior special needs cases,
which "fit within the closely guarded category of constitutionally
permissible suspicionless searches."[162] Citing an amicus brief by the
American Medical Association, the Court noted that "[t]he reasonable
expectation of privacy enjoyed by the typical patient undergoing

---

[155] Transcript of Oral Argument, Ferguson v. City of Charleston, 532 U.S. 67 (2001)
(No. 99-936), 2000 WL 1513143, at *3.

[156] *Id.*

[157] Telephone Interview with Priscilla Smith, *supra* note 145.

[158] *See generally* Transcript of Oral Argument, *supra* note 155.

[159] *Id.* at *5.

[160] *See id.* at *46–52.

[161] Ferguson v. City of Charleston, 532 U.S. 67, 86 (2001).

[162] *Id.* at 77.

diagnostic tests in a hospital is that the results of those tests will not be shared with nonmedical personnel without her consent."[163]

The Court noted that the Interagency Policy focused almost entirely on utilizing criminal prosecution as a cudgel to get women into treatment, as Charleston prosecutors and police were deeply involved in day-to-day administration of the policy.[164] Thus, the Court concluded that even if the ultimate goal of the policy was to get women who tested positive into substance abuse treatment in order to protect fetal life, "the immediate objective of the searches was to generate evidence for law enforcement purposes in order to reach that goal."[165] According to the Court, "[t]his fact distinguishes this case from circumstances in which physicians or psychologists, in the course of ordinary medical procedures aimed at helping the patient herself, come across information that under rules of law or ethics is subject to reporting requirements . . ."[166] The Court found such approach inconsistent with its Fourth Amendment jurisprudence and thus ruled that Interagency Protocol did not constitute a "special need."

Justice Kennedy filed a separate opinion concurring in the judgment, surprising Smith given his ambivalence toward abortion rights.[167] While Justice Kennedy agreed that the drug testing program was not justified by a special need, he wrote separately to emphasize the state's interest in protecting fetal health, which may be vindicated through penalties up to and including criminal punishment.[168] In other words, Kennedy seemingly endorsed the punitive approach undertaken by South Carolina even as he opposed the way in which it was carried out. Indeed, Kennedy emphasized the state's interest in fetal rights as he concluded his concurring opinion: "[t]here should be no doubt that South Carolina can impose punishment upon an expectant mother who has so little regard for her own unborn that she risks causing him or her lifelong damage or suffering."[169]

Justice Scalia, for his part, dissented from the judgment of the Court. Joined by Chief Justice Rehnquist and Justice Thomas, Scalia argued the drug testing program employed by MUSC did not violate the Fourth Amendment's ban on unreasonable search and seizure because the plaintiffs voluntarily gave MUSC urine samples as part of routine medical care.[170] That the women did not consent to the test for law enforcement purposes nor approve of the disclosure of their private medical information was irrelevant. Even if the drug test was a search,

---

[163] *Id.* at 78.

[164] *Id.* at 82–83.

[165] *Id.* at 83 (emphasis omitted).

[166] *Id.* at 80–81.

[167] Telephone Interview with Priscilla Smith, *supra* note 145.

[168] Ferguson v. City of Charleston, 532 U.S. 67, 88 (2001) (Kennedy, J., concurring).

[169] *Id.* at 89–90.

[170] *Id.* at 94–95 (Scalia, J., dissenting).

Scalia further concluded that the search would be justified by special needs independent of general law enforcement.[171]

FERGUSON'S LEGACY

In the immediate aftermath of the Supreme Court decision in favor of the plaintiffs, Lynn Paltrow and Priscilla Smith hailed it as a victory for all pregnant women. In comments to the *New York Times*, Paltrow described *Ferguson* as "a victory for all patients who are entitled to expect that when they go to the doctor they will receive medical care and not a search for police purposes."[172] Smith asserted that the Court's ruling would "stop an erosion of the privacy rights of pregnant women by recognizing that concern for the fetus doesn't override pregnant women's rights."[173] Their initial optimism about the effect of *Ferguson* was seemingly well-founded, as federal appellate courts relied on it to strike down programs that required welfare recipients to submit to drug tests or searches.[174]

The initial optimism of Paltrow and Smith faded, however, as similar accounts of pregnant women subject to arrest and prosecution multiplied. Thus, it became increasingly clear, as Linda Greenhouse presciently noted in her reporting on *Ferguson*, that the Court's decision "cannot provide an answer to the deeper questions raised by what happened in Charleston and what is happening in various contexts across the country."[175] Indeed, while *Ferguson* found that the hospital's testing of expectant mothers for drug use for law enforcement purposes violated the Fourth Amendment, the decision left significant room for the continued use of drug testing and criminal punishment of pregnant women because it did not place any substantive limits on the state's ability to criminalize pregnant women. Rather, the Court only held that the drug testing of pregnant women may not be done with or on behalf of law enforcement without consent or a warrant.

The continued use of drug tests and law enforcement to regulate the behavior of pregnant women is not merely anecdotal. A recent study conducted by Lynn Paltrow, who went on to establish the National Advocates for Pregnant Women, found that there have been over 413

---

[171] *Id.* at 101–03 (Scalia, J. dissenting with Rehnquist, C.J. and Thomas, J. joining).

[172] Linda Greenhouse, *Justices, 6–3, Bar Some Drug Tests*, N.Y. TIMES (Mar. 22, 2001), https://www.nytimes.com/2001/03/22/us/justices-6-3-bar-some-drug-tests.html.

[173] *Id.*

[174] *See, e.g.*, Lebron v. Sec'y of Fla. Dep't of Children & Families, 772 F.3d 1352 (11th Cir. 2014) (finding that mandatory drug testing of AFDC applicants was not justified by the "special needs" exception to the Fourth Amendment); Dubbs v. Head Start, Inc., 336 F.3d 1194, 1205 (10th Cir. 2003) (finding that intrusive physical examinations of children enrolled in Head Start was not justified by the "special needs" exception to the Fourth Amendment).

[175] Linda Greenhouse, *Should a Fetus's Well-Being Override a Mother's Rights?*, N.Y. TIMES (Sept. 9, 2000), https://www.nytimes.com/2000/09/09/arts/should-a-fetus-s-well-being-override-a-mother-s-rights.html?rref=collection%2Fbyline%2Flinda-greenhouse&action=click&contentCollection=undefined&region=stream&module=stream_unit&version=search&contentPlacement=1&pgtype=collection&mtrref=www.nytimes.com.

reported cases of arrest, incarceration or detention of pregnant women since 1973,[176] with one-third of the cases taking place since the Court's decision in *Ferguson*.[177] This includes arrests for failure to follow doctors' orders, imprisonment for drug use during pregnancy, and prosecutions for behavior alleged to have caused miscarriages or stillbirths.[178] Many of these cases emerge from the state of South Carolina, as the state supreme court deemed a viable fetus to be a "child" for purposes of state law in *Whitner v. State*.[179] According to the study, more than half of the individuals subject to pregnancy-related arrest, detention or prosecution were black women.[180] Black women, then, continue to be subjected to disproportionate rates of drug testing by medical professionals decades after the Court's ruling in *Ferguson*.

While *Ferguson* has had a limited effect on *legal* protections for pregnant women, it has, however, ignited debate among feminists regarding how to articulate demands for reproductive autonomy and liberty. Indeed, women of color have called upon feminists to abandon the traditional reproductive rights "choice" framework that has typically been preoccupied by the right not to have children.[181] Instead, they suggest a reproductive justice framework that highlights and challenges the various structural impediments to procreation and parenting that disproportionately burden the reproductive capacities of poor women, including racism, poverty, housing, healthcare, childcare, education, employment and access to affordable and nutritious food.[182]

Unfortunately, Crystal Ferguson did not live long enough to witness the impact of her resistance. She died on May 30, 2007, just six years after the Supreme Court ruled in her favor, killed in an arson fire.[183] Her family, particularly her daughter Annika, remember her as a fighter. As Annika noted, in Charleston, "[a]ll you see is either homeless people or something. Nobody wants to try. She wasn't like that. She wanted to try."[184]

---

[176] Paltrow & Flavin, *supra* note 60, at 309.

[177] *Id.* at 312; *see also* Maya Manian, *Lessons from Personhood's Defeat: Abortion Restrictions and Side Effects on Women's Health*, 74 OHIO ST. L.J. 75, 94 (2013).

[178] Manian, *supra* note 177 at 94–95.

[179] 492 S.E.2d 777, 778 (S.C. 1997).

[180] Paltrow & Flavin, *supra* note 60, at 311.

[181] *See, e.g.*, LORRETTA J. ROSS & RICKIE SOLINGER, REPRODUCTIVE JUSTICE: AN INTRODUCTION 238–39 (2017); ASIAN COMMUNITIES FOR REPROD. JUST., A NEW VISION FOR ADVANCING OUR MOVEMENT TOWARD REPRODUCTIVE HEALTH, REPRODUCTIVE RIGHTS AND REPRODUCTIVE JUSTICE 3–5 (2005).

[182] *See, e.g.*, ROSS & SOLINGER, at 238–66; *see also* ASIAN COMMUNITIES FOR REPROD. JUST., at 3–5.

[183] Psmith, *Good-bye: One Woman Drug War Victim Dies, Another is About To*, STOPTHEDRUGWAR.ORG (Jun. 14, 2007), https://stopthedrugwar.org/chronicle/2007/jun/14/goodbye_one_woman_drug_war_victi; *Crystal Ferguson Obituary*, POST & COURIER, http://www.legacy.com/obituaries/charleston/obituary.aspx?n=crystal-ferguson&pid=88684787 (last visited Dec. 9, 2018).

[184] Psmith, *supra* note 183.

9

Samuel R. Bagenstos*

Nevada Department of Human Resources v. Hibbs: Universalism and Reproductive Justice

The Family and Medical Leave Act (FMLA) was the first bill signed into law by President Bill Clinton—just two weeks after he took office.[1] Enactment of the statute was a longstanding goal of the Democratic Party.[2] It also represented a legislative victory for what I will call feminist universalism—the notion that sex equality is best served by rules and policies that reject differentiation between women and men. Ten years after Congress enacted the FMLA, the Supreme Court upheld the statute against a constitutional challenge in *Nevada Department of Human Resources v. Hibbs.*[3] The *Hibbs* Court, in a surprising opinion by Chief Justice Rehnquist, relied heavily on feminist universalist arguments. Even at the time of *Hibbs*, though, evidence was accumulating that the FMLA's universalist approach was not sufficient to achieve the underlying goals of feminist lawyers and activists: disestablishing gender-role stereotypes and promoting equal opportunities for women and men throughout society. *Hibbs* thus represents the triumph of feminist universalism, even as it highlights the limitations of the feminist universalist project.

THE FMLA AND FEMINIST UNIVERSALISM

Understanding where the FMLA came from—and the constitutional issues in *Hibbs*—requires examining what drew leading American feminists to frame the statute in universalist terms.

---

* Frank G. Millard Professor of Law, University of Michigan Law School.

[1] *See* RONALD D. ELVING, CONFLICT AND COMPROMISE: HOW CONGRESS MAKES THE LAW 11 (1995).

[2] *See, e.g., 1988 Democratic Party Platform*, AM. PRESIDENCY PROJECT, http://www. presidency.ucsb.edu/ws/index.php?pid=29609 ("We believe that Government should set the standard in recognizing that worker productivity is enhanced . . . by family leave policies that no longer force employees to choose between their jobs and their children or ailing parents . . . .").

[3] 538 U.S. 721 (2003).

Second-Wave Feminism and the Pregnancy Discrimination Act

From its start in the early 1960s, second-wave feminism aimed to untether the biological function of reproduction from social roles and social status. Key second-wave texts like Betty Friedan's *The Feminine Mystique* described a world in which women were largely confined to the tasks of raising children and managing the home. That world, they argued, improperly treated biology as destiny. It imposed significant psychological costs on individual women and deprived women as a group of full and equal status in society. Friedan, for example, wrote that a woman "who has no goal, no purpose, no ambition patterning her days into the future, making her stretch and grow beyond that small score of years in which her body can fill its biological function, is committing a kind of suicide."[4]

Feminist lawyers pursued three distinct but interlocking strategies to help ensure that a woman's biology would not be her destiny.[5] One strategy was to seek statutes and judicial rulings that promoted access to contraception and abortion. If women could choose whether and when to have children, they could time their parenting decisions to minimize interference with the educational and job prospects that were essential to full and equal status in the community. A second strategy was to seek federal programs that provided childcare directly. A federally funded network of childcare centers could remove both financial and social barriers to new mothers reentering the workforce. The third strategy focused not on the government but on private employers. Feminist lawyers sought legal regulation of the employment process to bar employers from treating mothers and pregnant women as second-class citizens. And because social stereotypes treated the ideal role of women as mothers and homemakers, this strategy naturally extended to barring discrimination against women in the workplace generally. As Professor Deborah Dinner has explained, "Upending the family-wage system would require more than the right to formal, equal treatment. Feminists also fought for the redistribution of childrearing labor between women and men in the home, as well as the redistribution of the costs of pregnancy, childbirth, and childrearing between the family and society."[6] The FMLA arose most directly from the third of these—feminist efforts to regulate the workplace.

Feminist lawyers initially relied on Title VII of the Civil Rights Act of 1964, which prohibits employment discrimination based not just on race but also on sex.[7] Although the Equal Employment Opportunity Commission (EEOC) and other elites initially treated the law's

---

[4]   BETTY FRIEDAN, THE FEMININE MYSTIQUE 280 (50th anniversary ed. 2013).

[5]   For an extensive discussion of the three prongs of this strategy, see Robert C. Post & Reva B. Siegel, *Legislative Constitutionalism and Section Five Power: Policentric Interpretation of the Family and Medical Leave Act*, 112 YALE L.J. 1943, 1986–89 (2003).

[6]   Deborah Dinner, *The Costs of Reproduction: History and the Legal Construction of Sex Equality*, 46 HARV. C.R.-C.L. L. REV. 415, 419 (2011).

[7]   42 U.S.C. § 2000e-2(a) (2012).

prohibition on sex discrimination as an accident or a joke, by the late 1960s the EEOC and the courts had begun to take that prohibition seriously.[8] Advocates used Title VII to challenge employers who attempted to force pregnant women to quit their jobs or take excessive leave.[9] And where the employer was the government—as in the large number of cases involving teachers driven out of their jobs once it became apparent they were pregnant—those lawyers made Fourteenth Amendment claims as well. These efforts had some initial success in the EEOC and the courts.[10]

But the Supreme Court ultimately ruled in 1974's *Geduldig v. Aiello*[11] that discrimination against pregnant women is not inherently sex discrimination for purposes of the Fourteenth Amendment. Two years later, in *General Electric Co. v. Gilbert*,[12] the Court applied the same analysis to Title VII. Rejecting the EEOC's interpretation, the Court held that the statute does not prohibit disparate treatment of pregnant women. As the Court explained, quoting its earlier opinion in *Geduldig*, pregnancy discrimination divides the workplace "into two groups— pregnant women and nonpregnant persons. While the first group is exclusively female, the second includes members of both sexes."[13]

Feminist lawyers immediately responded by urging passage of a new law that would expressly treat pregnancy discrimination as a form of sex discrimination.[14] They succeeded when Congress adopted the Pregnancy Discrimination Act (PDA) in 1978.[15] The PDA contained two key clauses. The first defined sex discrimination to include discrimination on the basis of pregnancy.[16] The second tied employers' treatment of pregnancy to their treatment of other disabilities in the workplace: "[W]omen affected

---

[8]   *See* HUGH DAVIS GRAHAM, THE CIVIL RIGHTS ERA: ORIGINS AND DEVELOPMENT OF NATIONAL POLICY, 1960–1972, at 207–11, 229–32 (1990); *see also* Cary Franklin, *Inventing the "Traditional Concept" of Sex Discrimination*, 125 HARV. L. REV. 1307, 1333–58 (2012).

[9]   *See* Deborah A. Widiss, *Gilbert Redux: The Interaction of the Pregnancy Discrimination Act and the Amended Americans with Disabilities Act*, 46 U.C. DAVIS L. REV. 961, 989–91 (2013).

[10]   *Cf.* Stanley Schair, *Sex Discrimination: The Pregnancy-Related Disability Exclusion*, 49 ST. JOHN'S L. REV. 684, 689–91 (1975) (describing how circuits were split on whether mandatory maternity leave policies for teachers violated the Fourteenth Amendment before the Supreme Court in *Cleveland Board of Education v. LaFleur* struck down a mandatory maternity regulation as unconstitutional under the Due Process Clause); Comment, *Mandatory Maternity Leave: Title VII and Equal Protection*, 14 WM. & MARY L. REV. 1026, 1026–27 (1973) (noting that before *LaFleur* and *Geduldig v. Aiello*, "the success of a constitutional attack on mandatory maternity leave policies necessarily depend[ed] upon the jurisdiction in which an action [was] brought").

[11]   417 U.S. 484 (1974). For discussion of *Geduldig*, see Deborah Dinner, *Sex Equality and the U.S. Welfare Regime: The Story of* Geduldig v. Aiello, *in* REPRODUCTIVE RIGHTS AND JUSTICE STORIES 77 (Melissa Murray, Katherine Shaw & Reva B. Siegel eds., 2019).

[12]   429 U.S. 125 (1976).

[13]   *Id.* at 135 (quoting *Geduldig*, 417 U.S. at 496 n.20).

[14]   *See* Dinner, *supra* note 6, at 469–70.

[15]   Pub. L. No. 95-555, 92 Stat. 2076 (1978) (codified at 42 U.S.C. § 2000(k) (2012)).

[16]   42 U.S.C. § 2000e(k) ("The terms 'because of sex' or 'on the basis of sex' include, but are not limited to, because of or on the basis of pregnancy, childbirth, or related medical conditions . . . .").

by pregnancy, childbirth, or related medical conditions shall be treated the same for all employment-related purposes, including receipt of benefits under fringe benefit programs, as other persons not so affected but similar in their ability or inability to work."[17] Taken together, these clauses overturned both the holding and the reasoning in *Gilbert*. They required employers who give leave or other accommodations to temporarily disabled employees to do the same for similarly-affected pregnant employees. And they barred employers from treating workers adversely simply because they are pregnant.

The congressional hearings on the PDA included testimony from a number of prominent feminist attorneys. These attorneys explained that the purpose of the law was not just to attack a narrow problem but to eliminate the broad stereotypes and practices that limited women's workplace opportunities generally. Georgetown Law Professor Wendy Williams, for example, identified employers' treatment of pregnancy as the keystone of workplace inequality. She testified that "the common thread of justification running through all the policies and practices that discriminate against women in the labor force rested ultimately on one fact: The capacity and reality of pregnancy."[18] Employers' "assumptions about pregnancy and its implications for the role of women, and the behavior of women, led to the view that women were marginal workers, not really deserving of the emoluments and pay of real workers."[19] And because all women of childbearing age are "viewed by employers among the potentially pregnant," the "stereotype that all women are marginal workers" had broad effects on "hiring, promotion, job assignments, and fringe benefits."[20]

The PDA rested heavily on the premises of feminist universalism. In particular, the statute seemed to incorporate a "sameness" feminism.[21] The second clause seemed to do so explicitly with its "shall be treated the same" language.[22] So long as women were the same as men, the statute appeared to say, they should be treated the same. Susan Deller Ross, then

---

[17]   *Id.*

[18]   *Legislation to Prohibit Sex Discrimination on the Basis of Pregnancy: Hearing on H.R. 5055 & H.R. 6075 Before the Subcomm. on Emp't Opportunities of the H. Comm. on Educ. & Labor*, 95th Cong. 43 (1977) [hereinafter *House Hearing*] (statement of Wendy Williams, Professor of Law, Georgetown Law School).

[19]   *Id.*

[20]   *Id.*

[21]   *Cf.* Dinner, *supra* note 6, at 444 (arguing that the turn toward formal equality arguments by feminist lawyers during this period is "better understood not as an ideological competition between difference and sameness feminism, special and equal treatment, but rather as a strategic conflict about how to remedy the economic costs that the family-wage system imposed on women"). *See generally* Mary Becker, *The Sixties Shift to Formal Equality and the Courts: An Argument for Pragmatism and Politics*, 40 WM. & MARY L. REV. 209 (1998) (arguing that by 1970, feminist lawyers had turned decisively toward sameness feminism).

[22]   § 2000e(k).

of the American Civil Liberties Union (ACLU),[23] underscored the theme in her testimony on the bill. "Most women are able to work through most of their pregnancies," she said. "They should be allowed to work like any other able workers."[24] At the same time, she recognized, "all pregnant women have some period of medical disability" from labor through "3 to 8 weeks after childbirth," and "[t]hese disabled women should likewise be given the same fringe benefits all other medically disabled workers get."[25]

Although proponents of the PDA aimed to eliminate important barriers to workplace equality, the model of sameness feminism seemed likely to have a limited impact. It would protect those women who could overcome employer-imposed barriers to succeeding in a man's world, but it would not change the background conditions that made it a man's world in the first place.[26]

Of course, most of the PDA's feminist advocates did not endorse such a narrow and formal approach to equality. Their efforts to secure the availability of abortion and childcare reflected a goal not just to require employers to treat women the same as men, but to change the social structures that created the context for workplace and other inequalities—in particular, the social structures that gave women sole or primary responsibility for childrearing. Still, as attempts to secure public funding for abortion ran aground and the push for a national childcare program stalled, the PDA's sameness model stood as the most powerful example of legal feminism in the statute books.

To be sure, feminists did not abandon efforts to move beyond the sameness model. As I show in the next section, intra-feminist debates on these questions remained robust—and played a crucial role in the development of the FMLA. And the limitations of a sameness approach were increasingly apparent. Biology aside, social norms meant that women were more likely to take time off to care for newborn children than men. This time off went beyond the "period of medical disability"[27] for which the PDA might provide some protection—it was about childcare, not physical recovery from pregnancy and childbirth. Unless employers were required to give new mothers maternity leave—and protect those new mothers against adverse treatment when they returned—women would face an obstacle to continuing in the workforce that men did not.

Pregnancy Leave Laws and the Move Toward the FMLA

Responding to this problem, activists in some states secured enactment of laws that required employers to provide maternity leave.[28]

---

[23]   *Susan Deller Ross*, ACLU WOMEN'S RTS. PROJECT, https://www.aclu.org/files/womensrights/tribute/3.html (last visited May 18, 2018).

[24]   *House Hearing, supra* note 18, at 48 (statement of Susan Deller Ross, ACLU).

[25]   *Id.*

[26]   *See* Catharine A. MacKinnon, *Reflections on Sex Equality Under Law*, 100 YALE L.J. 1281, 1287 (1991).

[27]   *House Hearing, supra* note 18, at 48 (statement of Susan Deller Ross, ACLU).

[28]   *See* Dinner, *supra* note 6, at 474.

Some of these statutes predated the PDA; others, like California's, were enacted later.[29] California's law, in particular, became a major focus of controversy. That law required employers to provide mothers up to four months of leave following childbirth.[30] Although the statute did not require employers to pay new mothers for their maternity leave time, it did prohibit them from firing or demoting new mothers for taking that leave.[31]

As Justice Ginsburg later explained, "[t]he California law sharply divided women's rights advocates":

> "Equal-treatment" feminists asserted it violated the Pregnancy Discrimination Act's (PDA) commitment to treating pregnancy the same as other disabilities. It did so by requiring leave only for disability caused by pregnancy and childbirth, thereby treating pregnancy as *sui generis*. "Equal-opportunity" feminists disagreed, urging that the California law was consistent with the PDA because it remedied the discriminatory burden that inadequate leave policies placed on a woman's right to procreate.[32]

When business groups filed suit to challenge the California maternity-leave mandate as preempted by the PDA, the competing groups of feminists filed competing briefs in the case.[33] Joan Bertin of the ACLU explained the position of the "equal treatment" feminists she represented: "The notion that pregnancy is a special disability is a stereotype, and stereotypes hurt us. The only way to eradicate that is to put pregnancy in the context of the whole range of things that happen to people over a lifetime."[34] But no less an icon than Betty Friedan took the other side of the argument:

> I think the time has come to acknowledge that women are different from men, and that there has to be a concept of equality that takes into account that women are the ones who have the babies. We shouldn't be stuck with always using a male model, trying to twist pregnancy into something that's like a hernia.[35]

---

[29]   *See* Brief for the National Conference of State Legislators *et al.* as *Amici Curiae* at 16–17, California Federal Savings & Loan Assn. v. Guerra, 1986 WL 728371 (June 12, 1986).

[30]   *See* Cal. Fed. Sav. & Loan Ass'n v. Guerra, 479 U.S. 272, 275–76 (1987) (describing California's Fair Employment and Housing Act, which had been amended in 1978 to prohibit employment discrimination on the basis of pregnancy).

[31]   *Id.*

[32]   Coleman v. Court of Appeals, 566 U.S. 30, 48 (2012) (Ginsburg, J., dissenting) (footnote omitted) (citations omitted).

[33]   *See* Tamar Lewin, *Maternity-Leave Suit Has Divided Feminists*, N.Y. TIMES (June 28, 1986), http://www.nytimes.com/1986/06/28/style/maternity-leave-suit-has-divided-feminists.html.

[34]   *Id.*

[35]   *Id.*

The Supreme Court ultimately upheld the California law on two alternative grounds that, together, might have bridged the internecine conflict among women's rights activists. The first ground, which resonated with the claims of the "equal opportunity" feminists, was that the state's maternity-leave law and the PDA "share a common goal" of "allow[ing] women, as well as men, to have families without losing their jobs."[36] The second, which accepted the "equal treatment" feminists' interpretation of the PDA for purposes of argument, was that employers could comply with both the state and federal statutes by granting four months' maternity leave and also giving "comparable benefits to other disabled employees."[37]

After the Supreme Court's decision, Representative Howard Berman, who had authored the California law when he was in the state legislature, sought to introduce a maternity-leave bill in Congress.[38] Feminist activists, aided in particular by Colorado Representative Pat Schroeder and Donna Lenhoff of the Women's Legal Defense Fund, successfully prevailed on Representative Berman to frame his federal bill consistently with feminist universalism—that is, by avoiding any legal distinction between men and women, whether pregnant or otherwise. That bill eventually became the Family and Medical Leave Act.[39] Rather than being limited to maternity leave, the new law guaranteed both mothers and fathers leave for the birth of a child.[40] It also guaranteed to workers, regardless of their sex, leave to take care of certain family members with "serious health condition[s]"—or to address their own "serious health condition[s]."[41] Covered employers were required to make a total of twelve weeks of unpaid leave available to each covered employee each year for these purposes.[42]

In framing the FMLA as a form of universal job protection, the goal of feminist lawyers was not to deny differences between women and men—or even to reject the proposition that employers should accommodate those differences. The goal was to broaden the frame, so that those differences could be accommodated in a way that didn't target women for special treatment.

Special treatment was seen as harmful to women in two ways. First, it entrenched social stereotypes that limited women's opportunities. A law guaranteeing parental leave to women, but not men, placed the imprimatur of the state on the proposition that taking care of children was women's work. By contrast, a law guaranteeing parental leave to all

---

[36] *Cal. Fed.*, 479 U.S. at 288, 289.

[37] *Id.* at 291.

[38] *See* ELVING, *supra* note 1, at 18–20.

[39] *See id.* at 20–23, 29–34.

[40] 29 U.S.C. § 2612(a)(1)(A) (2012).

[41] *Id.* § 2612(a)(1)(C)–(D).

[42] *Id.* § 2612(a)(1).

parents might shift caretaking patterns by removing an obstacle to men who wished to take time off to care for their family members.[43]

Second, and perhaps more concretely, special treatment encouraged discrimination against women by making them costlier to employ. If the law required parental leave for female but not male employees, an employer would have an incentive to hire only men so it could avoid that mandate. But if both men and women had the right to take leave, perhaps that would blunt the incentive to discriminate.[44] Of course, social norms would likely continue to mean that women would be more likely in practice to take parental or family-care leave. To address that concern, the statute's drafters also included personal-care leave in the FMLA's package of entitlements. The idea was that men would be at least as likely as women to take personal-care leave, so that the statute's new mandate would not, as a whole, give employers much incentive to discriminate against women.[45] The FMLA ultimately passed in this universalist form, though Congress limited the law to fairly large employers.[46]

WILLIAM HIBBS'S CASE

Hibbs's Accident and His Wife's Surgery

William Hibbs worked for the State of Nevada's welfare agency.[47] On Mother's Day of 1996, he was driving his Ford pickup truck with his family in Reno when another driver ran a red light and crashed into them.[48] William tore his rotator cuff in the crash, and his two children also experienced minor injuries.[49] His wife, Diane, was not so lucky. She seriously injured her neck and spine—and she required extensive treatment.[50] She had surgery in October 1996, but that did not alleviate her severe pain.[51] By the following spring, as William's lawyers explained in one of their briefs to the Supreme Court, Diane had "suffered a range of serious medical complications, including liver damage and addiction as a result of prescribed pain medication, anxiety attacks, clinical

---

[43]   *See* Donna Lenhoff & Claudia Withers, *Implementation of the Family and Medical Leave Act: Toward the Family-Friendly Workplace*, 3 J. GENDER & L. 39, 49–50 (1994).

[44]   *See* Dinner, *supra* note 6, at 475.

[45]   *See* Julie C. Suk, *Are Gender Stereotypes Bad for Women? Rethinking Antidiscrimination Law and Work-Family Conflict*, 110 COLUM. L. REV. 1, 43 (2010).

[46]   29 U.S.C. § 2611(4)(A)(i) (2012) (defining "employer" for the purposes of the act as "any person engaged in commerce or in any industry or activity affecting commerce who employs 50 or more employees for each working day during each of 20 or more calendar workweeks in the current or preceding calendar year").

[47]   Brief in Opposition at *2, Nev. Dep't of Human Res. v. Hibbs, 538 U.S. 721 (2003) (No. 01-1368), 2001 WL 34116242.

[48]   *Former State Worker Pitted Against Nevada in Supreme Court Family Leave Case*, LAS VEGAS SUN (Jan. 12, 2003, 7:30 AM), https://lasvegassun.com/news/2003/jan/12/former-state-worker-pitted-against-nevada-in-supre/ [hereinafter *Worker Pitted Against Nevada*].

[49]   *Id.* ("Hibbs tore a rotator cuff and his two younger children suffered scrapes and bruises . . . .").

[50]   *Id.*

[51]   Brief in Opposition, *supra* note 47, at *3.

depression, and suicidal tendencies, necessitating at one point that she be admitted to a hospital psychiatric unit."[52]

One condition in particular required further surgery: Diane "had a metal plate with screws in her neck from which the screws stripped and loosened to the point of pressing against her esophagus, requiring her to be extremely careful when moving her body so as to avoid a potentially fatal puncture."[53] The surgery could not be scheduled until November 1997, however, due to the specialist surgeon's availability.[54] During the interim period, William sought leave from his job to care for Diane.[55]

William requested the full twelve weeks of leave under the FMLA.[56] On June 23, 1997, his employer granted the request to take unpaid FMLA leave as needed to care for his spouse.[57] William took that leave intermittently until August 5, when he began taking the leave on a full-time basis.[58] On August 11, he began to receive paid leave donated by his coworkers pursuant to a workplace leave-bank program; at that point, he had used approximately three weeks of his twelve-week allocation of FMLA leave.[59] His coworkers donated just over nine weeks of paid leave, which William believed would not count against his FMLA allocation.[60] He planned to take the donated leave until it ran out in October, then revert to unpaid FMLA leave through the end of the year—which would cover Diane's surgery and initial recovery.[61]

Contrary to William's expectations, his employer *did* count the donated paid leave against his twelve-week FMLA allocation; under that calculation, his FMLA entitlement expired in October.[62] His employer ordered him to return to work by November 12 or face discipline.[63] When he did not return because he still needed to care for his wife, the employer fired him for being "absent without leave."[64]

Diane eventually had her surgery in December—one of "a dozen expensive operations in California and Arizona."[65] William found part-time work for the Federal Department of Housing and Urban Development, and the family had to survive on a combination of Diane's

---

[52] Id.
[53] Id. at *3–4 (citation omitted).
[54] Id. at *4.
[55] Id.
[56] Id.
[57] Id.
[58] Id. at *5.
[59] Id.
[60] Id. at *4–5.
[61] Id. at *5.
[62] Id. at *5–6.
[63] Id. at *7.
[64] Id. at *7–8.
[65] *Worker Pitted Against Nevada, supra* note 48.

disability payments and his $1,000 monthly wages from that job.[66] The Hibbses paid their bills "by selling off horses, three off-road vehicles, two classic cars, a truck, van, and eventually [William's] house near Virginia City. The family moved into a $6,500 mining home that had been abandoned for eight years."[67]

Hibbs's Lawsuit and the Supreme Court's Sovereign Immunity Cases

In April 1998, William Hibbs filed a lawsuit against the State of Nevada for violating his rights under the FMLA. By counting the banked leave donated by his coworkers against his twelve-week FMLA allocation without giving him sufficient advance notice, he alleged, the state had violated the statute. He also alleged that the state had violated the statute by retaliating against him for invoking his FMLA rights.[68] He sought reinstatement with back pay, plus damages.[69]

The FMLA provides for damages and back pay,[70] as well as injunctive relief.[71] And it treats state government employers, like William Hibbs's, identically to private employers.[72] When Congress adopted the statute in 1993, there was no legal reason for Congress to draw a distinction between public-sector and private-sector employment. The Supreme Court had held in *Garcia v. San Antonio Metropolitan Transit Authority* in 1985 that Congress can apply the same labor standards laws to state and local government employers as it applies to private employers.[73] And the Court had also held in *Pennsylvania v. Union Gas Co.* in 1989 that there is no constitutional bar to Congress authorizing suits against state governments for damages for violations of federal statutes.[74]

By the time William Hibbs filed his suit, though, a lot had changed. Under the leadership of Chief Justice Rehnquist, the Supreme Court had begun what many have called a "federalism revolution."[75] In 1996, Chief Justice Rehnquist's opinion for the Court in *Seminole Tribe of Florida v. Florida* overruled *Union Gas* and held that Congress could not authorize damages suits against states.[76] Rather, the Eleventh Amendment—or at

---

[66]   *Id.*

[67]   *Id.*

[68]   Brief in Opposition, *supra* note 47, at *8.

[69]   *Id.*

[70]   29 U.S.C. § 2617(a)(1)(A) (2012).

[71]   *Id.* § 2617(a)(1)(B).

[72]   *Id.* § 2611(4)(A)(iii) (defining "[t]he term 'employer'" to "include[ ] any 'public agency' ").

[73]   469 U.S. 528 (1985).

[74]   491 U.S. 1 (1989).

[75]   *See, e.g.,* MARK TUSHNET, A COURT DIVIDED: THE REHNQUIST COURT AND THE FUTURE OF CONSTITUTIONAL LAW 249 (2005); Linda Greenhouse, *The Revolution Next Time?*, N.Y. TIMES (Dec. 16, 2010, 8:00 PM), https://opinionator.blogs.nytimes.com/2010/12/16/the-revolution-next-time.

[76]   517 U.S. 44 (1996).

least the constitutional "presupposition" that the Eleventh Amendment "confirms"—provided that the state, as sovereign, was immune from such suits.[77]

Seminole Tribe reaffirmed the Court's prior holding that Congress could override a state's sovereign immunity if it acted under its power to enforce the Fourteenth Amendment.[78] But the very next year, the Court limited the circumstances in which Congress could exercise that power. In its 1997 decision in *City of Boerne v. Flores*,[79] the Court withdrew its prior suggestion that Congress had some authority to determine the *substantive* meaning of the Fourteenth Amendment.[80] Rather, *Boerne* held that Congress's enforcement power is tied to the Court's own interpretations of the Fourteenth Amendment: Congress can act to prevent, deter, or remedy conduct that the Court would believe to be in violation of that Amendment, but Congress cannot declare conduct to be a violation of the Amendment if the Court believes that conduct to be constitutional.[81]

The Case in the Lower Courts

Seminole Tribe and *Boerne* posed a problem for Hibbs's case. They meant that Hibbs could not recover damages from the state for his injuries unless the FMLA was "congruent and proportional" to Fourteenth Amendment violations recognized by the Supreme Court. And the FMLA's universal framing suggested that the statute went beyond simply prohibiting unconstitutional sex discrimination. If the problem was sex discrimination, a guarantee of 12 weeks of leave for every covered worker would seem to go well beyond solving that problem. A state could avoid unconstitutional discrimination by giving its workers *any* amount of leave—12 weeks, 6 weeks, or even no leave at all—so long as male and female workers got the same thing. Applying that logic, the district court ruled that Hibbs's FMLA claim against the state was barred by sovereign immunity.[82]

Hibbs appealed to the United States Court of Appeals for the Ninth Circuit. By the time the Ninth Circuit decided the case, seven other federal courts of appeals had addressed the question whether the FMLA was a valid exercise of Congress's power to enforce the Fourteenth

[77]   *Id.* at 54 (quoting Blatchford v. Native Vill. of Noatak, 501 U.S. 775, 779 (1991)).

[78]   *See id.* at 59 (citing Fitzpatrick v. Bitzer, 427 U.S. 445, 452–56 (1976)).

[79]   521 U.S. 507 (1997).

[80]   *See id.* at 527–28 ("There is language in our opinion in *Katzenbach v. Morgan*, 384 U.S. 641 (1966), which could be interpreted as acknowledging a power in Congress to enact legislation that expands the rights contained in § 1 of the Fourteenth Amendment. This is not a necessary interpretation, however, or even the best one.").

[81]   *Id.* at 519–20.

[82]   Transcript of Motion Nos. 54 and 55, Hibbs v. Dep't of Human Res., No. CV-N-98-205-HDM(PHA), 2004 WL 5267600 (D. Nev. June 3, 1999).

Amendment. All of them had held, consistent with the district court's decision, that it was not.[83]

But the Ninth Circuit panel that heard Hibbs's appeal consisted of three of the most liberal judges on the federal appellate bench. The most senior judge on the panel, Judge Stephen Reinhardt, a Carter appointee and former union-side labor lawyer, was perhaps the most outspoken liberal critic of the Rehnquist Court among sitting judges.[84] Not coincidentally, he was also one of the judges whose opinions were the most likely to be reversed by the Supreme Court.[85] The next-most-senior judge, Judge A. Wallace Tashima, a Clinton appointee, was a Japanese American who had been imprisoned in an internment camp as a child during World War II.[86] The third judge, Judge Marsha Berzon, served as Supreme Court Justice William Brennan's first female law clerk and participated in the drafting of and lobbying for the PDA as a young attorney before going on to a very successful career as one of the nation's most prominent union-side labor lawyers.[87] When President Clinton nominated Judge Berzon to the Ninth Circuit, the Senate dragged its feet for more than two years before finally confirming her by a vote of 64–34.[88]

The Ninth Circuit panel concluded that the FMLA was a valid exercise of Congress's Fourteenth Amendment enforcement power and thus held that Congress properly subjected state employers to monetary liability for violations of the statute. In the portion of the panel's opinion authored by Judge Tashima, the panel held that the FMLA was a congruent and proportional response to sex discrimination in the leave policies of public employers.[89] Judge Tashima endorsed the government's argument that "because women are regarded as having 'the primary responsibility for family caretaking' (both for infants and for sick family members), employers commonly offer less caretaking leave to men than to women." As a result, he explained,

---

[83]   See Hibbs v. Dep't. of Human Res., 273 F.3d 844, 850 (9th Cir. 2001) (collecting cases), aff'd sub nom. Nev. Dep't. of Human Res. v. Hibbs, 538 U.S. 721 (2003).

[84]   See William Overend, Stephen Reinhardt of Ninth Circuit: Liberal U.S. Judge Swims Against Conservative Tide, L.A. TIMES (Aug. 17, 1986), http://articles.latimes.com/1986-08-17/news/mn-16516_1_stephen-reinhardt.

[85]   See Maura Dolan, Stephen Reinhardt, 'Liberal Lion' of the Ninth Circuit, Dies at Eighty-Seven, L.A. TIMES (Mar. 29, 2018), http://www.latimes.com/local/lanow/la-me-ln-reinhardt-obit-20180329-story.html (noting that, when asked about his response to his opinions' frequent reversals by the Supreme Court, Judge Reinhardt said: "If they want to take away rights, that's their privilege. But I'm not going to help them do it.").

[86]   See David Margolick, Japanese-American Judges Reflect on Internment, N.Y. TIMES (May 19, 1995), https://www.nytimes.com/1995/05/19/us/japanese-american-judges-reflect-on-internment.html.

[87]   See 2007 Margaret Brent Awards, Marsha S. Berzon, AM. BAR ASS'N, https://www.americanbar.org/content/dam/aba/migrated/women/bios/BerzonBio.authcheckdam.pdf.

[88]   Neil A. Lewis, After Long Delays, Senate Confirms Two Judicial Nominees, N.Y. TIMES (Mar. 10, 2000), http://www.nytimes.com/2000/03/10/us/after-long-delays-senate-confirms-2-judicial-nominees.html.

[89]   Hibbs v. Dep't. of Human Res., 273 F.3d 844, 869–71 (9th Cir. 2001).

this kind of gender-discriminatory leave policy is harmful both to men—because they are not given enough leave to care for their families—and to women—because reduced leave for men forces women to spend more time taking care of their families, and women's consequently greater needs for caretaking leave make them less attractive job candidates than men.[90]

A flat requirement of twelve weeks' leave for both male and female employees responded directly to that discrimination.

A concurring opinion authored by Judge Berzon, but joined by the other two members of the panel, went much further. It concluded that the FMLA was a proper response not just to sex-discriminatory leave practices but to the entire edifice of state laws that had, until as late as the 1970s, limited the work opportunities of women and thus reinforced "the stereotypical assumption that women are marginal workers whose fundamental responsibilities are in the home."[91] Those state laws included protective labor legislation that limited the jobs women could perform or the hours they could work,[92] as well as laws governing workers' compensation and other public benefits[93]—laws that assumed that women, but not men, were economically dependent on their spouses. Those laws, Judge Berzon argued, continued to shape societal views about the proper roles of men and women.[94] And, as Judge Berzon wrote, the FMLA directly responded to them by requiring that both male and female workers receive twelve weeks of leave for caretaking.[95]

SUPREME COURT PROCEEDINGS

The Court Takes the Case

The Ninth Circuit's decision was an obvious candidate for Supreme Court review. By diverging from the rulings of other courts of appeals, the decision created a conflict in the circuits—one of the most common reasons the Supreme Court decides to hear a case.[96] And the decision seemed out of step with the jurisprudence that marked the Rehnquist Court's "federalism revolution." Indeed, in the four years that followed *Boerne*, the Court would consider the constitutionality, under Congress's Fourteenth Amendment enforcement power, of five more statutes—

---

[90]   *Id.* at 855.

[91]   *Id.* at 860.

[92]   *Id.* at 861–63.

[93]   *Id.* at 863.

[94]   *Id.* at 863–65 (noting that even as federal laws began to prohibit gender discrimination, decades of state laws based on "stereotypical beliefs about the appropriate roles of men and women" made up " 'volumes of history' of sex discrimination in the country").

[95]   *Id.* at 867.

[96]   *See* SUP. CT. R. 10 (noting that the existence of a circuit split can be considered as a factor in whether to grant certiorari); *see also* H.W. PERRY JR., DECIDING TO DECIDE: AGENDA SETTING IN THE UNITED STATES SUPREME COURT 246 (1991) ("Without a doubt, the single most important generalizable factor in assessing certworthiness is the existence of a conflict or 'split' in the circuits.").

including, notably, the Age Discrimination in Employment Act (ADEA) and the employment discrimination prohibitions of the Americans with Disabilities Act (ADA). In each instance, the Court held that the statute was not a valid exercise of Congress's power to enforce the Fourteenth Amendment.[97] That *Hibbs* had been decided by a notoriously liberal panel on a notoriously liberal circuit—at a time when the Supreme Court was tilting decidedly to the right—was the exclamation point at the end of the sentence.

The State of Nevada accordingly filed a petition for certiorari in the Supreme Court.[98] Even though the George W. Bush administration defended the FMLA and urged the Court to deny review of the Ninth Circuit's decision,[99] few observers expected the Court to take that path.[100] And indeed, the Court granted certiorari in June 2002, just as it was finishing its 2001 Term.[101] Argument was set for January 2003, with briefing to occur during the summer and fall of 2002.

The Oral Argument

When Nevada's attorney, Deputy Attorney General Paul Taggart, rose to argue the case on January 15, 2003,[102] he had every reason to expect that the wind would be at his back. The Court had not upheld a statute as valid Fourteenth Amendment enforcement legislation since *Boerne*. And the Court's post-*Boerne* cases seemed to adopt a requirement that Congress could not adopt such legislation without first establishing "a history and pattern" of constitutional violations by the states.[103] Although Congress plainly adopted the FMLA with sex equality in mind, the legislative history contained very little evidence of discriminatory conduct by state employers (as opposed to private employers).[104] And even if state employers did engage in unconstitutional discrimination in the

---

[97]   *See* Bd. of Trs. v. Garrett, 531 U.S. 356 (2001) (ADA); Kimel v. Fla. Bd. of Regents, 528 U.S. 62 (2000) (ADEA); United States v. Morrison, 529 U.S. 598 (2000) (Violence Against Women Act); Dickerson v. United States, 530 U.S. 428 (2000) (18 U.S.C. § 3501, which pertained to the admissibility of criminal confessions); Fla. Prepaid Postsecondary Educ. Expense Bd. v. Coll. Sav. Bank, 527 U.S. 627 (1999) (Patent and Plant Variety Protection Remedy Clarification Act).

[98]   Petition for a Writ of Certiorari, Dep't of Human Res. v. Hibbs, 538 U.S. 721 (2003) (No. 01-1368).

[99]   Brief for the United States in Opposition, *Hibbs*, 538 U.S. 721 (No. 01-1368).

[100]   *See, e.g.*, Edward Walsh, *Court Takes Up Family Medical Leave Act; Decision Could Restrict Federal Laws on States*, WASH. POST, June 25, 2002, at A6.

[101]   Nev. Dep't of Human Res. v. Hibbs, 536 U.S. 938 (2002).

[102]   Transcript of Oral Argument at *1–3, *Hibbs*, 538 U.S. 721 (No. 01-1368), 2003 WL 145272.

[103]   *Garrett*, 531 U.S. at 368 (holding that the employment provisions of the ADEA did not validly enforce the Fourteenth Amendment, in significant part because Congress did not identify such a pattern of constitutional violations by the states).

[104]   Justice Kennedy's *Hibbs* dissent emphasized the point. He urged the FMLA's legislative history was "devoid of any discussion of the relevant evidence" of a pattern of unconstitutional state activity. 538 U.S. at 746–49 (Kennedy, J., dissenting). *But see id.* at 730–35 (majority opinion) ("According to evidence that was before Congress when it enacted the FMLA, States continue to rely on invalid gender stereotypes in the employment context, specifically in the administration of leave benefits.").

granting of leave, the statute's universalism seemed to present a serious problem of proportionality: Why would the proper remedy for discrimination be a mandate that all workers receive twelve weeks of leave, rather than a mandate that whatever leave is granted to members of one sex must be granted to members of the other sex as well? Not surprisingly, Taggart emphasized these points in his argument.

About nine and a half minutes into Taggart's time, Justice O'Connor hit him with the question that would occupy much of the rest of his argument: what to do with the problematic case of *Fitzpatrick v. Bitzer*.[105] *Fitzpatrick* involved Congress's 1972 extension of Title VII of the Civil Rights Act to state employers.[106] Title VII prohibits, among other things, sex discrimination in employment.[107] Yet Congress did not amass any evidence of unconstitutional sex discrimination by state employers in 1972. Indeed, under the Supreme Court's jurisprudence at the time it was not at all clear what, if any, sex discrimination in employment violated the Fourteenth Amendment. Nevertheless, in the 1976 *Bitzer* case—in an opinion written by then-Justice Rehnquist—the Court upheld Title VII's extension to the states as valid Fourteenth Amendment enforcement legislation.[108] The *Bitzer* Court had reached that result with virtually no analysis, but even the Rehnquist Court's "Federalism Revolution" cases declined to call *Bitzer* into question.

Justice O'Connor asked Taggart whether *Bitzer* "would stand up" under his argument.[109] After all, she noted, in *Bitzer*, "the Court unanimously found Title VII was a valid abrogation of the Eleventh Amendment immunity, and there was no inquiry into the history of gender discrimination, it was just accepted."[110] Taggart responded that Title VII would survive even on his analysis because it "closely hewed" to the Court's interpretation of the Equal Protection Clause.[111] But Justice Ginsburg then jumped in to note that "part of [his] argument was, if the discrimination doesn't exist anymore in the State, even if it did at one time, then the provision would have to sunset."[112] Noting that "as far as [T]itle VII is concerned, many States, the vast majority of States have their own [T]itle VII laws," she concluded that "at this point in time," under Taggart's reasoning, *Bitzer* "would have to go."[113]

---

[105] 427 U.S. 445 (1976).

[106] Equal Employment Opportunity Act of 1972, Pub. L. No. 92-261, § 2(1), 86 Stat. 103, 103 (1972) (codified as amended at 42 U.S.C. § 2000(e)(a) (2012)) (amending Title VII's definition of "persons" counting as employers to include "governments," "governmental agencies" and "political subdivisions").

[107] 42 U.S.C. § 2000e–2(a) (2012).

[108] 427 U.S. at 456.

[109] Transcript of Oral Argument, *supra* note 102, at *10.

[110] *Id.*

[111] *Id.* at *11.

[112] *Id.*

[113] *Id.*

Justice Scalia threw Taggart a lifeline, suggesting that it was "general knowledge" that sex discrimination by state employers was widespread in 1972,[114] but that did not help. Justice Breyer asked Taggart whether he accepted the proposition that sex discrimination by state employers remained widespread in 1993, when the FMLA was passed.[115] When Taggart said that he did not, Justice Breyer remarked that he could not "see the distinction with Title VII. It's goodbye if I accept that argument, I think."[116] Although he spent some time at the end discussing the proportionality of the twelve-week requirement, the risk his position posed to Title VII had dominated his half of the oral argument.

In the Supreme Court, William Hibbs was represented by Cornelia T.L. Pillard, a Georgetown Law Professor and experienced Supreme Court advocate whom President Obama would later appoint to the United States Court of Appeals for the D.C. Circuit.[117] Chief Justice Rehnquist pressed her on the record of state discrimination in the granting of leave; Pillard responded with citations to the legislative history.[118] Justice Scalia suggested that it was entirely appropriate for states to give maternity leave to mothers without giving paternity leave to fathers, because only mothers had to recover physically from childbirth; Pillard responded that the states that offered maternity leave provided it for periods of time that vastly exceeded the time necessary to recover from pregnancy.[119] At that point, Justice Ginsburg stepped in to underscore that such long leave periods suggested that the states were indulging sex-role stereotypes regarding who does or should care for children.[120] Pillard seized the chance to reinforce the basic feminist argument for universalism in family and medical leave: "It's precisely these assumptions that have caused State employers and other employers to discriminate against women in hiring, promotion, and retention, and against men in the dispensing of leave, and these are really two sides of the same coin."[121]

The final advocate to speak was Viet Dinh. Dinh was Pillard's Georgetown Law colleague, but at the time he was on leave to serve as Assistant Attorney General for Legal Policy. Throughout the "Federalism Revolution," the Bush administration's Department of Justice had felt an institutional obligation to strongly defend the constitutionality of federal laws—a position that had put its lawyers at odds with the Rehnquist

---

[114] *Id.* at *13.

[115] *Id.* at *14.

[116] *Id.* at *14–15.

[117] *Professor Cornelia "Nina" Pillard Confirmed to D.C. Circuit*, GEO. L. (Dec. 12, 2013), https://www.law.georgetown.edu/news/press-releases/professor-nina-pillard-confirmed-dc-circuit.cfm.

[118] Transcript of Oral Argument, *supra* note 102, at *26–28.

[119] *Id.* at *28–31.

[120] *Id.* at *31.

[121] *Id.* at *31.

Court in some cases. Dinh spent much of his time at the lectern defending the appropriateness of the twelve-week leave period chosen by Congress.[122]

In an article reviewing the oral argument the next day, longtime *New York Times* Supreme Court reporter Linda Greenhouse suggested that the outcome of the case was still unclear. But she said that Justice O'Connor's questions about the case's implications for Title VII "offered a hint" of hope that Justice O'Connor might join the four more liberal Justices to uphold the FMLA. As Greenhouse observed, "it was hardly a secret in the courtroom that Justice O'Connor represented the[ ] only hope of picking up a fifth vote against a further expansion of state immunity."[123]

The Court's Decision

When the Court issued its decision on May 27, 2003, Justice O'Connor had indeed joined the four more liberal Justices to uphold the FMLA as valid Fourteenth Amendment enforcement legislation. But there was a surprise sixth vote for that position: Chief Justice Rehnquist, who had been the leader of the Court's federalism revolution. In an even more surprising turn, Chief Justice Rehnquist wrote the opinion for the Court. His opinion squarely endorsed the feminist universalist premises that underlay the statute. He explained that Congress had adopted the statute as a response to sex discrimination that was driven by "mutually reinforcing stereotypes":

> Stereotypes about women's domestic roles are reinforced by parallel stereotypes presuming a lack of domestic responsibilities for men. Because employers continued to regard the family as the woman's domain, they often denied men similar accommodations or discouraged them from taking leave. These mutually reinforcing stereotypes created a self-fulfilling cycle of discrimination that forced women to continue to assume the role of primary family caregiver, and fostered employers' stereotypical views about women's commitment to work and their value as employees. Those perceptions, in turn, Congress reasoned, lead to subtle discrimination that may be difficult to detect on a case-by-case basis.[124]

The universal twelve-week leave mandate, Chief Justice Rehnquist concluded, directly responded to both sides of this cycle of stereotypes: "By creating an across-the-board, routine employment benefit for all eligible employees, Congress sought to ensure that family-care leave would no longer be stigmatized as an inordinate drain on the workplace

---

[122] Transcript of Oral Argument, *supra* note 102, at *38–48.

[123] Linda Greenhouse, *The Supreme Court: Checks and Balances; Medical Leave Act Is Debated in Major Federalism Case*, N.Y. TIMES (Jan. 16, 2003), http://www.nytimes.com/2003/01/16/us/supreme-court-checks-balances-medical-leave-act-debated-major-federalism-case.html.

[124] Nev. Dep't of Human Res. v. Hibbs, 538 U.S. 721, 736 (2003).

caused by female employees, and that employers could not evade leave obligations simply by hiring men."[125]

Distinguishing the Court's earlier opinions involving the ADEA and the ADA, Chief Justice Rehnquist's opinion explained that "age- or disability-based distinctions" triggered only minimal rational basis scrutiny under the Fourteenth Amendment.[126] Gender discrimination, by contrast, "triggers a heightened level of scrutiny."[127] It is thus "easier for Congress to show a pattern of state constitutional violations," Chief Justice Rehnquist noted, in the gender discrimination context.[128] By making this move, Chief Justice Rehnquist effectively shielded all of Title VII—not just its sex discrimination provision—from challenge, as the statute bars discrimination based on race, sex, and religion, all forms of discrimination that trigger heightened constitutional scrutiny.

Justice Souter, joined by Justices Ginsburg and Breyer, filed a brief concurrence. Justice Souter emphasized that, by joining Chief Justice Rehnquist's majority opinion, he should not be understood as embracing the broader federalism jurisprudence on which that opinion relied.[129] Justice Stevens concurred in the judgment only. He argued that Congress had power under the Commerce Clause to abrogate Nevada's sovereign immunity, so he did not have to reach the question whether the FMLA was proper legislation to enforce the Fourteenth Amendment.[130]

Justices Scalia, Kennedy, and Thomas all dissented. The principal dissent, authored by Justice Kennedy, argued that Congress simply had not developed a sufficient record of unconstitutional state gender discrimination in the specific context of leave programs.[131] Justice Kennedy contended that the record amassed by Congress focused primarily on the actions of the private sector, not of states; that the evidence of state action simply involved the failure to provide adequate leave rather than sex-based discrimination under the Fourteenth Amendment; and that a universal 12-week mandate was not appropriately tied to any constitutional violation.[132] Justice Scalia added a brief dissent of his own to argue that, even if the FMLA validly abrogates state sovereign immunity in general (a proposition he rejected), Nevada should still have the opportunity to demand proof that it—and not other states—had committed sufficient constitutional violations to warrant abrogation of its sovereign immunity.[133]

---

[125] *Id.* at 737.

[126] *Id.* at 735.

[127] *Id.* at 736.

[128] *Id.*

[129] *See id.* at 740 (Souter, J., concurring).

[130] *See id.* at 740–741 (Stevens, J., concurring in the judgment).

[131] *Id.* at 744–59 (Kennedy, J., dissenting).

[132] *See id.* at 746–756.

[133] *See id.* at 741–744 (Scalia, J., dissenting).

THE AFTERMATH

In the immediate aftermath of the Court's decision, much of the commentary surrounding *Hibbs* focused on Chief Justice Rehnquist's surprising defection from his usual states'-rights position. Had Chief Justice Rehnquist begun to drift from the very federalism revolution that had been the centerpiece of his chief justiceship?

Greenhouse, for her part, suggested that the answer was "[n]ot evolution, perhaps, but life." She noted that Chief Justice Rehnquist's daughter was "a single mother who until recently held a high-pressure job and sometimes had child-care problems." "Several times" during the Term the Court decided *Hibbs*, Chief Justice Rehnquist was called upon to "le[ave] work early to pick up his granddaughters from school." These experiences, she offered, may have given him a newfound "solicitude for the usefulness of the Family and Medical Leave Act in erasing the 'pervasive sex-role stereotype that caring for family members is women's work.'"[134]

Yale Law Professor Robert Post, by contrast, suggested that the answer could be found in the topic that drew extensive discussion at oral argument—the concern that a ruling against the FMLA might call Title VII into question.[135] Title VII is the centerpiece of the Civil Rights Act of 1964, a statute that many across the political spectrum regard as something close to sacred.[136] Although Chief Justice Rehnquist's own jurisprudence had generally sought to narrow the application of Title VII, he might well have worried that encouraging a frontal attack on the constitutionality of the statute would invite widespread charges that the Court was acting illegitimately.[137]

But the future was not as kind to the feminist universalism that the Court endorsed in *Hibbs*. The year after the Court's decision in *Hibbs*, George Washington University Law Professor Michael Selmi wrote that it was "clear" that the FMLA had "not accomplished its goals with respect to combating stereotypes or discrimination against women in the

---

[134] Linda Greenhouse, *Ideas & Trends: Evolving Opinions; Heartfelt Words from the Rehnquist Court*, N.Y. TIMES (July 6, 2003), http://www.nytimes.com/2003/07/06/weekin review/ideas-trends-evolving-opinions-heartfelt-words-from-the-rehnquist-court.html.

[135] *See* Robert C. Post, *Foreword: Fashioning the Legal Constitution: Culture, Courts, and Law*, 117 HARV. L. REV. 4, 11–41 (2003).

[136] *See, e.g.*, Norbert Schlei, *Foreword* to BARBARA SCHLEI & PAUL GROSSMAN, EMPLOYMENT DISCRIMINATION LAW vii (2d ed. 1983) ("The Civil Rights Act of 1964 was the most important civil rights legislation of this century. Title VII of that Act . . . has been its most important part.").

[137] One model for this type of analysis employed by Chief Justice Rehnquist is his treatment of the decision in *Miranda v. Arizona*, 384 U.S. 436 (1966). Chief Justice Rehnquist, a longstanding critic of *Miranda*, consistently voted to narrow its application and to introduce and broaden exceptions to it. But when a frontal challenge to *Miranda* came before the Court in 2000, Chief Justice Rehnquist wrote the opinion for the Court rejecting the challenge. "*Miranda*," Chief Justice Rehnquist observed, "has become embedded in routine police practice to the point where the warnings have become part of our national culture." Dickerson v. United States, 530 U.S. 428, 443 (2000).

workplace."[138] If anything, he argued, "the statute has likely exacerbated both, though probably only to a socially insignificant degree."[139]

The universalist approach of the FMLA has had two evident limitations. First, even though the statute provides parental and family-care leave to all covered workers without regard to their gender, female workers continue to take the leave far more frequently than do male workers.[140] This pattern of female-dominated leave-taking persists across the world.[141] Some countries have made progress in addressing this imbalance, but have done so only by adopting policies that cut against the FMLA's universalist structure: either (a) abandoning universalism by specifically requiring fathers to take certain periods of leave; or (b) setting aside some leave periods for each parent, which may not be transferred to the other parent and will be forfeited if the assigned parent does not take them.[142] In contrast to those approaches, which effectively single out fathers and impose some cost on them for failing to take parental leave, the FMLA's universal model does little to alter the reality that women, far more than men, take that leave in our current world. That reality, in turn, is likely to entrench the stereotype that women, not men, take care of newborn children—despite the formally universal coverage of the statute.[143] To the extent that the feminist supporters of the FMLA thought that a universally framed law would avoid encouraging employers to discriminate against women, the actual pattern of leave-taking suggests that the law has fallen short of that goal.[144]

The drafters of the FMLA anticipated that women would likely continue to take more parental leave than men (though they do not seem

---

[138] Michael Selmi, *Is Something Better than Nothing? Critical Reflections on Ten Years of the FMLA*, 15 WASH. U. J.L. & POL'Y 65, 67 (2004).

[139] *Id.*

[140] *See* Wen-Jui Han & Jane Waldfogel, *Parental Leave: The Impact of Recent Legislation on Parents' Leave Taking*, 40 DEMOGRAPHY 191, 198 (2003) ("Our results for men indicate that the FMLA and state leave laws have not been associated with more leave taking or longer leaves by recent fathers. There is little or no indication in our data that more fathers take leaves or that they take longer leaves when they are entitled to more weeks of leave.").

[141] *See* Ariane Hegewisch & Janet C. Gornick, *The Impact of Work-Family Policies on Women's Employment: A Review of Research from OECD Countries*, 14 COMMUNITY, WORK & FAM. 119, 127–28 (2011) ("In principle, in many countries mothers and fathers are able to share their parental leave entitlement, yet in most countries women are not only more likely to take up leave but are also the sole participants in leave.").

[142] *See id.* at 127 (noting, for example, Portugal's obligatory five-day leave policy for new fathers, as well as Iceland's nine-month-per-child system, which provides three months for each parent and three months that may be divided among them).

[143] *See* Samuel R. Bagenstos, *Universalism and Civil Rights (With Notes on Voting Rights After* Shelby), 123 YALE L.J. 2838, 2864–66 (2014) (arguing that whether a law is understood as universal will often depend on its social meaning and impact on the world rather than its formal coverage).

[144] The effect cannot be great, however, as empirical evidence suggests that the FMLA, overall, had "no significant impacts . . . on women's employment or wages in the years after the policy went into effect." Maya Rossin-Slater, *Maternity and Family Leave Policy* 12 (IZA Inst. of Labor Econ., Discussion Paper No. 10500, 2017), http://www.nber.org/papers/w23069.pdf.

to have anticipated just how great the disparity would be). That is why they included self-care leave, along with parental and family-care leave, in the statute's twelve-week mandate. As we have seen, because the drafters expected that both men and women would take self-care leave, they believed that the FMLA as a whole would not give employers a meaningful incentive to discriminate against members of either gender.

To a large extent, the drafters' expectation has proven true. Leave to address an employee's own serious health condition has accounted for more than half of the leave taken under the FMLA.[145] But this has led to the second problem with the statute's universalist framing. Many employers complain that accommodating self-care leave is extremely burdensome, especially because such leave is likely to be taken intermittently and unpredictably, thus impeding efforts at workforce planning.[146] Because the statute ties self-care leave together with parental and family leave, employer discontent with self-care leave has fed a backlash against the FMLA as a whole. This backlash, in turn, creates obstacles to enacting in the United States the sorts of paid family leave policies embraced by most other industrialized countries—and it is precisely this type of leave that is most likely to open up employment opportunities to women.[147] The FMLA's universalist framing thus may be making it harder to adopt policies that could be more effective in promoting workplace equality.

The Supreme Court's most important post-*Hibbs* decision on the FMLA, in fact, involved the self-care leave provision. In *Coleman v. Court of Appeals of Maryland*, decided in 2012, the Court considered whether the self-care leave provision of the FMLA validly enforced the Fourteenth Amendment.[148] With Chief Justice Rehnquist and Justice O'Connor no longer on the bench, their replacements, Chief Justice Roberts and Justice Alito, joined the three *Hibbs* dissenters to hold that the self-care provision was not a proper exercise of the enforcement power.[149] Justice Kennedy's plurality opinion did not question *Hibbs*. But it held that the FMLA's self-care provision, unlike the family-care provision at issue in *Hibbs*, lacked a sufficient connection to gender discrimination.[150] In dissent, Justice Ginsburg cogently explained the universalist position taken by the statute's drafters—that the self-care provision was necessary to ensure that the FMLA did not lead to discrimination against women.[151] The *Coleman* decision thus further highlights the limits of the FMLA's feminist universalism.

---

[145] *See, e.g.*, Suk, *supra* note 45, at 19.

[146] *See id.* at 21–22.

[147] *See id.* at 46–49 (noting in particular that the "generous" maternity and parental leave policies available in France and Sweden are possible precisely because they are prioritized above and separated from other types of medical and family leave).

[148] 566 U.S. 30 (2012).

[149] *Id.* at 37–39, 44–45.

[150] *See id.* at 33–42.

[151] *See id.* at 47–51 (Ginsburg, J., dissenting).

* * *

Hibbs ultimately is a case with a mixed legacy. For the Supreme Court to embrace the key arguments of feminist universalism represented a triumph for an important school of thought within legal feminism. For the Court's opinion to be written by Chief Justice Rehnquist of all people was almost delicious. But the triumph came at a time when the limitations of the FMLA's approach were becoming apparent. To achieve the goals of justice and equality in and out of the workplace, feminists have increasingly realized that it is necessary to move beyond the universalist paradigm.

10

Katherine Shaw*

"Similar in Their Ability or Inability to Work": *Young v. UPS* and the Meaning of Pregnancy Discrimination

In 2002, Peggy Young began working for United Parcel Service (UPS) as a part-time early morning delivery driver, receiving and delivering packages that had arrived by air carrier overnight. She had worked for UPS since 1999, and she valued her job for the excellent insurance benefits it provided.[1]

In the summer of 2005, Young and her husband began attempting a pregnancy using in vitro fertilization (IVF). Young's first attempt resulted in a miscarriage, and her second attempt was unsuccessful.[2] In the summer of 2006 she decided to undergo a third round of IVF, and to take unpaid leave from her job at UPS while she did so.[3] This round was successful, and she became pregnant.[4]

When she was ready to return to work in October 2006, Young provided UPS with a note from her doctor recommending that she not lift more than 20 pounds for the duration of her pregnancy. This limitation did not strike her as significant. Most of her packages were quite light—envelopes, paychecks, and things of that nature—and, as she attested, she had virtually never needed to lift over 20 pounds on the job.[5] Young had two older children, and she assumed that during this pregnancy she

* Professor of Law and Co-Director, Floersheimer Center for Constitutional Democracy, Benjamin N. Cardozo School of Law. My thanks to Sam Stanton, Jess Honan, Patrick Glackin, and Shayna Byrne for terrific research assistance, to Reva Siegel, Melissa Murray, Deborah Dinner, and Douglas NeJaime for invaluable feedback on earlier drafts, and to Samuel Bagenstos, Sharon Fast Gustafson, and Peggy Peskey (formerly Peggy Young), for generously sharing their time and recollections with me.

[1] Affidavit of Plaintiff, Young v. United Parcel Service, Inc. (D. Md. Feb. 14, 2011) (No. DKC 08-2586), 2011 WL 665321, at *2 [hereinafter Young Affidavit].

[2] Telephone Interview with Peggy Peskey (Aug. 14, 2018) (formerly Peggy Young).

[3] Young Affidavit, *supra* note 1, at *2.

[4] *Id.*

[5] *Id.*

would work, as she had during her other pregnancies, until the day she went into labor.[6]

But UPS informed Young that in light of her lifting limitation she would not be able to perform the essential functions of her job as a driver, since the position technically required drivers to be able to "[l]ift, lower, push, pull, leverage and manipulate" packages "weighing up to 70 pounds" and to "[a]ssist in moving packages weighing up to 150 pounds."[7] Young explained that she was able and willing to continue with her regular job, and had secured assurances from colleagues that they could assist her with any heavy packages, or that alternatively she could take a "light duty assignment" that would not require heavy lifting. But Young's supervisors informed her that light duty assignments were not available for pregnant workers.[8] Indeed, under UPS policy, light duty assignments were available only to individuals who were temporarily disabled under the Americans with Disabilities Act (ADA), who had been injured on the job, or who had lost their Department of Transportation (DOT) certifications for any reason. Since Young's pregnancy did not place her in any of those categories, she was told she was ineligible for a light duty assignment.[9]

So Young went on unpaid leave, where she remained for the duration of her pregnancy, eventually losing the health insurance her UPS job provided.[10] She gave birth in April 2007, returned to work that June, and in July initiated a challenge that would strengthen the rights of pregnant workers nationwide.

Although *Young v. UPS* was not the Supreme Court's first encounter with the Pregnancy Discrimination Act (PDA), which in 1978 changed federal law to expressly include pregnancy discrimination within the meaning of sex discrimination,[11] it was arguably its most important case to interpret the PDA. Young's case required the Court to decide whether UPS's refusal to accommodate Young's pregnancy, even while it accommodated workers who were temporarily disabled for reasons other than pregnancy, violated the PDA's requirement that employers treat "women affected by pregnancy . . . the same for all employment-related purposes . . . as other persons not so affected but similar in their ability or inability to work."[12] And while the Court did not embrace a sweeping rule that would have required employers to automatically give pregnant workers the benefit of an accommodation given to any other worker,

---

[6]   Telephone Interview with Sharon Fast Gustafson, Attorney at Law, PLC (Mar. 14, 2018) [hereinafter Gustafson Interview].

[7]   Young v. United Parcel Serv., Inc., 135 S. Ct. 1338, 1344 (2015).

[8]   *Id.*

[9]   *Id.* at 1345.

[10]   *Id.*

[11]   Pub. L. No. 88-352, 78 Stat. 241 (1964), *amended by* Pub. L. No. 95-555, 92 Stat. 2076 (1978) (current version at 42 U.S.C. § 2000e(k) (2012)).

[12]   Young v. United Parcel Serv., Inc., 135 S. Ct. 1338, 1344 (2015) (citing 42 U.S.C. § 2000e(k) (2012)).

regardless of the source of the disability, it nevertheless clarified that employers could not evade their obligation of nondiscrimination by merely pointing to some difference between non-accommodated pregnant workers and accommodated nonpregnant workers. So, although the opinion did not mandate the accommodation of pregnancy under all circumstances, it nevertheless provided workers with a powerful tool for challenging a practice that was still far too common in 2006, and indeed in 2019—discrimination against employees on the basis of pregnancy.[13]

In addition, the story of *Young*—and indeed of the PDA itself—features a set of alliances that complicate the fault lines evident elsewhere in this volume. That is, the legal fight to protect women who not only become but remain pregnant, and who wish to continue working while pregnant, has produced coalitions of individuals and organizations that take starkly different views on many other issues involving reproductive rights and justice. So *Young* may point the way to the prospect of legal and political coalitions around issues like paid leave and subsidized childcare, where a wide array of actors may be able to work together both to promote women's autonomy and to facilitate family formation.

PREGNANCY DISCRIMINATION IN HISTORICAL CONTEXT

Feminists have long been divided about how best to protect pregnancy at work,[14] with the roots of the divide traceable to nineteenth and early twentieth century battles over protective labor legislation. A number of early feminists and other Progressive Era reformers advocated for special workplace protections for women, in part as a strategy to establish the permissibility of broader regulation of workplace conditions in the face of a *Lochner*-era Court resistant to such interventions. As Deborah Dinner explains, these reformers used "maternal gender ideologies as a wedge with which to crack Lochnerism."[15] These efforts

---

[13] For a harrowing recent account of the discrimination many pregnant workers continue to face, see Jessica Silver-Greenberg & Natalie Kitroff, *Miscarrying at Work: The Physical Toll of Pregnancy Discrimination*, N.Y. TIMES (Oct. 21, 2018), http://www.nytimes.com/interactive/2018/10/21/business/pregnancy-discrimination-miscarriages.html; Rebecca Traister, *Why Women Can't Break Free from the Parent Trap*, THE NEW REPUBLIC (Feb. 2, 2015), https://newrepublic.com/article/120939/maternity-leave-policies-america-hurt-working-moms ("[T]he simple—and celebrated—act of having a baby turns out to be a stunningly precarious economic and professional choice.").

[14] *See* Stephanie Wildman, *Pregnant and Working: The Story of* California Federal Savings v. Guerra, *in* WOMEN AND THE LAW STORIES 254, 268–70 (Elizabeth M. Schneider & Stephanie Wildman eds., 2011).

[15] Deborah Dinner, *Strange Bedfellows at Work: Neomaternalism in the Making of Sex Discrimination Law*, 91 WASH. U. L. REV. 453, 462 (2014); *see also* Reva B. Siegel, *She the People: The Nineteenth Amendment, Sex Equality, Federalism, and the Family*, 115 HARV. L. REV. 947, 1046 (2002); Joan G. Zimmerman, *The Jurisprudence of Equality: The Women's Minimum Wage, the First Equal Rights Amendment, and* Adkins v. Children's Hospital, *1905–1923*, 78 J. AM. HIST. 188 (1991). Muller v. Oregon, 208 U.S. 412 (1908), in which the Court upheld a state maximum-hours law for women, represented a major victory for this approach. *Id.* at 422–23 ("The two sexes differ in structure of body, in the functions to be performed by each. . . . This difference justifies a difference in legislation.").

were largely successful: in *Muller v. Oregon*, the Court upheld a state law that prohibited women—but not men—from working more than ten hours per day in any "mechanical establishment, or factory, or laundry."[16] Despite the judicial endorsement of this mode of protective legislative, some women's rights advocates, including supporters of the first Equal Rights Amendment, soon began to distance themselves from such protectionist ideologies, particularly after the ratification of the Nineteenth Amendment.[17] By the 1970s, legal feminists began advancing new understandings of the Constitution's equality guarantees, with various sex-based distinctions falling under the weight of their arguments.[18] And, as women's participation in labor markets increased dramatically during this period, so too did the stakes of workplace treatment of pregnancy.[19]

As feminist reformers recognized, pregnancy discrimination could appear in both overt and more covert forms, ranging from refusal to hire pregnant applicants and outright termination upon the announcement of a pregnancy—less common today, though far from eradicated[20]—to more indirect tactics, like the failure to accommodate the specific physical limitations pregnancies can sometimes impose.[21] Over the course of the 1970s, advocates began challenging these forms of pregnancy discrimination under both the Constitution and federal statutes.

As Deborah Dinner details elsewhere in this volume, in the 1974 case *Geduldig v. Aiello*, the Supreme Court rejected an equal protection challenge to California's exclusion of pregnancy from its otherwise comprehensive temporary disability insurance policy.[22] *Geduldig* largely closed the door to recourse under the federal Constitution for pregnancy discrimination, but it did not speak directly to what *statutes* might require of employers—in particular, Title VII of the Civil Rights Act of 1964, which makes it an unlawful employment practice for an employer "to discriminate against any individual with respect to . . . . compensation, terms, conditions, or privileges of employment, because of

---

[16]   *Muller*, 208 U.S. at 416.

[17]   As Reva Siegel explains, "Many in the suffrage movement had supported protective labor legislation for women . . . but in the immediate aftermath of the Nineteenth Amendment's ratification, some in the movement were beginning to question the wisdom of supporting sex-differentiated legislation." Siegel, *supra* note 15, at 1014.

[18]   *See, e.g.*, Reed v. Reed, 404 U.S. 71, 76–77 (1971).

[19]   Dinner, *supra* note 15, at 471 ("Women between the ages of twenty and thirty-four accounted for the greatest increase in labor-force participation among women during the period from 1960 to 1974.").

[20]   *See* Natalie Kitroeff and Jessica Silver-Greenberg, *Pregnancy Discrimination is Rampant Inside America's Largest Companies*, N.Y. TIMES (June 15, 2018), https://www.ny times.com/interactive/2018/06/15/business/pregnancy-discrimination.html.

[21]   Deborah A. Widiss, *Gilbert Redux: The Interaction of the Pregnancy Discrimination Act and the Amended Americans with Disabilities Act*, 46 U.C. DAVIS L. REV. 961, 972 (2013).

[22]   *See generally* Deborah Dinner, *Sex Equality and the U.S. Welfare Regime: The Story of* Geduldig v. Aiello, *in* REPRODUCTIVE RIGHTS AND JUSTICE STORIES 77 (Melissa Murray, Katherine Shaw & Reva B. Siegel eds., 2019).

such individual's . . . . sex[.]"²³ Indeed, even as the Court was considering *Geduldig*, a Title VII challenge to pregnancy discrimination was making its way through the lower courts. The litigation effort in that Title VII case, *General Electric Co. v. Gilbert*,²⁴ involved an unlikely coalition of feminists and pro-life activists; as the *New York Times* reported at the time, "A cause that has managed to unite women from feminists to members of the Right to Life movement is the right to disability benefits for time lost due to pregnancy."²⁵

In *Gilbert*, a group of female employees challenged General Electric (GE)'s temporary disability scheme under Title VII. The GE scheme was exceptionally broad, providing "nonoccupational sickness and accident benefits" in the amount of 60% of typical weekly pay,²⁶ and covering everything from sports injuries to cosmetic surgery to "injuries incurred in the commission of a crime or during a fight."²⁷ Despite this broad coverage, GE excluded from its plan temporary disabilities caused by pregnancy.²⁸

In ruling on the challenge to GE's policy, the *Gilbert* Court explained that the case was not directly controlled by the constitutional holding of *Geduldig*. Nevertheless, because *Geduldig* involved "a strikingly similar disability plan," the Court concluded that its reasoning was "quite relevant in determining whether or not the pregnancy exclusion did discriminate on the basis of sex."²⁹ Accordingly, the *Gilbert* Court hewed closely to *Geduldig*'s logic, concluding that discrimination on the basis of pregnancy was not discrimination on the basis of sex under Title VII. As the Court explained, GE's benefits package was "facially nondiscriminatory in the sense that there is no risk from which men are protected and women are not. Likewise, there is no risk from which women are protected and men are not."³⁰ Rather than discriminating against women, the Court explained, the policy merely divided workers "into two groups—pregnant women and nonpregnant persons. While the first group is exclusively female, the second includes members of both sexes."³¹

---

²³   42 U.S.C. § 2000e–2(a)(1) (2012).

²⁴   429 U.S. 125 (1976).

²⁵   Virginia Lee Warren, *The Fight for Disability Benefits in Pregnancy*, N.Y. TIMES (Sept. 16, 1975), https://www.nytimes.com/1975/09/16/archives/the-fight-for-disability-benefits-in-pregnancy.html.

²⁶   Gen. Elec. Co. v. Gilbert, 429 U.S. 125, 128 (1976).

²⁷   *Id.* at 151 (Brennan, J., dissenting).

²⁸   *Id.* at 129–31.

²⁹   *Id.* at 133.

³⁰   *Id.* at 138. The Court continued: "It is impossible to find any gender-based discriminatory effect in this scheme simply because women disabled as a result of pregnancy do not receive benefits; that is to say, gender-based discrimination does not result simply because an employer's disability-benefits plan is less than all-inclusive." *Id.*

³¹   *Id.* at 135 (quoting *Geduldig*, 417 U.S. at 496 n.20).

One significant distinction between *Geduldig* and *Gilbert* was that *Gilbert* involved not only a statute but an agency's interpretation of that statute. But the Court, while clearly importing the logic of its constitutional decision in *Geduldig*, disregarded the Equal Employment Opportunity Commission (EEOC)'s interpretation of Title VII—an interpretation informed by distinct constitutional commitments.[32] The EEOC's 1975 guidelines took the position that "[d]isabilities caused or contributed to by pregnancy, miscarriage, abortion, childbirth, and recovery therefrom are, for all job-related purposes, temporary disabilities and should be treated as such under any health or temporary disability insurance or sick leave plan."[33] But the Court concluded that the EEOC's guidance was entitled to very limited weight.[34]

Following the loss in *Gilbert,* the locus of advocacy around pregnancy and work largely shifted to the legislative arena, where advocates sought to correct through legislation the Court's wrong in *Gilbert* (and, indirectly, *Geduldig*) by making explicit that discrimination against pregnant women *did* constitute discrimination on the basis of sex.[35] In March of 1977, just four months after the decision in *Gilbert*, legislators introduced "[a] bill to amend title VII of the Civil Rights Act of 1964 to prohibit sex discrimination on the basis of pregnancy." As Senator Harrison Williams, one of the lead sponsors of the bill that would become the PDA, explained as he opened debate on the measure, "*Gilbert* came as a deep disappointment to working women across the nation." He continued, explaining that the decision represented "a serious setback to women's rights and to the development of antidiscrimination law" as well as "pos[ing] a serious threat to the security of the family unit."[36]

---

[32]   WILLIAM N. ESKRIDGE, JR. & JOHN FEREJOHN, A REPUBLIC OF STATUTES 73, 451 (2010) ("[H]owever defensible *Geduldig* was under a cautious and deliberation-respecting theory of judicial review, *Gilbert* was less defensible, because the EEOC had engaged in a thoughtful deliberative process in its role implementing Title VII."); Sophia Z. Lee, *Race, Sex, and Rulemaking: Administrative Constitutionalism and the Workplace, 1960 to the Present*, 96 VA. L. REV. 799, 886 (2010).

[33]   29 C.F.R. § 1604.10(b) (1975).

[34]   *Gilbert*, 429 U.S. at 141–43.

[35]   In shifting their efforts from courts to the legislature, PDA advocates engaged in an important form of what Robert Post and Reva Siegel have described as "legislative constitutionalism"; Robert C. Post & Reva B. Siegel, *Legislative Constitutionalism and Section Five Power: Policentric Interpretation of the Family and Medical Leave Act*, 112 YALE L. J. 1943, 1945 (2003) (describing Section 5 of the 14th Amendment as "link[ing] the legal interpretations of courts to the constitutional understandings of the American people, as expressed through their chosen representatives"); *id.* at 2013 (describing the legislative debates over the PDA as having "clear constitutional overtones"). *See also* Mary Ziegler, *Choice at Work: Young v. United Parcel Service, Pregnancy Discrimination, and Reproductive Liberty*, 93 DENV. L. REV. 219, 246 (2015); Cary Franklin, *Inventing the "Traditional Concept" of Sex Discrimination*, 125 HARV. L. REV. 1307, 1358–67 (2012); Reva B. Siegel, Note—*Employment Equality Under the Pregnancy Discrimination Act of 1978*, 94 YALE L. J. 929, 938 (1985) ("Congress acted to provide women raising pregnancy claims the benefits of full Title VII protection because, unlike the Court, it understood that pregnancy played a central role in the logic of sex-based employment discrimination").

[36]   95 CONG. REC. 7, 539–40 (daily ed. Mar. 15, 1977) (statement of Sen. Williams).

Williams's twin focus on women's autonomy and family creation was likely no accident, for the legislative advocacy effort drew support from a broad and sometimes surprising coalition of forces, including a number of anti-abortion and pro-life voices. The Campaign to End Discrimination Against Pregnant Workers, an organization formed in the wake of *Gilbert*, featured participants from across the political spectrum.[37] Legal feminists and grassroots advocates were primary drivers behind the bill: law professor and feminist litigator Wendy Williams, for example, helped draft the bill and argued in her testimony that women should not be compelled to "forgo a fundamental right," like the right to bear children, "as a condition precedent to the enjoyment of . . . employment free from discrimination."[38] But the bill also drew support from religious and conservative organizations, some of which were animated by a belief that employment-related antidiscrimination measures would economically empower women to continue their pregnancies, and thus decrease the incidence of abortion. An especially important conservative proponent of the PDA was American Citizens Concerned for Life (ACCL). The organization's founder, Marjory Mecklenberg, publicly endorsed the PDA,[39] and representatives from the organization testified in support of the bill.[40] This was especially significant because some iterations of the PDA expressly required employers to cover treatment, conditions, or leave related to abortion, as well as childbirth (although the final version of the bill did not include that language).[41] And both Democrats and Republicans made arguments that sounded in antidiscrimination principles, the protection of families, and at times the goal of reducing or removing incentives to abortion.[42]

After a protracted legislative process, the PDA was enacted in 1978 with bipartisan support.[43] The final language actually consisted of two

---

[37]   ESKRIDGE & FEREJOHN, *supra* note 32, at 71.

[38]   *Discrimination on the Basis of Pregnancy, 1977: Hearings on S. 995 Before the Subcomm. on Labor of the S. Comm. on Human Res.*, 95th Cong. 137 (1977) (statement of Wendy W. Williams, Assistant Professor of Law, Georgetown University Law Center).

[39]   DANIEL K. WILLIAMS, DEFENDERS OF THE UNBORN: THE PRO-LIFE MOVEMENT BEFORE *ROE. V. WADE* 217 (2016).

[40]   *Legislation to Prohibit Sex Discrimination on the Basis of Pregnancy Part 2: Hearing on H.R. 5055 and H.R. 6075 Before the Subcomm. on Emp't Opportunities of the H. Comm. on Educ. and Labor*, 95th Cong. 66 (1977) (statement of Dr. Dorothy Czarnecki, M.D., American Citizens Concerned for Life); *see also Legislation to Prohibit Sex Discrimination on the Basis of Pregnancy: Hearing on H.R. 5055 and H.R.6075 Before the Subcomm. on Emp't Opportunities of the H. Comm. on Educ. and Labor*, 95th Cong. 60–61 (1977) (statement of Dr. Andre Hellegers, M.D., Director, Joseph and Rose Kennedy Institute, Georgetown University).

[41]   Ziegler, *supra* note 35, at 246.

[42]   *See, e.g.,* 123 CONG. REC. S4142-45 (daily ed. Mar. 15, 1977) (statement of Sen. Brooke) ("[F]aced with the dual cost of being forced to pay their medical costs plus losing their wages, many low-income women may come to feel that their only alternative is an abortion."). *See also* Deborah Dinner, *Strange Bedfellows at Work: Neomaternalism in the Making of Sex Discrimination Law*, 91 WASH. U. L. REV. 453, 498-503 (2014).

[43]   S. 995, 95th Cong. (1978) (codified as amended at 42 U.S.C. § 2000e(k) (2012)); *see also* William N. Eskridge, Jr., *Title VII's Statutory History and the Sex Discrimination Argument for LGBT Equality*, 127 YALE L. J. 322, 354 (2017).

separate clauses. The first amended Title VII's definitions section to provide that "the terms 'because of sex' or 'on the basis of sex' include, but are not limited to, because of or on the basis of pregnancy, childbirth, or related medical conditions."[44] The second, more opaque, clause—the one squarely at issue in *Young*—provided that "women affected by pregnancy, childbirth, or related medical conditions shall be treated the same for all employment-related purposes . . . as other persons not so affected but similar in their ability or inability to work."[45]

The Supreme Court's first significant encounter with the PDA came nearly a decade after the law's enactment, in the 1987 case *California Federal Savings & Loan Association v. Guerra (Cal. Fed)*.[46] At issue in *Cal. Fed* was whether a California law that prohibited pregnancy discrimination, and included within that prohibition a requirement of reasonable pregnancy-related leave, was preempted by the PDA. The Court rejected the preemption argument, finding that the PDA and the California law shared a common goal, the eradication of employment barriers for women, with the PDA merely representing "a floor below which pregnancy benefits may not drop—not a ceiling above which they may not rise."[47] Then in 1991, the Court confronted the PDA more directly in *UAW v. Johnson Controls*, a challenge to a company policy that restricted the employment of all women (but not men) of child-bearing age from work that might involve lead exposure, unless they could prove infertility; the Court had no trouble concluding that this policy violated Title VII as amended by the PDA.[48]

Despite these signals from the Supreme Court, in the years that followed, federal appeals courts nearly invariably sided with employers in cases brought by pregnant workers alleging failure to accommodate pregnancy. These courts fixated on "techniques of comparison" between pregnant and nonpregnant workers,[49] typically concluding that where an employer failed to accommodate *some* nonpregnant workers, that denial insulated the employer from liability for failing to accommodate pregnant

---

[44]   42 U.S.C. § 2000e(k).

[45]   *Id.*

[46]   *See generally* Stephanie M. Wildman, *The Story of* California Federal Savings v. Guerra, *in* WOMEN AND THE LAW STORIES 254 (Elizabeth M. Schneider & Stephanie Wildman eds., 2011). California Fed. Sav. & Loan Ass'n v. Guerra, 479 U.S. 272 (1987).

[47]   *Id.* at 280. The Court rejected the argument made for Cal. Fed. Savings by Ted Olson, who insisted that the case featured a choice between "equal treatment" and "special treatment," and linked California's scheme to stereotype-based protective legislation. As he described it, "The question presented by this case is whether the federal mandate of equal protection prevails over the state policy of special protection." Oral Argument at 00:47, California Fed. Sav. & Loan Ass'n v. Guerra, 479 U.S. 272 (1987) (No. 85-494) https://www.oyez.org/cases/1986/85-494.

[48]   UAW v. Johnson Controls, Inc., 499 U.S. 187, 211 (1991) ("It is no more appropriate for the courts than it is for individual employers to decide whether a woman's reproductive role is more important to herself and her family than her economic role. Congress has left this choice to the woman as hers to make.").

[49]   Reva B. Siegel, *Pregnancy as a Normal Condition of Employment*, 59 WM. & MARY L. REV. 971, 976 (2018) (In this era, "courts reasoned as if the wrong of pregnancy discrimination could be defined solely through techniques of comparison.").

workers. In a classic formulation of this view, Judge Richard Posner wrote in 1994 that under the PDA, "[e]mployers can treat pregnant women as badly as they treat similarly affected but nonpregnant employees."[50] It was against this backdrop that Peggy Young's case arose.

YOUNG V. UPS

UPS's denial of Peggy Young's request to accommodate her 20-pound weight limitation came as a genuine surprise to her, particularly in light of the kinds of accommodations the company *did* provide to other workers—those with on-the-job injuries, ADA disabilities, or anyone who had lost a commercial driver's license. As Young's lawyer Sharon Gustafson later described the third category, "[T]hey accommodated *anybody* who couldn't keep their commercial driver's license [(CDL)], for any reason! Alcohol related reasons. Sleep apnea. Emotional reasons. . . . if you could not keep your commercial driver's license, they would accommodate you by bringing you inside for a spell. Well, almost anything gave you the ability to go and say 'take my CDL away from me.' Except for pregnancy. You just never lost a CDL because you were pregnant."[51]

For Young, unpaid leave and the loss of her health insurance were no small matters. She explained that "one of the primary reasons" she worked at UPS was for the benefits: "I have worked many part-time jobs in my life, and this is the only part-time job I have ever found that provided good benefits."[52] After losing her UPS benefits, she went on her husband's military benefits, but she found those benefits inferior to those she would have received had she continued on her UPS plan; although she had intended to get maternity care through a hospital "with a maternity ward that has an excellent reputation and is only twenty minutes from my house," she instead "had to receive medical care at either Andrews Air Force Base or Bethesda Naval Hospital," which required her to travel up to two hours in each direction.[53]

In April 2007, with the birth of her daughter approaching, Young contacted attorney Sharon Gustafson, a solo practitioner who specialized in employment discrimination claims, in particular pregnancy discrimination.[54] Young initially sought help with short-term disability benefits, for which she had attempted to qualify after being told she could not return to work. As Gustafson recounts, during their initial consultation, she asked Young, "What is it you really want?" According to Gustafson, Young responded: "Well I don't really even want disability benefits. What I want is to be able to work. But they won't let me work."[55]

---

[50]   Troupe v. May Dep't Stores Co., 20 F.3d 734, 738 (7th Cir. 1994).

[51]   Gustafson Interview, *supra* note 6.

[52]   Young Affidavit, *supra* note 1, at *8.

[53]   *Id.*

[54]   SHARON FAST GUSTAFSON, http://www.sharonfastgustafson.com (last visited Nov. 27, 2018).

[55]   Gustafson Interview, *supra* note 6.

Gustafson found, and still finds, UPS's resistance to Young's request baffling: "I really just feel like sometimes I can't understand what companies are thinking. And this is one of those cases. Because my client—what she was asking for—it wasn't just reasonable. It was ludicrously reasonable."[56]

Young gave birth at the end of April 2007, and in June returned to her job at UPS. In July she filed an EEOC charge, arguing that UPS's denial of her request for an accommodation was discrimination on the basis of sex and on the basis of pregnancy. She received a Right to Sue letter, and she and Gustafson filed a lawsuit in federal district court.[57]

Young primarily framed her case as a "disparate treatment" claim, arguing that UPS intentionally discriminated against her because of her pregnancy and that, in addition, she could make a prima facie showing of discrimination under the burden-shifting framework announced in *McDonnell Douglas v. Green*,[58] under which a plaintiff must establish "(1) membership in a protected class; (2) satisfactory job performance; (3) adverse employment action; and (4) that similarly situated employees outside the protected class received more favorable treatment."[59] The district court granted UPS's motion for summary judgment, and Young appealed.

The Fourth Circuit affirmed the district court, rejecting Young's argument that the UPS policy represented discrimination on the basis of pregnancy. Instead, the appellate court concluded that the UPS policy was pregnancy-blind, in that it "treat[ed] pregnant workers and nonpregnant workers alike."[60] In effect, the court concluded, Young was treated no *worse* than any other worker with an injury or condition acquired off the job, and who did not qualify for an accommodation by virtue of the ADA or because of the loss of a commercial driver's license,

---

[56]   *Id.*

[57]   Young v. United Parcel Serv., Inc., No. DKC 08-2586, 2011 WL 665321 (D. Md. Feb. 14, 2011). Young initially also pursued claims under ERISA not relevant to this discussion, and a claim of race discrimination—Young is white and argued that UPS had accommodated African-American employees with pregnancy limitations—but she voluntarily dismissed the race discrimination claim before the district court had ruled on it. *Id.* at *7.

[58]   McDonnell Douglas Corp. v. Green, 411 U.S. 792 (1973).

[59]   Young v. United Parcel Serv., Inc., 707 F.3d 437, 449–50 (4th Cir. 2013), *vacated and remanded*, 135 S. Ct. 1338 (2015), *amended by*, 784 F.3d 192 (4th Cir. 2015). Although Young's attorney believed she had preserved a disparate impact claim, the district court ruled that she had not done so, and when she attempted to later amend her complaint to more explicitly allege disparate impact, the district court denied her motion. 707 F.3d at 442.

[60]   *See id.* at 449. *See also id.* at 446 ("By limiting accommodations to those employees injured on the job, disabled as defined under the ADA, and stripped of their DOT certification, UPS has crafted a pregnancy-blind policy.").

and so the denial of her request for a light-duty assignment was not discrimination on the basis of pregnancy.[61]

Young's loss in the Fourth Circuit caught the attention of University of Michigan law professor Sam Bagenstos; after reading the opinion, Bagenstos immediately called Gustafson to find out whether she planned to seek Supreme Court review. As Bagenstos explained, when he read the decision, he thought "this was a case that you might get even a conservative Supreme Court to rule for a civil rights plaintiff, which is rare."[62] Bagenstos had been following lower court cases on the PDA, and believed that many, including the Fourth Circuit opinion in Young's case, "were totally inconsistent with the statute—both its language and what the statute was about."[63]

Although Gustafson had very much wanted to continue pursuing the case, as a solo practitioner without Supreme Court experience, she had been hesitant after the Fourth Circuit loss. So when Bagenstos offered his assistance, Gustafson enthusiastically accepted. Together they drafted a petition for certiorari that asked the Court to take up the case in order to answer the question "Whether and in what circumstances, an employer that provides work accommodations to nonpregnant employees with work limitations must provide work accommodations to pregnant employees who are 'similar in their ability or inability to work.' "[64] The petition argued that the Fourth Circuit's reading was flatly inconsistent with the text of the PDA, as well as the statute's purpose and legislative history. The Court granted the petition.[65]

In their briefs before the Supreme Court, Bagenstos and Gustafson argued on behalf of Peggy Young that by failing to provide Young with the same kind of accommodation it provided to employees whose limitations derived from sources other than pregnancy, UPS violated the PDA's mandate that pregnant workers be treated the same as others who were "similar in their ability or inability to work."[66]

In its briefing, UPS reprised familiar arguments that Young was seeking preferential treatment (what it termed "most-favored-nation status" for pregnant workers[67]), insisting that the PDA "does not

---

[61]   *Id.* at 450. For a detailed description of the Fourth Circuit oral argument and opinion, *see* GILLIAN THOMAS, BECAUSE OF SEX: ONE LAW, TEN CASES, AND FIFTY YEARS THAT CHANGED AMERICAN WOMEN'S LIVES AT WORK 215–16 (2016).

[62]   Telephone Interview with Professor Samuel Bagenstos, Univ. of Mich. (Feb. 16, 2018).

[63]   *Id.*

[64]   Petition for Writ of Certiorari, Young v. United Parcel Service, 707 F.3d 437 (4th Cir. 2014) (No. 11-2078), 2013 WL 1462041, at *i [hereinafter Cert. Petition].

[65]   Cert. Petition, *supra* note 64; Young v. United Parcel Service, 134 S. Ct. 2898, *cert. granted*, (2014).

[66]   42 U.S.C. § 2000e(k) (2012).

[67]   *See* Brief of Respondent at 13, 28, Young v. United Parcel Serv., 135 S. Ct. 1338 (No. 12-1226). Under UPS's characterization of Young's argument—which Professor Bagenstos vigorously resisted at oral argument—any employer that chose to accommodate a single nonpregnant employee would be thereby compelled to extend the same or similar

mandate accommodations or other special treatment for pregnant employees." It further argued that "because UPS treated [Young] the same as it did other employees with similar lifting restrictions from an off-the-job injury or condition," UPS had not discriminated against Young on the basis of her pregnancy.[68]

Young was joined in her arguments by a broad array of outside groups, who provided "friend of the court" briefs supporting Young's argument that UPS's refusal to accommodate her pregnancy, even while it accommodated wide swaths of other employees, was a clear violation of the PDA. In many ways, the support for Young resembled the diverse coalition that had come together to enact the PDA nearly forty years earlier. The conservative organization Americans United for Life, together with 22 other pro-life groups, filed a brief in support of Young, arguing that "[e]conomic pressure is a significant factor in many women's decision to choose abortion over childbirth. . . Protecting the ability to work can increase true freedom for women, promote the common good, and protect the most vulnerable among us."[69] Meanwhile, the ACLU, along with a number of other organizations with progressive and pro-choice leanings, took up Young's position on the ground that policies like UPS's "relegate[ ] women to second-class status in the workplace and to economic disadvantage over the long term."[70]

These strange bedfellows not only recalled the PDA's enacting coalition, but were also a direct reflection of Young's legal team: Sharon Gustafson identifies as a "pro-life feminist" (though she also says "I know people disagree with whether there is such a thing"),[71] while Professor Bagenstos is a progressive law professor and civil rights litigator, who

---

accommodations to *all* pregnant employees with comparable limitations. *See* Oral Argument at 2:50, Young v. United Parcel Serv., 135 S. Ct. 1338 (2015) (No. 12-1226) https://www.oyez.org/cases/2014/12-1226. (Justice Scalia: "[I]f you have your senior employees driven to work when . . . they are unable to drive themselves, you have to do the same for pregnant women. Would you say that's the case?" Samuel R. Bagenstos: "No, we would not say that.").

[68]   Brief of Respondent at 9–10, Young v. United Parcel Serv., 135 S. Ct. 1338 (No. 12-1226).

[69]   Brief for 23 Pro-Life Organizations & the Judicial Education Project as Amici Curiae Supporting Petitioner, Young v. United Parcel Serv., 135 S. Ct. 1338 (2015) (No. 12-1226.) There were, however, conservative voices on the other of the case, including a brief filed by Phyllis Schlafly's Eagle Forum, which argued that in enacting the PDA, "Congress never intended: (1) to eliminate stereotypes of husband-breadwinner, wife-homemaker families; (2) to have women return to work immediately after giving birth to the exclusion of caring for their newborns; (3) to have pregnant women work as package-delivering truck drivers." Brief for Eagle Forum Education & Legal Defense Fund, Inc., as Amicus Curiae Supporting Respondent at 27, Young v. United Parcel Serv., 135 S. Ct. 1338 (2015) (No. 12-1226).

[70]   Brief for American Civil Liberties Union et al., as Amici Curiae Supporting Petitioner, Young v. United Parcel Serv., 135 S. Ct. 1338 (2015) (No. 12-1226).

[71]   Gustafson Interview, *supra* note 6; *see also* Sharon Fast Gustafson, *Anti-Abortion Feminism*, GEO. L. WKLY. (Jan. 22, 1990), https://repository.library.georgetown.edu/handle/10822/1047996 [http://hdl.handle.net/10822/1047996].

clerked for Justice Ruth Bader Ginsburg and liberal Ninth Circuit Judge Stephen Reinhardt.

The broad coalition the case and its lawyers attracted may well have had some impact on both the outcome in the case and the Court's final vote. For, although the 6–3 decision finding for Peggy Young was not endorsed by *all* of the conservative members of the Court, both Chief Justice Roberts and Justice Alito voted in Young's favor (with Alito concurring in the judgment), no small accomplishment in an employment discrimination case. And Justice Anthony Kennedy, though he dissented, acknowledged in his opinion that "the difficulties pregnant women face in the workplace are and do remain an issue of national importance;"[72] he also approvingly cited state laws prohibiting pregnancy discrimination, writing that such laws "honor and safeguard the important contributions women make to both the workplace and the American family."[73]

Justice Breyer's opinion for a majority that included both Chief Justice Roberts and Justice Ruth Bader Ginsburg was in many ways a consummate compromise. In an attempt to chart a middle path, the majority gave Young the chance to proceed with her claim in the lower courts, but stopped short of a rule that would have required all employers that accommodated some workers to extend comparable accommodations "to *all* pregnant workers (with comparable physical limitations), irrespective of the nature of their jobs, the employer's need to keep them working, their ages, or any other criteria."[74]

The Court focused its reading on the meaning of the second clause of the PDA, which provides that "women affected by pregnancy, childbirth, or related medical conditions shall be treated the same for all employment-related purposes . . . as other persons not so affected but similar in their ability or inability to work."[75] The key interpretive question, as the Court saw it, was what the statute required where an employer accommodated *some* but not *all* workers disabled for conditions unrelated to pregnancy—precisely as UPS's policy did. UPS urged a reading under which a court was to inquire merely whether "an employer provides pregnant women with the accommodations it provides to others *within* a facially neutral category (such as those with off-the-job injuries) to determine whether the employer has violated Title VII."[76] Young, by contrast, argued that as long as "an employer accommodates . . . a subset of workers with disabling conditions," "pregnant workers who are similar in the ability to work [must] receive the same treatment even if still other

---

[72] Young v. United Parcel Serv., 135 S. Ct. 1338, 1367 (2015) (Kennedy, J., dissenting).

[73] *Id.*

[74] *Id.* at 1349–50.

[75] 42 U.S.C. § 2000e(k) (2012).

[76] *Young*, 135 S. Ct. at 1349.

nonpregnant workers do not receive accommodations."[77] This reading, she contended, would ensure that "women as capable of doing their jobs as their male counterparts . . . not be forced to choose between having a child and having a job."[78] As *amicus curiae*, the United States echoed Young's argument, insisting that nothing in the PDA directs courts to find discrimination only where a pregnant worker "receives less favorable treatment than every other employee who is similar in his ability to inability to work," but rather prevents employers from offering benefits to *some* employees "who are limited in their ability to work" but denying those same benefits "to pregnant employees who are similarly limited."[79] It also urged the Court to pay special attention, under *Skidmore v. Swift*,[80] to the EEOC's position that employers must treat pregnant workers as they did "other employees similarly unable to perform their jobs, whether by providing modified tasks, alternative assignments, or fringe benefits[.]"[81] And, significantly, the EEOC guidance was clear that employers could *not* refuse to accommodate pregnant workers by "relying on a policy that makes distinctions based on the source of an employee's limitations,"[82] as UPS did.

Rejecting all of these formulations, the Court instead concluded that *McDonnell Douglas* supplied the proper framework for assessing the sort of disparate-treatment pregnancy discrimination claim Young advanced. This meant, in the pregnancy discrimination context, that a plaintiff could make a prima facie case by showing "that she belongs to the protected class, that she sought accommodation, that the employer did not accommodate her, and that the employer did accommodate others 'similar in their ability or inability to work.' "[83] The employer could then respond with a "legitimate, nondiscriminatory reason" for refusing the accommodation, though, importantly, mere expense or inconvenience would ordinarily *not* supply a sufficient reason to justify the refusal[84]—a significant component of the decision that takes off the table one of the key justifications employers have historically offered when challenged for their refusals to accommodate pregnancy. The Court also explained that a plaintiff could get to a jury by showing that the employer's reasons were not strong enough to justify the burden, *or* by showing that an employer

---

[77]   Brief for Petitioner at 28, Young v. United Parcel Serv., Inc., 135 S. Ct. 1338 (No. 12-1226).

[78]   *Id.* at 19–20.

[79]   Brief for United States at 16, Young v. United Parcel Serv., Inc., 135 S. Ct. 1338 (No. 12-1226).

[80]   323 U.S. 134 (1944).

[81]   *Id.* at 26–29.

[82]   EEOC Compl. Man. (BNA) § 626-I(A)(5) (July 2014); 2 EEOC Compl. Man. (BNA) § 626-I(C) (July 2014).

[83]   *Young*, 135 S. Ct. at 1354.

[84]   *Id.*

accommodated a large percentage of nonpregnant workers but *not* a large percentage of pregnant workers.[85]

Justice Scalia wrote the lead dissent, arguing that the Fourth Circuit should be affirmed and blasting the majority's conclusion as "splendidly unconnected with the text and even the legislative history of the Act."[86]

AFTER *YOUNG*

After the Supreme Court's decision in *Young*, the Fourth Circuit remanded the case to the district court, where the parties entered into settlement negotiations and eventually agreed to dismiss the case.[87] By then—actually by the time the case was before the Supreme Court—UPS had changed its policy to allow pregnant workers with limitations like Young's to be temporarily reassigned to light-duty work.[88]

The legal and political landscape had changed in other ways in the immediate run-up to *Young*, and, as a result of both those developments and *Young* itself, pregnancy discrimination claims have fared comparatively well in the lower courts in the aftermath of the case. One study of lower-court cases in the year following *Young*—albeit one featuring small sample sizes—found that while pre-*Young* dismissal or summary judgment rates for pregnancy discrimination claims had been around 70%, in the year following *Young*, a full 73% of such cases had been allowed to proceed to trial.[89] And this data may not capture the full extent of *Young*'s impact on workplace treatment of pregnancy; in Gustafson's experience, *Young* has empowered pregnant workers to demand and receive accommodations from employers, obviating the need to pursue litigation at all. "I think it has made a difference," she explains. When employees initially approach her for possible representation, she says, she advises them first to bring *Young* to the attention of employers, counseling them to say something like this: " 'I don't know if you're aware

---

[85]   *Id.* at 1354–55.

[86]   *Id.* at 1361 (Scalia, J., dissenting). Significantly, however, Justice Scalia seemed to suggest that Young should have pursued her case as a disparate impact claim—perhaps implicitly recognizing that Young did identify a genuine harm, merely pursued the wrong theory of liability. *Id.* at 1365–66.

[87]   Judge Deborah K. Chasanow approved the stipulation in October 2015. Order Approving Stipulation of Dismissal with Prejudice, 135 S. Ct. 1338 (2015); *see also* Ben James, *UPS Settles Pregnancy Bias Case That Went To High Court*, LAW360 (Oct. 1, 2015, 5:13 PM), https://www.law360.com/articles/709843/ups-settles-pregnancy-bias-case-that-went-to-high-court.

[88]   Brigid Schulte, *With Supreme Court Case Pending, UPS Reverses Policy on Pregnant Workers*, WASH. POST (Oct. 29, 2014), https://www.washingtonpost.com/blogs/she-the-people/wp/2014/10/29/with-supreme-court-case-pending-ups-reverses-policy-on-pregnant-workers/.

[89]   *Pregnancy Accommodation in the Courts One Year After* Young v. UPS, NAT'L WOMEN'S L. CTR. (June 2016), https://nwlc.org/resources/pregnancy-accommodation-in-the-courts-one-year-after-young-v-ups/; *see also* Lynn Ridgeway Zehrt, *A Special Delivery: Litigating Pregnancy Accommodation Claims After The Supreme Court's Decision In* Young v. United Parcel Service, Inc., 68 RUTGERS U. L. REV. 683 (2016); Joanna L. Grossman, *Expanding the Core: Pregnancy Discrimination Law As It Approaches Full Term*, 52 IDAHO L. REV. 825, 860 (2016).

of this *Young v. UPS* case, but it's pretty clear now that if you're making accommodations for other people with similar needs, you need to make them for pregnancy too.' " And, she reports, "People do it! So I think it's made a real difference."[90]

In addition, the 2008 amendments to the ADA may well impact the legal status of pregnancy accommodations in the post-*Young* era. The events in *Young* took place before the effective date of the ADA Amendments Act (ADAAA), so the interaction between the two statutory regimes was not squarely presented in *Young*, but the Court itself noted that the amendments might "limit the future significance of our interpretation of the [PDA]."[91] The amendments and the EEOC's interpreting regulations expand the definition of "disability," which is now defined as "[a] physical or mental impairment that substantially limits one or more of the major life activities,"[92] with "major life activity" defined as including "standing, sitting, reaching, lifting, [and] bending."[93] Many of the accommodations pregnant women seek at work could potentially fall under this expanded definition of "disability," which in some cases might eliminate the need to engage in PDA analysis at all.

Both before and in the years since *Young*, pregnancy discrimination has been the subject of active lawmaking at the state and local level, and currently, nearly half of the states have codified some form of workplace pregnancy protection.[94] California passed its state law in 1999, and over the ensuing years, as courts narrowly construed the provisions of the PDA, other states and localities followed suit. State "Pregnant Worker Fairness Acts" typically impose a broad requirement that employers provide reasonable accommodations to pregnant workers; significantly, this eliminates the need to identify 'comparators.' The California law, for example, makes it an unlawful employment practice "[f]or an employer to refuse to provide reasonable accommodation for an employee for a condition related to pregnancy, childbirth, or a related medical condition, if she so requests, with the advice of her health care provider."[95]

---

[90]   Gustafson Interview, *supra* note 6.

[91]   Young v. United Parcel Serv., Inc., 135 S. Ct. 1338, 1348 (2015) ("We note that statutory changes made after the time of Young's pregnancy may limit the future significance of our interpretation of the Act. In 2008, Congress expanded the definition of 'disability' under the ADA to make clear that "physical or mental impairment[s] that substantially limi[t]" an individual's ability to lift, stand, or bend are ADA-covered disabilities.").

[92]   Americans with Disabilities Act (ADA) Amendments Act of 2008, 42 U.S.C. § 12102(1)(A) (2008); 29 C.F.R. § 1630.2 (g)(1)(i) (2018).

[93]   42 U.S.C. § 12102(2)(A); 29 C.F.R. § 1630.2 (i)(1)(i).

[94]   *See* A BETTER BALANCE, *Pregnant Worker Fairness Legislative Success* (Nov. 20, 2017),   https://www.abetterbalance.org/resources/pregnant-worker-fairness-legislative-successes/; U.S. DEP'T OF LAB., EMPLOYMENT PROTECTIONS FOR WORKERS WHO ARE PREGNANT OR NURSING, (last visited Feb. 1, 2019) https://www.dol.gov/wb/state_protection_summary_508_txt.htm; Reva Siegel, *Pregnancy as a Normal Condition of Employment*, 59 WM. & MARY L. REV. 971, 976 n. 14 (2018).

[95]   CAL. GOV'T CODE § 12945 (West 1999).

Maryland—Young's home state—enacted its own pregnancy discrimination law in response to the Fourth Circuit opinion ruling against Young.[96] The state's "Reasonable Accommodations for Disabilities Due to Pregnancy Act," which took effect on October 1, 2013, amended Maryland's Fair Employment Practices Act to require employers, upon a pregnant employee's request for a reasonable accommodation, to "explore with the employee all possible means of providing the reasonable accommodation."[97] In certain circumstances the law also requires employers to transfer a pregnant employee to a less strenuous or less hazardous position for the duration of her pregnancy.[98]

Young herself, together with representatives from the ACLU and other groups, testified in favor of the law.[99] In her written testimony, Young described her experiences with UPS and her (at that point unsuccessful) legal challenge to her treatment; she concluded by arguing that "Pregnant employees should be protected from discrimination."[100] Opponents of the bill, including the Chamber of Commerce, argued that the law would unduly burden businesses and that it was unnecessary in light of the PDA;[101] to this, a State Senator responded that the Fourth Circuit's ruling against Young had made apparent the need for a state law, and that California's law, after which the Maryland law had been modeled, had not led to an increase in discrimination complaints, but rather, a decrease in them.[102]

Proponents of the bill ultimately prevailed. At the signing ceremony, Young stood behind Maryland Governor Martin O'Malley as he signed into law the bill her story had inspired.[103]

THE LESSONS OF *YOUNG V. UPS*

The story of pregnancy discrimination and the law is a story as much about legislatures as courts. As Mary Ziegler explains, pregnancy is a domain in which the elaboration of constitutional values has largely

[96] Andrea K. Walker, *Maryland General Assembly Close to Passing Bill to Strengthen Rights of Pregnant Women in the Workplace*, BALT. SUN (Mar. 22, 2013) http://www.baltimoresun.com/health/bs-hs-pregnant-worker-law-20130322-story.html.

[97] MD. CODE ANN., State Gov't § 20–609 (LexisNexis 2009 & Supp. 2018).

[98] *Id.*

[99] *Reasonable Accommodations for Disabilities Due to Pregnancy Act, Hearing on S.B. 784 Before the Sen. Jud. Proc. Comm.* (Md. 2013) (written testimony of Peggy S. Young) [hereinafter Young Testimony]; Ariela Migdal & Lenora M. Lapidus, *States Fight Back Against Pregnancy Discrimination*, ACLU.ORG (Apr. 18, 2013) https://www.aclu.org/blog/womens-rights/pregnancy-and-parenting-discrimination/states-fight-back-against-pregnancy?redirect=blog/womens-rights/states-fight-back-against-pregnancy-discrimination.

[100] Young Testimony, *supra* note 99.

[101] Walker, *supra* note 96.

[102] *Id.*

[103] Darcy Spencer, *The Voice of Maryland's Pregnant Worker Protection Law*, NBC WASH. (May 16, 2013) https://www.nbcwashington.com/news/local/The-Voice-of-Marylands-Pregnant-Worker-Protection-Law-207801311.html.

happened in legislatures, both state and federal;[104] so, although *Young* is technically a statutory case, it is both a product of, and will have continuing influence on, constitutional values and constitutional mobilization.[105] Moreover, the Constitution figures quite differently in the law of pregnancy discrimination than in areas like contraception and abortion. After *Geduldig*, the Constitution is unlikely to serve as a shield against state and federal attacks on pregnant women's rights. Rather, the Constitution functions more as a sword: as the source of principles and values that are subsequently expressed through statutory enactments, with their own enforcement mechanisms.

Beyond its relationship to the Constitution, *Young* is a remarkable story of coalition-building, one in which pro-life voices—including self-identified pro-life feminists—and pro-choice feminists joined together to pursue an outcome that would significantly improve pregnant workers' ability to remain in the work force while taking steps toward parenthood. This coalition both reflected and forged anew the alliance that enacted the Pregnancy Discrimination Act nearly forty years earlier. And it may point the way to other possibilities for compromise and coalition around pregnancy and leave;[106] as *Young* shows, at least some self-identified pro-life individuals and organizations appear to believe that supporting pregnant women, and not merely opposing abortion, is an important component of an agenda committed to life.[107]

---

[104] Ziegler, *supra* note 35, at 221 (describing the PDA as the product of a "successful legislative constitutional project"); *see also* Cary Franklin, *The Anti-Stereotyping Principle in Constitutional Sex Discrimination Law*, 85 N.Y.U. L. REV. 83, 150 (2010) ("The women's movement had always viewed legislation as a central part of the anti-stereotyping project.").

[105] *Cf.* Reva B. Siegel, *You've Come A Long Way, Baby: Rehnquist's New Approach to Pregnancy Discrimination in* Hibbs, 58 STAN. L. REV. 1871 (2006).

[106] *See generally* Reva B. Siegel, *ProChoiceLife: Asking Who Protects Life and How— and Why It Matters in Law and Politics*, 93 IND. L. J. 207 (2018).

[107] Claire Cain Miller, *What a Bipartisan Paid Leave Plan Might Look Like*, N.Y. TIMES (June 6, 2017), https://www.nytimes.com/2017/06/06/upshot/what-a-bipartisan-paid-leave-plan-might-look-like.html; Eugene Scott, *If Working Mothers Want Paid Family Leave, They'll Likely Need a Bipartisan Solution*, WASH. POST (Feb. 6, 2018), https://www. washingtonpost.com/news/the-fix/wp/2018/02/06/if-working-mothers-want-paid-family-leave-theyll-likely-need-a-bipartisan-solution/?utm_term=.4973f89a5003; *cf.* Elizabeth Dias, *Beto O'Rourke May Benefit from an Unlikely Support Group: Evangelical Women*, N.Y. TIMES (Oct. 9, 2018) (" 'I care as much about babies at the border as I do about babies in the womb,' said Tess Clarke . . . . confessing that she was 'mortified' at how she used to vote, because she had only considered abortion policy. 'We've been asleep. Now, we've woke up.' ").

11

Cary Franklin*

Whole Woman's Health v. Hellerstedt and What It Means to Protect Women

The obvious place to begin, when telling the story of *Whole Woman's Health v. Hellerstedt*,[1] is June 25, 2013. That is the day Wendy Davis, a little-known state senator from Fort Worth, Texas, embarked on an epic filibuster of the law that became known as H.B. 2.[2] Ostensibly an effort to protect women's health, H.B. 2 required, among other things, that abortion providers obtain admitting privileges at nearby hospitals and that abortion clinics outfit themselves as ambulatory surgical centers.[3] Because hospitals only rarely grant admitting privileges to abortion providers and ambulatory surgical centers are prohibitively expensive, the law would have closed all but a handful of abortion clinics in the state of Texas.[4]

The odds of a successful filibuster were long. Davis would have to refrain from eating, drinking, using the bathroom, sitting, or leaning on her desk for thirteen hours, while talking continuously and in relevant ways about the proposed legislation.[5] But Davis had stamina, and as she talked, support for her efforts snowballed. By nightfall, thousands of supporters had gathered in the Capitol building in Austin and hundreds of thousands of people around the world watched her via livestream.[6] Ten

---

*   W. H. Francis, Jr. Professor, University of Texas School of Law. Thank you to everyone involved in this volume for their helpful comments, and especially to Melissa Murray, Kate Shaw, and Reva Siegel for their insights and their dedication to this project.

[1]   136 S. Ct. 2292 (2016).

[2]   Manny Fernandez, *In Battle Over Texas Abortion Bill, Senator's Stand Catches the Limelight*, N.Y. TIMES, June 27, 2013, at A18.

[3]   *Whole Woman's Health*, 136 S. Ct. at 2300.

[4]   *Id.* at 2301–03, 2312 (observing that the district court found that the admitting privileges requirement, which briefly took effect, reduced the number of abortion clinics in Texas from approximately forty to approximately twenty, and that if the surgical center requirement took effect, that number would fall to seven or eight).

[5]   For the rules governing filibusters in the Texas Senate in 2013, see Senate Rules 4.01, 4.03 S. Res. 4, 83rd Leg., Reg. Sess. (Tex. 2013), *available at* http://www.lrl.state.tx.us/scanned/Rules/83-0/83_Senate_Rules.pdf. Under these rules, a filibustering senator may be forced to yield after three infractions. *See id.* at R. 4.03.

[6]   Dan Solomon, *The Long Tale of HB2 Comes to a Close*, TEX. MONTHLY (June 27, 2016), https://texasmonthly.com/the-daily-post/long-tortured-tale-hb2-comes-close/.

hours into her filibuster, the President of the United States tweeted his encouragement (#standwithwendy).[7]

At the eleventh hour, however, the Lieutenant Governor—a vocal proponent of the bill—cited Davis for her third infraction and declared the filibuster over.[8] That is when the real drama began: Davis's supporters chanted so loudly ("let her speak!") that the legislators struggled to hold a vote.[9] The midnight deadline came and went, and for hours, it was unclear whether the bill had passed.[10] The official record showed the vote had begun at 11:59 p.m.: on time.[11] But then Democrats discovered that the record had been tampered with—someone had moved the start time to make it appear that the vote had occurred before midnight.[12] The undoctored record showed the vote had actually commenced at 12:02 a.m.: too late.[13] The bill was defeated. Undeterred, Governor Rick Perry convened another special legislative session the following month, during which the bill passed.[14] Yet, in the end, supporters of abortion rights triumphed. In 2016, the Supreme Court declared H.B. 2's admitting privileges and surgical center requirements unconstitutional.[15]

That is one way of telling the story of *Whole Woman's Health*. It is a story journalists have told many times, and it will soon be told in a movie,

---

[7] Barack Obama (@BarackObama), TWITTER (June 25, 2013, 8:40 PM), https://twitter.com/BarackObama/status/349703625616011264. The President's tweet read: "Something special is happening in Austin tonight." *Id.* House Minority Leader Nancy Pelosi and half a million others also deployed the hashtag #standwithwendy—coined by the ACLU's Texas branch—on Twitter that night. *See* Nancy Pelosi (@NancyPelosi), TWITTER (June 25, 2013, 5:53 PM), https://twitter.com/nancypelosi/status/349661603102330880; Caitlin Dewey, *Wendy Davis 'Tweetstorm' Was Planned in Advance*, WASH. POST: THE FIX (June 26, 2013, 5:16 PM), http://www.washingtonpost.com/blogs/the-fix/wp/2013/06/26/this-tweetstorm-was-planned-in-advance.

[8] Manny Fernandez, *Filibuster in Texas Senate Tries to Halt Abortion Bill*, N.Y. TIMES, June 26, 2013, at A14. For more on Davis's ostensible infractions, see *infra* text accompanying notes 96–99.

[9] WENDY DAVIS, LET HER SPEAK: TRANSCRIPT OF TEXAS STATE SENATOR WENDY DAVIS'S JUNE 25, 2013, FILIBUSTER OF THE TEXAS STATE SENATE 206 (2013); Sonia Smith & Erica Grieder, *A Bill Is Killed, A Star Is Born*, TEX. MONTHLY (June 26, 2013), https://www.texasmonthly.com/politics/a-bill-is-killed-a-star-is-born/.

[10] Smith & Grieder, *supra* note 9.

[11] WENDY DAVIS, FORGETTING TO BE AFRAID: A MEMOIR 286 (2014); Peter Weber, *Wendy Davis' Stunning Filibuster of a Texas Abortion Bill*, THE WEEK, June 26, 2013, http://theweek.com/articles/462815/wendy-davis-stunning-filibuster-texas-abortion-bill.

[12] Weber, *supra* note 11; *see also* Julián Aguilar et al., *Liveblog: Abortion Bill Fails Amid Midnight Chaos After Filibuster*, TEX. TRIB. (June 26, 2013), https://www.texastribune.org/2013/06/26/dems-approach-abortion-victory-special-session-wan/.

[13] Weber, *supra* note 11; Elise Hu, *Clock Runs Out on Controversial Texas Abortion Bill*, NPR (June 26, 2013), https://www.npr.org/sections/thetwo-way/2013/06/26/195758145/clock-runs-out-on-controversial-texas-abortion-bill.

[14] Karen McVeigh, *Rick Perry Signs Wide-Ranging Texas Bill to Limit Access to Abortion*, THE GUARDIAN (July 18, 2013), https://www.theguardian.com/world/2013/jul/18/rick-perry-texas-abortion-bill.

[15] Whole Woman's Health v. Hellerstedt, 136 S. Ct. 2292, 2300 (2016).

called *Let Her Speak*, starring Sandra Bullock as Wendy Davis.[16] It is a perfect Hollywood story, complete with a compelling heroine, a mobilized social movement, suspense, intrigue, and a triumphant ending. But H.B. 2's defeat is only half of the story, and it is not even clear that it is the more important half. The story of how the Texas legislature came to pass a law that would have left vast swathes of one of the largest states in the union without any abortion providers is, in its own way, just as compelling as the story of Davis's filibuster—and, ultimately, just as relevant to the future of abortion law.

This chapter aims to tell that other half of the story. Davis's filibuster made news around the world, but it is the equally impassioned, though less publicized, efforts of the *pro-life* movement that have dramatically altered the landscape of abortion provision in the United States in recent years. A substantial part of that success has to do with the movement's evolving legal and political strategy. In the years after *Roe v. Wade*,[17] the predominant and immediate aim of many pro-life advocates was to overturn the Court's decision.[18] More recently, a different, more incremental strategy has gained favor—particularly among the leaders of the influential pro-life advocacy group Americans United for Life (AUL). AUL works at the state level, not to ban abortion, but to inundate it with regulation.[19] Charmaine Yoest, President of AUL from 2008 to 2016, explained that, by subjecting abortion to increasingly burdensome forms of regulation, "we end up hollowing out *Roe*, even without the Supreme Court."[20] Her former colleague at AUL, Dan McConchie, amplified that idea: "States can't outlaw abortion. That does not mean there's a constitutional right to abortion being convenient."[21] At the same time, an AUL lawyer explained, the organization's legislative strategy "is carefully designed to present particular abortion issues to the courts that test Supreme Court doctrine and that will encourage the

---

[16]   Justin Kroll, *Sandra Bullock to Star as Filibustering Senator Wendy Davis in "Let Her Speak,"* VARIETY (Nov. 9, 2017), http://variety.com/2017/film/news/sandra-bullock-wendy-davis-let-her-speak-1202585780/.

[17]   410 U.S. 113 (1973).

[18]   In addition to trying to persuade the Court to overrule *Roe*, many pro-life advocates in the 1970s and early 1980s threw their energies into the passage of a Human Life Amendment, which would also have overturned the Court's decision. For more on these efforts see, James Bopp, Jr., *An Examination of Proposals for a Human Life Amendment, in* RESTORING THE RIGHT TO LIFE: THE HUMAN LIFE AMENDMENT 3 (James Bopp, Jr. ed., 1984).

[19]   Erica Hellerstein, *Inside the Highly Sophisticated Group That's Quietly Making It Much Harder to Get an Abortion*, THINK PROGRESS (Dec. 2, 2014), https://thinkprogress.org/inside-the-highly-sophisticated-group-thats-quietly-making-it-much-harder-to-get-an-abortion-9db723232471/ (observing that "AUL's role in shifting the abortion debate to a 'death by 1000 cuts' strategy has proven effective").

[20]   Emily Bazelon, *Charmaine Yoest's Cheerful War on Abortion*, N.Y. TIMES MAG. (Nov. 4, 2012), http://www.nytimes.com/2012/11/04/magazine/charmaine-yoests-cheerful-war-on-abortion.html.

[21]   Olga Khazan, *Planning the End of Abortion*, THE ATLANTIC (July 16, 2015), http://www.theatlantic.com/politics/archive/2015/07/what-pro-life-activists-really-want/398297/. For more on AUL's strategy, see Linda Greenhouse & Reva B. Siegel, *The Difference a Whole Woman Makes: Protection for the Abortion Right After* Whole Woman's Health, 126 YALE L.J. F. 149, 151–53 (2016).

courts, and ultimately the Supreme Court, to cut back on *Roe v. Wade* or to readdress and overrule it."[22]

In developing this incrementalist legal strategy, AUL has had to contend with *Planned Parenthood of Southeastern Pennsylvania v. Casey*, the 1992 decision that has governed the regulation of abortion for the past generation. The Court held in *Casey* that laws regulating abortion are subject to an "undue burden" test.[23] *Casey* defined an undue burden as "a state regulation [that] has the purpose or effect of placing a substantial obstacle in the path of a woman seeking an abortion of a nonviable fetus."[24] The decision further specified that when the state seeks to vindicate its interest in *protecting fetal life*, the means it chooses to accomplish that end "must be calculated to inform the woman's free choice, not hinder it."[25] States may seek to protect fetal life by trying to dissuade women from having abortions, but not by trying to impede their access to the procedure.

One of the linchpins in AUL's campaign to limit the right to abortion in the wake of *Casey* has been legislation referred to by its critics as Targeted Regulation of Abortion Providers, or TRAP laws. Abortion, like all medical procedures, is subject to reasonable health and safety regulation. But TRAP laws—of which H.B. 2 is one[26]—single out abortion providers and impose on them burdens different from, and far weightier than, those imposed on providers of healthcare services of comparable risk.[27] In so doing, such laws threaten to drive abortion providers out of business, seriously constricting women's access to abortion without formally banning the procedure.[28]

---

[22] Clarke D. Forsythe, *A Legal Strategy to Overturn* Roe v. Wade *After* Webster*: Some Lessons from Lincoln*, 1991 BYU L. REV. 519, 534 (1991). *See also* AUL, *Accomplishments*, https://aul.org/what-we-do/achievements/ ("AUL's specific strategy works to save lives today while undermining [abortion-protective doctrine] adopted by the Supreme Court [in the past]. . . .").

[23] 505 U.S. 833, 876 (1992).

[24] *Id.* at 877.

[25] *Id.*

[26] *See* Whole Woman's Health v. Hellerstedt, 136 S.Ct. 2292, 2321 (2016) (Ginsburg, J., concurring) (characterizing H.B. 2 as a TRAP law).

[27] For further discussion of the way in which TRAP laws single out abortion providers for onerous regulation not imposed on providers of comparably risky—or indeed, more risky—procedures, see *infra* notes 71–72 and accompanying text.

[28] For more on the design and function of TRAP laws, see Bonnie S. Jones, Sara Daniel & Lindsay K. Cloud, *State Law Approaches to Facility Regulation and Other Office Interventions*, 108 AM. J. PUB. HEALTH 486, 491 (Apr. 2018); GUTTMACHER INST., *State Policies in Brief: Targeted Regulation of Abortion Providers* (June 1, 2018), at http://www. guttmacher.org/statecenter/spibs/spib_TRAP.pdf. *See also* Linda Greenhouse & Reva B. Siegel, Casey *and the Clinic Closings: When "Protecting Health" Obstructs Choice*, 125 YALE L.J. 1428, 1446 (2016) (explaining that TRAP laws single out abortion in various contexts, including the licensing of clinics and the regulation of telemedicine, admitting privileges, and off-label drug prescriptions).

Critics of TRAP laws argue that they violate *Casey* because they have the purpose and effect of impeding women's access to abortion.[29] But advocates of such laws argue that their primary aim is not to hinder women, but to protect them.[30] Indeed, advocates (when they stay on message[31]) argue that TRAP laws are not intended primarily to protect fetal life, but to *safeguard maternal health*—to protect pregnant women from dangerous providers and to ensure that abortion is performed in safe environments.[32] These advocates argue that legislators ought to be given wide latitude—indeed, near-total judicial deference—to regulate abortion when they are acting to vindicate the state's interest in protecting women's health.[33]

Were courts to accept this logic, it would create a major conduit around the constitutional limitations *Roe* and *Casey* imposed on the regulation of abortion. Thus, when the controversy over H.B. 2 reached the Court, the implications of the case extended far beyond Texas. The Court in *Whole Woman's Health* had to decide whether it would grant the pro-life movement's bid effectively to eviscerate the constitutional protections *Roe* and *Casey* established—or whether it would reaffirm the idea, embedded in American law for nearly half a century, that the Constitution meaningfully limits how far the state may go in cutting off women's access to abortion.

THE QUIET TRIUMPHS OF AMERICANS
UNITED FOR LIFE

The passage of H.B. 2 in the summer of 2013 was not a bolt from the blue. The trend over the preceding decades had been toward tighter restrictions on abortion, and this trend accelerated dramatically in the wake of the 2010 midterm elections. Those elections swept into office scores of Tea Party and other conservative candidates for whom ending abortion was a key priority.[34] Emboldened by their collective victories, those legislators took aim at abortion. States passed more laws regulating

---

[29]   *See, e.g.*, Jones, Daniel & Cloud, *supra* note 28, at 491 (finding that "TRAP laws make abortions less accessible to patients (especially poor and low-income patients) by reducing the number of facilities that provide abortion services" (footnote omitted)).

[30]   *See, e.g.*, Press Release, AUL, *AUL Represents State Legislators in Historic Supreme Court Case, Fights to Protect Health and Safety Standards for Women Vulnerable to Abortion Industry Abuses* (Feb. 3, 2016), http://www.aul.org/blog/aul-represents-state-legislators-in-historic-supreme-court-case-fights-to-protect-health-and-safety-standards-for-women-vulnerable-to-abortion-industry-abuses/.

[31]   As this chapter shows, politicians who campaign and vote for TRAP laws do not always hew to AUL's carefully constructed message that the aim of these laws is to protect women's health. For examples of TRAP law proponents candidly discussing their fetal-protective motivations in advocating for these laws, see *infra* text accompanying notes 58–60.

[32]   *See, e.g.*, Brief for Respondents at 31–40, Whole Woman's Health v. Hellerstedt, 136 S.Ct. 2292 (2016) (No. 15-274).

[33]   *Id.* at 20–28.

[34]   *See* Robert Pear, *Push for Stricter Abortion Limits is Expected in House*, N.Y. TIMES, Dec. 12, 2010, at A34 (noting that, in the House, "[o]pponents of abortion gained about 45 seats in the midterm elections").

abortion in 2011 than in any other year in American history.[35] Indeed, nearly a third of *all* abortion regulations passed in the decades since *Roe* were passed between 2010 and 2016.[36] These new laws were notable not simply for their quantity, but also for their character. While many were aimed explicitly at protecting fetal life, an increasing number were aimed (at least ostensibly) at protecting women's health[37]—and many of these ostensible health protections were strikingly similar to one another, as if they had been drafted by the same hand.

Both the woman-protective focus and the striking similarity of the new abortion restrictions reflected the ascendance of AUL, an organization that describes itself (quite fairly) as "the nation's premier pro-life legal team."[38] AUL was founded in 1971 in response to the liberalization of abortion laws at the state level.[39] One thing that has distinguished AUL from other leading pro-life organizations is its "uniquely effective 'mother-child strategy.'"[40] In the late 1970s and 1980s, when the pro-life movement became a dominant force in American culture, the focus was on the fetus.[41] The movement relied heavily on gruesome images of aborted fetuses and heaped condemnation on women seeking to end pregnancies.[42] But focus groups conducted by pro-life leaders in the early 1990s revealed that Americans were uncomfortable with this overt vilification of women and that angry fetal-focused tactics were costing the movement mainstream support.[43] Some pro-life leaders, including those at AUL, adapted to this information by rejecting the dominant fetal-protective strategy in favor of a strategy that treated pregnant women and fetuses alike as victims of a dangerous and greedy

---

[35]   Sarah Kliff, *2011: The Year of the Abortion Restrictions*, WASH. POST (Dec. 29, 2011), https://www.washingtonpost.com/blogs/wonkblog/post/2011-the-year-of-the-abortion -restrictions/2011/12/29/gIQAbJqjOP_blog.html; Alastair Gee, *Anti-Abortion Laws Gain More Ground in the USA*, 377 LANCET 1992 (2011).

[36]   GUTTMACHER INST., *Last Five Years Account for More Than One-Quarter of All Abortion Restrictions Enacted Since* Roe (Jan. 13, 2016), https://www.guttmacher.org/ article/2016/01/last-five-years-account-more-one-quarter-all-abortion-restrictions-enacted-roe.

[37]   Greenhouse & Siegel, *supra* note 28, at 1430.

[38]   AUL, *About*, https://aul.org/about/.

[39]   AUL, *Americans United for Life: Defending Life Since 1971*, http://www.aul.org/ about-aul/history/; JOSHUA C. WILSON, THE NEW STATES OF ABORTION POLITICS 72 (2016).

[40]   AUL, DEFENDING LIFE 302 (2019), *available at* https://aul.org/wp-content/ uploads/2018/12/Defending-Life-2019.pdf.

[41]   Reva B. Siegel, *The Right's Reasons: Constitutional Conflict and the Spread of Woman-Protective Antiabortion Argument*, 57 DUKE L.J. 1641, 1660–62 (2008).

[42]   JOHANNA SCHOEN, ABORTION AFTER *ROE* 150–51 (2015) (explaining that in the 1980s, "antiabortion activists sharpened their depiction of abortion as the murder of a child in both narrative and visual form," and "fetal images became a mainstay on picket lines and at marches").

[43]   *See* John Willke & Barbara Willke, *Why Can't We Love Them Both?*, 7 LIFE & LEARNING 10, 18–20 (1997), *available at* http://www.uffl.org/vol%207/willke7.pdf (describing the pro-life movement's use of focus groups and what they revealed: that Americans balked at supporting the pro-life movement because they felt it was not "compassionate to women").

abortion industry.[44] The way to convince Americans to reject abortion was not to vilify pregnant women, AUL concluded, but to persuade them that abortion hurts women as much as it hurts fetuses.[45] Instead of framing abortion regulations as a means of protecting fetuses from callous women, AUL decided to frame such regulations as woman-protective—a means of shielding pregnant women from unscrupulous men and an industry that preys on society's most vulnerable members in a ruthless quest to enrich itself.[46]

Reframing abortion restrictions as woman-protective was not AUL's only innovation. In the early 1970s, at the time AUL was founded, a conservative political entrepreneur named Paul Weyrich and a group of conservative lawmakers founded the American Legislative Exchange Council (ALEC), a nonprofit organization that develops model legislation.[47] ALEC has been spectacularly successful in converting its model legislation into law.[48] It has produced model bills on a broad range of topics, but historically its focus has been on reducing individual and corporate taxation, combatting environmental regulation, stopping illegal immigration, strengthening voter identification laws, weakening labor unions, privatizing education, and opposing gun control.[49] AUL, which is loosely affiliated with ALEC, has replicated this strategy in the abortion context.[50] Every year, it publishes a lengthy pro-life "playbook" called *Defending Life*.[51] The first half of *Defending Life* ranks states

---

[44] *See id.* at 19–20 (describing the early days of this transformation); Siegel, *supra* note 41, at 1680–81 (discussing AUL's embrace of a "woman-protective" approach).

[45] *See* Bazelon, *supra* note 20 (describing AUL President Charmaine Yoest's efforts "to make the case that being anti-abortion is being pro-woman").

[46] *See, e.g., Statement by Dr. Charmaine Yoest at Selma Project Rally*, AUL (June 20, 2015), http://www.aul.org/2015/06/statement-by-dr-charmaine-yoest-at-selma-project-rally/ ("Today, we stand in solidarity with women throughout America, and in a special way minority and poor women who are routinely targeted and exploited by Big Abortion. . . . [W]e are here to remember the names of precious women, who lost their lives in an under-regulated, callous, profit-centered industry sometimes protected deliberately or negligently by political officials. We are here to say, their lives mattered.").

[47] *See* Brendan Greeley & Alison Fitzgerald, *Pssst. . . Wanna Buy A Law?*, BLOOMBERG BUSINESSWEEK (Dec. 1, 2011), https://www.bloomberg.com/news/articles/2011-12-01/pssst-dot-wanna-buy-a-law; Nancy Scola, *Exposing ALEC: How Conservative-Backed State Laws Are All Connected*, THE ATLANTIC (Apr. 14, 2012), https://www.theatlantic.com/politics/archive/2012/04/exposing-alec-how-conservative-backed-state-laws-are-all-connected/255869/.

[48] *See* Olivia Ward, *America's Secret Political Power*, TORONTO STAR (Dec. 17, 2011), https://www.thestar.com/news/world/2011/12/17/americas_secret_political_power.html.

[49] For more on ALEC's agenda, see its website at https://www.alec.org.

[50] For more on AUL's affiliation with ALEC, see Katrina vanden Heuvel, *"There Are States Where It's Not Safe to Be a Woman,"* THE NATION (Apr. 8, 2013), https://www.thenation.com/article/there-are-now-states-where-its-not-safe-be-woman/; Michael King, *United Defense of the Fetus*, AUSTIN CHRON. (July 19, 2013), https://www.austinchronicle.com/news/2013-07-19/point-austin-united-defense-of-the-fetus/. Representative Jodie Laubenberg, who introduced the AUL-inspired H.B. 2 in the House, was named ALEC's Texas State Chair around the time she introduced the law. *See* Press Release, TEXAS HOUSE OF REPRESENTATIVES, *Laubenberg Named Texas State Chair of the American Legislative Exchange Council* (Feb. 5, 2013), http://www.house.state.tx.us/news/press-releases/?id=4269.

[51] *Defending Life* is available for download on AUL's website. *See supra* note 40.

according to their hostility to abortion and encourages them to compete with one another to become the most restrictive. The second half provides legislators with dozens of model anti-abortion statutes ready to be introduced in statehouses throughout the country. "[O]ur model legislation enables legislators to easily introduce bills without needing to research and write the bills themselves," AUL explains.[52] Its model statutes look like Mad Libs, the phrasal template game that prompts players to supply words to substitute for blanks in a story. Often, all legislators need to do before introducing one of these statutes is to fill in the blanks with the name of their state.

AUL's involvement in the unprecedented wave of anti-abortion legislation enacted in the wake of the 2010 midterms is hardly a secret. Each year, AUL claims credit in *Defending Life* for a substantial portion of the abortion restrictions passed in the previous year.[53] On the front page of its website, it proudly quotes *Rolling Stone* magazine, which in 2014 published an article, "The Stealth War on Abortion," that attributes much of the pro-life movement's post-2010 success to AUL's "highly successful under-the-radar strategy."[54] The 2014 edition of *Defending Life*, published shortly after the passage of H.B. 2, opens with a letter from then-Texas Governor Rick Perry, thanking AUL for its help in restricting abortion in his state.[55] Indeed, H.B. 2 was drawn from the section of model statutes in *Defending Life* that AUL now refers to as its Women's Protection Project.[56] Generally, however, AUL stays in the background: working with state legislators to craft new regulations, sending its representatives to testify in favor of those regulations, and writing briefs on behalf of its legislative allies when those regulations are challenged in court.[57]

---

[52] AUL, *Legislation*, https://aul.org/what-we-do/legislation/.

[53] *See, e.g.*, AUL, DEFENDING LIFE ix (2016), *available at* http://perma.cc/7TYJ-Z834 (claiming credit for a third of the abortion regulations passed in 2015); AUL, DEFENDING LIFE xii (2015), *available at* http://perma.cc/8FR3-6Y7K (claiming credit for a third of the abortion regulations passed between 2011 and 2015).

[54] *See* www.aul.org (quoting Janet Reitman, *The Stealth War on Abortion*, ROLLING STONE, Jan. 30, 2014) [https://perma.cc/ZAG7-7FTW].

[55] Rick Perry, *Letter*, in AUL, DEFENDING LIFE 4–5 (2014), *available at* http://perma.cc/3EHF-FP97.

[56] *See* AUL, *Abortion Patients' Enhanced Safety Act*, in DEFENDING LIFE 225–28 (2013), *available at* http://perma.cc/8M6M-VXLF (model legislation requiring abortion clinics to be licensed as ambulatory surgical centers); AUL, *Women's Health Protection Act*, in DEFENDING LIFE 229–37 (2013) (model legislation requiring abortion clinics to meet the same standards as ambulatory surgical centers and to employ at least one physician who possesses admitting privileges at a hospital within thirty miles of the clinic); AUL, *Abortion Providers' Privileging Act*, in DEFENDING LIFE 238–40 (2013) (model legislation requiring that a physician with admitting privileges at a hospital within thirty miles be present at any clinic where abortions are performed).

[57] AUL was involved in all of these ways in the passage and defense of H.B. 2. *See, e.g.*, Hearing on S.B. 24 and S.B. 5 Before the Tex. Senate Comm. on Health & Human Services, 83rd Leg., 1st Sess. (June 13, 2013) (statement of Abby Johnson, AUL Senior Policy Advisor) (advocating on behalf of the passage of the law that became H.B. 2) (recording available at https://senate.texas.gov/av-archive.php?yr=2013; transcript on file with author); Brief for 44 Texas Legislators as Amici Curiae in Support of Defendants-

This strategy is not without its pitfalls—most of them having to do with the fact that state lawmakers do not always get the messaging right. The day after the Texas Senate approved the admitting privileges and surgical center requirements, Lieutenant Governor David Dewhurst tweeted a map of Texas depicting all of the clinics that would be forced to close as a result. "We fought to pass S.B. 5 thru the Senate last night, & this is why!" he exclaimed.[58] During the House floor debate over H.B. 2, Representative Chris Turner reported:

> There is a member on this floor earlier who bragged [ ]: 'I can't wait for two weeks from now when this bill makes it to the governor's desk and we can finally stop saying this is about women's health and talk about what it is, which is shutting down abortion clinics. I can't wait to go back to my constituents and be able to say that.'[59]

In early 2013, in calling for the law that became H.B. 2, Governor Perry himself declared that his goal was to "make abortion, at any stage, a thing of the past," and that until we live in an "ideal world . . . without abortion," Texas's aim should be to "continue to pass laws to ensure abortions are as rare as possible."[60]

This strategy gives rise to other problems as well. Representative Jodie Laubenberg, who introduced H.B. 2 in the Texas House, struggled to offer even basic information about the bill.[61] Faced with a barrage of

---

Appellants and Reversal of the District Court, Whole Woman's Health v. Lakey, 769 F.3d 285 (5th Cir. 2014) (No. 14-50928) (authored by Mailee R. Smith, AUL Staff Counsel).

[58] David Dewhurst (@DavidHDewhurst), TWITTER (June 19, 2013, 9:41 AM), http://twitter.com/DavidHDewhurst/status/347363342497302528/photo/1; see also Jim Vertuno, *Dewhurst Tweet Says Bill Attempt To Close Clinics*, AUSTIN AM. STATESMAN (June 19, 2013), https://www.statesman.com/article/20130619/NEWS/306199682 ("[A] tweet Wednesday from Republican Lt. Gov. David Dewhurst suggested supporters of the measure hope to close clinics and all but ban the procedure in the state."). Apparently recognizing his mistake, Dewhurst sent a second tweet not long thereafter explaining that he was "unapologetically pro-life AND a strong supporter of protecting women's health." David Dewhurst (@DavidHDewhurst), TWITTER (June 19, 2013, 12:06 PM), http://twitter.com/DavidHDewhurst/status/347400087191814145.

[59] Tex. House Floor Debate, 83rd Leg., 2d Sess., at S134–35 (July 9, 2013) (statement of Rep. Chris Turner), *available at* http://www.journals.house.state.tx.us [hereinafter House Floor Debate].

[60] Rick Perry, Keynote Address, *We Must Continue Working to Make Abortion a Thing of the Past*, Texas Alliance for Life Rally (Jan. 26, 2013), http://www.lrl.state.tx.us/legeLeaders/governors/displayDocs.cfm?govdoctypeID=6&governorID=44. For more on public officials' tendency to characterize admitting privileges and surgical center requirements as about protecting fetal life, as well as maternal health, see Greenhouse & Siegel, *supra* note 28, at 1452–53, 1470.

[61] Mary Tuma, *Notorious Abortion Bill Inspired By Draft Legislation From National Anti-Abortion Group*, SAN ANTONIO CURRENT (July 2, 2013), https://www.sacurrent.com/sanantonio/notorious-abortion-bill-inspired-by-draft-legislation-from-national-anti-abortion-group/Content?oid=2248521 (reporting that Laubenberg "oftentimes fumbled [her] responses, evaded definitive answers or simply didn't have the knowledge or data to back them up, making for some cringe-worthy exchanges under the Capitol dome"); *id.* (noting that Laubenberg seemed so flummoxed by questions regarding basic facts about H.B. 2 that "an astonished state representative asked Laubenberg outright on the House floor, 'How do you not know this?' ").

questions about the projected costs to women's (and men's) healthcare of closing dozens of reproductive health clinics throughout the state, Laubenberg simply repeated, in almost rote fashion, that the bill was designed to protect women's health.[62] She could not cite any statistics to substantiate her claim that abortion posed a significant health risk to women; nor was she able to describe the kinds of casualties the admitting privileges and surgical center requirements would avert.[63] Ultimately, however, these lapses were not enough to cost AUL its bill or to prevent Texas politicians from insisting that they had acted to protect women's health.

WHAT IT MEANS TO PROTECT WOMEN

Supporters of H.B. 2 frequently adverted to Kermit Gosnell, the Pennsylvania doctor who was charged in 2010 with crimes in the practice of abortion, and ultimately sentenced to life in prison without the possibility of parole for, among other things, killing three infants born alive, negligently causing the death of an adult woman, and violating laws barring late-term abortions.[64] H.B. 2's supporters used the example of Gosnell to argue that abortion was a dangerous business and that it was important to crack down on the plethora of substandard abortion clinics that were no better than back alleys. If the admitting privileges and surgical center requirements saved the life of even one woman, supporters argued, those measures would be worth taking.[65]

The bill's opponents countered those claims by arguing—with the support of the American College of Obstetricians and Gynecologists, the Texas Medical Association, and the Texas Hospital Association—that there was no health justification for H.B. 2.[66] Lawmakers who opposed the bill drew on testimony by the Texas Hospital Association (THA) to argue that requiring abortion providers to obtain admitting privileges would do nothing to increase their patients' wellbeing.[67] The reason most abortion providers lack admitting privileges, the THA explained, is that such privileges are reserved for doctors who regularly admit and treat patients in hospitals,[68] something abortion providers almost never need

---

[62] *See* Hearing on H.B. 2 Before the Tex. House Comm. on State Affairs, 83rd Leg., 2d Sess. (July 2, 2013) [hereinafter House Comm. Hearing, 2d Sess.] (recording available at http://www.house.state.tx.us/video-audio/committee-broadcasts/83/; transcript on file with author).

[63] *Id.*

[64] *See, e.g.*, Sonia Smith, *Special Procedures*, TEX. MONTHLY (June 19, 2013), https://www.texasmonthly.com/politics/special-procedures/; Matthew Waller, *Texas Legislature: Abortion Regulations Join Session*, SAN ANGELO STANDARD-TIMES (June 11, 2013), http://archive.gosanangelo.com/news/texas-legislature-abortion-regulations-join-session-ep-4386 11632-355551901.html/.

[65] Chuck Lindell, *Tougher Abortion Standards Clear Panel*, AUSTIN AM. STATESMAN, Mar. 31, 2013, at B1.

[66] *See* DAVIS, *supra* note 9, at 9–30 (reading into the legislative record statements by these three organizations opposing H.B. 2).

[67] *See, e.g., id.* at 15–18.

[68] *Id.* at 15–16.

to do.[69] Moreover, the THA observed, the fact that a doctor has admitting privileges does not mean he or she will be present when a patient arrives at the hospital. Patients who arrive at hospitals with abortion-related complications are treated by staff doctors irrespective of who treated them originally.[70]

Likewise, legislators opposed to H.B. 2 argued, there is no health-based reason to require abortion clinics to outfit themselves as ambulatory surgical centers. These legislators observed that the state allows a significant number of medical procedures that present greater health risks than abortion to be performed outside of ambulatory surgical centers. Indeed, they observed, the rate of major complications arising from abortion is vanishingly small—slightly lower than the rate for colonoscopies and considerably lower than the rate for routine dental work.[71] Yet Texas does not require those procedures (and other procedures more risky than abortion, such as vasectomies and plastic surgery) to take place in ambulatory surgical centers.[72] This is because there is no evidence that requiring such procedures to take place in hospital-like settings, with extra-wide hallways and state-of-the-art ventilation systems, would further reduce already-low complication rates.[73] Indeed, lawmakers argued, the surgical center requirement would hurt women because it would drive reproductive healthcare clinics out of business, leaving vast numbers of women—particularly those who live in rural areas and/or lack financial resources—without access to care.[74] If the law were permitted to take effect, the best estimates suggested that two million Texas women of reproductive age would be required to drive more than fifty miles to reach a provider, and nearly one

---

[69] *See* Hearing on H.B. 2 Before the Tex. House Comm. on State Affairs, 83rd Leg., 1st Sess. (June 20, 2013) (recording available at http://www.house.state.tx.us/video-audio/committee-broadcasts/83/; transcript on file with author) (statement of Rep. Jessica Farrar) (noting "that fewer than .3% of abortion patients experience a complication that requires a hospitalization"); House Floor Debate at S62 (statement of Rep. Donna Howard) (noting that admitting privileges are reserved for doctors who treat patients in hospitals with some regularity and that abortion-related "complications are so rare" providers cannot satisfy this requirement).

[70] *See* DAVIS, *supra* note 9, at 16.

[71] *See, e.g.,* Mandy Oaklander, *Abortion Complication Rates Are 'Lower Than That For Wisdom Tooth Extraction,' Study Says,* TIME (Dec. 9, 2014), http://time.com/3623572/abortion-safe-complications/ (comparing the complication rates of abortion and other common medical procedures); Ushma Upadhyay et al., *Incidence of Emergency Department Visits and Complications After Abortion,* 125 OBSTETRICS & GYNECOLOGY 175, 175 (2015) (examining the healthcare received by approximately 55,000 women in the six weeks after their abortions and finding a 0.23% major complications rate, "comparable to previously published rates").

[72] *See, e.g.,* Tex. Senate Floor Debate, 83rd Leg., 1st Sess. (June 18, 2013) (recording available at https://senate.texas.gov/av-archive.php?yr=2013; transcript on file with author) [hereinafter Senate Floor Debate] (statement of Sen. Wendy Davis).

[73] *Id.* ("I still have yet to have anyone provide empirical data to me that would demonstrate that [imposing ambulatory surgical center requirements would] create[ ] a safer environment than patients are currently receiving for all of these services in the state of Texas today.").

[74] *See, e.g.,* House Floor Debate at S35–37 (statement of Rep. Jose Menéndez).

million women would be required to drive more than one hundred fifty miles to do so.[75]

Legislators who opposed H.B. 2 argued that if pro-life lawmakers were truly motivated by a desire to safeguard women's health, they would not single out abortion with unnecessary and even counter-productive regulation, but would instead direct their attention to the abysmal state of women's health and healthcare in Texas.[76] The bill's opponents repeatedly observed that Texas was at or near the bottom in a broad range of categories related to reproductive health and women's wellbeing more generally. They noted that Texas ranks dead last when it comes to the percentage of state residents with health insurance.[77] They noted that the rate of teen pregnancy is higher in Texas than in almost every other state, and that the rate of repeat teen pregnancy is higher in Texas than anywhere else.[78] They also called attention to the state's high maternal mortality rates.[79]

H.B. 2's opponents argued that, for all its purported concern about women's health, the Texas legislature had done little to address these statistics, and in fact had made matters worse. They pointed out that Texas is one of the minority of states that rejected the Affordable Care Act's Medicaid expansion.[80] Had the legislature chosen to participate in the expansion, over a million uninsured Texans would have become eligible for coverage.[81] In large part due to its low health insurance rates, Texas ranks forty-seventh among states when it comes to meeting the contraceptive needs of poor women.[82] In terms of policies affecting women's health more generally, it ranks fiftieth.[83] Yet, as Wendy Davis and others noted, the legislature in 2011 dramatically slashed family

---

[75] Whole Woman's Health v. Lakey, 46 F.Supp.3d 673, 681 (W.D. Tex. 2014).

[76] For a scholarly version of this argument, see Reva B. Siegel, *ProChoiceLife: Asking Who Protects Life and How—and Why It Matters in Law and Politics*, 93 IND. L. J. 207 (2018).

[77] *See, e.g.*, Senate Floor Debate (statement of Sen. Sylvia Garcia); House Floor Debate at S121 (statement of Rep. Jessica Farrar).

[78] *See, e.g.*, House Floor Debate at S134 (statement of Rep. Chris Turner).

[79] *See, e.g., id.* at S121 (statement of Rep. Jessica Farrar) (noting that maternal mortality rates in Texas far exceed the national average and have worsened significantly since the mid-1990s).

[80] *See, e.g.*, Senate Floor Debate (statement of Sen. Rodney Ellis); House Floor Debate at S134 (statement of Rep. Chris Turner).

[81] *See* House Floor Debate at S134 (statement of Rep. Chris Turner); Wade Goodwyn, *Texas Loses Billions to Treat the Poor By Not Expanding Medicaid, Advocates Say*, NPR (May 29, 2015), https://www.npr.org/2015/05/29/410470081/texas-didn-t-expand-medicaid-advocates-say-money-is-being-left-on-the-table.

[82] UNITED HEALTH FOUND., 2016 HEALTH OF WOMEN AND CHILDREN REPORT, available at http://www.americashealthrankings.org/explore/2016-health-of-women-and-children-report/measure/Family_planning/state/TX (measuring the percentage of need for contraceptive services among women with a family income below 250% of the federal poverty level and women younger than age twenty that is met by publicly-funded providers).

[83] UNITED HEALTH FOUND., 2016 HEALTH OF WOMEN AND CHILDREN REPORT, available at https://www.americashealthrankings.org/explore/2016-health-of-women-and-children-report/measure/policy_women_mch/state/TX (assessing a broad range of women's-health-related policies in effect in each state).

planning services.[84] It cut over seventy million dollars from the state's family planning budget (a two-thirds reduction) and redistributed the remaining funds away from dedicated family planning providers.[85] Eighty-two family planning clinics closed in response to those cuts.[86] Moreover, sex education bills routinely die in Austin, with the result that a majority of Texas school districts offer only abstinence-only programs and many offer no sex education at all.[87]

Legislators who opposed H.B. 2 argued that its chief supporters had been on the wrong side of all of these issues from a women's health perspective. Representative Laubenberg, who introduced H.B. 2 in the House, not only voted to cut family planning services and to reject the Medicaid expansion, but also proposed an amendment to a 2007 appropriations bill that would have required pregnant women to wait three months before qualifying for prenatal and perinatal care under Texas's Children's Health Insurance Program.[88] When challenged, Laubenberg vehemently insisted that pregnant women should not qualify for CHIP funds because their children "aren't born yet."[89] Laubenberg's history of voting against funding for women's healthcare prompted one witness who testified against H.B. 2 to remark: "[I]f this is really about women's safety you have picked the worst bill author in the Texas legislature."[90]

Recognizing that H.B. 2 was almost certain to pass, legislators who opposed the bill offered a series of amendments designed to blunt its impact on women's access to reproductive healthcare. One such amendment required the state to cover the cost of converting abortion

---

[84]   *See, e.g.*, Senate Floor Debate (statement of Sen. Wendy Davis); House Floor Debate at S98 (statement of Rep. Dawnna Dukes).

[85]   Kari White et al., *Cutting Family Planning in Texas*, 367 NEW ENG. J. MED. 1179, 1179 (2012).

[86]   Amanda J. Stevenson et al., *Effect of Removal of Planned Parenthood From the Texas Women's Health Program*, 374 NEW ENG. J. MED. 853, 854 (2016).

[87]   *See* House Floor Debate at S80, 82 (statement of Rep. Ruth McClendon) (noting that "in 1995, Texas made a big push to institute abstinence as the only sex education in [its] public schools" and arguing that state legislators ought to reverse this if they wish to curb teen pregnancy and abortion); *see also* Cassandra Pollock, *Study: A Quarter of Texas Public Schools No Longer Teach Sex Ed*, TEX. TRIB. (Feb. 14, 2017), https://www.texas tribune.org/2017/02/14/texas-public-schools-largely-teach-abstinence-only-sex-education-repor/ (noting that, during the 2015–2016 school year, a quarter of Texas public school districts offered no sex education and well over half offered only abstinence-only programs).

[88]   Jennifer Bendery, *Texas Abortion Bill Author In 2007: No Health Care For Unborn Because "They're Not Born Yet,"* HUFFINGTON POST (July 9, 2013), https://www. huffingtonpost.com/2013/07/09/texas-abortion-bill-author_n_3570588.html.

[89]   *Id.*

[90]   House Comm. Hearing, 2d Sess. (statement of Bill Kelley, former chief of staff to Texas Rep. Ellen Cohen). Kelley also noted Representative Laubenberg's assertion, during the debate over H.B. 2, that rape and incest exceptions to abortion laws are unnecessary because "[i]n the emergency room they have what's called rape kits, where a woman can get cleaned out." That assertion made the national news. See Alexander Abad-Santos, *Sponsor of New Texas Anti-Abortion Bill Thinks Rape Kits Are Contraceptives*, THE ATLANTIC (June 24, 2013), https://www.theatlantic.com/politics/archive/2013/06/new-texas-anti-abortion-bill-rape-kits/313947/.

clinics into ambulatory surgical centers, so that the regulation would not cause clinics to close.[91] Another would have conditioned H.B. 2's requirements on the state's acceptance of the Medicaid expansion[92]; yet another would have barred H.B. 2 from taking effect until the rate of uninsured Texans fell below five percent.[93] One amendment would have rendered pregnant women eligible to receive Temporary Assistance to Needy Families (TANF) benefits, food stamps, and Medicaid after the twentieth week of gestation and would have raised the Medicaid coverage ceiling from 185 to 250 percent of the poverty line.[94] Another would have required that the sex education curriculum offered in Texas schools be evidence-based.[95]

It is unlikely that the legislators who proposed these amendments believed they would pass. The idea was to lay a foundation for the inevitable constitutional challenge to H.B. 2. If H.B. 2's proponents claimed that their motivation was to protect women's health, its opponents sought to undermine that claim by showing that the only step H.B. 2's backers were willing to take to operationalize their purported commitment to women's health was closing abortion clinics.

In fact, it was this line of argument that led to the premature end of Wendy Davis's filibuster. Filibusterers in Texas get three strikes, and then they are out. Davis received one strike when someone helped her into a back brace (illicit assistance from a colleague).[96] But the other two strikes were substantive. She received one strike for referencing the 2011 cuts to Texas's family planning program,[97] and another for invoking the state's sonogram law, which imposes a twenty-four-hour waiting period on women seeking abortions.[98] Davis's aim, in the first instance, was to raise questions about the legislature's commitment to women's health; her aim in the second instance was to suggest that H.B. 2 would interact with other regulations in ways that would make it exceedingly difficult for poor and rural women to obtain abortions. In both cases, the Lieutenant Governor, who presides over the Texas Senate, determined that Davis had strayed too far from the matter at hand. He deemed her interventions "not germane" to the debate over H.B. 2.[99] As we shall see, however, the Lieutenant Governor's pronouncements about what was germane to discussions about H.B. 2 were not the last word on the matter.

---

[91] *See* House Comm. Hearing, 2d Sess. (statement of Rep. Sylvester Turner).

[92] *See* Senate Floor Debate (statement of Sen. Rodney Ellis).

[93] *See id.* (statement of Sen. Wendy Davis).

[94] *See, e.g.*, House Floor Debate at S74 (statement of Rep. Dawnna Dukes).

[95] *See* Senate Floor Debate (statement of Sen. Kirk Watson).

[96] For more on the strikes that ended Davis's filibuster, see DAVIS, *supra* note 11, at 276–82.

[97] *Id.* at 276–77.

[98] *Id.* at 281–82.

[99] *Id.* at 276–82; *see also* Smith & Grieder, *supra* note 9.

TAKING A REAL LOOK AT ABORTION REGULATION

Founded in 2003 by Amy Hagstrom Miller, Whole Woman's Health is a privately-owned group of women's clinics that provides comprehensive gynecological services, including abortion.[100] It bills itself as "a woman-owned, woman-centered, progressive business"—one that starts from the premise that "each woman must be at the center of her own healthcare decisions" and works to destigmatize abortion.[101] When H.B. 2 went into effect, forcing two of its clinics to close,[102] Whole Woman's Health filed a lawsuit, challenging the constitutionality of the law's admitting privileges and surgical center requirements.[103]

In the most immediate sense, the lawsuit concerned the clinic closures in Texas. But the fear among abortion rights advocates like Hagstrom Miller was that "[w]hat's happening in Texas won't stay in Texas."[104] She and others were concerned that laws like H.B. 2 would be replicated in state houses throughout the nation, leaving vast numbers of American women seeking abortions with nowhere to turn. The broader question in *Whole Woman's Health* was whether the Court would look the other way and allow this clinic-closing campaign to continue, or whether it would reaffirm the idea, at the heart of *Roe* and *Casey*, that the Constitution meaningfully constrains the kinds of abortion regulation states may enact.

One of the key controversies in *Whole Woman's Health* involved the standard of review that applies to abortion regulation. The Court in *Roe* applied strict scrutiny.[105] But *Casey* replaced *Roe*'s strict scrutiny framework with an "undue burden" test often equated with intermediate scrutiny.[106] Post-*Casey*, states may regulate abortion throughout pregnancy to vindicate their legitimate interests in protecting fetal life and safeguarding maternal health.[107] But they may not place "a substantial obstacle in the path of a woman seeking an abortion of a nonviable fetus," and when they act to protect fetal life, the means they

---

[100] *See* WHOLE WOMAN'S HEALTH, About Us, https://wholewomanshealth.com/about-us/ (last visited Oct. 18, 2018).

[101] *Id.*

[102] Alexandra Sifferlin, *Texas Abortion Clinic at Center of Historic Supreme Court Decision Reopens*, TIME (Apr. 28, 2017), http://time.com/4759278/texas-abortion-clinic-whole-womans-health-supreme-court/.

[103] *See* Whole Woman's Health v. Lakey, 46 F.Supp.3d 673 (W.D. Tex. 2014).

[104] Lauren Kelly, *Meet the Woman Behind the Supreme Court's High-Stakes Abortion Case*, ROLLING STONE (Mar. 2, 2016), https://www.rollingstone.com/politics/news/meet-the-woman-behind-the-supreme-courts-high-stakes-abortion-case-20160302.

[105] 410 U.S. 113, 164–66 (1973).

[106] *See, e.g.*, Planned Parenthood Se., Inc. v. Strange, 33 F. Supp. 3d 1330, 1337–38 (M.D. Ala. 2014) (describing the undue burden standard as a "middle ground between those who would impose strict-scrutiny review of such regulations and those who would require only a rational basis" (quotation marks omitted)); AUL, CONSTITUTIONAL LAW AND ABORTION PRIMER 24, available at https://aul.org/wp-content/uploads/2018/10/Constitutional-Law-and-Abortion-Primer-SCAN.pdf (observing that the Court has repeatedly and "expressly readopted Casey and its undue-burden, intermediate standard of review").

[107] Planned Parenthood of Se. Pa. v. Casey, 505 U.S. 833, 875–76 (1992).

choose "to further th[is] interest . . . . must be calculated to inform the woman's free choice, not hinder it."[108] The state of Texas and advocacy groups such as AUL seized on the opportunity presented by the H.B. 2 litigation to try to persuade the Court to lower the standard of review even further, to rational basis.[109] Rational basis is the most lenient form of judicial review; it is the level of scrutiny courts apply when reviewing ordinary social and economic legislation unconnected to constitutional rights. Because this standard is so deferential to lawmakers—asking only whether the government has a legitimate interest in enacting a piece of legislation and could rationally have believed that the legislation furthered that interest—laws subject to rational basis almost always survive constitutional review.

The district court in *Whole Woman's Health* rejected the invitation to apply rational basis review. It applied *Casey*'s undue burden test and found that H.B. 2 constituted a substantial obstacle to abortion because "the severity of the burden imposed by both requirements [wa]s not balanced by the weight of the interests underlying them."[110] If H.B. 2 was intended to protect fetal life, it was clearly unconstitutional because it did "not counsel against the decision to seek an abortion," but simply made it more difficult for women to obtain abortions.[111] Likewise, the court found, "[t]he primary interest proffered for the act's requirements . . . [namely,] concerns over the health and safety of women seeking abortions," did not justify the law.[112] The court found that the clinic closures caused by these requirements "would operate for a significant number of women in Texas just as drastically as a complete ban on abortion,"[113] and that the requirements themselves would do nothing to enhance women's safety, in part because "abortion in Texas was [already] extremely safe."[114]

The Fifth Circuit reversed. It concluded that the district court had overestimated the size of the burden H.B. 2 imposed by improperly taking account of factors like women's own inability to secure childcare, transportation, time off work, and funds to make multiple trips to distant clinics.[115] The Fifth Circuit held that when determining whether a law violates the right to abortion, courts should consider only those burdens directly attributable to the "law itself."[116] Put differently, the court essentially adopted the Lieutenant Governor's narrow assessment of

---

[108] *Id.* at 877.

[109] *See, e.g.*, Brief for Respondents, Whole Woman's Health v. Hellerstedt, 136 S.Ct. 2292 (2016) (No. 15-274); Brief for 44 Texas Legislators as Amici Curiae in Support of Defendants-Appellants and Reversal of the District Court, Whole Woman's Health v. Lakey, 769 F.3d 285 (5th Cir. 2014) (No. 14-50928) (authored by Mailee R. Smith, AUL Staff Counsel).

[110] Whole Woman's Health v. Lakey, 46 F.Supp.3d 673, 684 (W.D. Tex. 2014).

[111] *Id.*

[112] *Id.*

[113] *Id.* at 682.

[114] *Id.* at 684.

[115] Whole Woman's Health v. Cole, 790 F.3d 563, 589 (5th Cir. 2015).

[116] *Id.*

what was germane to the discussion of H.B. 2. Even conceding that H.B. 2 would close clinics and thereby increase some patients' travel time, the Fifth Circuit concluded that the "law itself" did not impose a substantial obstacle to abortion.[117]

Perhaps even more importantly, the Fifth Circuit adopted the highly deferential rational basis standard of review, finding that H.B. 2's requirements "were rationally related to a legitimate state interest" and that the district court erred by "substituting its own judgment for that of the legislature."[118] In other related rulings on H.B. 2, the Fifth Circuit asserted that "[n]othing in the Supreme Court's abortion jurisprudence deviates from the essential attributes of the rational basis test."[119] The court claimed that because a "law based on rational speculation unsupported by evidence or empirical data satisfies rational basis review,"[120] judges have no business "evaluat[ing] whether [health-justified abortion restrictions] would actually improve women's health and safety."[121] On the Fifth Circuit's account, when a legislature asserts that an abortion restriction promotes women's health, courts must defer to that judgment and inquire only whether the legislature could rationally have supposed its actions would further that asserted purpose.[122]

In support of these propositions, the court cited *Gonzales v. Carhart*, a 2007 Supreme Court decision upholding the federal Partial-Birth Abortion Ban Act.[123] In several instances in *Carhart*, the Court deployed keywords associated with the rational basis test.[124] But the Court in *Carhart* did not apply rational basis: It applied *Casey*'s undue burden test.[125] The Court made it clear in *Carhart* that under this test, courts "retain[ ] an independent constitutional duty to review factual findings where constitutional rights are at stake," and that "[u]ncritical deference to [the legislature's] factual findings . . . is inappropriate."[126] Thus, the

---

[117] *Id.* at 588–90.

[118] *Id.* at 584, 587.

[119] Planned Parenthood of Greater Tex. Surgical Health Servs. v. Abbott (Abbott II), 748 F.3d 583, 594 (5th Cir. 2014).

[120] *Id.* (quotation marks omitted).

[121] Whole Woman's Health v. Lakey, 769 F.3d 285, 297 (5th Cir.), *vacated in part*, 135 S. Ct. 399 (2014).

[122] *See, e.g.*, Abbott II, 748 F.3d at 596 ("The first-step in the analysis of an abortion regulation . . . is rational basis review, not empirical basis review."); Lakey, 769 F.3d at 297 (stating that "[i]n our circuit, we do not balance the wisdom or effectiveness of a[n] [abortion] law against the burdens the law imposes," because to do so would "ratchet[ ] up rational basis review into a pseudo-strict-scrutiny approach by examining whether the law advances the State's asserted purpose").

[123] 550 U.S. 124 (2007).

[124] *See, e.g., id.* at 158 ("Where it has a rational basis to act, and it does not impose an undue burden, the State may use its regulatory power to bar certain procedures and substitute others, all in furtherance of its legitimate interests in regulating the medical profession in order to promote respect for life, including life of the unborn.").

[125] *Id.* at 146.

[126] *Id.* at 165–66. For more on the Fifth Circuit's mischaracterization of Carhart, see Greenhouse & Siegel, *supra* note 28, at 1433–34, 1467–69. Greenhouse and Siegel observe

Fifth Circuit's application of the rational basis test and its assertions about the proper standard of review in abortion cases were less a statement of existing precedent than they were an invitation to the Court to reconsider its prior rulings and ratchet down the level of scrutiny that applies in the context of abortion.

This was precisely the kind of holding AUL and its allies hoped to win from the courts. AUL's aim in promoting requirements like those of H.B. 2 has long been to erode abortion rights, lowering the amount of constitutional protection they receive, rather than advocating for explicit bans on abortion that may not survive in court.[127] Charmaine Yoest, who was President of AUL during the litigation over H.B. 2, explained the organization's strategy this way: "In terms of social change you have to think about what's the next move. You're not going to capture the queen in one fell swoop."[128] The Fifth Circuit's decision did not (and could not) formally overrule *Roe* and *Casey*—but it hollowed out those decisions. If the Supreme Court had adopted the Fifth Circuit's reasoning, it would not have granted states permission to ban abortion. But it would have effectively withdrawn judicial oversight of abortion regulations styled as protective of maternal health. This would have allowed states to render abortion practically inaccessible to vast numbers of women by passing ostensibly health-justified laws that would make it impossible for abortion providers to operate.

Thus, when commentators refer to *Whole Woman's Health* as "the most important abortion case on reproductive rights . . . in twenty-five years,"[129] it is not simply because the Court declared the two controverted provisions of H.B. 2 unconstitutional. It is because the Court declined the Fifth Circuit's invitation to grant near-total deference to legislatures when they offer health justifications for abortion regulations. The Court held in *Whole Woman's Health* that the Fifth Circuit was "wrong to equate the judicial review applicable to the regulation of a constitutionally protected personal liberty with the less strict review

---

that Carhart concerned a regulation designed to protect fetal life, not maternal health—one that did not restrict access to abortion pre-viability, close any clinics, or leave women and their doctors without alternative procedures for terminating a pregnancy. The Fifth Circuit, however, elided these distinctions, treating the reasoning in Carhart as if it were perfectly applicable to cases involving health-justified abortion regulations. *Id.* at 1466–73.

[127] *See* Charlotte Hays, *Behind the Pro-Life Victories of 2011*, NAT. CATH. REG. (Oct. 5, 2011), http://www.ncregister.com/daily-news/behind-the-pro-life-victories-of-2011 (quoting Yoest, who said of AUL's constitutional strategy: "For us, it's very much a military strategy. . . . We don't make frontal attacks. . . . We don't want to re-create Pickett's Charge at Gettysburg. We pick our battles. What we do is very much under the radar screen and not very sexy."). For an early statement of AUL's incrementalist strategy, see Victor G. Rosenblum & Thomas J. Marzen, *Strategies for Reversing* Roe v. Wade *Through the Courts*, in ABORTION AND THE CONSTITUTION: REVERSING *ROE V. WADE* THROUGH THE COURTS 195, 196–97 (Dennis J. Horan et al. eds., 1987).

[128] *See* Khazan, *supra* note 21.

[129] Dahlia Lithwick, *The Right to Abortion: War of Attrition*, PROSPECT (Feb. 13, 2017), https://www.prospectmagazine.co.uk/magazine/right-to-abortion-women-feminism-gender-donald-trump-attrition.

applicable where, for example, economic legislation is at issue."[130] When faced with health-justified abortion regulation, the Court explained, judges should not simply defer to legislatures but should determine, based on their own assessment of the facts, whether the regulation actually serves health-related interests.[131] Applying this heightened standard of review, the Court found no support for the proposition that H.B. 2 vindicated Texas's asserted interest in protecting maternal health—especially in light of the state's approach to protecting its citizens' health outside of the abortion context.[132]

The Court also rejected the Fifth Circuit's method of assessing the magnitude of the burden H.B. 2 imposed. The Fifth Circuit held that barriers to abortion that arose from women's own lack of financial resources were irrelevant to assessing H.B. 2's constitutionality. The Supreme Court rejected that reasoning, holding that women's lived experience of exercising the right to abortion was central to the analysis of an abortion regulation's constitutionality. The Court reaffirmed its holding in *Casey* that when assessing the size of the burden an abortion regulation imposes, the constitutional analysis begins with the subset of women actually burdened by the regulation—even if their own life circumstances are what make the statute burdensome.[133] This attentiveness to women's actual experience of the abortion right also manifested itself in the Court's discussion of the real-world impact of Texas's clinic closures.[134] "[I]n the face of no threat to women's health," the Court observed,

> Texas seeks to force women to travel long distances to get abortions in crammed-to-capacity superfacilities. Patients seeking these services are less likely to get the kind of individualized attention, serious conversation, and emotional support that doctors at less taxed facilities may have offered. . . . Surgical centers attempting to accommodate sudden, vastly increased demand . . . may find that quality of care declines.[135]

---

[130] Whole Woman's Health v. Hellerstedt, 136 S.Ct. 2292, 2309 (2016).

[131] *Id.* at 2310 ("The statement that legislatures, and not courts, must resolve questions of medical uncertainty is . . . inconsistent with this Court's case law. Instead, the Court, when determining the constitutionality of laws regulating abortion procedures, has placed considerable weight upon evidence and argument presented in judicial proceedings.").

[132] *Id.* at 2311–12 (finding no health benefits stemming from admitting privileges requirement); id. at 2315–16 (finding no health benefit from surgical center requirement); *see also id.* at 2315 (observing that Texas permits childbirth and colonoscopies—procedures with considerably higher complication rates than abortion—to take place outside of surgical centers and concluding that the state imposed the surgical center requirement on abortion providers for reasons other than its purported interest in protecting women's health).

[133] *Id.* at 2320. For more on the significance of this holding, see Cary Franklin, *The New Class Blindness*, 128 YALE L.J. 2 (2018).

[134] *See* Greenhouse & Siegel, *supra* note 21, at 162 (observing that the Court in Whole Woman's Health considers abortion "restrictions cumulatively and in context, describing how, taken as a whole, they will alter the lived conditions of exercising the abortion right").

[135] Whole Woman's Health, 136 S.Ct. at 2318.

This eyes-wide-open analysis is in keeping with the Court's determination that judges should examine whether health-justified abortion regulations actually yield any health benefits. Here, and throughout its decision in *Whole Woman's Health*, the Court engages in forms of constitutional analysis that are attentive to the effects that barriers to abortion have on the women whose paths they impede.

CONCLUSION

Whole Woman's Health was an important victory for supporters of abortion rights. If H.B. 2 was not an attempt to capture the queen, it was at least an attempt to take the bishop. Had the Court retreated from scrutinizing health-justified abortion regulations, there would be little constitutional impediment to pro-life legislatures using such regulations to drive abortion clinics out of business. But to portray *Whole Woman's Health* as a simple victory for abortion rights would be to miss half the story. Before being ruled unconstitutional, H.B. 2's admitting privileges requirement briefly took effect. About half of Texas's forty abortion clinics closed in that brief period, and most have not reopened.[136] Nor did the Court's decision slow down AUL or the Texas legislature. The year after the Court decided *Whole Woman's Health*, Texas passed an AUL-inspired law requiring abortion providers to bury or cremate fetal remains.[137] In 2017, AUL responded to the Court's decision with a "re-envisioned" Women's Protection Project that contains new model laws focusing on "the criminal, civil, and administrative enforcement of all abortion related statutes" and "enhanced inspection requirements for abortion facilities."[138] Most of the attention *Whole Woman's Health* has received in the media has focused on Wendy Davis, her allies, and their triumphant vindication at the Supreme Court. But the story of how H.B. 2 came to be enacted in the first place, and the renewed determination of AUL and other pro-life advocates in the wake of the Court's decision, is no less compelling and at least as consequential for the future of abortion law in this country.

Indeed, the Court's recent shift to the right following the appointment of Justice Kavanaugh[139] gives AUL and other pro-life advocates every reason to persist in their campaign to restrict abortion

---

[136] Aneri Pattani, *Don't Expect Shuttered Texas Abortion Clinics to Reopen Soon*, TEX. TRIB. (June 27, 2016), https://www.texastribune.org/2016/06/27/dont-expect-shuttered-abortion-clinics-reopen-soon/; *see also id.* (reporting that some of the shuttered clinics may never reopen due to high start-up costs and onerous regulations).

[137] Marissa Evans, *Texas Fetal Remains Burial Rule Blocked By Federal Court Again*, TEX. TRIB. (Jan. 29, 2018), https://www.texastribune.org/2018/01/29/texas-fetal-remains-burial-rule-blocked-federal-court-again/ (reporting that the law has been blocked twice by federal courts but that the state is continuing to fight for it).

[138] AUL, DEFENDING LIFE 309–10 (2017), available at https://perma.cc/XWY3-2DXX.

[139] Robert Barnes, *The Kavanaugh Court is Decades in the Making for Conservatives—How Fast Will It Shift Right?*, CHI. TRIB. (Oct. 6, 2018), http://www.chicago tribune.com/news/nationworld/politics/ct-kavanaugh-court-conservatives-20181006-story. html ("The Kavanaugh court will be the one conservatives have worked for decades to construct . . . with velocity the only question about the Supreme Court's advance to the right.").

rights. *Whole Woman's Health* preserved a half-century of constitutional jurisprudence promising meaningful constitutional review of abortion regulation. But the future of that jurisprudence is now deeply uncertain. The Court in *Whole Woman's Health* rejected the Fifth Circuit's characterization of *Gonzales v. Carhart* as a rational basis decision. But it is only a matter of time before a new invitation to lower the standard of review in abortion cases reaches the Court, and it is not clear that the current Justices will continue to hold the line. Were the Court to adopt a rational basis approach mandating judicial deference to legislative judgments, it would effectively end meaningful judicial review of abortion regulation.

As the story of *Whole Woman's Health* shows, the adoption of such a rational basis framework would leave abortion providers in states with pro-life legislatures almost completely unprotected. In many regions of the country, it would place the abortion right squarely in the hands of legislators determined to eviscerate that right. At that point, it might not matter whether *Roe* remains on the books: In many places, the so-called right to abortion would already have ceased to offer women any meaningful protection.

12

Douglas NeJaime*

The Story of *Brooke S.B. v. Elizabeth A.C.C.*: Parental Recognition in the Age of LGBT Equality

Questions of reproductive rights are often entangled with questions of equality. An important and voluminous scholarly literature examines how the regulation of pregnancy, contraception, and abortion relates to questions of sex equality.[1] In mapping parenthood onto evolving principles of sexual orientation equality, this chapter explores a connection between reproduction and equality that has received less explicit attention. It does so not by way of a U.S. Supreme Court opinion or a case decided on constitutional grounds—although the Court's marriage equality precedents, and the constitutional values those precedents expressed, shape approaches to parental recognition. Instead, this chapter tells the story of a family law matter resolved in state court. *Brooke S.B. v. Elizabeth A.C.C.*,[2] a 2016 decision of New York's highest court, broke new ground on a critical question: Who is a parent?[3] The case

---

* Professor of Law, Yale Law School. I am grateful to the editors for including me in this volume. For helpful comments, I thank Khiara Bridges, Maya Manian, Serena Mayeri, Melissa Murray, Kate Shaw, Neil Siegel, Reva Siegel, and Cilla Smith. For invaluable research support, I thank Rachel Granetz and Callie Wilson, as well as Lora Johns at Yale's Lillian Goldman Law Library. For her time and generosity, I thank Susan Sommer.

[1] *See, e.g.*, Cary Franklin, *The Anti-Stereotyping Principle in Constitutional Sex Discrimination Law*, 85 N.Y.U. L. REV. 83 (2010); Melissa Murray, *Overlooking Equality on the Road to* Griswold, 124 YALE L.J. F. 324 (2015), http://www.yalelawjournal.org/forum/overlooking-equality-on-the-road-to-griswold; Reva Siegel, *Reasoning from the Body: A Historical Perspective on Abortion Regulation and Questions of Equal Protection*, 44 STAN. L. REV. 261 (1992).

[2] 61 N.E.3d 488 (N.Y. 2016). Cases involving parentage are generally not publicly available. In addition to relying on published opinions by the New York courts, this chapter draws on redacted versions of the briefs in the case. I am grateful to Susan Sommer, who represented Brooke, for providing me with redacted materials. In this chapter, I use only the women's first names, which appeared in the published opinion, and I refer to the child only as "M.B.," which also appeared in the published opinion.

[3] The *Brooke S.B.* case was consolidated with another case involving a nonbiological lesbian co-parent. In *Estrellita A. v. Jennifer L.D.*, two women decided to have a child together through donor insemination. *Id.* at 491–92. Over the first three years of the child's life, the couple resided together and co-parented the child. *Id.* at 492. After the couple separated, the nonbiological mother continued to see the child. *Id.* The biological mother

illustrates both the opportunities and limitations that arise when parentage law embraces sexual orientation equality.

By relating conflict over parental recognition to the evolving status of same-sex-couples' families, this chapter shows how law may recognize nonbiological parents in an effort to vindicate sexual orientation equality.[4] Yet, the emphasis on LGBT equality can shape approaches to parental recognition in ways that yield recognition for some families— namely, same-sex couples and those using assisted reproductive technologies (ART)—while leaving other families in an uncertain state— namely, families in which the nonbiological parent did not participate in the plan to have the child but nonetheless raised the child. This distinction captures differences between *intent* and *function*— increasingly important concepts in parentage law. An intentional approach to determining parental status focuses on adults' plans with respect to parenting, typically looking to decisions made well before the child's conception.[5] A functional approach focuses on events that occur after the child is born, such as whether there is an existing parent-child relationship, and whether, with the consent of the legal parent, the individual claiming parental rights formed a bonded parental relationship with the child.[6] In short, intentional parenthood focuses on the decision to have a child, while functional parenthood focuses on the act of raising the child.

In deciding *Brooke S.B.*, the court followed the intentional approach, although it did not discount entirely the value of a more functional approach. By focusing on the parties' intent, the decision closely tracks same-sex family formation and thus vindicates sexual orientation equality. Yet, the decision fails to fully capture functional bonds that exist in a range of families, only some of which include LGBT parents.[7]

---

then commenced a proceeding seeking child support, and the nonbiological mother filed a petition seeking visitation. *Id.* at 491–92. The lower court recognized the nonbiological mother's standing based on judicial estoppel; since the biological mother successfully sought child support by claiming that the nonbiological mother was in fact a legal parent, she could not then take a contrary position in opposing the nonbiological mother's visitation petition. *Id.* at 492, 501; *see also* Estrellita A. v. Jennifer D., 963 N.Y.S.2d 843, 844 (Fam. Ct. 2013). The New York intermediate and high courts affirmed that decision. *Brooke S.B.*, 61 N.E.3d at 493, 501.

[4] I have been writing on this topic over a series of articles and essays. *See* Douglas NeJaime, *The Nature of Parenthood*, 126 YALE L.J. 2260 (2017); Douglas NeJaime, *Marriage Equality and the New Parenthood*, 129 HARV. L. REV. 1185 (2016); *see also* Douglas NeJaime, *Differentiating Assimilation*, 75 STUDIES IN LAW, POLITICS AND SOCIETY 1 (2018); Douglas NeJaime, *The Family's Constitution*, 32 CONST. COMMENT. 413 (2017); Douglas NeJaime, Griswold's *Progeny: Assisted Reproduction, Procreative Liberty, and Sexual Orientation Equality*, 124 YALE L.J. F. 340 (2015), http://www.yalelawjournal.org/forum/griswolds-progeny.

[5] *See infra* notes 111–112 and accompanying text.

[6] *See infra* notes 113–114 and accompanying text.

[7] The privileging of an intentional approach over a functional one may, especially outside of the same-sex-couple population, further inequalities based on race and class, since intentional standards benefit individuals with access to ART. *See* Dorothy E. Roberts, *The Social Context of Oncofertility*, 61 DEPAUL L. REV. 777, 791, 794 (2012) (identifying "the huge lacuna between the ART available to rich and poor women" and describing "evidence

Importantly, a functional standard may eventually find a home in New York law, as the *Brooke S.B.* court left open the possibility of a functional test that would reach beyond the same-sex parents before it.

THE FACTS[8]

Brooke and Elizabeth's story sounds much like those of many other same-sex couples who for decades had been forming families with children. Since the 1970s and 1980s, lesbian couples had turned to donor insemination to have children. For years, those couples who broke up during the children's minority did so within a hostile legal regime that viewed the biological mother as the legal mother and the nonbiological mother as a legal stranger. Without recognition as a legal parent, an individual generally cannot seek custody or visitation. Accordingly, if the biological mother refused to allow her former partner access to the child, the nonbiological mother's relationship with the child would end.

In those cases that were litigated, often by leading national LGBT rights organizations, the nonbiological mother told a familiar story of family formation—a committed relationship, a decision to have a child together, and a joint effort to raise the child. Quotidian details of family life became critical facts meant to convince the court that the two women intended to create a family together and then functioned as a family until—and often even in the years following—their break-up. The law, the nonbiological mother urged, should abandon its reflexive attachment to parental recognition organized around biological connection and instead recognize the parent-child relationship that exists in fact. Following this pattern, Brooke and Elizabeth's story reveals features that had confronted courts for decades.

Brooke and Elizabeth began dating in 2006 and eventually moved in together.[9] By 2007, they were engaged to be married—anticipating a time when New York would open marriage to same-sex couples.[10] Elizabeth wore an engagement ring and "referred to herself in front of Brooke and others as Brooke's 'wife.'"[11] Eventually, Brooke and Elizabeth decided to

---

that many women of color wish to use ART but are prevented by impediments to access"). Moreover, functional recognition is most relevant to nonmarital families, which tend to be less white and have lower incomes than marital families. *See* Linda C. McClain, *The Other Marriage Equality Problem*, 93 B.U. L. REV. 921, 943 (2013) (explaining the contemporary marriage gap along lines of both race and class).

[8]   The facts, some of which are also recited in the court's opinion, are drawn primarily from Brooke's brief. Of course, some of these facts were contested by Elizabeth. Confidential Brief for Petitioner-Respondent at 6–23, Brooke S.B. v. Elizabeth A.C.C., 61 N.E.3d 488 (N.Y. 2016) (No. APL-2015-00236); Confidential Brief for Respondent-Respondent at 11–12, Brooke S.B. v. Elizabeth A.C.C., 61 N.E.3d 488 (N.Y. 2016) (No. APL-2015-00236).

[9]   Confidential Brief for Petitioner-Respondent, *supra* note 8, at 8 (internal citations omitted).

[10]   *Id.* (internal citations omitted).

[11]   *Id.* at 8–9 (internal citations omitted).

have a child together. Elizabeth, they agreed, "would conceive their child
using donor insemination," and a mutual friend donated sperm.[12]

After Elizabeth became pregnant, the couple prepared together for
their new addition. They "decorated the nursery for their expected child
in the home they shared."[13] Friends and family threw them a baby
shower.[14] Medical care was a joint effort, as "Brooke accompanied
Elizabeth to every pre-natal care appointment."[15] When Elizabeth went
into premature labor and was flown to a hospital, "Brooke drove there to
join her at her bedside, remaining with her through the entire hospital
stay."[16] After that point, "Elizabeth had almost daily pre-natal care
appointments, and Brooke was by Elizabeth's side for every single one."[17]
Indeed, the attending nurse described Brooke as "very attentive to
[Elizabeth] and very excited over the pregnancy."[18] When the big day
arrived in June 2009, Brooke was by Elizabeth's side as she gave birth;
indeed, Brooke cut the umbilical cord.[19] Brooke's last name appeared as
their son's last name on the birth certificate.[20]

Once they took their son, M.B., home, Brooke was a "fully involved"
parent.[21] She bathed and fed the boy.[22] She took him to doctors'
appointments and arranged visits with extended family.[23] In fact, Brooke
became the child's primary caretaker.[24] She "left her job and stayed home
to care for M.B." when Elizabeth's maternity leave ended.[25] Even as she
focused on caregiving, Brooke also contributed to the family's financial
support—spending "her own money on clothes, toys, diapers, and other
expenses for M.B."[26]

Elizabeth, Brooke, and M.B. held themselves out as a family.[27]
Elizabeth frequently used Brooke's last name as her last name.[28] When
M.B. was baptized, the certificate listed Brooke and Elizabeth as his
"parents."[29] The couple represented Brooke as M.B.'s mother not only to

---

[12] *Id.* at 9 (internal citations omitted).

[13] *Id.* at 10 (internal citations omitted).

[14] *Id.* (internal citations omitted).

[15] *Id.* at 9.

[16] *Id.* at 9–10 (internal citations omitted).

[17] *Id.* at 10 (internal citations omitted).

[18] *Id.* (internal citations omitted).

[19] Brooke S.B. v. Elizabeth A.C.C., 61 N.E.3d 488, 491 (N.Y. 2016).

[20] Confidential Brief for Petitioner-Respondent, *supra* note 8, at 11 (internal
citations omitted).

[21] *Id.* at 7.

[22] *Id.*

[23] *Id.*

[24] *Id.* at 7, 12 (internal citations omitted).

[25] *Id.* at 12 (internal citations omitted).

[26] *Id.* at 7, 13.

[27] *Id.* at 11.

[28] *Id.* (internal citations omitted).

[29] *Id.* at 13 (internal citations omitted).

their families and their faith community but also to healthcare professionals and government workers.[30] "Both Elizabeth and Brooke were listed on the enrollment contract as M.B.'s parents" for the state-provided subsidized childcare for which they qualified.[31]

Elizabeth and Brooke ended their relationship in 2010.[32] They agreed to share parenting, with Brooke having their son overnight on Tuesdays and Thursdays as well as time on weekends.[33] Brooke also had "almost daily lunch time visits" with M.B,[34] who called her "Mama B."[35] When M.B. began to attend school—a free program for which he qualified—Brooke was responsible for dropping him off in the morning and would frequently pick him up later in the day.[36] "Brooke continued to attend M.B.'s doctors' appointments, was deeply involved in his daycare and schooling, and provided financially for M.B."[37]

Eventually, Elizabeth found a new partner, and they married in the wake of New York's passage of the Marriage Equality Act.[38] Brooke and her parents—M.B.'s "Mimi" and "Papa"—attended the wedding, where M.B. "spent practically the entire event glued to [Brooke's] side."[39]

Brooke, too, began a new relationship.[40] But when Brooke's new partner, along with the partner's son, moved into Brooke's home, "Elizabeth gave Brooke an ultimatum—[the new partner] and her son must leave."[41] Brooke acquiesced to preserve a good relationship with Elizabeth—and thereby provide a healthy environment for M.B.[42]

---

[30]   *Id.* at 14 (internal citations omitted).

[31]   *Id.* at 15 (internal citations omitted). Elizabeth and Brooke defied the popular— and largely inaccurate—image of same-sex couples with children. They were a low-income couple living in New York's westernmost county, Chautauqua. While media images may focus on affluent, urban same-sex couples raising children, research from the Williams Institute suggests a different picture. Same-sex couples raising children report lower household incomes than comparable different-sex couples, and LGBT individuals raising children, either as single parents or in two-adult households, are more likely than their non-LGBT counterparts to report household incomes near the poverty line. *See* GARY J. GATES, WILLIAMS INST., LGBT PARENTING IN THE UNITED STATES 1 (2013), https://williams institute.law.ucla.edu/wp-content/uploads/LGBT-Parenting.pdf. Moreover, childrearing among same-sex couples is most common, not in the Northeast and West Coast, but instead in the South, Mountain West, and Midwest. *Id.*

[32]   Brooke S.B. v. Elizabeth A.C.C., 61 N.E.3d 488, 491 (N.Y. 2016).

[33]   Confidential Brief for Petitioner-Respondent, *supra* note 8, at 17 (internal citations omitted).

[34]   *Id.* (internal citations omitted).

[35]   *Brooke S.B.*, 61 N.E.3d at 491.

[36]   Confidential Brief for Petitioner-Respondent, *supra* note 8, at 20.

[37]   *Id.* at 17 (internal citations omitted).

[38]   *Id.* at 20.

[39]   *Id.* (internal citations omitted).

[40]   *Id.* at 21.

[41]   *Id.* (internal citations omitted).

[42]   *Id.* (internal citations omitted).

Brooke and Elizabeth both remained in M.B.'s life for approximately three years after they broke up.[43] But in mid-2013, Elizabeth terminated Brooke's contact with M.B.[44] Brooke filed a petition for joint custody and regular visitation.[45] Unable to afford her own attorney, Brooke represented herself.[46] The family court appointed an attorney for M.B. The attorney determined that regular visitation with Brooke would further M.B.'s best interests.[47] Elizabeth moved to dismiss Brooke's petition on the ground that Brooke did not qualify as a parent under state law and thus did not have standing to seek custody or visitation.[48]

Elizabeth's contention relied on the continuing validity of *Alison D. v. Virginia M.*,[49] a 1991 case in which New York's high court denied standing to a nonbiological lesbian co-parent in similar circumstances.[50] The court had affirmed *Alison D.* as recently as 2010.[51] The family court judge found Brooke's case "heartbreaking,"[52] noting how M.B. tried "to communicate in some way with [Brooke's] picture because he recognizes this person as one of his mothers."[53] Nonetheless, the judge dismissed the petition under *Alison D.*,[54] explaining that "[t]here's nothing I can do about this in terms of the law."[55]

M.B.'s attorney appealed, and the intermediate appellate court affirmed.[56] Again, Brooke appeared *pro se*, drafting briefs on her own behalf as she tried to gain access to her son.[57] The Court of Appeals, New York's highest court, then granted leave to appeal to the attorney for the child.[58]

Brooke "had been casting her net looking for help."[59] At that point, Lambda Legal, the nation's largest LGBT rights legal organization, stepped in, along with the LGBT Bar Association of Greater New York and Blank Rome, a New York law firm that offered pro bono

---

[43]   Brooke S.B. v. Elizabeth A.C.C., 61 N.E.3d 488, 491 (N.Y. 2016).

[44]   *Id.*

[45]   *Id.*

[46]   Telephone Interview with Susan Sommer, former Dir. of Constitutional Litig., Lambda Legal (Oct. 18, 2017).

[47]   *Brooke S.B.*, 61 N.E.3d at 491. R. Thomas Rankin of Goodell & Rankin represented the child. *Id.* at 489.

[48]   *Id.* at 491.

[49]   572 N.E.2d 27 (N.Y. 1991).

[50]   *Brooke S.B.*, 61 N.E.3d at 491.

[51]   *See* Debra H. v. Janice R., 930 N.E.2d 184, 188 (N.Y. 2010).

[52]   *Brooke S.B.*, 61 N.E.3d at 491.

[53]   Confidential Brief for Petitioner-Respondent, *supra* note 8, at 25 (quoting transcript of oral argument).

[54]   *Brooke S.B.*, 61 N.E.3d at 491.

[55]   Confidential Brief for Petitioner-Respondent, *supra* note 8, at 25 (quoting transcript of oral argument).

[56]   *Brooke S.B.*, 61 N.E.3d at 491.

[57]   Telephone interview with Susan Sommer, *supra* note 46.

[58]   *Brooke S.B.*, 61 N.E.3d at 491.

[59]   Telephone interview with Susan Sommer, *supra* note 46.

representation.[60] Susan Sommer, then Lambda Legal's head of constitutional litigation working out of the organization's New York City headquarters, argued Brooke's case in the Court of Appeals.[61]

PARENTAL RECOGNITION AND LGBT EQUALITY OVER TWENTY-FIVE YEARS

The discussion that follows situates Brooke's fight for parental recognition—and thus for a continuing relationship with her son—within the nation's emerging recognition of the equal status of gays and lesbians. While sounding primarily in the register of state family law, Brooke's claim gained strength from—and tested the limits of—federal constitutional decisions protecting the rights of same-sex couples. In particular, *Obergefell v. Hodges*,[62] the 2015 U.S. Supreme Court decision opening marriage to same-sex couples, recognized the equal status of same-sex couples' families.[63]

Alison D.: *Biological Connection and the Meaning of "Parent"*[64]

To vindicate Brooke's parental relationship, her lawyers would have to convince the court to abandon *Alison D.* The facts of *Alison D.* closely resembled the facts of *Brooke S.B.* Two women started dating, moved in together the following year, and eventually decided to have a child through donor insemination. They functioned as a family, co-parenting the child for more than two years until their relationship ended. Even then, they continued to share parental responsibilities and abided by a visitation schedule. Eventually, though, the biological mother, Virginia, cut off contact between the child and the nonbiological mother, Alison.[65] When Alison went to court to establish her status as a legal parent, Lambda Legal represented her.[66]

---

[60]   *Brooke S.B.*, 61 N.E.3d at 489.

[61]   Telephone interview with Susan Sommer, *supra* note 46; *see also id.* at 488.

[62]   135 S. Ct. 2584 (2015).

[63]   The Court later affirmed *Obergefell*'s application to parental recognition for married same-sex couples in 2017's *Pavan v. Smith*, 137 S. Ct. 2075 (2017). Brooke's claim, in contrast, asked the New York courts to vindicate unmarried same-sex couples' interest in family-based equality.

[64]   I am grateful to Anthony Maccarini, the lawyer who represented the biological mother, Virginia, in *Alison D.*, for supplying me with materials from the case. Again, because briefs in the case are not publicly available and to protect the parties involved, I adopt the Court of Appeals' usage of the women's first names and last initial. Notably, Maccarini "personally never felt" that the case was "a 'gay rights' case." Letter from Anthony G. Maccarini, Attorney at Law, to Lora Johns, Yale Law School Library (Sept. 11, 2017) (on file with author). In fact, according to Maccarini, after the case, "a lesbian couple retained [him] to petition for the adoption by one of the other's natural child," and after a trial court's denial, he "contacted [his] adversary on the prior case (The Lambda Legal Defense & Education Fund, Inc.) and informed them of the result. They then took over the case and subsequently brought it to the Court of Appeals" in what became the case establishing second-parent adoption in New York. *Id.*

[65]   Alison D. v. Virginia M., 572 N.E.2d 27, 28–29 (N.Y. 1991).

[66]   For a detailed account of the case, including Lambda Legal's role, see Suzanne B. Goldberg, *Family Law Cases as Law Reform Litigation: Unrecognized Parents and the Story of* Alison D. v. Virginia M., 17 COLUM. J. GENDER & L. 307 (2008).

In 1991, the legal landscape for same-sex couples was hostile. No state provided relationship recognition. Marriage equality in any state would not arrive for more than a decade. Indeed, same-sex sex remained criminal in many states. States denied recognition not only to the adult relationships but also to the parent-child relationships of same-sex couples. No state appellate court had ruled that same-sex couples could engage in second-parent adoptions.[67] And gays and lesbians continued to struggle for the right to foster and adopt as individuals. In 1991, vindicating sexual orientation equality was not a judicial priority.

Accordingly, framing Alison's parental claim as grounded in LGBT equality would hardly have been a wise strategy. Rather than urge the court to view the matter primarily as an LGBT rights case, lawyers framed the issue around family diversity and child welfare. Continuation of the child's relationship with both parents—regardless of the parents' sexual orientation—would promote the child's best interest.[68]

Alison D. ultimately turned on interpretation of § 70 of the state Domestic Relations Law, which provides:

> Where a minor child is residing within this state, either *parent* may apply to the supreme court for a writ of habeas corpus to have such minor child brought before such court; and on the return thereof, the court, on due consideration, may award the natural guardianship, charge and custody of such child to either parent for such time, under such regulations and restrictions, and with such provisions and directions, as the case may require[.][69]

While the law only allowed a parent to petition for custody or visitation, it did not define the term "parent." That task, then, was left to the courts.[70]

Ultimately, in the nation's first state high court decision adjudicating the parental claim of a nonbiological lesbian mother, the court rejected Alison's claim. The court ruled that despite Alison's "close and loving relationship with the child, she is not a parent within the meaning of Domestic Relations Law § 70."[71] Because she was "a biological stranger to [the] child,"[72] she was a nonparent—merely a third party attempting to encroach on the biological mother's rights.[73]

---

[67] Nonetheless, trial courts in some states had begun to grant second-parent adoptions to same-sex couples in the mid-1980s. *See* NANCY D. POLIKOFF, BEYOND (STRAIGHT AND GAY) MARRIAGE 53 (2008).

[68] Petitioner-Appellant's Brief at 12–14, Alison D. v. Virginia M., 572 N.E.2d 27 (N.Y. 1991) (No. 000692-88).

[69] N.Y. DOM. REL. LAW § 70(a) (McKinney 2017) (emphasis added).

[70] Brooke S.B. v. Elizabeth A.C.C., 61 N.E.3d 488, 493 (N.Y. 2016).

[71] *Alison D.*, 572 N.E.2d at 28.

[72] *Id.*

[73] *See id.* at 29 ("We decline petitioner's invitation to read the term parent in section 70 to include categories of nonparents who have developed a relationship with a child or

In a prescient dissent, Chief Judge Judith Kaye focused on the harm specifically inflicted on children of same-sex couples and other relationships featuring a nonbiological parent. "[T]he impact of today's decision," she warned, "falls hardest on the children of those relationships, limiting their opportunity to maintain bonds that may be crucial to their development."[74]

Debra H.: *Something Old and Something New*

In *Debra H. v. Janice R.*, almost twenty years after *Alison D.*, the Court of Appeals again considered the status of an unmarried, nonbiological co-parent in a same-sex couple.[75] The environment for LGBT people had certainly improved. The U.S. Supreme Court had struck down sodomy prohibitions.[76] Some states had opened marriage to same-sex couples. Others offered various forms of nonmarital relationship recognition. Many states extended parental rights to nonbiological lesbian co-parents. For its part, New York authorized second-parent adoption, and thus allowed an unmarried, nonbiological parent to adopt her partner's biological child.[77]

Nonetheless, the law continued to treat same-sex couples and their families as outsiders. New York had failed to provide any statewide system to recognize same-sex couples' relationships. And the Court of Appeals had rejected same-sex couples' marriage claims under the state constitution, reasoning that the legislature could act on the "commonsense premise that children will do best with a mother and father in the home."[78]

The situation in *Debra H.* looked familiar. Two women began a relationship and eventually decided to have a child, with Janice conceiving by donor insemination.[79] They raised the child together for more than two years before breaking up; even after they separated, Janice allowed Debra access to the child for another two years before cutting off contact.[80] Lambda Legal again stepped in to represent the nonbiological mother.[81]

One crucial difference, however, was that Janice and Debra had traveled out-of-state to obtain government recognition of their relationship—entering into a civil union in Vermont when Janice was eight months pregnant.[82] This fact became critical to the New York high

---

who have had prior relationships with a child's parents and who wish to continue visitation with the child.").

[74] *Id.* at 30 (Kaye, J., dissenting).

[75] 930 N.E.2d 184 (N.Y. 2010).

[76] Lawrence v. Texas, 539 U.S. 558 (2003).

[77] Matter of Jacob, 660 N.E.2d 397 (N.Y. 1995).

[78] Hernandez v. Robles, 855 N.E.2d 1, 8 (N.Y. 2006).

[79] *Debra H.*, 930 N.E.2d at 186.

[80] *Id.*

[81] *Id.* at 185.

[82] *Id.* at 200.

court, which ruled in Debra's favor. The nonbiological mother, the court reasoned, qualifies as the child's parent under Vermont law,[83] and "New York will recognize parentage created by a civil union in Vermont."[84] Importantly, the court rejected Debra's "invitation to distinguish or overrule *Alison D.*",[85] instead endorsing "a bright-line rule that promotes certainty in the wake of domestic breakups."[86]

Brooke S.B.: *Parental Recognition in the Age of LGBT Equality*

By 2015, when lawyers were submitting their briefs to the Court of Appeals in *Brooke S.B.*, they were working in a legal environment in which important protections had been extended to the families of same-sex couples. Whereas lawyers in *Alison D.* deemphasized sexual orientation, instead universalizing the parent-child relationship at issue against the backdrop of pervasive sexual orientation discrimination, lawyers in *Brooke S.B.* could persuasively frame the issue around the rights of same-sex couples.[87]

The New York legislature passed marriage equality in 2011.[88] In 2013, in *United States v. Windsor*, the U.S. Supreme Court struck down section 3 of the federal Defense of Marriage Act, thereby requiring the federal government to treat same-sex couples lawfully married under state law as married for federal purposes as well.[89] In 2015, in *Obergefell v. Hodges*, the Court struck down state marriage bans on both liberty and equality grounds, thereby opening marriage to same-sex couples nationwide.[90] These developments, Brooke's lawyers argued, "affirmed that the families formed by lesbian and gay couples deserve the same respect and legal protections others receive."[91] Appealing to the child-centered justifications that underwrote *Windsor* and *Obergefell*, the lawyers criticized *Alison D.*'s bright-line rule as "a boundary line enforcing a legacy of stigma for children of same-sex parents."[92] Further,

---

[83]   *Id.* at 196.

[84]   *Id.* at 197. For criticism of the court's reasoning, including its interpretation of Vermont law, see Nancy D. Polikoff, *The New "Illegitimacy": Winning Backward in the Protection of the Children of Lesbian Couples*, 20 AM. U. J. GENDER SOC. POL'Y & L. 721 (2012).

[85]   *Debra H.*, 930 N.E.2d at 194.

[86]   *Id.* at 191.

[87]   *See, e.g.*, Brief for The New York Bar Association, as Amicus Curiae Supporting Petitioner-Respondent at 13, Brooke S.B. v. Elizabeth A.C.C., 61 N.E.3d 488 (N.Y. 2016) (No. APL-2015-00236) ("[T]he restrictive definition of who is a 'parent' fails to protect the best interests of tens of thousands of children living in households headed by same-sex couples.").

[88]   Marriage Equality Act, 2011 N.Y. Sess. Laws. Ch. 95 (A. 8354) (McKinney) (codified at N.Y. DOM. REL. LAW, ART. 3, § 10–A).

[89]   570 U.S. 744 (2013).

[90]   135 S. Ct. 2584 (2015).

[91]   Confidential Brief for Petitioner-Respondent, *supra* note 8, at 4.

[92]   *Id.*

lawyers supporting Brooke argued that New York parentage law unconstitutionally discriminated based on sexual orientation.[93]

Not only had the nation come to recognize same-sex couples' right to marry, but courts and legislatures in many states had recognized the rights of *unmarried*, nonbiological parents in same-sex couples.[94] As Lambda Legal's Sommer described it, "There had been decisions from states like Oklahoma and Kansas . . . . There had been great evolution and progress in all corners of the country."[95] Since New York looked increasingly like an outlier, lawyers could argue that the court "should bring New York into the mainstream."[96]

These two developments—marriage equality and the recognition of nonbiological parents—were related. The law's embrace of marriage for same-sex couples did not simply signify respect for same-sex couples' families; it vindicated *nonbiological* parent-child bonds in particular.[97] As the child's attorney argued, "[t]he concept that a 'parent' is defined chiefly through a person's biological connection to a child is no longer viable in the wake of [the Marriage Equality Act] and *Obergefell*."[98] "Any definition of parent," the attorney urged, "must reflect this new legal and social reality."[99] Critically, marriage equality informed but did not resolve questions of parental recognition; that is, "the availability of marriage . . . did not eliminate the need to afford standing to non-biological parents."[100]

THE COURT RULES: SEXUAL ORIENTATION EQUALITY AND NONBIOLOGICAL PARENTHOOD

In a groundbreaking opinion written by Judge Sheila Abdus-Salaam,[101] the court overturned *Alison D.* and extended parental recognition to an unmarried, nonbiological parent. In doing so, it articulated a standard to be applied to the situation before it: "where a partner shows by clear and convincing evidence that the parties agreed to conceive a child and to raise the child together, the non-biological, non-

---

[93]   *See, e.g.*, Brief for The National Center for Lesbian Rights et al. as Amici Curiae Supporting Petitioner-Respondent at 25, Brooke S.B. v. Elizabeth A.C.C., 61 N.E.3d 488 (N.Y. 2016) (No. APL-2015-00236) ("Denying Brooke (and unmarried non-biological parents like her) the ability to establish parentage . . . discriminat[es] against Brooke based on both method of conception and sexual orientation.").

[94]   *See* NeJaime, *The Nature of Parenthood, supra* note 4, at 2370–72.

[95]   Telephone interview with Susan Sommer, *supra* note 46.

[96]   Confidential Brief for Petitioner-Respondent, *supra* note 8, at 32.

[97]   *See* NeJaime, *Marriage Equality and the New Parenthood, supra* note 4, at 1190–91.

[98]   Confidential Brief for Appellant Attorney for the Child at 53, Brooke S.B. v. Elizabeth A.C.C., 61 N.E.3d 488 (N.Y. 2016) (No. APL-2015-00236).

[99]   *Id.* at 54.

[100]   Confidential Brief for Petitioner-Respondent, *supra* note 8, at 82.

[101]   Tragically, Judge Abdus-Salaam, the first black woman to serve on the Court of Appeals, was later found dead in the Hudson River in an apparent suicide. Her successor, Judge Paul Feinman, became the first openly gay judge on the Court of Appeals. *See* Alan Feuer, *Death of Judge is Ruled Suicide, Ending a Mystery*, N.Y. TIMES, July 27, 2017, at A24.

adoptive partner has standing to seek visitation and custody under Domestic Relations Law § 70."[102]

The court's reasoning reflected the significant shift toward LGBT equality since *Alison D.* That decision was outmoded not simply because it harmed existing parent-child relationships in a range of families, but because it reflected a legal regime of LGBT discrimination that had been repudiated. Marriage equality, the court explained, rendered "*Alison D.*'s foundational premise of heterosexual parenting and nonrecognition of same-sex couples . . . unsustainable."[103]

While courts in other states had ruled that unmarried, nonbiological co-parents could be recognized as legal parents, the New York court broke new ground by explicitly acknowledging that sexual orientation equality requires parental recognition that does not hinge on biological connection. In a concurring opinion, Judge Pigott agreed with the result because Brooke and Elizabeth could not have gotten married.[104] Going forward, in his view, marriage and second-parent adoption solved the dilemma faced by same-sex couples.[105] But the majority rejected this position, acknowledging that marriage and second-parent adoption did not by themselves furnish genuine equality for same-sex couples. "[W]here both partners in a heterosexual couple are biologically related to the child," the court explained, "both former partners will have standing regardless of marriage or adoption."[106] But, "[u]nder the current legal framework, which emphasizes biology, it is impossible—without marriage or adoption—for both former partners of a same-sex couple to have standing, as only one can be biologically related to the child."[107] Because different-sex and same-sex couples are differently situated with respect to biological connection, "a proper test for standing that ensures equality for same-sex parents" requires paths to nonbiological parentage outside of marriage and adoption.[108]

On this view, to treat same-sex couples as truly belonging, the state must move away from a parentage regime designed around the heterosexual family and thus designed around biological relationships.[109] That was the regime inside which *Alison D.* was decided, and it did not reflect contemporary principles of sexual orientation equality. The critical question then becomes: What follows from the recognition that sexual

---

[102] Brooke S.B. v. Elizabeth A.C.C., 61 N.E.3d 488, 490 (N.Y. 2016).

[103] *Id.* at 498.

[104] *Id.* at 504 (Pigott, J., concurring).

[105] *Id.* ("[A]n unmarried individual who lacks a biological or adoptive connection to a child conceived after 2011 does not have standing under Domestic Relations Law § 70, regardless of gender or sexual orientation.").

[106] *Id.* at 498 (majority opinion).

[107] *Id.*

[108] *Id.* at 498–99.

[109] *See* NeJaime, *The Nature of Parenthood, supra* note 4, at 2333.

orientation equality requires a parentage regime untethered from biological connection?

INTENT, FUNCTION, AND EQUALITY

Two related—and often complementary—approaches to parental recognition protect nonbiological parent-child relationships: intent and function.[110] Intentional parenthood focuses on the intent to be a parent of the child. This approach, which traces its origins to married, different-sex couples using assisted reproductive technologies (ART),[111] today reaches a much broader swath of families using ART to have children. Consider this Maine law: "a person who consents to assisted reproduction by a woman . . . with the intent to be the parent of a resulting child is a parent of the resulting child."[112] Functional parenthood, by contrast, focuses on the act of raising the child.[113] This approach emerged to address the range of households in which an individual who is not the child's biological parent functions as a parent—including not only same-sex but also different-sex cohabiting partners, as well as relatives and stepparents. Consider Delaware's de facto parent law: Provided the legal parent "fostered the formation and establishment of a parent-like relationship between the child and the de facto parent," parental status can be established by a showing that the de facto parent "exercised parental responsibility for the child" and "acted in a parental role for a length of time sufficient to have established a bonded and dependent relationship with the child that is parental in nature."[114]

In practice, intentional and functional approaches to parenthood often bleed together. After all, when individuals jointly plan to have a child together, they usually raise that child together. Evidence of parental conduct may be relevant to determinations of intent, and manifestations of intent may be relevant to the criteria in functional standards.[115] In my own work, I have linked intentional and functional concepts and have connected them to the acceptance and recognition of same-sex parenting.[116] Both approaches can accommodate same-sex couples who have used donor insemination or other forms of ART to have children.

---

[110] *See* NeJaime, *Marriage Equality and the New Parenthood, supra* note 4, at 1187–89.

[111] *See id.* at 1195–96, 1208–12.

[112] ME. REV. STAT. ANN. tit. 19-A, § 1923 (2017).

[113] *See* NeJaime, *Marriage Equality and the New Parenthood, supra* note 4, at 1188–89. Nonetheless, functional standards generally include the biological or adoptive parent's consent as a way to mediate concerns about constitutional parental rights—effectively showing that she waived her right to exclude the individual seeking parental recognition. *See* Carlos A. Ball, *Rendering Children Illegitimate in Former Partner Parenting Cases: Hiding Behind the Façade of Certainty*, 20 AM. U. J. GENDER SOC. POL'Y & L. 623, 632–33 (2012).

[114] DEL. CODE ANN. tit. 13, § 8–201(c) (West 2017).

[115] *See* Ball, *supra* note 113, at 659; Richard F. Storrow, *Parenthood by Pure Intention: Assisted Reproduction and the Functional Approach to Parentage*, 53 HASTINGS L.J. 597, 674–75 (2002).

[116] *See* NeJaime, *The Nature of Parenthood, supra* note 4; NeJaime, *Marriage Equality and the New Parenthood, supra* note 4.

The nonbiological lesbian co-parent who finds that her relationship has ended after the child's birth can ordinarily show facts necessary to satisfy either an intentional or functional test.

But the trajectory from *Alison D.* to *Brooke S.B.* suggests the need to disentangle intent and function—to appreciate the potential and limitations of each and to recognize how each relates to emergent principles of sexual orientation equality. Because it focuses on the parties' intentions prior to conception, an intentional standard favors same-sex family formation and recognizes each partner as a parent at the time of the child's birth.[117] Indeed, if a same-sex couple broke up during a pregnancy, courts following an intentional approach would likely conclude that both parties were legal parents. By contrast, a functional standard favors those who have developed a parent-child bond. It captures most same-sex-couple-headed families, given that the nonbiological co-parent is serving, or has served, as a parent. But in focusing on post-birth conduct, it does not offer certainty to the nonbiological parent at the moment of birth. Accordingly, if a same-sex couple ended their relationship during the pregnancy, a functional approach would likely not confer parental status on the individual who lacks a biological connection to the child.[118] Critically, unlike the intentional standard, which favors lesbian and gay parents and those who use ART, a functional standard captures a broader range of families.[119]

The path from *Alison D.* to *Brooke S.B.* shows how as sexual orientation equality became an objective for the law of parental recognition, an intentional approach began to overshadow a functional approach. Against a legal backdrop hostile to same-sex couples, lawyers logically argued in a more universalist register that emphasized function. But as the legal regime embraced same-sex couples, advocates for same-sex parents shifted into a more LGBT-specific register that made concepts of intent increasingly salient. That shift has consequences for the law of parental recognition.

---

[117] While many same-sex couples are raising children from previous different-sex relationships, here I am tracking what researchers have termed "*planned* LGB-parent families." *See* ABBIE E. GOLDBERG, NANETTE K. GARTRELL, & GARY GATES, WILLIAMS INST., RESEARCH REPORT ON LGB-PARENT FAMILIES 5 (2014), https://williamsinstitute.law.ucla.edu/wp-content/uploads/lgb-parent-families-july-2014.pdf.

[118] *Cf.* Transcript of Oral Argument at 7, Brooke S.B. v. Elizabeth A.C.C., 61 N.E.3d 488 (N.Y. 2016) (No. APL-2015-00236) (the lawyer for the child's attorney explaining why a "[breakup] during the pregnancy" would not be covered by the functional standard).

[119] *See* Martha Minow, *All in the Family & in All Families: Membership, Loving, and Owing*, 95 W. VA. L. REV. 275, 284–86 (1992–93); Martha L. Minow, *Redefining Families: Who's In and Who's Out?*, 62 U. COLO. L. REV. 269, 278–84 (1991); Melissa Murray, *The Networked Family: Reframing the Legal Understanding of Caregiving and Caregivers*, 94 VA. L. REV. 385, 386–88 (2008); Nancy D. Polikoff, *This Child Does Have Two Mothers: Redefining Parenthood to Meet the Needs of Children in Lesbian-Mother and Other Nontraditional Families*, 78 GEO. L.J. 459, 542–43 (1990).

First, consider *Alison D.* Lawyers supporting the nonbiological mother urged a "functional definition of parent."[120] Lambda Legal lawyers emphasized parental conduct, explaining that Alison "functioned as a parent and was a parent to [the child]."[121] The primary analogy was to stepparents—that is, families in which the nonbiological parent assumed parental responsibilities after the child's birth.[122] Sexual orientation seemed beside the point. Indeed, rather than urge a result because it would protect same-sex couples, the New York City Bar Association cautioned that "[t]he fact that this case presents the Court with two lesbian parents should not change the rules of analysis."[123] Nonetheless, the court rejected a functional approach to parental recognition and announced a bright-line rule that turned on biology or adoption—and thus excluded nonbiological parents in same-sex couples.[124]

Not only was sexual orientation equality not a legal priority at the time *Alison D.* was decided, intent-based standards in parentage law also were relatively limited—primarily reaching married couples who used donor insemination. Generally, the husband of a married woman who conceived with donor sperm would be recognized as the legal father of the resulting child if he consented to his wife's insemination. In this way, intent-based understandings of parenthood existed in law, but only for married, heterosexual men. In the early 1990s, other forms of ART, including *in vitro* fertilization (IVF) and gestational surrogacy, were just beginning to take hold. Only after *Alison D.* did a state supreme court first announce a principle of intentional parenthood with respect to motherhood—and only for a woman biologically connected to the child. In a dispute involving gestational surrogacy, the California Supreme Court ruled that the genetic mother, and not the gestational surrogate, was the legal mother because she was the intended mother.[125] (Eventually, in California, concepts of intent began to shape determinations of motherhood for those with neither a gestational nor genetic connection to the child.[126]).

---

[120] Petitioner-Appellant's Brief, *supra* note 68, at 20; *see also* Brief for the Association of the Bar of the City of New York as Amicus Curiae Supporting Petitioner-Appellant at 4, Alison D. v. Virginia M., 572 N.E. 2d 27 (N.Y. 1991) (No. 000692-88); Brief for NOW Legal Defense and Education Fund and National Organization for Women of New York State as Amici Curiae Supporting Petitioner-Appellant at 7–8, Alison D. v. Virginia M., 572 N.E. 2d 27 (N.Y. 1991) (No. 000692-88).

[121] Petitioner-Appellant's Brief, *supra* note 68, at 23. The "indicia of parenthood" included "express agreement" by the biological parent. *Id.* For explanation, see *supra* note 113.

[122] *See id.* at 14–15.

[123] Brief for the Association of the Bar of the City of New York as Amicus Curiae Supporting Petitioner-Appellant, *supra* note 120, at 5.

[124] At that point, the court had not approved second-parent adoption; it did so five years later. *See* Matter of Jacob, 660 N.E.2d 397 (N.Y. 1995).

[125] *See* Johnson v. Calvert, 851 P.2d 776, 782 (Cal. 1993).

[126] *See In re* Marriage of Buzzanca, 72 Cal. Rptr. 2d 280, 293 (Ct. App. 1998).

By the time the New York Court of Appeals took up *Debra H.*, almost twenty years after *Alison D.*, distinctions between functional and intentional approaches to parental recognition had surfaced.[127] In *Debra H.*, the court refused "to replace the bright-line rule in *Alison D.* with a complicated and nonobjective test for determining so-called functional or de facto parentage" and instead derived Debra's parentage from the couple's Vermont civil union.[128] But concurring opinions advocated standards that would recognize Debra as a parent regardless of the couple's civil union. Judge Carmen Beauchamp Ciparick urged the court to abandon *Alison D.* and to adopt a "functional approach" to parental recognition, relying on a groundbreaking 1995 Wisconsin decision that articulated a functional standard as it extended visitation rights to a nonbiological lesbian co-parent.[129] Judge Robert Smith, in contrast, urged the court to adopt an intent-based approach tailored specifically to same-sex couples—who were ineligible for marriage in many jurisdictions, and therefore unable to establish parentage under the rules governing married couples using donor sperm. Under Judge Smith's approach, "where a child is conceived through [donor insemination] by one member of a same-sex couple living together, with the knowledge and consent of the other, the child is as a matter of law . . . the child of both."[130] Because "gay and straight couples face different situations, both as a matter of law and as a matter of biology," Judge Smith viewed their differential treatment as warranted and thus proposed a rule that "would apply only to same-sex couples—indeed, only to lesbian couples."[131]

In *Brooke S.B.*, tensions between intentional and functional standards structured the litigation and, ultimately, the court's approach. Brooke's lawyers did not distance same-sex couples from the full range of nonbiological parents. Nonetheless, the group that figured most centrally were not stepparents, as had been the case in *Alison D.*, but those using ART—a population that had exploded in recent years and had gained greater protection in the law of parental recognition. "The widespread use of ART," lawyers asserted, "has rendered obsolete the automatic assumption that a child is the genetic offspring of the parents who rear him or her."[132] While ART encompassed a larger universe of families, same-sex couples represented a population dependent on ART for non-adoptive family formation.[133]

[127] *See* Ball, *supra* note 115, at 656–61.

[128] Debra H. v. Janice R., 930 N.E.2d 184, 192 (N.Y. 2010).

[129] *Id.* at 202–203 (Ciparick, J., concurring) (citing *In re* Custody of H.S.H.-K., 533 N.W.2d 419, 421 (Wis. 1995)).

[130] *Id.* at 205 (Smith, J., concurring).

[131] *Id.*

[132] Confidential Brief for Petitioner-Respondent, *supra* note 8, at 38.

[133] *See id.* at 26 ("*Alison D.*'s narrow reading of the statutory term 'parent' . . . has not kept pace with the reality for thousands of children, particularly those raised by committed same-sex couples, many of whom conceived through assisted reproductive technology ('ART').").

Parental recognition that could accommodate ART, and thus accommodate same-sex family formation, drew on notions of intent. For example, lawyers explained that many of the families using ART "are formed by same-sex couples, who use donor gametes with the full *intention* that both partners in the couple will parent the resulting child."[134] Ultimately, in linking respect for same-sex couples' families to recognition of parents who use ART, lawyers made intent a critical aspect of parental recognition.

Still, even as LGBT advocates consistently appealed to intent, they continued to argue for a functional test that would reach a broader swath of families.[135] At oral argument, Lambda Legal's Sommer articulated a standard that sounded more like Delaware's de facto parent law than Maine's intentional rule:

> The standard that we suggest is that a person can be established as a parent if, one, the child's already legally recognized parent, the biological or adoptive parent, consented to and fostered the formation of the parent-child bond, and, two, that person did take on . . . the role of a parent, performing the tasks and taking the financial responsibility of parenthood.[136]

The child's attorney, too, argued for a functional test.[137]

While LGBT advocates appealed to both intent and function on Brooke's behalf, a key supporter of Brooke's parental claim starkly distinguished between the two concepts. In an *amicus curiae* brief supporting Brooke, a group of domestic violence organizations, led by Sanctuary for Families, urged an intent-based standard. They proposed "an interpretation of the word 'parent' . . . that would include an adult who can show by clear and convincing evidence that she and her partner *jointly planned and explicitly agreed to the conception* of a child with the *intention* of raising the child as co-parents."[138] Critically, they framed their solution as an LGBT-equality measure—aimed at "establishing parity for LGBT parents."[139]

Not only did the Sanctuary for Families brief propose and endorse an intentional test, it rejected a functional one as "overbroad."[140] Such a test, the brief warned, would inevitably involve judges in "cumbersome

---

[134] *Id.* at 38 (emphasis added).

[135] *Id.* at 5 (focusing on "whether a person who has functioned as a child's intended second parent with the deliberate agreement of a biological parent, as Brooke has, should be accorded the status of parent for purposes of custody and visitation").

[136] Transcript of Oral Argument, *supra* note 118, at 16.

[137] *Id.*

[138] Brief for Sanctuary for Families, et al., as Amici Curiae for Petitioner-Respondent at 9, Brooke S.B. v. Elizabeth A.C.C., 61 N.E.3d 488 (N.Y. 2016) (No. APL-2015-00236) (emphasis added).

[139] *Id.*

[140] *Id.*

inquir[ies] into post-conception facts."[141] More specifically, they worried that a "functional approach, requiring a case-by-case analysis, would empower former abusive partners with no biological or adoptive connection to a child to claim parental rights as a way to continue threatening their victims."[142]

Even though it came from a pro-LGBT perspective that supported Brooke, the Sanctuary for Families brief found common ground with the biological mother's position. Situating the dispute within broader questions over functional parental recognition, Elizabeth's lawyers claimed that "this is not solely an issue for same-sex couples."[143] Adopting a functional test, they cautioned, would lead to claims by "step-parents, long term girlfriends, and long term boyfriends, aunts, uncles and grandparents who have assumed parental duties in an effort to care for a child."[144] For many years, disputes over functional recognition of same-sex parents had featured this slippery-slope concern,[145] even though courts had shown themselves capable of distinguishing between parental and non-parental claims.[146] Of course, in seeking to exclude Brooke, Elizabeth's lawyers rejected not only a functional approach but also an intentional standard.[147]

The intentional approach advanced by the Sanctuary for Families brief would constitute an important advance for many families, including specifically those formed by same-sex couples. Still, it would not accommodate the full range of nonbiological parent-child relationships that lacked legal recognition. Noting that her "client would prevail" under an intentional standard, Sommer nonetheless explained that even as an intentional standard "captures a substantial segment of New York families that had been falling through the cracks, . . . it doesn't address the needs of all of them."[148]

At oral argument, Judge Abdus-Salaam, who would author the court's opinion, specifically cited the Sanctuary for Families brief and probed the lawyers about the intent-based test it proposed.[149] Sommer responded by describing the standard as "a good test" but cautioned that

---

[141] *Id.*

[142] *Id.* at 8.

[143] Confidential Brief for Respondent-Respondent, *supra* note 8, at 22, at 23.

[144] *Id.*

[145] *See* NeJaime, *Marriage Equality and the New Parenthood*, *supra* note 4, at 1204, 1224, 1227.

[146] *See* Ball, *supra* note 115, at 653–56.

[147] Elizabeth's brief situated marriage as the solution for same-sex couples. *See* Confidential Brief for Respondent-Respondent, *supra* note 8, at 22 ("The passage of the Marriage Equality Act in New York State is a positive step in the direction for same sex [sic] couples. . . . As we move forward, it seems likely that children born during the marriage of a same-sex couple can be viewed [as] a child of both.").

[148] Telephone interview with Susan Sommer, *supra* note 46.

[149] Transcript of Oral Argument, *supra* note 118, at 24 ("[Sanctuary for Families] proposed a test based on the intent of the two partners and their joint agreement to conceive and raise a child. Do you support that . . . ?").

"no test should exclusively hinge on the consent to conceive the child, because there may be occasions . . . where the second parent enters the child's life, or the family's life, right after conception."[150] For his part, the lawyer arguing on behalf of M.B.'s attorney[151] echoed these concerns. At oral argument, he described the Sanctuary for Families proposal as "a bright-line rule that really pertains to lesbian couples" and warned that it "talks about a contract rather than . . . really looking at the relationship between the child and the parent."[152]

Ultimately, the court adopted the intent-based standard, even quoting the Sanctuary for Families brief.[153] Since Brooke alleged that she and Elizabeth "entered into a pre-conception agreement to conceive and raise a child as co-parents," she would, upon establishing such allegations, have standing as a parent.[154] To be sure, the intent-based test that the court announced constitutes a landmark advance not only for the legal status of same-sex couples but also for the law of parental recognition more broadly. Of particular importance is the fact that the court did not limit its ruling to couples who could not have married. And the test is not limited to same-sex couples. Parental recognition is available to those nonbiological parents, whether in same-sex or different-sex couples, who could have married but did not.

TOWARD FUNCTION

Importantly, the court adopted the intent-based standard without, as the Sanctuary for Families brief hoped, foreclosing a functional test in other circumstances.[155] "[R]eject[ing] the premise that we must now declare that one test would be appropriate for all situations," the court expressly noted that it did "not . . . decide whether, in a case where a biological or adoptive parent consented to the creation of a parent-like relationship between his or her partner and child *after conception*, the partner can establish standing to seek visitation and custody."[156]

The fact that the court "left the door open for future cases presenting different scenarios," Sommer remarked, was itself "a major breakthrough"—a "judicious but also quite sweeping move."[157] Family court judges are now authorized to evaluate individual cases and protect existing parent-child relationships—a result that *Alison D.* had essentially foreclosed. Since *Brooke S.B.*, cases that rely on more

---

[150] *Id.* at 24–25.

[151] At the Court of Appeals, Eric Wrubel of Warshaw Burstein argued on behalf of the child's attorney. *Id.* at 2.

[152] *Id.* at 40–41.

[153] Brooke S.B. v. Elizabeth A.C.C., 61 N.E.3d 488, 500 (N.Y. 2016) (citation omitted).

[154] *Id.*

[155] Brief for Sanctuary for Families, et al., as Amici Curiae for Petitioner-Respondent, *supra* note 138, at 38–43.

[156] *Brooke S.B.*, 61 N.E.3d at 500–01 (emphasis added).

[157] Telephone interview with Susan Sommer, *supra* note 46.

functional than intentional criteria have "start[ed] to percolate up."[158] In September 2017, a family court applied a functional test to a same-sex couple without a pre-conception agreement, concluding that the nonbiological mother "was essentially a parent" and that the biological mother "fostered, furthered, and nurtured a parent-like relationship."[159]

While cases that call for a functional standard feature both LGBT and non-LGBT parents, there is reason to believe that respect for families formed by same-sex couples may lead to more expansive recognition of functional parent-child relationships in New York. As the *Brooke S.B.* court itself articulated, valuing same-sex parenting requires valuing nonbiological bonds—recognition that parental attachments derive from relationships, rather than genetics. A parentage regime capable of accommodating the full range of nonbiological parent-child relationships requires not only intentional but functional criteria.

Consider developments from outside New York. The recently approved Uniform Parentage Act (UPA)—UPA (2017)—aims to revise parentage law to "ensure the equal treatment of children born to same-sex couples."[160] It includes numerous provisions codifying intent-based principles.[161] It also includes provisions aimed at functional recognition. The *de facto* parent section allows an individual to establish her status as a legal parent based on a "bonded and dependent relationship with the child which is parental in nature," provided the other parent "fostered or supported the ... relationship."[162] The intentional and functional concepts embedded in the UPA (2017) grew out of efforts to protect families formed by same-sex couples, whose equality interests are understood as bound up in the protection of nonbiological parent-child relationships.[163] As the UPA (2017) demonstrates, both intentional and functional standards are necessary to provide comprehensive protection for nonbiological parents.

As for Brooke, in the wake of the court's decision, Blank Rome successfully represented her in family court.[164] Brooke was reunited with her son and shares parenting with Elizabeth.[165] As Elizabeth had, Brooke too married her new partner.[166] Finally, Brooke is *functioning* as she *intended*—as a parent.

---

[158] *Id. See also* Ian Parker, *Are You My Mother?*, NEW YORKER, May 22, 2017, at 46.

[159] J.C. v. N.P., 2017 NYLJ LEXIS 2831, at *14–15 (Fam. Ct. Nassau Cty. Sep. 27, 2017).

[160] UNIF. PARENTAGE ACT prefatory note (UNIF. LAW COMM'N 2017).

[161] *See id.* at §§ 703, 809.

[162] *Id.* at § 609(d). *See also id.* at § 204(a)(2) (gender-neutral "holding out" presumption).

[163] *See* Courtney G. Joslin, *Nurturing Parenthood Through the UPA (2017)*, 127 YALE L.J. F. 589, 599; 599 nn. 60–62 (2018), https://www.yalelawjournal.org/forum/nurturing-parenthood-through-the-upa-2017.

[164] Telephone interview with Susan Sommer, *supra* note 46.

[165] *Id.*

[166] *Id.*

Acknowledgments

We received a great deal of help with this book along the way. Yale law student Dylan Cowit, NYU law student Caitlin Millat, and Cardozo law students Patrick Glackin and Shayna Byrne provided superb editorial assistance on a number of these chapters. Cilla Smith was critical throughout the editorial process, including her work organizing a conference that brought contributors together at Yale Law School in December 2017 to discuss the draft chapters and the themes of the volume as a whole. Yale law students Rebecca Chan, Rachel Frank, Rachel Luban, Laura McCready, Laura Portuondo, and Faren Tang helped record and preserve the work of that conference. And many of the individual chapters benefited from the insights and recollections of attorneys and parties to the cases described here; we are grateful to them for sharing their stories with us.